Collins *Street Atlas*

GLASGOW

D1147386

Contents

Key to map symbols	1
Key to map pages	2-3
City centre map	4-5
Map pages	6-73
Local information	74-76
Index to place names	77-78
Index to street names	78-125
Rail network map	126

Published by Collins
An imprint of HarperCollins*Publishers*
77-85 Fulham Palace Road, Hammersmith, London W6 8JB

www.collins.co.uk

Mapping generated from Collins/Bartholomew digital databases

This product uses map data licensed from Ordnance Survey® with the permission of the Controller of Her Majesty's Stationery Office. © Crown copyright. Licence number 399302

Printed in Hong Kong

ISBN 0 00 714700 7   Imp 001   PI11321   EDU

e-mail: roadcheck@harpercollins.co.uk

Key to map symbols ①

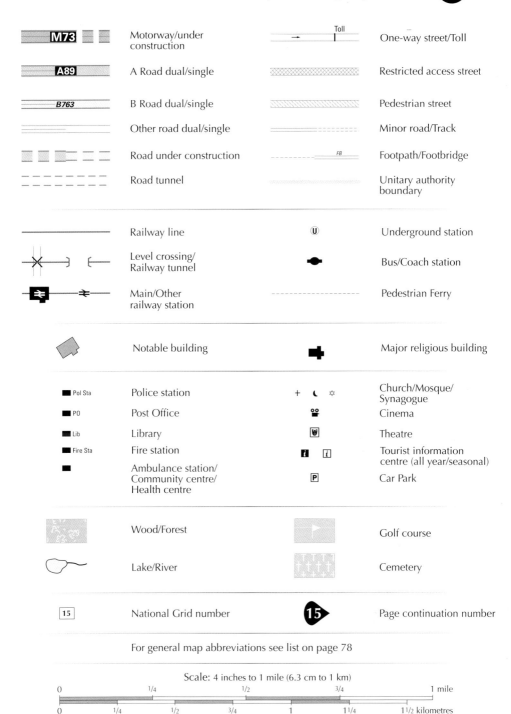

M73	Motorway/under construction
A89	A Road dual/single
B763	B Road dual/single
	Other road dual/single
	Road under construction
	Road tunnel
	Railway line
	Level crossing/Railway tunnel
	Main/Other railway station
	Notable building
Pol Sta	Police station
PO	Post Office
Lib	Library
Fire Sta	Fire station
	Ambulance station/Community centre/Health centre
	Wood/Forest
	Lake/River
15	National Grid number

	One-way street/Toll
	Restricted access street
	Pedestrian street
	Minor road/Track
	Footpath/Footbridge
	Unitary authority boundary
Ⓤ	Underground station
	Bus/Coach station
	Pedestrian Ferry
	Major religious building
+ ☾ ✡	Church/Mosque/Synagogue
	Cinema
	Theatre
ⓘ ⓘ	Tourist information centre (all year/seasonal)
Ⓟ	Car Park
	Golf course
	Cemetery
⑮▶	Page continuation number

For general map abbreviations see list on page 78

Scale: 4 inches to 1 mile (6.3 cm to 1 km)

0   1/4   1/2   3/4   1 mile

0   1/4   1/2   3/4   1   11/4   11/2 kilometres

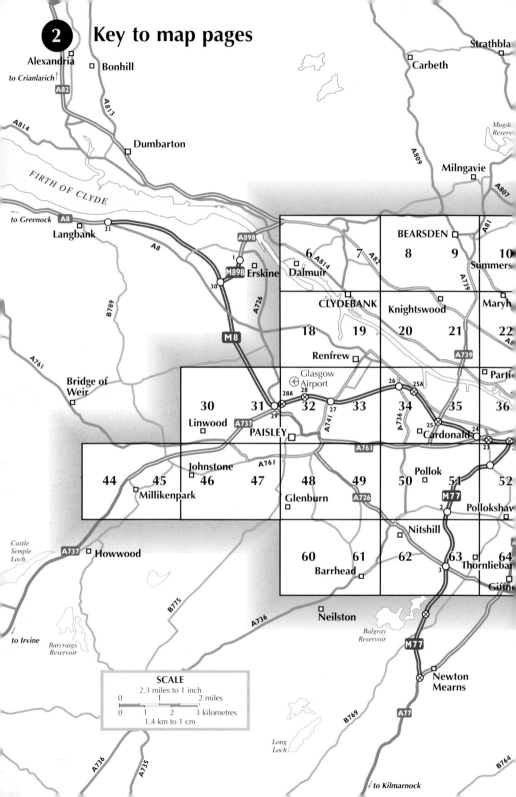

2 Key to map pages

Alexandria
Bonhill
to Crianlarich
A82
A813
A814
Dumbarton

Strathbla
Carbeth
A809
Milngavie
A807
Mugdo
Reserv

FIRTH OF CLYDE

to Greenock
A8
Langbank
A898
M898
Erskine
Dalmuir
31
30
A8
B789
A726
M8
A761
Bridge of Weir
B789

BEARSDEN
A81
8 9 10
Summers

6 A814 7 A82
CLYDEBANK
Knightswood
Maryh
18 19 20 21 22
Renfrew
A739
A739
Parti

Glasgow Airport
28A 28
30 31 32 33 34 35 36
Linwood
A737
PAISLEY
29
A741
26 25A
A736
25 Cardonald 24
23

Johnstone
A761
44 45 46 47 48 49 50 51 52
Millikenpark
Glenburn
A726
Pollok
M77
Pollokshav
2

Castle Semple Loch
A737
Howwood
Nitshill
60 61 62 63 64
Barrhead
Thornlieban
Giffne
3

B775
Neilston
Balgray Reservoir
M77

to Irvine
Barcraigs Reservoir
A736
Newton Mearns
A77

SCALE
2.3 miles to 1 inch
0   1   2 miles
0   1   2   3 kilometres
1.4 km to 1 cm

Long Loch
B769
A77
to Kilmarnock
A736
A735
B764

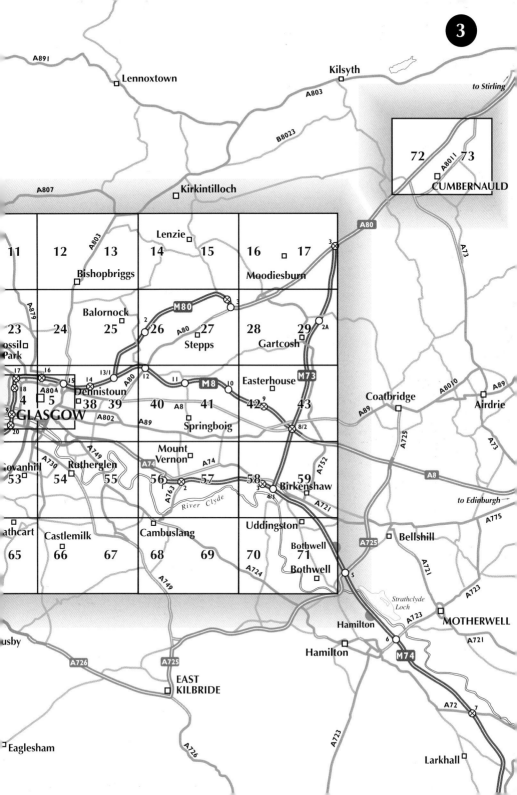

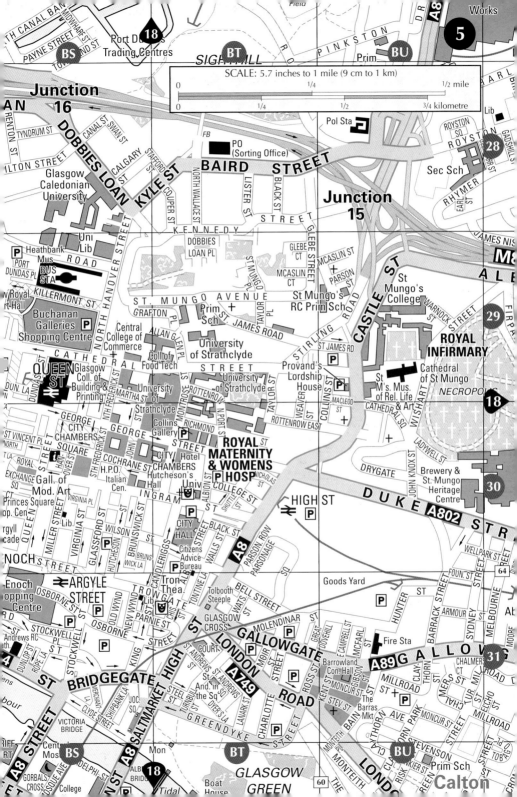

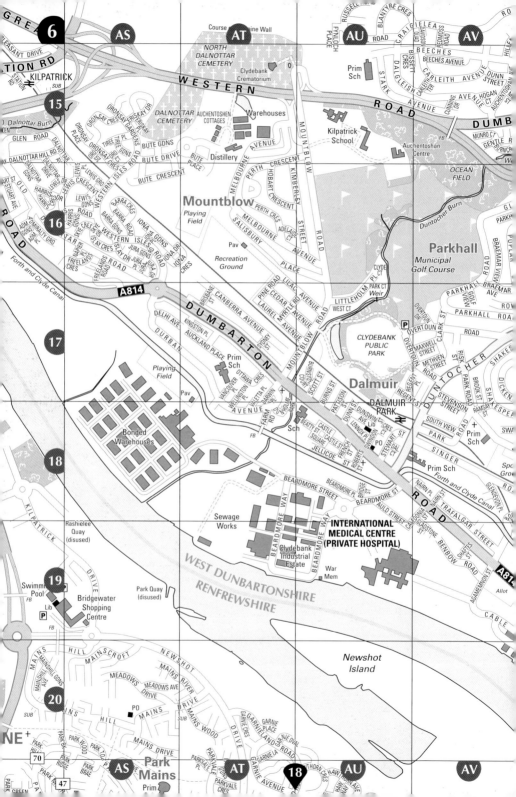

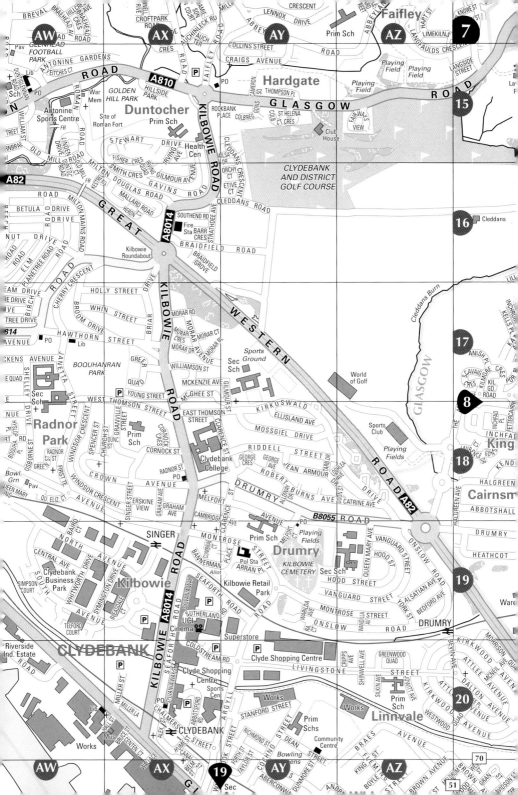

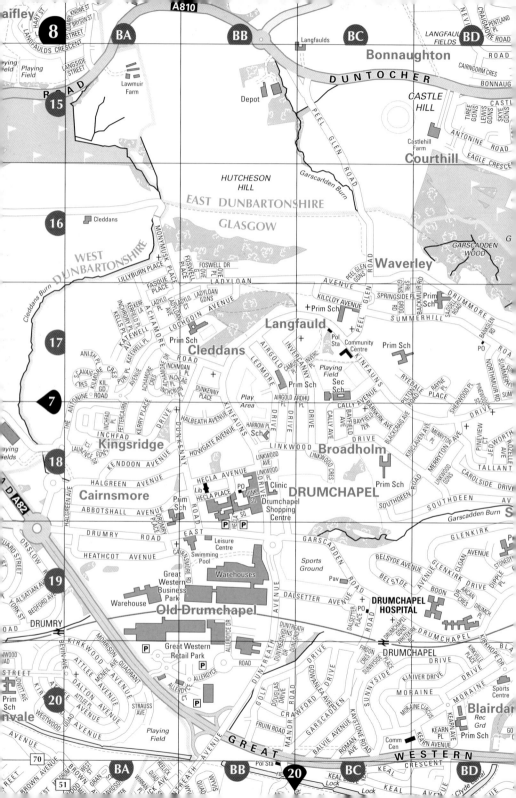

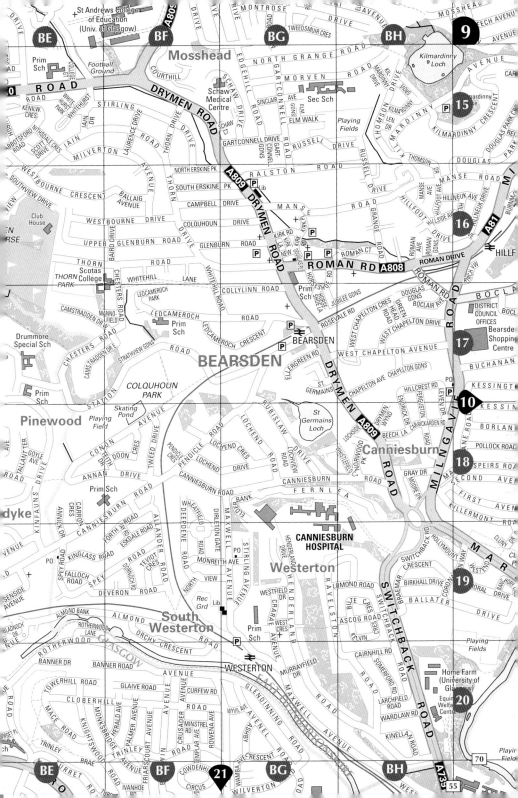

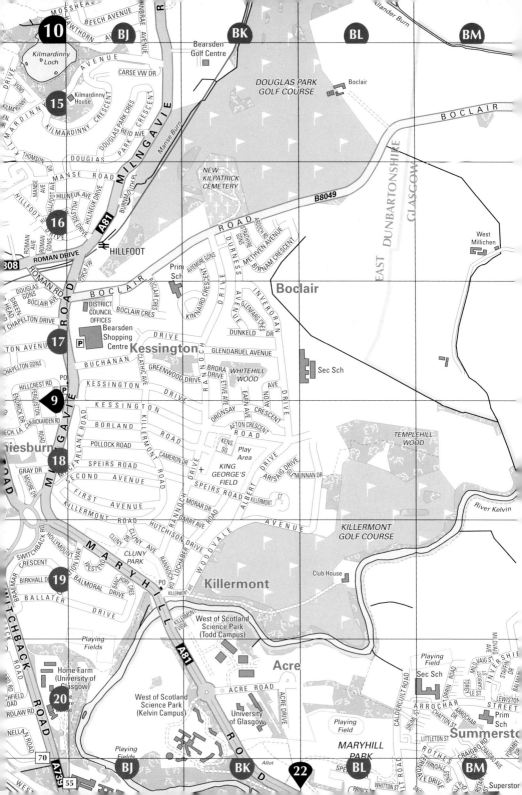

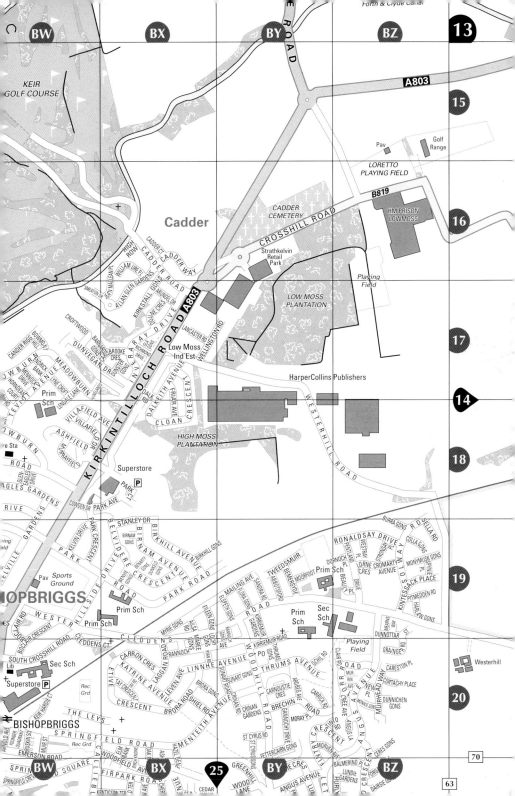

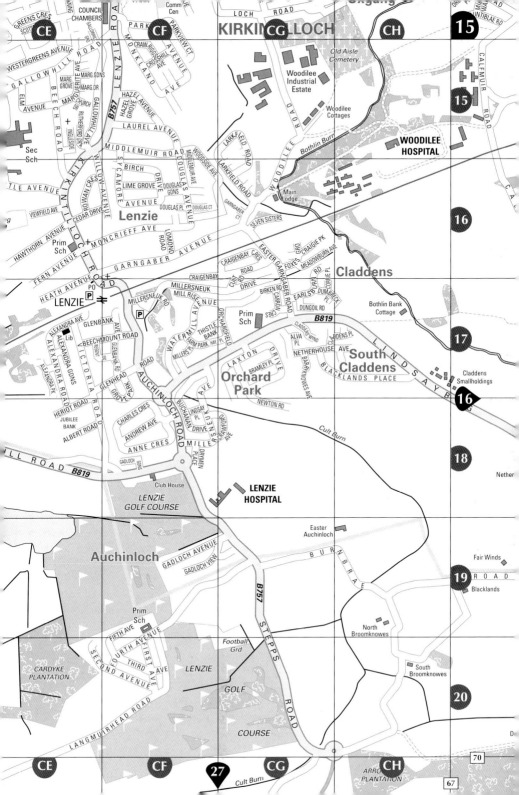

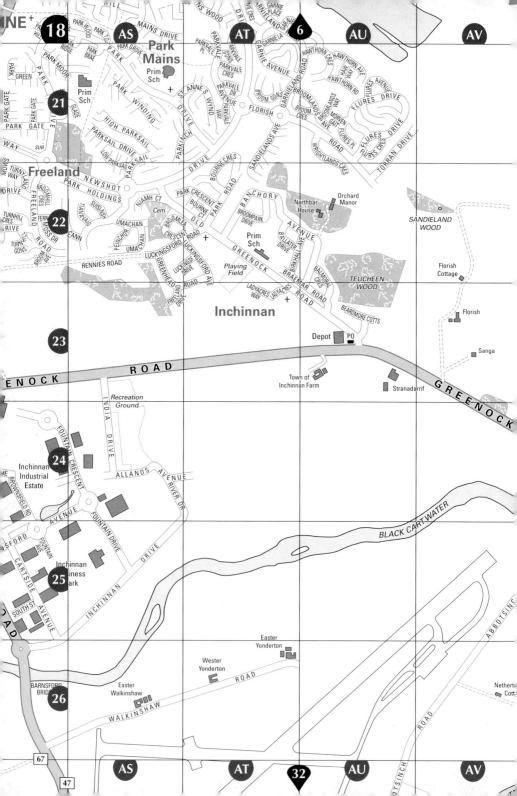

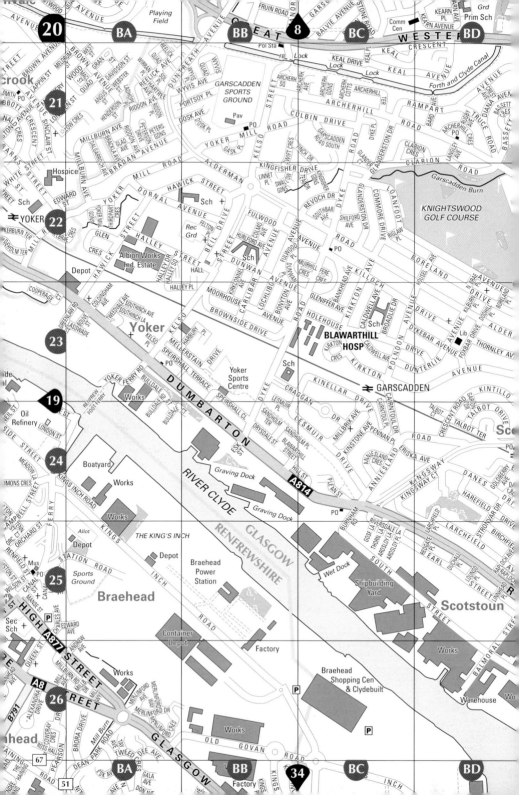

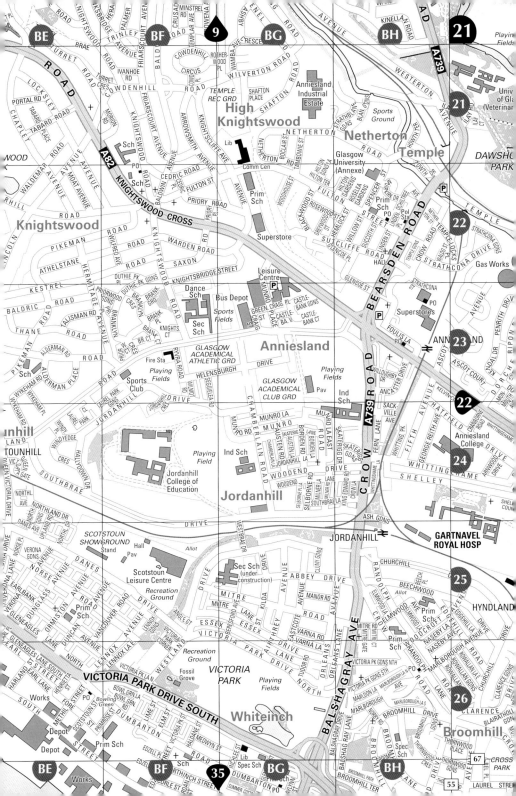

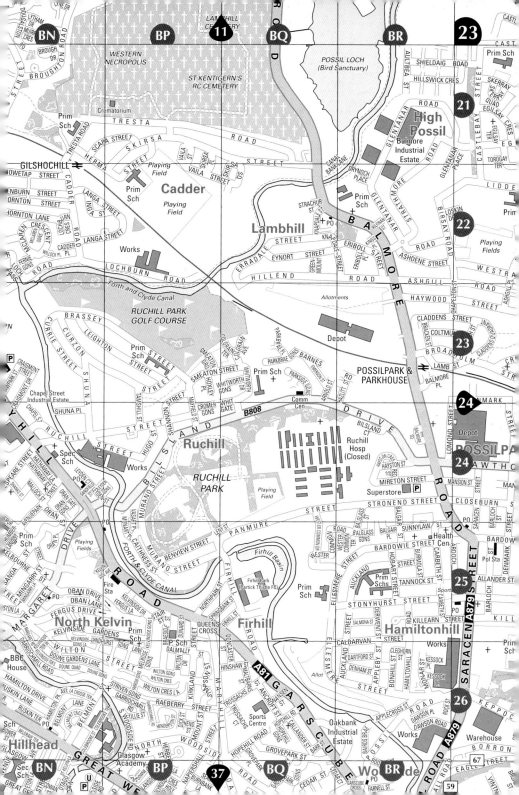

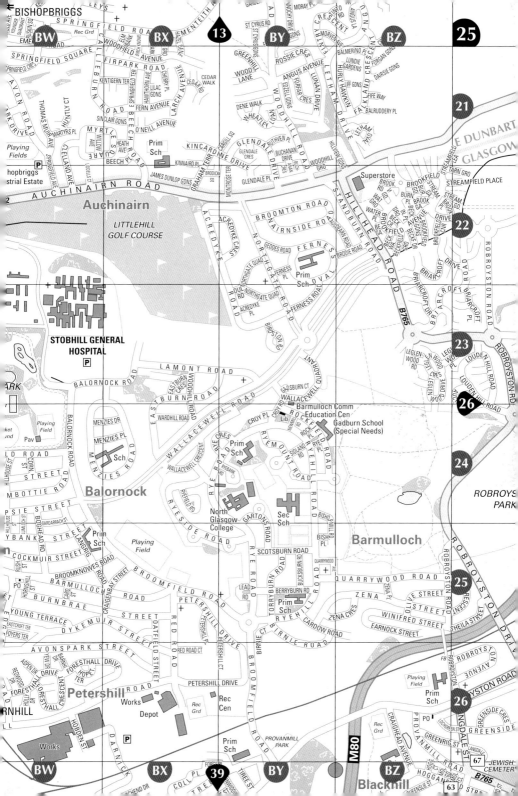

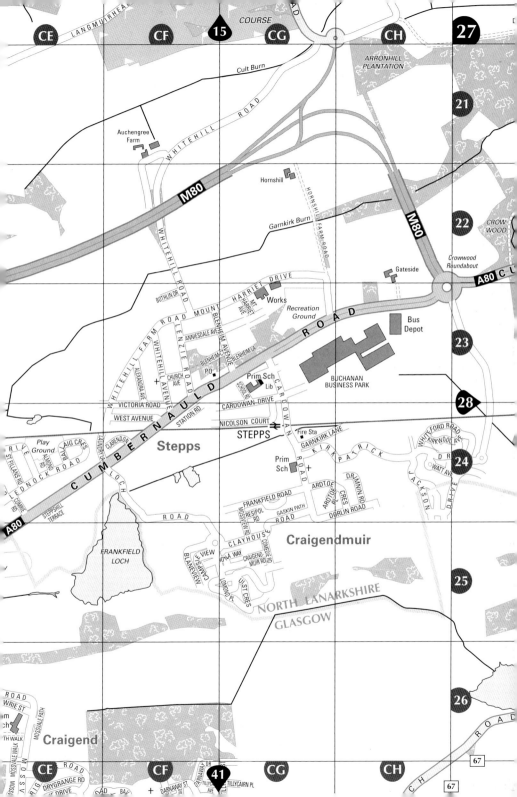

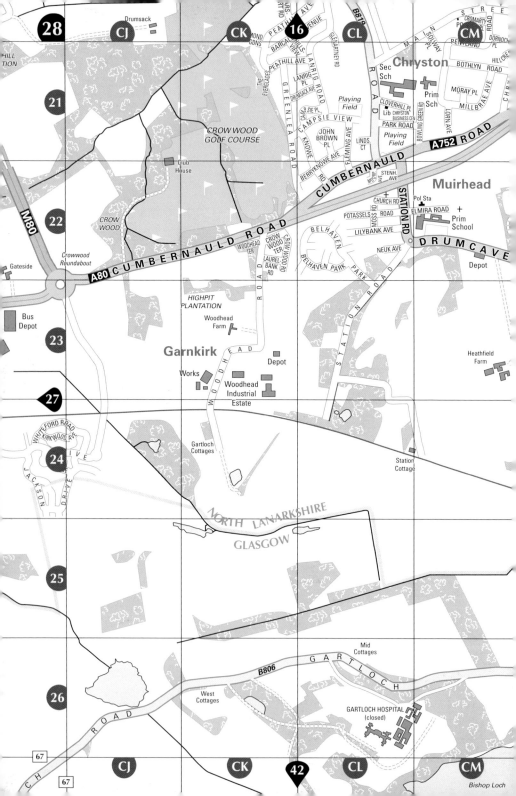

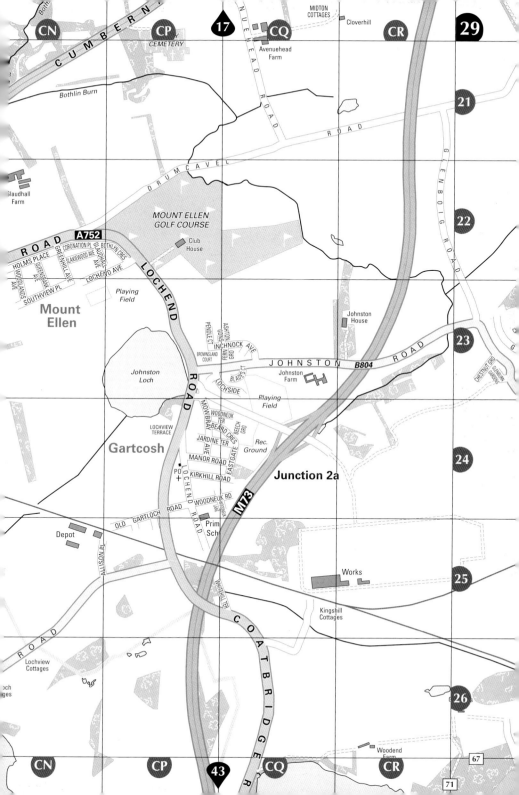

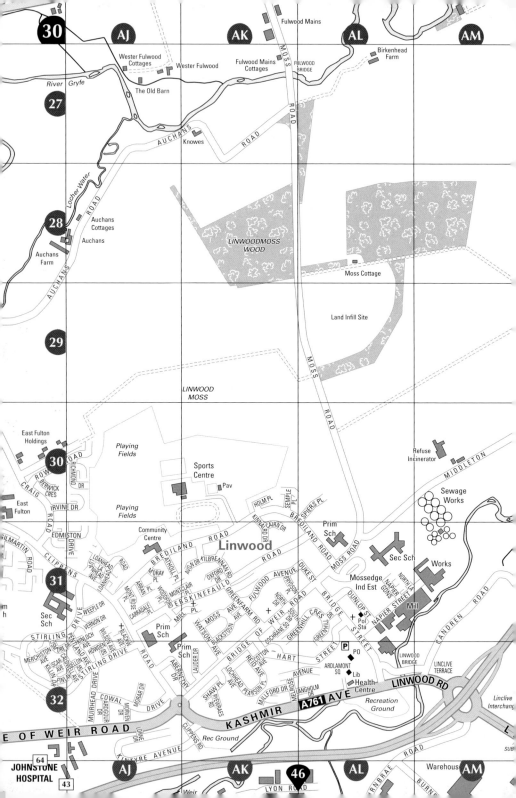

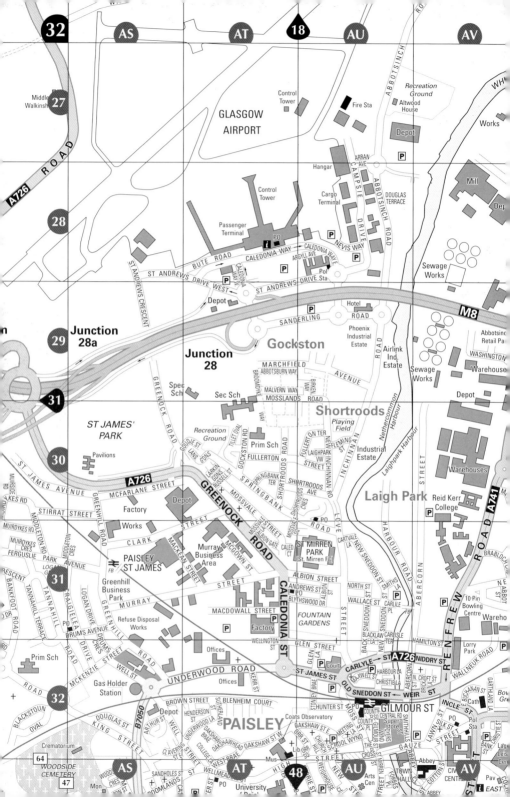

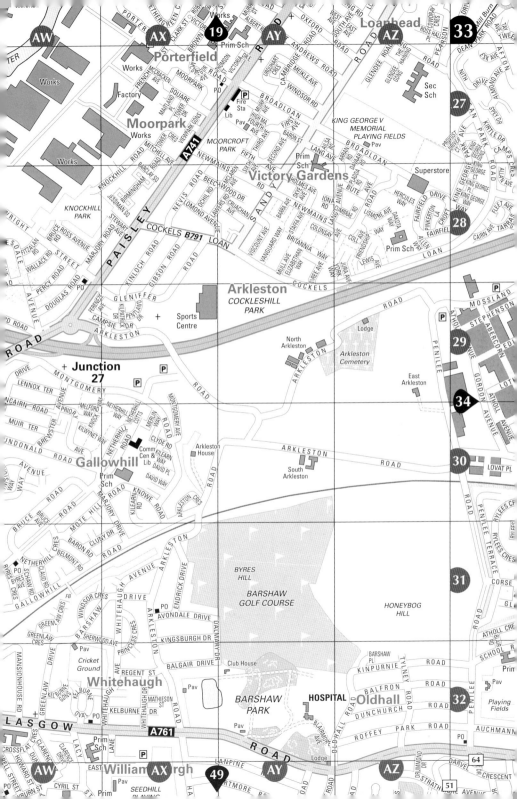

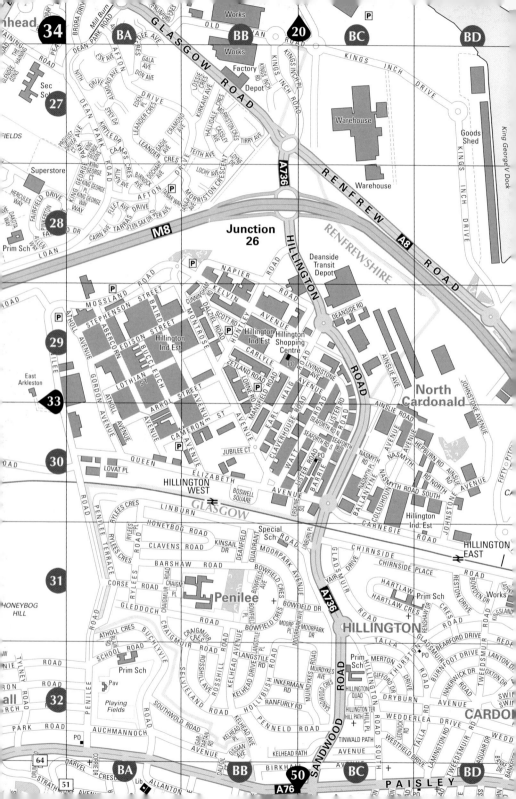

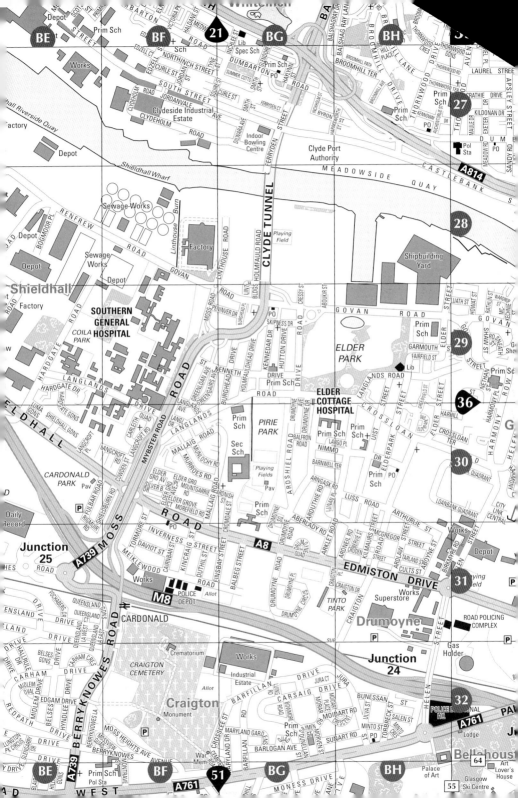

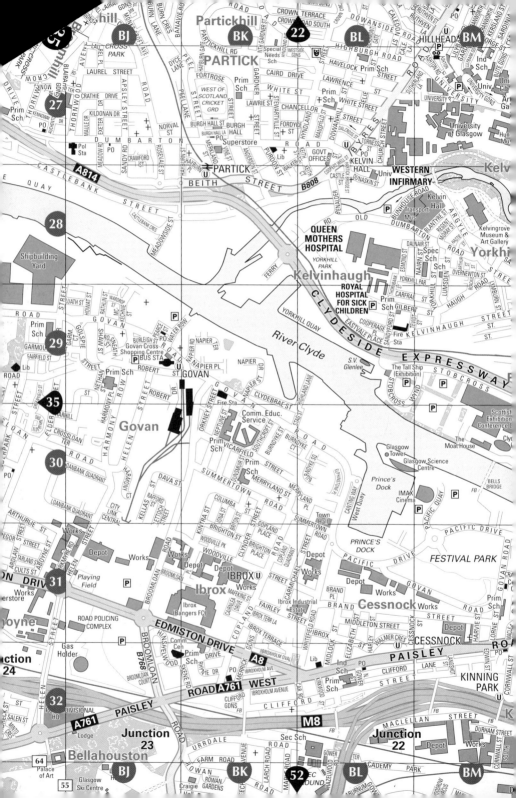

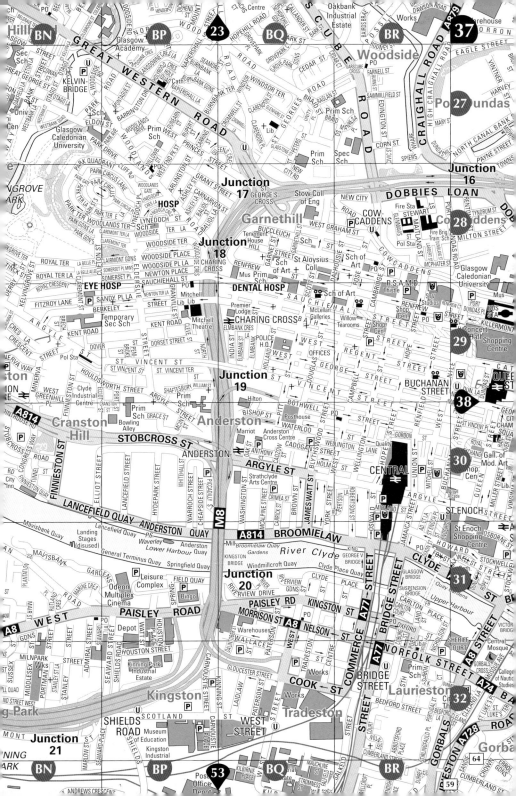

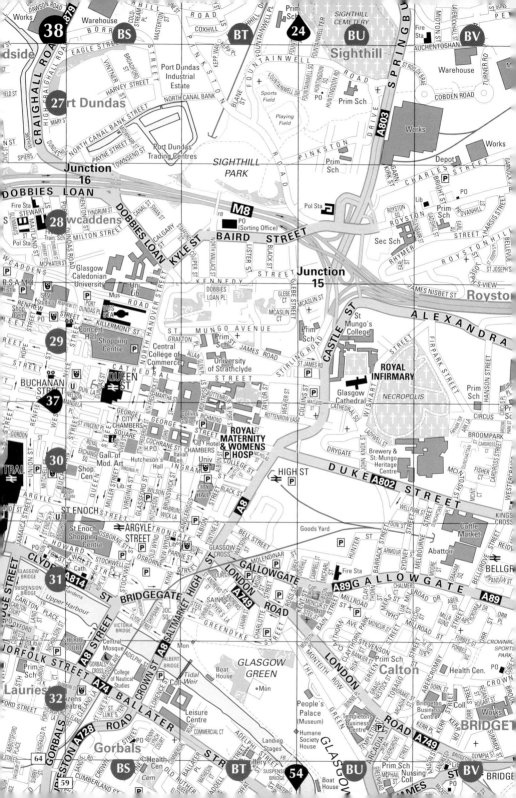

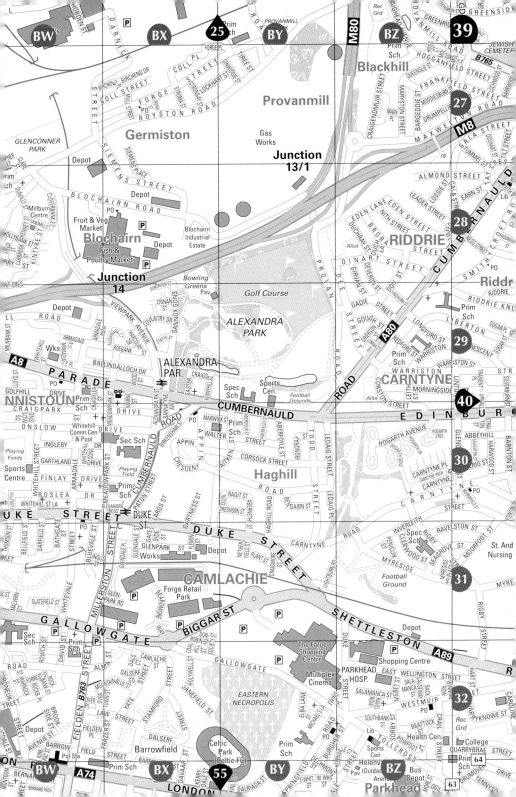

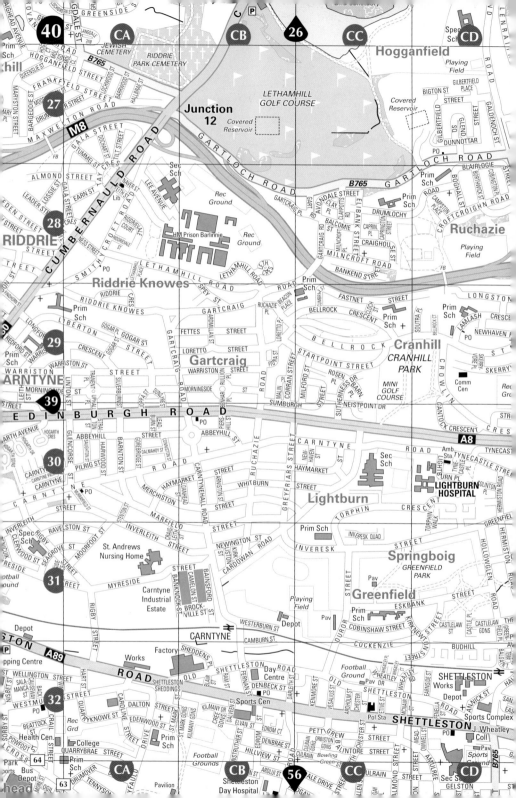

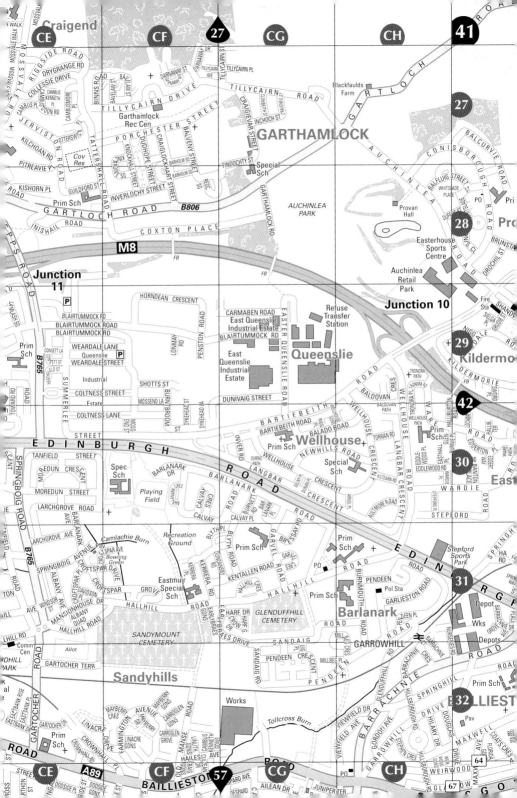

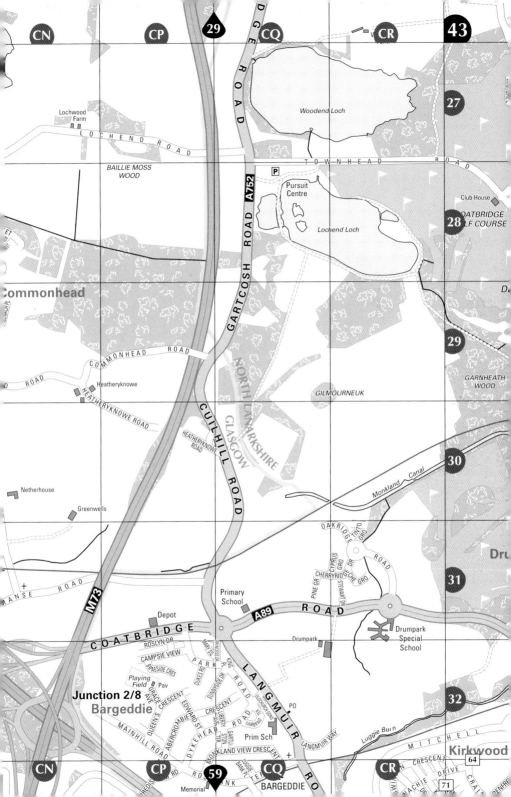

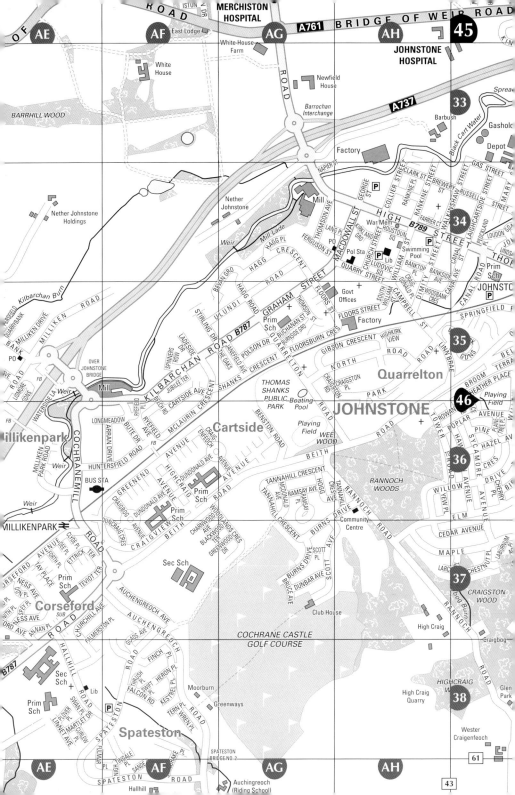

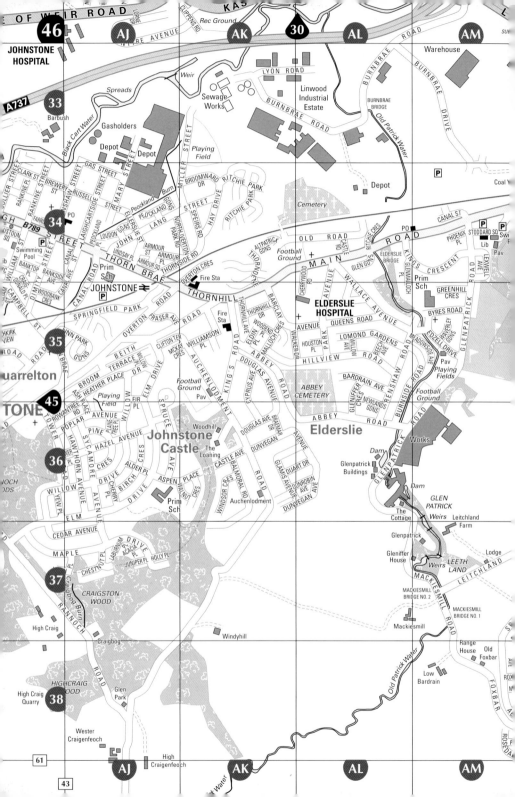

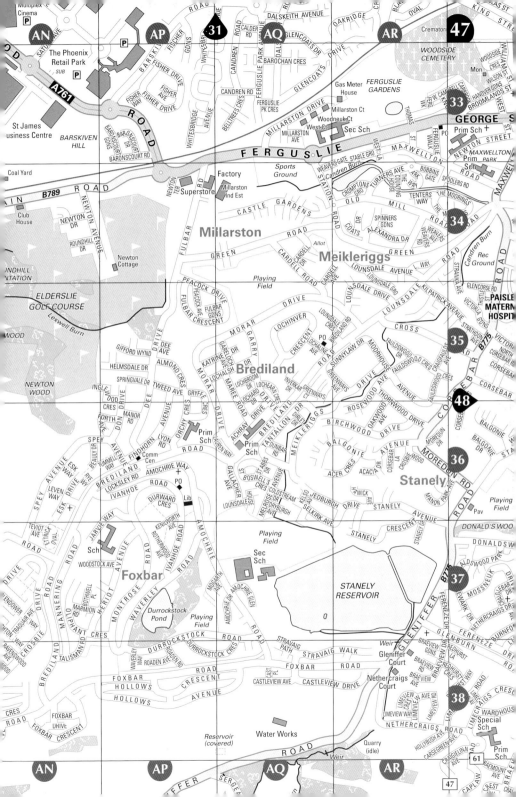

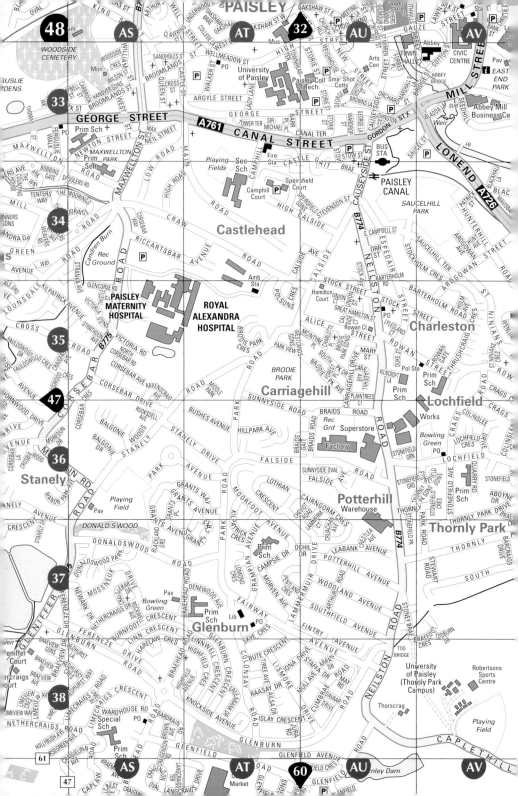

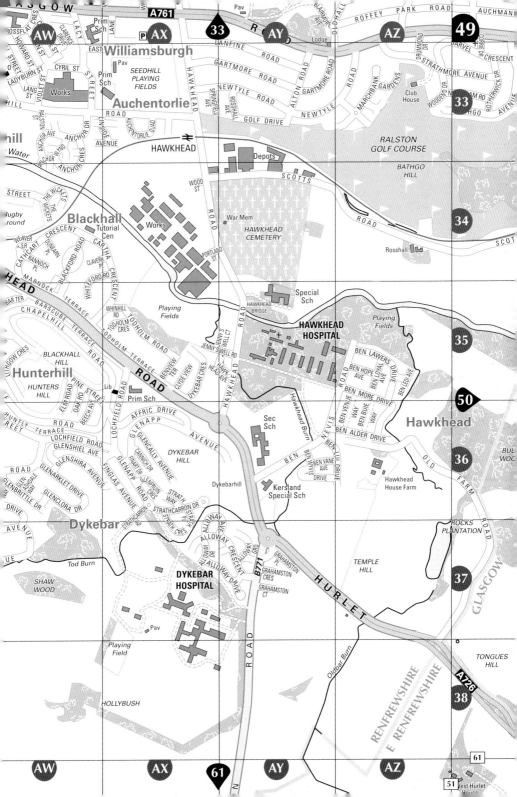

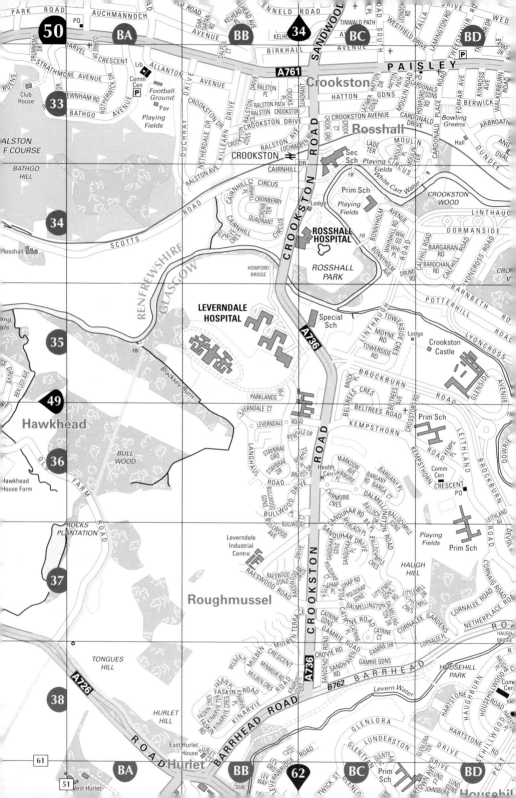

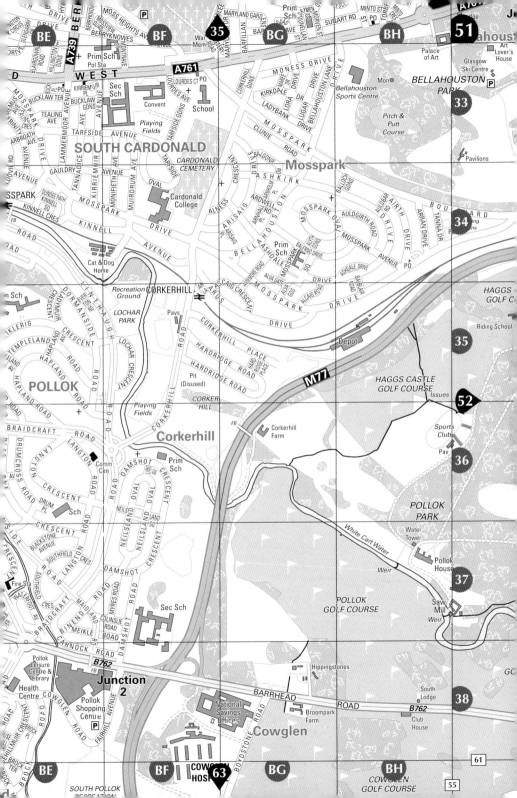

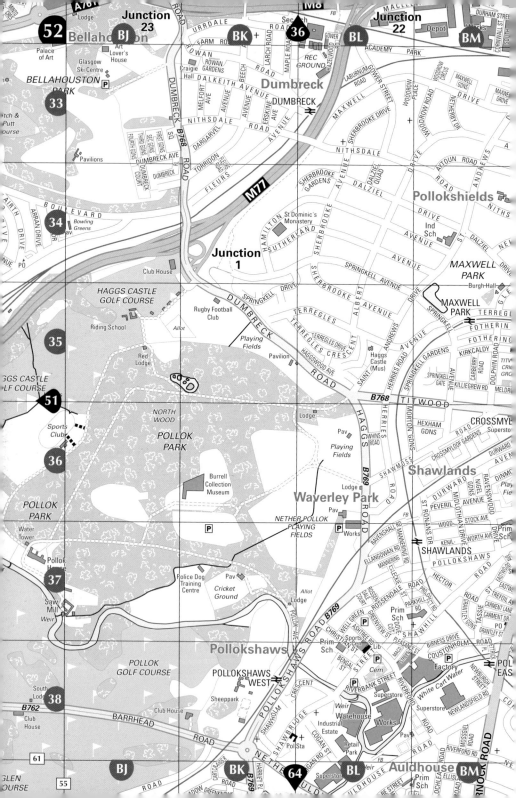

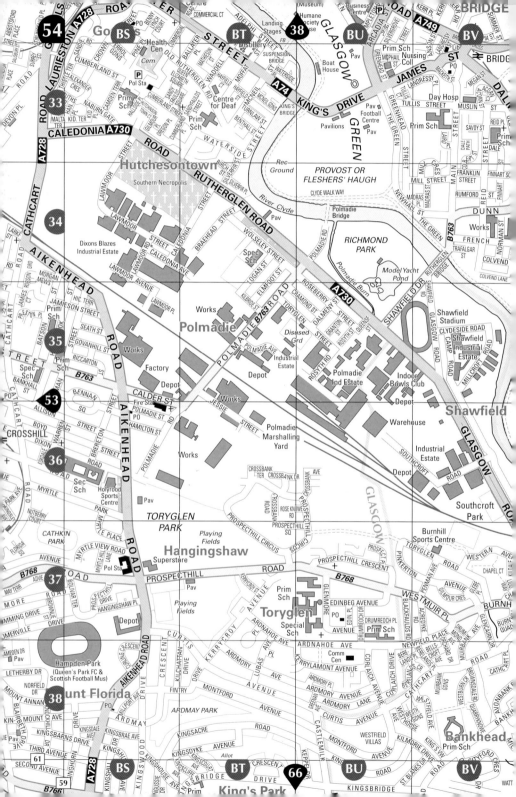

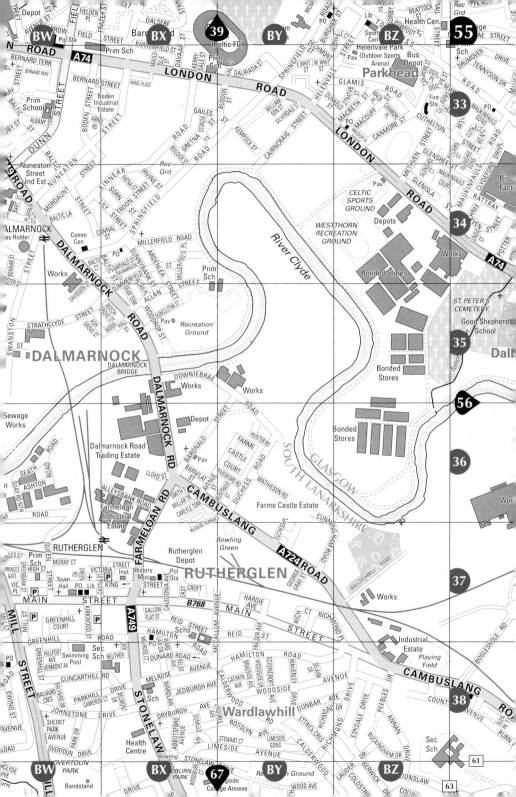

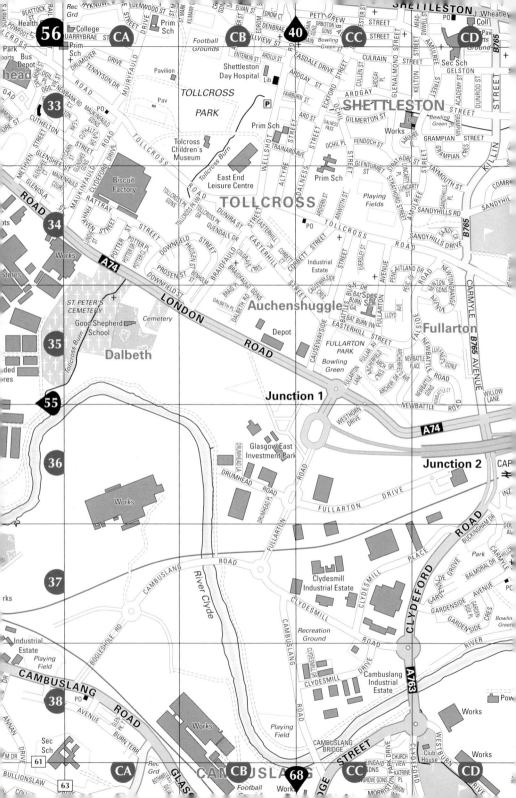

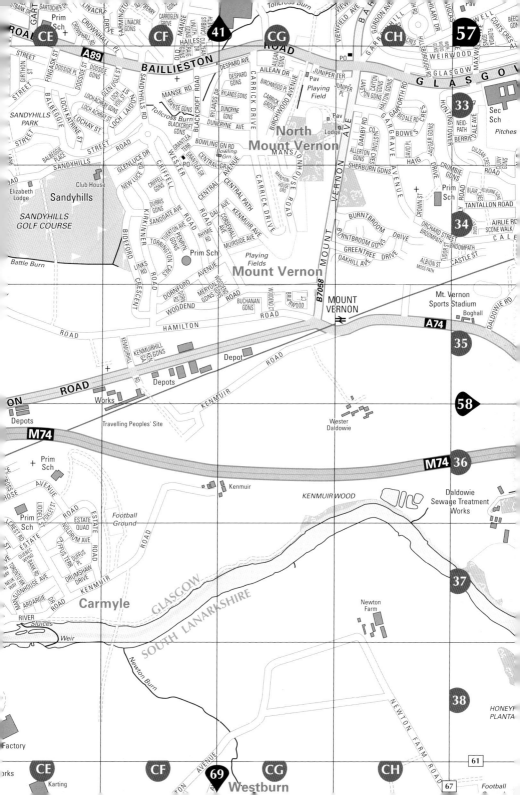

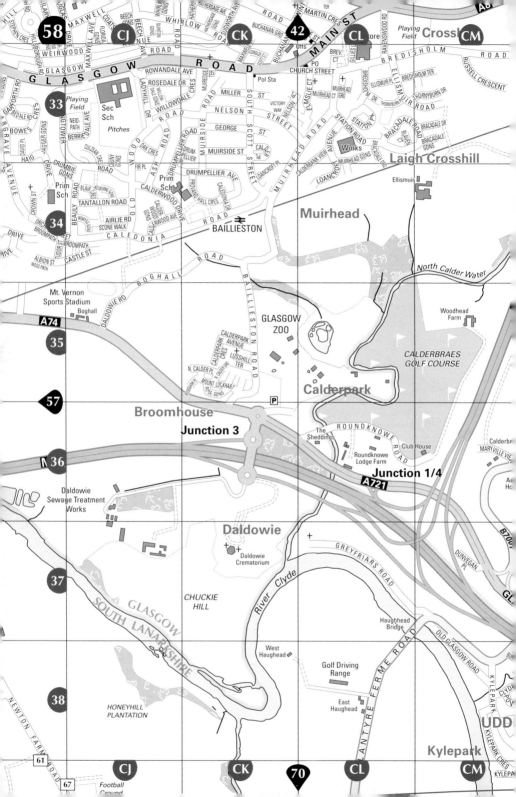

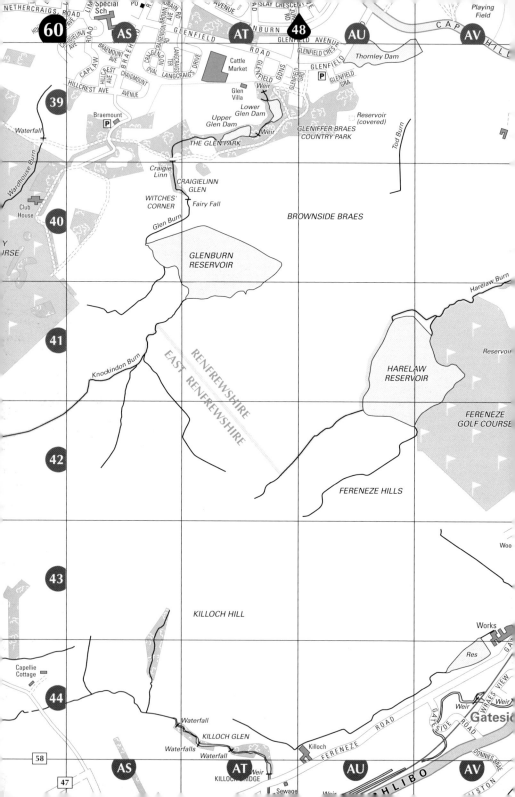

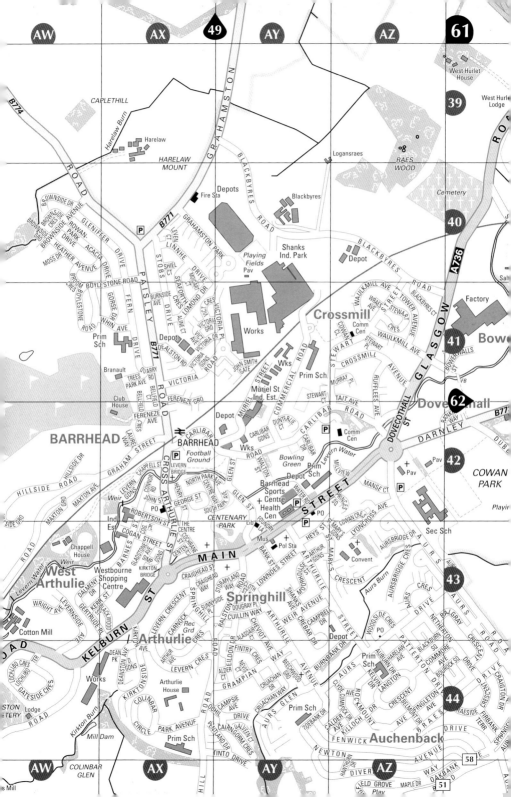

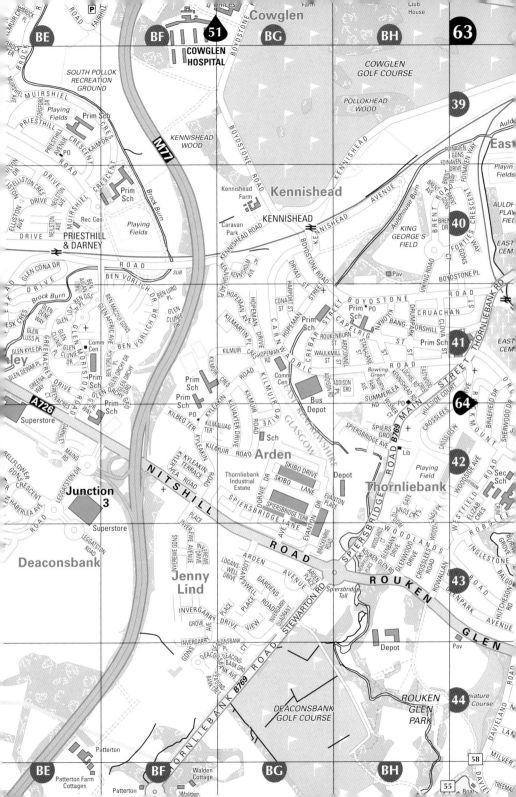

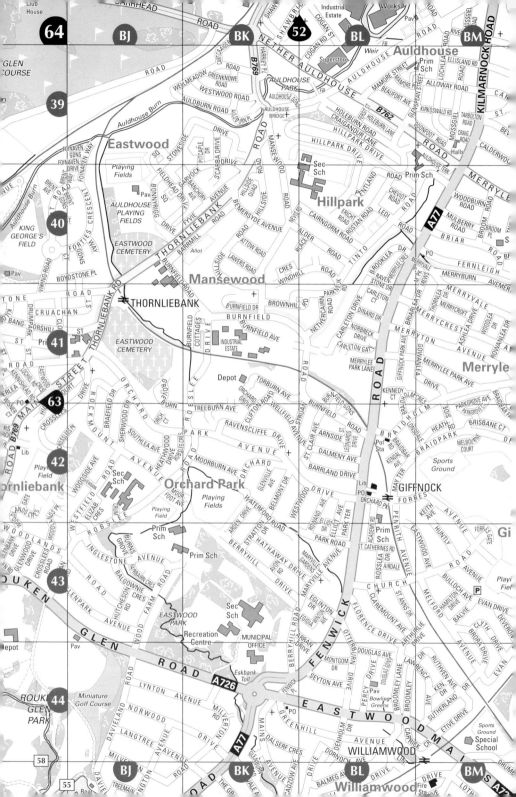

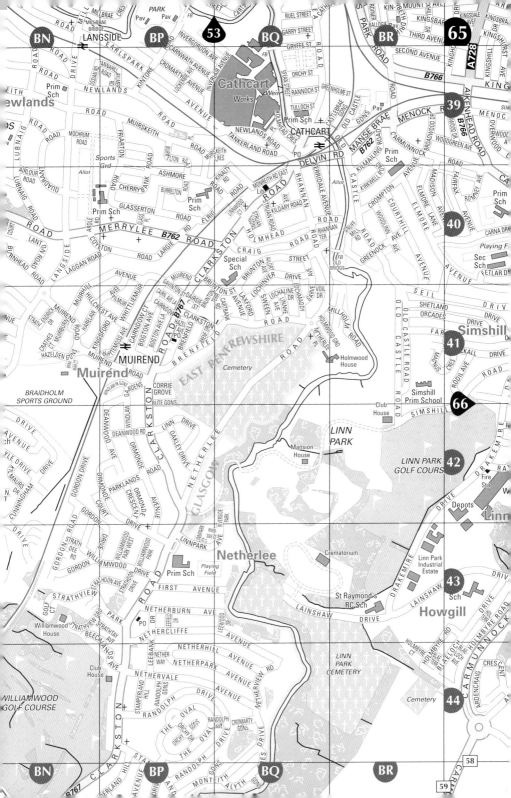

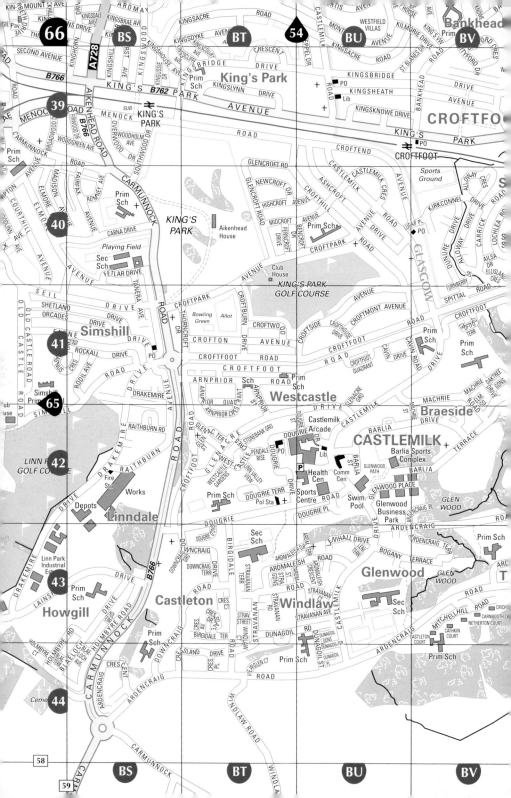

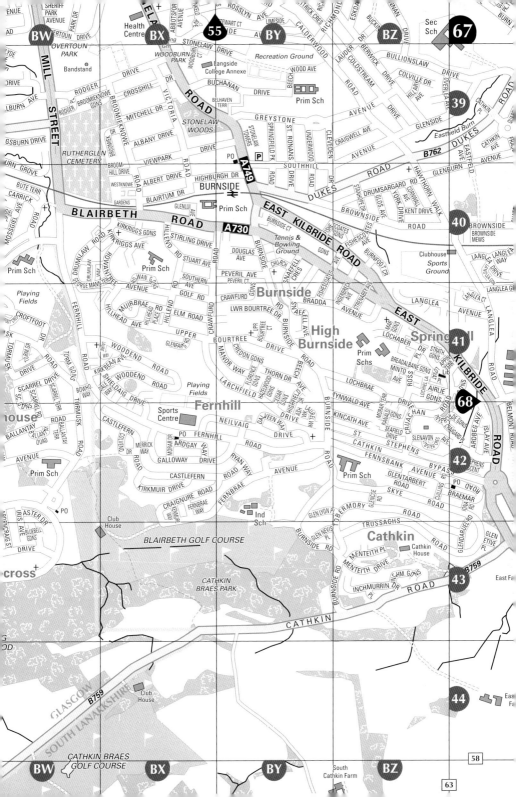

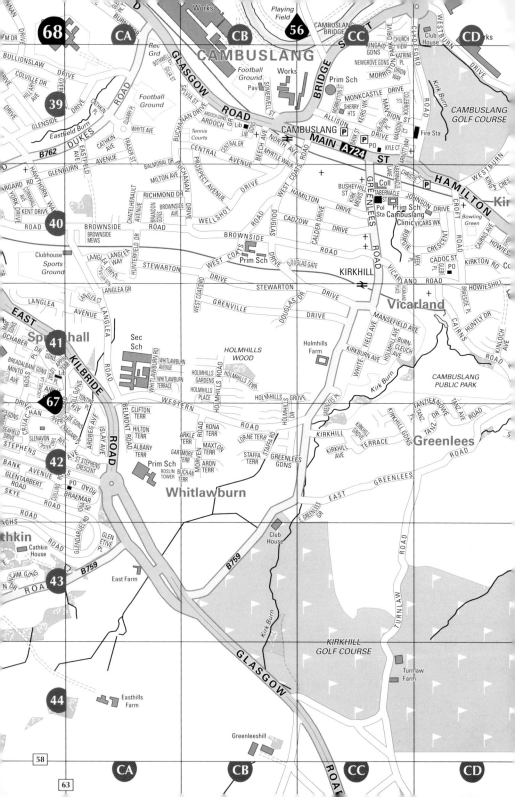

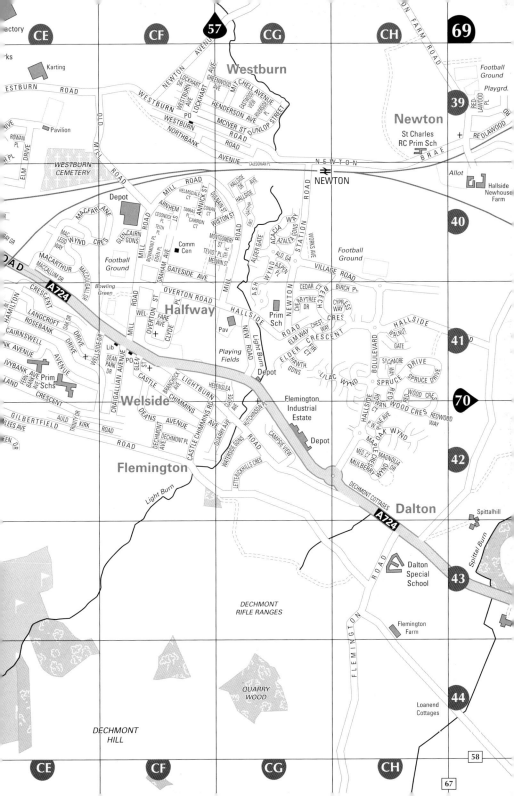

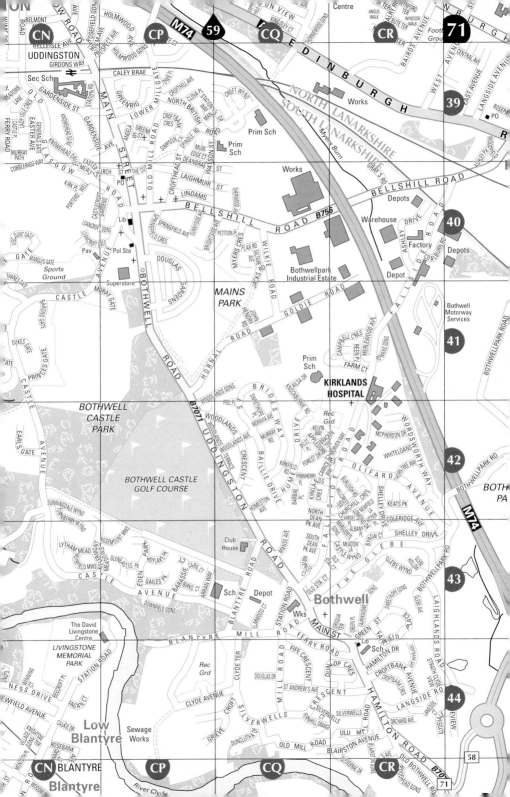

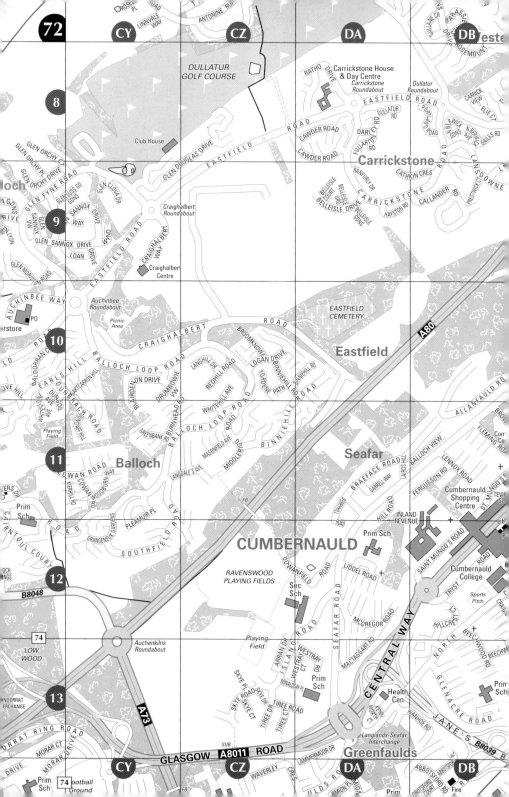

Local information

Useful Information
Area of City 79 sq. miles (approx)

Population (Glasgow City 1999) 611,440

Electricity 240 volts A.C.

Emergency Services
Police, Fire and Ambulance. Dial 999 on any telephone.

Licensing Hours
Public Houses
City Centre
Daily except Sundays 11a.m. – 12midnight
Sundays 12.30p.m. – 12midnight

Restaurants, hotels and public houses with catering facililities; same as above but can be extended for drinks with meals.

Tourist Information Centres
11 George Square, G2 1DY
0141 204 4400

Town Hall, 9a Gilmour Street,
Paisley, PA1 1DD
0141 889 0711

Glasgow International Airport (Abbotsinch), Paisley,
PA3 2ST
0141 848 4440

Road Chef Services, M74 Northbound, Hamilton
ML 6JW 01698 285590

Post Offices
St. Vincent Street Branch Office
47 St. Vincent Street, G2 5QX
Open Monday to Friday 8.30a.m. – 5.45p.m.
Saturdays 9a.m. – 5.30p.m.

City Branch Office
87-91 Bothwell Street, G2 7AA
Monday to Friday 9.00a.m. – 5.30p.m.

Hope Street Branch Office
228 Hope Street, G2 3PN
Monday to Thursday 8.30a.m. – 5.30p.m.
Friday 9.00a.m. – 5.30p.m.
Saturday 8.30a.m. – 5.30p.m.

Post Office Counters Ltd
0845 7223344

Entertainment

As Scotland's commercial and industrial capital, Glasgow offers a good choice of leisure activities. The city now has many theatres where productions include serious drama, pantomime, pop and musicals. The Theatre Royal, Hope Street is Scotland's only opera house and has been completely restored to its full Victorian splendour. The Royal Scottish National Orchestra gives classical music concerts at the Glasgow Royal Concert Hall between October and April and is the venue for the proms in June. Cinemas are still thriving in Glasgow, as are the many public houses, some of which provide meals and live entertainment. In the city centre and Byres Road, West End, there is a fair number of restaurants where

traditional home cooking, as well as international cuisines, can be sampled. More night life can be found at the city's nightclubs, discos and dance halls.

Outdoors, apart from the many parks and nature trails, there is Calderpark Zoological Gardens, situated 6 miles from the centre between Mount Vernon and Uddingston. Here you may see white rhinos, black panthers and iguanas among many species. Departing from Anderston Quay, you can also cruise down the Clyde in 'P.S. Waverley' – the last sea-going paddle-steamer in the world.

Cinemas

Glasgow Film Theatre 12 Rose Street, G3 6RB
0141 332 8128
Grosvenor Ashton Lane, G12 8SJ
0141 339 4298
IMAX 50 Pacific Quay, G51 1EA
0141 420 5000
Odeon Springfield Quay, Paisley Road, G5 8NP
08705 050007
Odeon 56 Renfield Street, G2 1NF
08705 050007

Showcase Barrbridge Road, Bargeddie, G69 7TZ
01236 438 880
Showcase Phoenix Business Park, Paisley, PA1 2BH
0141 887 0011
UGC The Forge Shopping Centre, 1221 Gallowgate,
G31 4EB. 08701 555136
UGC 145-159 West Nile Street, G1 2RL
08709 070789
UCI Clyde Shopping Centre, Britannia Way,
Clydebank, G81 2RZ. 08700 10 20 30

Theatres

Arches Theatre
30 Midland Street, G1 4PR
09010 220300
Citizens' Theatre
119 Gorbals Street, G5 9DS
0141 429 0022
King's Theatre
297 Bath Street, G2 4JN
0845 330 3511
Mitchell Theatre and Moir Hall
Granville Street, G3
0141 287 5511
New Athenaeum Theatre
100 Renfrew Street, G2 3DB
0141 332 5057

Pavilion Theatre
121 Renfield Street, G2 3AX
0141 332 1846
Theatre Royal
282 Hope Street, G2 3QA
0845 330 3511
Tramway
25 Albert Drive, G41 2PE
0845 330 3511
Tron Theatre
63 Trongate, G1 5HB
0141 552 4267

Halls

Glasgow Royal Concert Hall
2 Sauchiehall Street, G2 3NY
0141 353 8000
Henry Wood Hall,
73 Claremont Street, G3 7JB
0141 225 3555
Scottish Exhibition Conference Centre,
G3 8YW
0141 248 3000

For more information about the following G.C.C.
halls contact;
Cultural and Leisure Services,
3rd Floor, 20 Trongate, G1 5ES. 0141 287 8931
City Halls, Candleriggs, G1
Couper Institute, 86 Clarkston Road, G44
Langside Hall, 5 Langside Avenue, G41
Partick Burgh Hall, 9 Burgh Hall Street, G11
Shettleston Hall, Wellshot Road, G32
Woodside Hall, Glenfarg Street, G20

Transport

The City of Glasgow has one of the most advanced, fully integrated public transport systems in the whole of Europe. The Strathclyde Transport network consists of: the local railway network, the local bus services and the fully modernised Glasgow

Underground, with links to Glasgow International Airport and the Steamer and car ferry services. See the Strathclyde Passenger Transport (SPT) rail network map on page 126 and for information contact them on 0141 332 6811.

Bus Services

Long Distance Coach Service
Citylink 08705 505050
National Express 08705 808080

Scottish Citylink Coaches Ltd and National Express provide rapid services to London and most parts of Scotland.

Local Bus Services

Traveline Scotland (timetable only) 0870 6082608
A comprehensive network of local bus services is provided by a variety of operators within the City of Glasgow and also direct to a number of surrounding towns. These services depart from City Centre bus stops or from Buchanan Bus Station, Killermont Street, G2. 0141 333 3708

Railway Services

National Rail (timetable only): 08457 484 950
ScotRail (telesales only): 08456 550033
Arriva Trains Northern: 08706 023322
G.N.E.R. (timetable & telesales): 08457 225225
Virgin (timetable & telesales): 08457 222333

ScotRail trains serve over 170 stations in Glasgow and Strathclyde (see map on page 126) and operate to most destinations in Scotland.
Arriva Trains Northern, G.N.E.R. & Virgin operate services to England.
Use Glasgow Queen Street station for services to the north east of Glasgow and use Glasgow Central station for services to the west and south of Glasgow and England.

Taxis

Glasgow has over 1400 traditional London type taxis, all licensed by the Glasgow District Council. At the time of publishing, a three mile journey costs approximately £5. The total price of each journey is shown on the meter and is calculated by distance or time or a combination of both. The major taxi companies offer City tours at fixed prices, listing the places of interest to be visited, leaflets are available at all major hotel reception areas. Tours vary from 1 to 3 hours and in price between £15 and £45.
A tour "Glasgow by Night" is also available.

Any passenger wishing to travel to a destination outside the Glasgow District Boundary should ascertain from the driver the fare to be charged.

Complaints

Any complaints regarding the conduct of a taxi driver should be addressed to:
The Taxi Enforcement Officer,
City Building Department,
73 Hawthorn Street, G22 6HY.
0141 287 3326

Glasgow International Airport

Located eight miles (13km) west of Glasgow along-side the M8 motorway at Junction 28 & 28A this air-port is linked by a bus service to Buchanan Bus Station, which runs every 15 minutes from 6.30am – 6.00pm Monday to Saturday and every 30 minutes at off peak times. There is a frequent coach service link-ing the Airport with all major bus and rail terminals in the city. Coach and bus tickets along with rail infor-mation can be obtained from the SPT travel desk, door 5 on the ground floor.
Car parking is available with a graduated scale of charges.
The Airport telephone number is 0141 887 1111

Aer Lingus Flights to: Dublin
Reservations 08450 844 444
Air Canada Flights to: Toronto
Reservations 08705 247226

British Airways Flights to: Belfast, Birmingham, Bristol, Gatwick, Heathrow, Londonderry, Manchester, Southampton and Inter Scottish Routes
Reservations 0845 77 333 77
British European Flights to: Birmingham
Reservations 08705 676 676
British Midland Flights to: East Midlands, Heathrow, Jersey, Copenhagen, Leeds Bradford, and Manchester
Reservations 0870 607 0555
Continental Flights to: New York
Reservations 0800 776 464
Easy Jet Flights to: Belfast and Luton
Reservations 0870 600 0000
Go Flights to: Belfast, East Midlands and Stansted
Reservations 0870 607 6543
Icelandair Flights to: Reykjavik
Reservations 08457 581 111
KLM U.K. Flights to: Amsterdam
Reservations 08705 074 074
Manx Airlines Flights to: Isle of Man
Reservations 08457 256 256

Prestwick International Airport

Also offers access to Glasgow via a 45 minute train journey. Flights from and to Brussels, Dublin, Franfurt, Oslo, Paris and Stansted,. Discounted rail fares to Glasgow Central station are available for air passengers.

Prestwick International Airport 01292 511000

Ryanair
Reservations 0871 246 0000

Index to place names

A

Abronhill 73 DF9
Acre 10 BK20
Anderston 4 BP30
Anniesland 21 BG23
Arden 63 BG42
Arkleston 33 AY29
Arthurlie 61 AX44
Auchenback 61 AZ44
Auchenshuggle 56 CB35
Auchentorlie 49 AX33
Auchinairn 25 BW22
Auchinloch 15 CE19
Auldhouse 64 BL39

B

Baillieston 41 CH32
Balgrayhill 24 BV23
Balloch 72 CY11
Balornock 25 BW24
Bankhead 54 BV38
Bargeddie 43 CN32
Barlanark 41 CH31
Barmulloch 25 BZ25
Barrhead 61 AW42
Battlefield 53 BQ38
Bearsden 9 BF17
Bellahouston 36 BJ32
Birkenshaw 59 CP36
Bishopbriggs 12 BV19
Bishoploch 42 CL28
Blackhall 49 AW34
Blackhill 39 BZ27
Blairdardie 8 BD20
Blairtummock 42 CJ29
Blochairn 39 BW28
Blysthwood 19 AY24
Boclair 10 BK17
Bonnaughton 8 BC15
Bothwell 71 CQ43
Bowerwalls 62 BA41
Bowhouse 67 BW42
Braehead 20 BA25
Braeside 66 BV42
Brediland 47 AQ35
Bridgend 17 CN18
Bridgeton 38 BV32
Broadholm 8 BC18
Broomhill 21 BH26
Broomhouse 58 CJ36
Burnside 67 BY41

C

Cadder, G23 23 BP22
Cadder, G64 13 BX16
Cairnsmore 8 BA18
Calderbraes 59 CN37
Calderpark 58 CL35
Calton 38 BU32
Cambuslang 68 CB39
Camlachie 39 BX31
Canniesburn 9 BH18
Carbrain 73 DC12
Cardonald 34 BD32
Cardowan 27 CF24
Carmyle 57 CE37
Carntyne 39 BZ29
Carriagehill 48 AT35
Carrickstone 72 DA9
Cartside 45 AF36
Castlehead 48 AT34
Castlemilk 66 BU42
Castleton 66 BS43
Cathcart 65 BQ39
Cathkin 67 BZ43
Cessnock 36 BL31
Charleston 48 AU35
Chryston 28 CL21
Claddens 15 CH16
Cleddans 8 BB17
Clydebank 7 AV20
Colston 24 BV22
Commonhead 43 CN29
Coresford 45 AE37
Corkerhill 51 BE36
Courthill 8 BC15
Cowcaddens 4 BR28
Cowglen 51 BG38

Cowlairs 24 BT25
Craigend 27 CE26
Craigendmuir 27 CG25
Craigton 35 BF32
Cranhill 40 CC29
Cranston Hill 37 BN30
Croftfoot 66 BV39
Crookston 50 BC33
Crosshill, G42 53 BQ36
Crosshill, G69 42 CM32
Crossmill 61 AY41
Crossmyloof 52 BM35
Cumbernauld 72 CZ12
Cumbernauld Village 73 DE8

D

Dalbeth 56 CA35
Daldowie 58 CK37
Dalmarnock 55 BW35
Dalmuir 6 AU17
Dalton 69 CH42
Darnley 63 BE41
Deaconsbank 63 BE43
Dennistoun 39 BW29
Dovecothall 61 AZ42
Dowanhill 22 BL26
Drumchapel 8 BB18
Drumoyne 35 BH31
Drumry 7 AY19
Dumbreck 52 BK33
Duntocher 7 AX15
Dykebar 49 AW37

E

Easterhouse 42 CL29
Eastfield 72 DA10
Easthall 42 CJ30
Eastwood 64 BJ39
Elderslie 46 AL36

F

Ferguslie Park 31 AP32
Fernhill 67 BX42
Finnieston 36 BM29
Firhill 23 BQ25
Flemington 69 CF42
Foxbar 47 AP37
Freeland 18 AS22
Fullarton 56 CD35

G

Gallowhill 33 AW30
Garnethill 4 BQ28
Garnkirk 28 CJ23
Garrowhill 41 CG32
Gartcosh 29 CP24
Gartcraig 40 CB29
Garthamlock 41 CG27
Gateside 60 AV44
Germiston 39 BX27
Giffnock 64 BM43
Gilshochill 22 BM22
Glenburn 48 AT37
Glenwood 66 BU43
Gockston 32 AT29
Gorbals 38 BS32
Govan 36 BJ30
Govanhill 53 BQ35
Greenfaulds 72 DA13
Greenfield 40 CC31
Greenlees 68 CD42

H

Haghill 39 BY30
Halfway 69 CF41
Hallside 69 CH41
Hamiltonhill 23 BR25
Hanginghaw 54 BS37
Hardgate 7 AY15
Hawkhead 49 AZ36
High Burnside 67 BY41
High Gallowhill 14 CC15
High Knightswood 21 BG21
High Possil 23 BR21
Hillhead 23 BN26
Hillington 34 BC31
Hillpark 64 BL40

Hogganfield 40 CC27
Househillwood 62 BD39
Howgill 65 BR43
Hunterhill 49 AW35
Hurlet 62 BA39
Hutchesontown 54 BS34
Hyndland 22 BJ26

I

Ibrox 36 BK31
Inchinnan 18 AT23

J

Jenny Lind 63 BF43
Johnstone 45 AH36
Johnstone Castle 46 AJ36
Jordanhill 21 BG24

K

Kelvindale 22 BK23
Kelvingrove 36 BM28
Kelvinhaugh 36 BK28
Kelvinside 22 BK25
Kennishead 63 BG40
Kessington 10 BJ17
Kilbarchan 44 AD34
Kilbowie 7 AX19
Kildermorie 42 CJ29
Kildrum 73 DD10
Killermont 10 BK19
King's Park 66 BT39
Kingsridge 8 BA18
Kingston 37 BP32
Kinning Park 36 BM32
Kirkhill 68 CD40
Kirklandneuk 19 AW26
Knightswood 21 BE22
Kylepark 58 CM38

L

Laigh Crosshill 58 CL33
Laigh Park 32 AU30
Lambhill 23 BQ22
Langfauld 8 BB17
Langmuir 59 CP33
Langside 53 BN37
Laurieston 37 BR32
Lenzie 15 CF16
Lenziemill 73 DC13
Lightburn 40 CC30
Linndale 66 BS42
Linnvale 7 AZ20
Linwood 30 AK31
Loanhead 19 AZ26
Lochfield 48 AV36
Low Blantyre 71 CN44

M

Mansewood 64 BK40
Maryhill 22 BK22
Meikleriggs 47 AQ34
Merrylee 64 BM41
Millarston 47 AP34
Millerston 26 CC25
Millikenpark 45 AE36
Milton 24 BS22
Moodiesburn 16 CM19
Moorpark 33 AX27
Mosshead 9 BF15
Mosspark 51 BG34
Mountblow 6 AT16
Mount Ellen 29 CN23
Mount Florida 53 BR38
Mount Vernon 57 CG34
Muirend 65 BN41
Muirhead, (Baill.) G69 58 CL33
Muirhead, (Chry.) G69 28 CM22

N

Netherlee 65 BQ43
Netherton 23 BH21
Newlands 65 BN39
Newton 69 CH39
Nitshill 62 BB40
North Cardonald 34 BD29
North Kelvin 23 BN25

North Mount Vernon 57 CG33

O

Old Drumchapel 8 BA19
Oldhall 33 AZ32
Orchard Park, G46 64 BJ42
Orchard Park, G66 15 CG17

P

Paisley 32 AT32
Parkhall 6 AV16
Parkhead 55 BZ33
Parkhouse 24 BT23
Park Mains 18 AS21
Partick 36 BK27
Partickhill 22 BK26
Penilee 34 BB31
Petershill 25 BW26
Pinewood 9 BE18
Pollok 51 BE35
Pollokshaws 52 BK38
Pollokshields 52 BM34
Polmadie 54 BT35
Port Dundas 37 BR27
Port Eglinton 53 BP33
Porterfield 33 AX27
Possilpark 24 BS24
Potterhill 48 AU36
Priesthill 62 BD39
Provanhall 42 CJ28
Provanmill 39 BY27

Q

Quarrelton 45 AH35
Queenslie 41 CG29

R

Radnor Park 7 AW18
Renfrew 19 AY26
Riddrie 39 BZ28
Riddrie Knowes 40 CA29
Robroyston 26 CA23
Rogerfield 42 CL30
Rosshall 50 BC33
Roughmussel 50 BB37
Roystonhill 38 BV29
Ruchazie 40 CD28
Ruchill 23 BP24
Rutherglen 55 BX37

S

Sandyhills 41 CF32
Scotstoun 20 BD25
Scotstounhill 20 BD24
Seafar 72 DA11
Seedhill 48 AV33
Shawfield 54 BV36
Shawlands 52 BL36
Shettleston 56 CC33
Shieldhall 35 BE29
Shortroods 32 AU30
Sighthill 38 BU27
Simshill 66 BS41
South Cardonald 51 BE33
South Claddens 15 CH17
South Nitshill 62 BC41
South Westerton 9 BF19
Spateston 45 AF38
Spittal 66 BV40
Springboig 40 CC31
Springburn 24 BV25
Springhall 67 BZ41
Springhill 61 AY43
Stanely 47 AR36
Stepps 27 CF24
Stonedyke 8 BD18
Strathbungo 53 BN35
Summerston 10 BM20
Swinton 42 CL31

T

Tannochside 59 CR37
Temple 21 BH21
Templecross 66 BV43
Thornliebank 63 BH42
Thornly Park 48 AV37

Tollcross	56	CB34		Victory Gardens	33	AY28		Westburn	69	CG39		Woodside	37	BQ27
Toryglen	54	BT37		**W**				Westcastle	66	BT41		Wyndford	22	BM24
Tradeston	37	BQ32		Wardlawhill	55	BY38		Westerton	9	BG19		**Y**		
U				Waverley	8	BC16		Whitecrook	19	AZ21		Yoker	20	BA23
Uddingston	58	CM38		Waverley Park	52	BK36		Whitehaugh	33	AW32		Yorkhill	36	BM28
V				Wellhouse	41	CG30		Whiteinch	21	BG26				
Vicarland	68	CC41		Welside	69	CF42		Whitlawburn	68	CA42				
				West Arthurlie	61	AW43		Williamsburgh	49	AX33				
								Windlaw	66	BT43				

Index to street names

General abbreviations

All	Alley	Cors	Corners	Gra	Grange	N	North	St.	Saint
Allot	Allotments	Cotts	Cottages	Grd	Ground	NTS	National Trust	St	Street
Amb	Ambulance	Cov	Covered	Grds	Grounds		for Scotland	Sta	Station
App	Approach	Crem	Crematorium	Grn	Green	Nat	National	Sts	Streets
Arc	Arcade	Cres	Crescent	Grns	Greens	PH	Public House	Sub	Subway
Av/Ave	Avenue	Ct	Court	Gro	Grove	PO	Post Office	Swim	Swimming
Bdy	Broadway	Cts	Courts	Gros	Groves	Par	Parade	TA	Territorial
Bk	Bank	Ctyd	Courtyard	Gt	Great	Pas	Passage		Army
Bldgs	Buildings	Dep	Depot	Ho	House	Pav	Pavilion	TH	Town Hall
Boul	Boulevard	Dev	Development	Hos	Houses	Pk	Park	Tenn	Tennis
Bowl	Bowling	Dr	Drive	Hosp	Hospital	Pl	Place	Ter	Terrace
Br	Bridge	Dws	Dwellings	Hts	Heights	Pol	Police	Thea	Theatre
Cath	Cathedral	E	East	Ind	Industrial	Prec	Precinct	Trd	Trading
Cem	Cemetery	Ed	Education	Int	International	Prim	Primary	Twr	Tower
Cen	Central/	Elec	Electricity	Junct	Junction	Prom	Promenade	Twrs	Towers
	Centre	Embk	Embankment	La	Lane	Pt	Point	Uni	University
Cft	Croft	Est	Estate	Las	Lanes	Quad	Quadrant	Vil	Villas
Cfts	Crofts	Ex	Exchange	Lib	Library	RC	Roman	Vil	Villa
Ch	Church	Exhib	Exhibition	Lo	Lodge		Catholic	Vw	View
Chyd	Churchyard	FB	Footbridge	Ln	Loan	Rd	Road	W	West
Cin	Cinema	FC	Football Club	Lwr	Lower	Rds	Roads	Wd	Wood
Circ	Circus	Fld	Field	Mag	Magistrates	Rec	Recreation	Wds	Woods
Cl/Clo	Close	Flds	Fields	Mans	Mansions	Res	Reservoir	Wf	Wharf
Co	County	Fm	Farm	Mem	Memorial	Ri	Rise	Wk	Walk
Coll	College	Gall	Gallery	Mkt	Market	S	South	Wks	Works
Comm	Community	Gar	Garage	Mkts	Markets	Sch	School	Yd	Yard
Conv	Convent	Gdn	Garden	Ms	Mews	Sec	Secondary		
Cor	Corner	Gdns	Gardens	Mt	Mount	Shop	Shopping		
Coron	Coroners	Govt	Government	Mus	Museum	Sq	Square		

Post town abbreviations

Bell.	Bellshill		Ersk.	Erskine		Renf.	Renfrew
Clyde.	Clydebank		John.	Johnstone			
Coat.	Coatbridge		Pais.	Paisley			

District abbreviations

Abbots.	Abbotsinch		Cumb.V.	Cumbernauld Village		Linw.	Linwood
Baill.	Baillieston		Dunt.	Duntocher		Millik.	Millikenpark
Barr.	Barrhead		Elder.	Elderslie		Miln.	Milngavie
Bears.	Bearsden		Gart.	Gartcosh		Mood.	Moodiesburn
Bishop.	Bishopbriggs		Giff.	Giffnock		Muir.	Muirhead
Blan.	Blantyre		Hous.	Houston		Neil.	Neilston
Both.	Bothwell		How.	Howwood		Old Kil.	Old Kilpatrick
Camb.	Cambuslang		Inch.	Inchinnan		Ruther.	Rutherglen
Chry.	Chryston		Kilb.	Kilbarchan		Thornlie.	Thornliebank
Clark.	Clarkston		Kirk.	Kirkintilloch		Udd.	Uddingston
Cumb.	Cumbernauld		Lenz.	Lenzie			

This index contains streets that are not named on the map due to insufficient space. For each of these cases the nearest street that does appear on the map is listed in *italics*.

A

			Abbotsburn Way, Pais. PA3	32	AT29		Abbot St, Pais. PA3	32	AV31
Abbey Cl, Pais. PA1	32	AU32		Abbotsford, (Bishop.) G64	13	BY19		Abbott Cres, Clyde. G81	19	AZ21
Abbeycraig Rd, G34	42	CM28		Abbotsford Av, (Ruther.) G73	55	BX38		Aberconway St, Clyde. G81	19	AY21
Abbeydale Way, (Ruther.) G73	67	BY42		Abbotsford Cres, Pais. PA2	46	AM38		Abercorn Av, G52	34	BA29
off Neilvaig Dr				Abbotsford Pl, G5	37	BR32		Abercorn Pl, G23	11	BN20
Abbey Dr, G14	21	BG25		Abbotsford Rd, (Bears.) G61	9	BE15		Abercorn St, Pais. PA3	32	AV31
Abbeygreen St, G34	43	CN28		Abbotsford Rd, Clyde. G81	7	AX20		Abercromby Dr, G40	38	BV31
Abbeyhill St, G32	40	CA30		Abbotshall Av, G15	8	BA18		Abercromby Sq, G40	38	BV31
Abbey Mill Business Cen,	48	AV33		Abbotsinch Retail Pk, Pais. PA3	32	AV29		Abercromby St, G40	38	BV32
Pais. PA1				Abbotsinch Rd, Pais. PA3	32	AU27		Aberdalgie Path, G34	42	CK29
Abbey Rd, (Elder.) John. PA5	46	AK35		Abbotsinch Rd, Renf. PA4	18	AV25		Aberdalgie Rd, G34	42	CK29
Abbey Wk, (Baill.) G69	43	CP32		Abbot St, G41	53	BN36		Aberdour St, G31	39	BY30
off Sunnyside Dr				*off Frankfort St*						

Street		
Aberfeldy St, G31	39	BY30
Aberfoyle St, G31	39	BY30
Aberlady Rd, G51	35	BG31
Abernethy Dr, (Linw.) Pais. PA3	30	AJ32
Abernethy St, G31	39	BY30
Aberuthven Dr, G32	56	CD34
Abiegail Pl, (Blan.) G72	70	CM44
Aboukir St, G51	35	BG29
Aboyne Dr, Pais. PA2	48	AW40
Aboyne St, G51	35	BH31
Acacia Dr, (Barr.) G78	61	AW40
Acacia Dr, Pais. PA2	47	AR36
Acacia Pl, John. PA5	46	AJ37
Acacia Way, (Camb.) G72	69	CG40
Academy Pk, G51	52	BL33
Academy Rd, (Giff.) G46	64	BL43
Academy St, G32	56	CD33
Acer Cres, Pais. PA2	47	AQ36
Achamore Cres, G15	8	BA17
Achamore Dr, G15	8	BA17
Achamore Rd, G15	8	BA17
Achray Dr, Pais. PA2	47	AQ36
Acorn Ct, G40	54	BV33
Acorn St, G40	54	BV33
Acre Dr, G20	10	BK20
Acredyke Cres, G21	25	BY22
Acredyke Pl, G21	25	BY22
Acredyke Rd, G21	25	BX22
Acredyke Rd, (Ruther.) G73	54	BV37
Acre Rd, G20	10	BK20
Adams Ct La, G1	4	BR31
Adamswell St, G21	24	BU26
Adamswell Ter, (Mood.) G69	17	CQ19
Addiewell St, G32	40	CC30
off Cardowan Rd		
Addison Gro, (Thornlie.) G46	63	BH41
Addison Pl, (Thornlie.) G46	63	BH41
Addison Rd, G12	22	BM25
Addison Rd, (Thornlie.) G46	63	BG41
Adelaide Ct, Clyde. G81	6	AT16
Adelphi St, G5	38	BT32
Admiral St, G41	37	BN32
Advie Pl, G42	53	BR37
Affric Dr, Pais. PA2	49	AX36
Afton Cres, (Bears.) G61	10	BK18
Afton Dr, Renf. PA4	34	BA27
Afton Rd, (Cumb.) G67	73	DD10
Afton St, G41	53	BN37
Agamemnon St, Clyde. G81	6	AV19
Agnew La, G42	53	BQ36
Aigas Cotts, G13	21	BH24
off Fern La		
Aikenhead Rd, G42	53	BR34
Aikenhead Rd, G44	66	BS39
Ailean Dr, G32	57	CG33
Ailean Gdns, G32	57	CG33
Ailort Av, G44	65	BQ40
off Lochinver Dr		
Ailsa Dr, G42	53	BP38
Ailsa Dr, (Both.) G71	71	CQ41
Ailsa Dr, (Ruther.) G73	66	BV40
Ailsa Dr, Clyde. G81	7	AY15
Ailsa Dr, Pais. PA2	48	AT38
Ailsa Rd, (Bishop.) G64	13	BX19
Ailsa Rd, Renf. PA4	33	AY27
Ainslie Av, G52	34	BC29
Ainslie Rd, G52	34	BC29
Ainslie Rd, (Cumb.) G67	73	DE10
Airdale Av, (Giff.) G46	64	BL43
Aird's La, G1	5	BS31
off Bridgegate		
Airgold Dr, G15	8	BB17
Airgold Pl, G15	8	BB17
Airlie Gdns, (Ruther.) G73	67	BZ41
Airlie La, G12	22	BK25
Airlie Rd, (Baill.) G69	58	CJ34
Airlie St, G12	22	BJ26
Airlink Ind Est, Pais. PA3	32	AU29
Airlour Rd, G43	65	BN40
Airth Dr, G52	51	BH34
Airth La, G52	51	BH34
off Mosspark Dr		
Airth Pl, G52	51	BH34
off Mosspark Dr		
Airthrey Av, G14	21	BG26
Airthrey La, G14	21	BG25
off Airthrey Av		
Aitkenhead Av, Coat. ML5	59	CR33
Aitkenhead Rd, (Udd.) G71	59	CQ36
Aitken St, G31	39	BY30
Alasdair Ct, (Barr.) G78	61	AY43
Albany Av, G32	41	CE31
Albany Cotts, G13	21	BH24
off Fern La		
Albany Dr, (Ruther.) G73	67	BX39
Albany Pl, (Both.) G71	71	CR43
off Marguerite Gdns		
Albany Quad, G32	41	CE31
Albany St, G40	55	BW33
Albany Ter, (Camb.) G72	68	CA42
Albany Way, Pais. PA3	32	AU29
off Abbotsburn Way		
Albert Av, G42	53	BQ36
Albert Br, G1	38	BS32
Albert Br, G5	38	BS32
Albert Cross, G41	53	BP34
Albert Dr, G41	52	BL35
Albert Dr, (Bears.) G61	10	BK18
Albert Dr, (Ruther.) G73	67	BX40
Albert Rd, G42	53	BQ36
Albert Rd, (Lenz.) G66	15	CE18
Albert Rd, Clyde. G81	7	AW18
Albert Rd, Renf. PA4	19	AY26
Albion Gate, G1	5	BT30
off Albion St		
Albion Gate, Pais. PA3	32	AT31
Albion St, G1	5	BT31
Albion St, (Baill.) G69	57	CH34
Albion St, Pais. PA3	32	AT31
Albion Wks Ind Est, G13	20	BA22
Alcaig Rd, G52	51	BG35
Alder Av, (Kirk.) G66	14	CD16
Alder Ct, (Barr.) G78	61	AY44
Alder Gate, (Camb.) G72	69	CG40
Alderman Pl, G13	21	BE23
Alderman Rd, G13	20	BB21
Alder Pl, G43	64	BK40
Alder Pl, John. PA5	46	AJ36
Alder Rd, G43	64	BL40
Alder Rd, (Cumb.) G67	73	DF11
Alder Rd, Clyde. G81	6	AV16
Alderside Pl, (Both.) G71	71	CR42
off Churchill Cres		
Aldersyde Gdns, (Udd.) G71	59	CN38
Aldersyde Pl, (Blan.) G72	70	CL44
Alexander Cres, G5	54	BS33
Alexander St, Clyde. G81	7	AX20
Alexandra Av, (Stepps) G33	27	CF23
Alexandra Ct, G31	39	BX29
Alexandra Cross, G31	39	BX30
Alexandra Dr, Pais. PA2	47	AR34
Alexandra Gdns, (Kirk.) G66	15	CE17
Alexandra Par, G31	5	BU29
Alexandra Pk, (Kirk.) G66	15	CE17
Alexandra Pk St, G31	39	BX30
Alexandra Rd, (Lenz.) G66	15	CE17
Alford St, G21	24	BT26
Alfred La, G12	22	BM26
Alfred Ter, G12	23	BN26
Algie St, G41	53	BP37
Alice St, Pais. PA2	48	AU35
Aline Ct, (Barr.) G78	61	AX41
off Lomond Dr		
Allan Av, Renf. PA4	34	BA28
Allander Gdns, (Bishop.) G64	12	BV17
Allander Rd, (Bears.) G61	9	BF18
Allander St, G22	24	BS25
Allander Wk, (Cumb.) G67	72	DB12
off Cumbernauld Shop Cen		
Allands Av, (Inch.) Renf. PA4	18	AS24
Allanfauld Rd, (Cumb.) G67	72	DB11
Allan Glen Gdns, (Bishop.) G64	13	BX17
Allan Glen Pl, G4	5	BT29
Allan Pl, G40	55	BX34
Allan St, G40	55	BX35
Allanton Av, Pais. PA1	50	BA33
Allanton Dr, G52	34	BD32
Allen Way, Renf. PA4	33	AZ28
Allerdyce Ct, G15	8	BA20
Allerdyce Dr, G15	8	BB20
Allerdyce Rd, G15	8	BB20
Allerton Gdns, (Baill.) G69	57	CH33
Alleysbank Rd, (Ruther.) G73	55	BX36
Allison Dr, (Camb.) G72	68	CC30
Allison Pl, G42	53	BQ35
off Prince Edward St		
Allison Pl, (Gart.) G69	29	CN25
Allison St, G42	53	BQ35
Allnach Pl, G34	43	CN29
Alloway Av, Pais. PA2	49	AX37
Alloway Cres, (Ruther.) G73	66	BV40
Alloway Cres, Pais. PA2	49	AX37
Alloway Dr, (Ruther.) G73	66	BV40
Alloway Dr, Clyde. G81	7	AY18
Alloway Dr, Pais. PA2	49	AX37
Alloway Gro, Pais. PA2	49	AY37
Alloway Rd, G43	64	BM39
Alma St, G40	39	BW32
Almond Av, Renf. PA4	34	BA27
Almond Bk, (Bears.) G61	9	BE19
Almond Cres, Pais. PA2	47	AP35
Almond Dr, (Kirk.) G66	14	CD16
Almond Rd, G33	27	CE24
Almond Rd, (Bears.) G61	9	BF19
Almond St, G33	39	BZ28
Almond Vale, (Udd.) G71	59	CQ38
off Hamilton Vw		
Alness Cres, G52	51	BF34
Alpine Gro, (Udd.) G71	59	CP38
Alsatian Av, Clyde. G81	7	AZ19
Alston La, G40	5	BU31
off Claythorn St		
Altnacreag Gdns, (Mood.) G69	17	CQ18
Alton Rd, Pais. PA1	49	AY33
Altpatrick Gdns, (Elder.) John. PA5	46	AK34
Altyre St, G32	56	CB34
Alva Gdns, G52	51	BG35
Alva Gate, G52	51	BG34
Alva Pl, (Lenz.) G66	15	CG17
Alyth Gdns, G52	51	BG34
Ambassador Way, Renf. PA4	33	AZ28
off Cockels Ln		
Amisfield St, G20	23	BN24
Amochrie Dr, Pais. PA2	47	AQ37
Amochrie Glen, Pais. PA2	47	AQ37
Amochrie Rd, Pais. PA2	47	AP37
Amochrie Way, Pais. PA2	47	AP36
Amulree Pl, G32	56	CC33
Amulree St, G32	40	CD32
Ancaster Dr, G13	21	BH23
Ancaster La, G13	21	BH23
off Great Western Rd		
Anchor Av, Pais. PA1	49	AW33
Anchor Cres, Pais. PA1	49	AW34
Anchor Dr, Pais. PA1	49	AW33
Anchor La, G1	5	BS30
off St. Vincent Pl		
Anchor Wynd, Pais. PA1	49	AW34
Ancroft St, G20	23	BQ26
Anderson Dr, Renf. PA4	19	AZ25
Anderson Gdns, (Blan.) G72	71	CN44
off Station Rd		
Anderson St, G11	36	BK27
Anderston Cross Cen, G2	4	BQ30
Anderston Quay, G3	4	BP31
Andrew Av, (Lenz.) G66	15	CF18
Andrew Av, Renf. PA4	20	BA26
Andrew Dr, Clyde. G81	19	AY21
Andrew Sillars Av, (Camb.) G72	68	CD40
Andrews St, Pais. PA3	32	AT31
Angela Way, (Udd.) G71	71	CP39
Angle Gate, G14	21	BF25
Angus Av, G52	50	BD33
Angus Av, (Bishop.) G64	25	BY21
Angus Gdns, (Udd.) G71	59	CP37
Angus La, (Bishop.) G64	13	BZ20
Angus Oval, G52	50	BD33
Angus Pl, G52	50	BD33
Angus Pl, G21	24	BU25
Angus St, Clyde. G81	20	BA21
Angus Wk, (Udd.) G71	59	CR38
Anish Pl, G15	8	BA17
Annandale St, G42	53	BR34
Annan Dr, (Bears.) G61	9	BE18
Annan Dr, (Ruther.) G73	55	BZ38
Annan Pl, John. PA5	45	AE37
Annan St, G42	53	BQ37
Annan Way, (Cumb.) G67	72	DB12
off Cumbernauld Shop Cen		
Annbank Pl, G31	38	BV31
Annbank St, G31	38	BV31
Anne Av, Renf. PA4	19	AZ25
Anne Cres, (Lenz.) G66	15	CF18
Annette St, G42	53	BQ35
Annfield Gdns, (Blan.) G72	70	CK44

Street	Pg	Ref
Annfield Pl, G31	38	BV30
Annick Dr, (Bears.) G61	9	BE18
Annick Ind Est, G32	41	CE32
Annick St, G32	40	CD32
Annick St, (Camb.) G72	69	CF40
Anniesdale Av, (Stepps) G33	27	CF23
Anniesland Cres, G14	20	BC24
Anniesland Ind Est, G13	21	BG21
Anniesland Mans, G13	21	BH23
off Ancaster Dr		
Anniesland Rd, G13	20	BD24
Anniesland Rd, G14	20	BC24
Anson St, G40	54	BV33
Anson Way, Renf. PA4	33	AY28
off Britannia Way		
Anstruther St, G32	56	CB33
Anthony St, G2	4	BQ30
Antonine Gdns, Clyde. G81	7	AW15
Antonine Rd, (Bears.) G61	8	BD15
Antonine Rd, The, G15	8	BA18
Anwoth St, G32	56	CC34
Apartments, The, (Giff.) G46	64	BK44
off Milverton Rd		
Appin Cres, G31	39	BX30
Appin Rd, G31	39	BX30
Appin Ter, (Ruther.) G73	67	BZ41
Appin Way, (Both.) G71	71	CQ42
off Bracken Ter		
Appleby St, G22	23	BR26
Applecross Gdns, (Mood.) G69	17	CP18
Applecross St, G4	23	BR26
Appledore Cres, (Both.) G71	71	CQ42
Apsley La, G11	36	BJ27
off Apsley St		
Apsley St, G11	36	BJ27
Aranthrue Cres, Renf. PA4	19	AY25
Aranthrue Dr, Renf. PA4	19	AY25
off Aranthrue Cres		
Aray St, G20	22	BM22
Arbroath Av, G52	50	BD33
Arcadia Pl, G40	38	BU32
Arcadia St, G40	38	BU32
Arcan Cres, G15	8	BD19
Archerfield Av, G32	56	CC35
Archerfield Cres, G32	56	CC35
Archerfield Dr, G32	56	CC35
Archerfield Gro, G32	56	CC35
Archerhill Av, G13	20	BC21
Archerhill Cotts, G13	20	BC21
Archerhill Cres, G13	20	BD21
Archerhill Gdns, G13	20	BC21
Archerhill Rd, G13	20	BC21
Archerhill Sq, G13	20	BB21
Archerhill Ter, G13	20	BC21
Ardargie Dr, G32	57	CE37
Ardargie Gro, G32	57	CE37
off Ardargie Dr		
Ardargie Pl, G32	57	CE37
off Ardargie Dr		
Ardbeg Av, (Bishop.) G64	13	BY20
Ardbeg Av, (Ruther.) G73	68	CA42
Ardbeg La, G42	53	BQ35
Ardbeg St, G42	53	BQ35
Ardconnel St, (Thornlie.) G46	63	BH41
Arden Av, (Thornlie.) G46	63	BG43
Ardencraig Cres, G45	66	BS44
Ardencraig Dr, G45	66	BV43
Ardencraig Pl, G45	66	BU42
Ardencraig Quad, G45	66	BV43
Ardencraig Rd, G45	66	BS44
Ardencraig St, G45	67	BW42
Ardencraig Ter, G45	66	BV43
Arden Dr, (Giff.) G46	64	BK43
Ardenlea, (Udd.) G71	59	CP38
Ardenlea St, G40	55	BX34
Arden Pl, (Thornlie.) G46	63	BG43
Ardery St, G11	36	BJ27
off Apsley St		
Ardessie Pl, G20	22	BM24
Ardessie St, G23	10	BM20
off Torrin Rd		
Ardfern St, G32	56	CC34
Ardgay Pl, G32	56	CC33
Ardgay St, G32	56	CC33
Ardgay Way, (Ruther.) G73	67	BX42
Ardgour Dr, (Linw.) Pais. PA3	30	AJ32
Ardgowan Av, Pais. PA2	48	AV34
Ardgowan Ct, Pais. PA2	49	AX34
off Cartha Cres		
Ardgowan Dr, (Udd.) G71	59	CP38
Ardgowan St, Pais. PA2	48	AV35
Ardholm St, G32	40	CC32
Ardhu Pl, G15	8	BC17
Ardlamont Sq, (Linw.) Pais. PA3	30	AL32
Ardlaw St, G51	35	BH31
Ardle Rd, G43	65	BN40
Ardlui St, G32	56	CB33
Ardmaleish Cres, G45	66	BU43
Ardmaleish Dr, G45	66	BT43
Ardmaleish Rd, G45	66	BT43
Ardmaleish St, G45	66	BT43
Ardmaleish Ter, G45	66	BU43
Ardmay Cres, G44	54	BS38
Ardmillan St, G33	40	CB29
Ardmory Av, G42	54	BT38
Ardmory La, G42	54	BU38
Ardmory Pl, G42	54	BU38
Ardnahoe Av, G42	54	BT37
Ardnahoe Pl, G42	54	BT37
Ardneil Rd, G51	35	BH31
Ardnish St, G51	35	BG30
Ardoch Gdns, (Camb.) G72	68	CB39
Ardoch Gro, (Camb.) G72	68	CB39
Ardoch Rd, (Bears.) G61	10	BK16
Ardoch St, G22	24	BS25
Ardoch Way, (Chry.) G69	17	CP19
off Braeside Av		
Ardo Gdns, G51	36	BJ32
off Hinshelwood Dr		
Ard Rd, Renf. PA4	19	AX25
Ardshiel Rd, G51	35	BG30
Ardsloy La, G14	20	BC25
Ardsloy Pl, G14	20	BC25
Ard St, G32	56	CC33
Ardtoe Cres, G33	27	CG24
Ardtoe Pl, G33	27	CG24
Arduthie Rd, G51	35	BG30
Ardwell Rd, G52	51	BG34
Argosy Way, Renf. PA4	33	AY28
off Britannia Way		
Argyle St, G2	4	BQ30
Argyle St, G3	36	BM28
Argyle St, Pais. PA1	48	AT33
Argyll Arc, G2	5	BS30
Argyll Av, (Abbots.) Pais. PA3	32	AT28
Argyll Av, Renf. PA4	19	AX25
Argyll Rd, (Bears.) G61	9	BG15
Argyll Rd, Clyde. G81	7	AY20
Arisaig Dr, G52	51	BG34
Arisaig Dr, (Bears.) G61	10	BK18
Arisaig Pl, G52	51	BG34
Ark La, G31	38	BV30
Arkleston Ct, Pais. PA3	33	AX29
off Montgomery Rd		
Arkleston Cres, Pais. PA3	33	AX30
Arkleston Rd, Pais. PA1	33	AX31
Arkleston Rd, Pais. PA3	33	AX30
Arkleston Rd, Renf. PA4	33	AW29
Arkle Ter, (Camb.) G72	68	CB42
Arklet Rd, G51	35	BG31
Arkwrights Way, Pais. PA1	47	AR34
off Turners Av		
Arlington St, G3	4	BP28
Armadale Ct, G31	39	BW29
Armadale Path, G31	39	BW29
Armadale Pl, G31	39	BW29
Armadale St, G31	39	BW30
Armour Pl, John. PA5	46	AJ34
Armour Sq, John. PA5	46	AJ34
Armour St, G31	5	BU31
Armour St, John. PA5	46	AJ34
Armstrong Cres, (Udd.) G71	59	CQ37
Arngask Rd, G51	35	BG30
Arnhall Pl, G52	51	BG34
Arnhem St, (Camb.) G72	69	CF40
Arnholm Pl, G52	51	BG34
Arnisdale Pl, G34	42	CJ29
Arnisdale Rd, G34	42	CJ29
Arnisdale Way, (Ruther.) G73	67	BX42
off Shieldaig Dr		
Arniston St, G32	40	CB30
Arnold Av, (Bishop.) G64	13	BW20
Arnold St, G20	23	BQ23
Arnol Pl, G33	41	CH30
Arnott Way, (Camb.) G72	68	CC39
Arnprior Cres, G45	66	BT42
Arnprior Gdns, (Chry.) G69	17	CP19
off Braeside Av		
Arnprior Quad, G45	66	BT41
Arnprior Rd, G45	66	BT41
Arnprior St, G45	66	BT41
Arnside Av, (Giff.) G46	64	BL42
Arnwood Dr, G12	22	BJ24
Aron Ter, (Camb.) G72	68	CB42
Aros Dr, G52	51	BF35
Aros La, G52	51	BF35
Arran Av, (Abbots.) Pais. PA3	32	AU27
Arran Dr, (Giff.) G46	64	BK43
Arran Dr, G52	51	BH34
Arran Dr, (Cumb.) G67	72	CZ13
Arran Dr, John. PA5	45	AF36
Arran Dr, Pais. PA2	48	AU38
Arran La, (Chry.) G69	17	CQ19
Arran Pl, Clyde. G81	7	AY19
Arran Pl, (Linw.) Pais. PA3	30	AJ31
Arran Rd, Renf. PA4	33	AZ27
Arran Ter, (Ruther.) G73	66	BV40
off Carrick Rd		
Arran Way, (Both.) G71	71	CP43
Arrochar Ct, G23	22	BM21
Arrochar Dr, G23	10	BM20
Arrochar Path, G23	10	BM20
off Chatton St		
Arrochar St, G23	22	BM21
Arrol Pl, G40	55	BX33
Arrol Rd, G40	55	BW33
Arrol St, G52	34	BA30
Arrowsmith Av, G13	21	BF21
Arthur Av, (Barr.) G78	61	AX44
Arthurlie Av, (Barr.) G78	61	AY43
Arthurlie Dr, (Giff.) G46	64	BL44
Arthurlie Gdns, (Barr.) G78	61	AY43
Arthurlie St, G51	35	BH30
Arthurlie St, (Barr.) G78	61	AY43
Arthur Rd, Pais. PA2	48	AU37
Arthur St, G3	36	BM28
Arthur St, Pais. PA1	32	AS32
Arundel Dr, G42	53	BQ38
Arundel Dr, (Bishop.) G64	13	BX17
Asbury Ct, (Linw.) Pais. PA3	30	AL32
off Melrose Av		
Ascaig Cres, G52	51	BF35
Ascog Rd, (Bears.) G61	9	BH19
Ascog St, G42	53	BQ35
Ascot Av, G12	21	BH23
Ascot Ct, G12	22	BJ23
Ashburton La, G12	22	BK23
Ashburton Rd, G12	22	BJ23
Ashby Cres, G13	9	BG20
Ashcroft Dr, G44	66	BU40
Ashdale Dr, G52	51	BG34
Ashdene St, G22	23	BR22
Ashfield, (Bishop.) G64	13	BW18
Ashfield St, G22	24	BS25
Ashgill Pl, G22	24	BS23
Ashgill Rd, G22	23	BR22
Ash Gro, (Bishop.) G64	13	BX20
Ash Gro, (Kirk.) G66	14	CD16
Ashgrove, (Mood.) G69	17	CP19
off Deepdene Rd		
Ash Gro, (Udd.) G71	59	CR37
Ashgrove St, G40	55	BW35
Ashkirk Dr, G52	51	BG34
Ashlea Dr, (Giff.) G46	64	BM41
Ashley Dr, (Both.) G71	71	CR40
Ashley La, G3	4	BP28
Ashley St, G3	4	BP28
Ashmore Rd, G43	65	BP40
Ashmore Rd, G44	65	BP40
Ash Pl, John. PA5	46	AJ35
Ash Rd, (Cumb.) G67	73	DF8
Ash Rd, (Baill.) G69	58	CJ34
Ash Rd, Clyde. G81	6	AV16
Ashton Gdns, (Gart.) G69	29	CP23
Ashton La, G12	36	BM27
Ashton La, N, G12	36	BM27
off Ashton La		
Ashton Rd, G12	36	BM27
Ashton Rd, (Ruther.) G73	55	BW36
Ashton Way, Pais. PA2	47	AN37
Ashtree Rd, G43	52	BL37
Ashvale Cres, G21	24	BU24
Ash Wk, (Ruther.) G73	67	BY42
Ashwood Gdns, G13	21	BH24
Ash Wynd, (Camb.) G72	69	CG41
Aspen Dr, G21	25	BW26

Aspen Pl, (Camb.) G72 69 CG40
Aspen Pl, John. PA5 46 AJ36
Aster Dr, G45 67 BW42
Aster Gdns, G53 62 BD42
off Waukglen Cres
Athelstane Rd, G13 21 BE22
Athena Way, (Udd.) G71 59 CQ38
Athole Gdns, G12 22 BL26
Athole La, G12 22 BL26
Atholl Av, G52 34 BA29
Atholl Cres, Pais. PA1 34 BA31
Atholl Gdns, (Bishop.) G64 12 BV18
Atholl Gdns, (Ruther.) G73 68 CA42
Atholl La, (Mood.) G69 17 CQ19
Atholl Pl, (Linw.) Pais. PA3 30 AJ31
Atholl Ter, (Udd.) G71 59 CP36
Atlas Ind Est, G21 24 BV25
Atlas Pl, G21 24 BV26
Atlas Rd, G21 24 BU25
Atlas Sq, G21 24 BV25
off Ayr St
Atlas St, Clyde. G81 19 AX21
Attlee Av, Clyde. G81 8 BA20
Attlee Pl, Clyde. G81 8 BA20
Attow Rd, G43 64 BK40
Auburn Dr, (Barr.) G78 61 AZ44
Auchans Rd, (Hous.) John. 30 AJ27
PA6
Auchenbothie Cres, G33 25 BZ23
Auchenbothie Pl, G33 26 CA24
off Auchenbothie Cres
Auchencrow St, G34 42 CM29
Auchengeich Rd, (Mood.) G69 16 CM17
Auchengreoch Av, John. PA5 45 AF37
Auchengreoch Rd, John. PA5 45 AF37
Auchengreoch Rd, (How.) 45 AF37
John. PA9
Auchenkilns Roundabout, 72 CY13
(Cumb.) G67
Auchenlodment Rd, John. PA5 46 AK35
Auchentorlie Quad, Pais. PA1 49 AX33
Auchentorlie St, G11 35 BH27
Auchentoshan Av, Clyde. G81 6 AV15
Auchentoshan Ter, G21 38 BV27
Auchentoshen Cotts, (Old Kil.) 6 AT15
G60
Auchinairn Rd, (Bishop.) G64 25 BW22
Auchinbee Roundabout, 72 CY10
(Cumb.) G68
Auchingill Path, G34 42 CM28
off Auchingill Rd
Auchingill Pl, G34 42 CM28
Auchingill Rd, G34 42 CL28
Auchinlea Retail Pk, G34 41 CH28
Auchinlea Rd, G34 41 CH27
Auchinleck Av, G33 26 CA23
Auchinleck Cres, G33 26 CA23
Auchinleck Dr, G33 26 CA23
Auchinleck Gdns, G33 26 CA23
Auchinleck Rd, G33 26 CB22
Auchinloch Rd, (Lenz.) G66 15 CF17
Auchinloch St, G21 24 BV26
Auchmannoch Av, Pais. PA1 34 BA32
Auckland Pl, Clyde. G81 6 AT17
Auckland St, G22 23 BR26
Auldbar Rd, G52 51 BH34
Auldbar Ter, Pais. PA2 49 AW35
Auldburn Pl, G43 64 BK39
Auldburn Rd, G43 64 BK39
Auldearn Rd, G21 25 BY22
Auldgirth Rd, G52 51 BH34
Auldhouse Av, G43 64 BK39
off Thornliebank Rd
Auldhouse Ct, G43 64 BK39
off Stoneside Dr
Auldhouse Gdns, G43 64 BK39
Auldhouse Rd, G43 64 BL39
Auldhouse Ter, G43 64 BM39
Auld Kirk Rd, (Camb.) G72 69 CE42
Auld Rd, The, (Cumb.) G67 73 DC9
Auld St, Clyde. G81 6 AU18
Aultbea St, G22 23 BR21
Aultmore Rd, G33 41 CH30
Aursbridge Cres, (Barr.) G78 61 AZ43
Aursbridge Dr, (Barr.) G78 61 AZ43
Aurs Cres, (Barr.) G78 61 AZ43
Aurs Dr, (Barr.) G78 61 AZ43
Aurs Glen, (Barr.) G78 61 AY44
Aurs Pl, (Barr.) G78 62 BA43
Aurs Rd, (Barr.) G78 61 AZ43

Austen La, G13 21 BG24
off Skaterig La
Austen Rd, G13 21 BG24
Avenel Rd, G13 9 BG20
Avenue, The, (Kilb.) John. PA10 44 AD35
off Low Barholm
Avenue End Rd, G33 26 CD25
Avenuehead Rd, (Chry.) G69 17 CQ20
Avenuepark St, G20 23 BN25
Avenue St, G40 39 BW32
Avenue St, (Ruther.) G73 55 BX36
Aviemore Gdns, (Bears.) G61 10 BK16
Aviemore Rd, G52 51 BG35
Avoch Dr, (Thornlie.) G46 63 BG42
Avoch St, G34 42 CK28
off Dubton St
Avon Av, (Bears.) G61 10 BK18
Avonbank Rd, (Ruther.) G73 54 BV38
Avondale Dr, Pais. PA1 33 AX31
Avondale St, G33 40 CC28
Avon Dr, (Bishop.) G64 25 BW21
Avon Dr, (Linw.) Pais. PA3 30 AK31
Avon Rd, (Giff.) G46 64 BK43
Avon Rd, (Bishop.) G64 25 BW21
Avonspark St, G21 25 BW26
Avon Wk, (Cumb.) G67 72 DB12
off Cumbernauld Shop Cen
Aylmer Rd, G43 65 BP39
Ayr St, G21 24 BU26
Aytoun Rd, G41 52 BM34
Azalea Gdns, (Camb.) G72 69 CG40

B
Back Causeway, G31 39 BZ32
Backmuir Rd, G15 8 BD17
Back Sneddon St, Pais. PA3 32 AU32
Bagnell St, G21 24 BV24
Baillie Dr, (Both.) G71 71 CQ42
Baillieston Rd, G32 57 CK33
Baillieston Rd, (Udd.) G71 58 CK34
Baillie Wynd, (Udd.) G71 59 CQ37
Bainsford St, G32 40 CB31
Bain Sq, G40 5 BU31
off Bain St
Bain St, G40 5 BU31
Baird Av, G52 34 BA29
Baird Ct, Clyde. G81 7 AW19
Baird Dr, (Bears.) G61 9 BF16
Bairds Av, (Udd.) G71 71 CR39
Bairds Brae, G4 23 BR26
Baird St, G4 5 BT28
Baker Pl, G41 53 BN36
off Baker St
Baker St, G41 53 BN36
Bakewell Rd, (Baill.) G69 42 CJ32
Balaclava St, G2 4 BQ30
off McAlpine St
Balado Rd, G33 41 CG30
Balbeggie Pl, G32 57 CE33
Balbeggie St, G32 57 CE33
Balbeg St, G51 35 BG31
Balblair Rd, G52 51 BH34
Balcarres Av, G12 22 BL24
Balcomie St, G33 40 CC28
Balcurvie Rd, G34 42 CJ27
Baldinnie Rd, G34 42 CK29
Baldovan Cres, G33 41 CH29
Baldovan Path, G33 41 CH30
Baldovie Rd, G52 51 BE34
Baldragon Rd, G34 42 CK28
Baldric Rd, G13 21 BE23
Baldwin Av, G13 21 BF21
Balerno Dr, G52 51 BG34
Balfluig St, G34 41 CH28
Balfour St, G20 22 BM23
Balfron Rd, G51 35 BG30
Balfron Rd, Pais. PA1 33 AZ32
Balgair Dr, Pais. PA1 33 AX32
Balgair Pl, G22 23 BR25
Balgair St, G22 23 BR24
Balgair Ter, G32 40 CD32
Balglass Gdns, G22 23 BR25
Balglass St, G22 23 BR25
Balgonie Av, Pais. PA2 47 AQ36
Balgonie Dr, Pais. PA2 48 AS36
Balgonie Rd, G52 51 BG33
Balgonie Wds, Pais. PA2 48 AS36
Balgraybank St, G21 24 BV25

Balgray Cres, (Barr.) G78 61 AZ43
Balgrayhill Rd, G21 24 BV24
Balintore St, G32 40 CC32
Baliol La, G3 4 BP28
Baliol St, G3 4 BP28
Ballaig Av, (Bears.) G61 9 BF16
Ballaig Cres, (Stepps) G33 27 CE24
Ballantay Quad, G45 67 BW42
Ballantay Rd, G45 67 BW42
Ballantay Ter, G45 67 BW42
Ballantyne Av, G52 34 BC30
Ballater Dr, (Bears.) G61 9 BH19
Ballater Dr, Pais. PA2 48 AV36
Ballater Dr, (Inch.) Renf. PA4 18 AT22
Ballater Pl, G5 54 BT33
Ballater St, G5 38 BS32
Ballayne Dr, (Chry.) G69 17 CQ18
Ballindalloch Dr, G31 39 BW29
Ballindarroch La, G31 39 BW29
off Armadale St
Balloch Gdns, G52 51 BH34
Balloch Loop Rd, (Cumb.) G68 72 CY10
Ballochmill Rd, (Ruther.) G73 55 BZ37
Ballochmyle Cres, G53 50 BC37
Ballochmyle Dr, G53 50 BC36
Ballochmyle Gdns, G53 50 BC36
Ballochmyle Pl, G53 50 BC36
Balloch Vw, (Cumb.) G67 72 DB11
Ballogie Rd, G44 53 BR38
Balmartin Rd, G23 10 BM20
Balmerino Pl, (Bishop.) G64 25 BZ21
Balmoral Cres, (Inch.) Renf. 18 AU22
PA4
Balmoral Dr, G32 56 CD37
Balmoral Dr, (Bears.) G61 10 BJ19
Balmoral Dr, (Camb.) G72 68 CA40
Balmoral Gdns, (Udd.) G71 59 CP36
Balmoral Gdns, (Blan.) G72 70 CL43
Balmoral Rd, (Elder.) John. 46 AK36
PA5
Balmoral St, G14 20 BD26
Balmore Pl, G22 23 BR23
Balmore Rd, G22 23 BR22
Balmore Rd, G23 11 BQ18
Balmore Rd, (Miln.) G62 11 BP15
Balmore Sq, G22 23 BR24
Balmuildy Rd, G23 11 BQ17
Balmuildy Rd, (Bishop.) G64 12 BV18
Balornock Rd, G21 25 BW24
Balornock Rd, (Bishop.) G64 25 BW23
Balruddery Pl, (Bishop.) G64 25 BZ21
Balshagray Av, G11 21 BG26
Balshagray Cres, G14 35 BG27
off Dumbarton Rd
Balshagray Dr, G11 21 BG26
Balshagray La, G11 35 BH27
Balshagray Pl, G11 21 BH26
off Balshagray Dr
Baltic Ct, G40 55 BW34
off Baltic St
Baltic La, G40 55 BW34
Baltic Pl, G40 55 BW33
Baltic St, G40 55 BW33
Balvaird Cres, (Ruther.) G73 55 BW38
Balvaird Dr, (Ruther.) G73 55 BW38
Balveny St, G33 41 CF27
Balvicar Dr, G42 53 BP36
Balvicar St, G42 53 BP36
Balvie Av, G15 8 BC20
Balvie Av, (Giff.) G46 64 BM43
Banavie La, G11 22 BK26
off Banavie Rd
Banavie Rd, G11 22 BJ26
Banchory Av, G43 64 BK40
Banchory Av, (Inch.) Renf. PA4 18 AT22
Banchory Cres, (Bears.) G61 10 BJ19
Banff St, G33 40 CD27
off Gilbertfield St
Bangorshill St, (Thornlie.) G46 63 BH41
Bankbrae Av, G53 62 BC39
Bankend St, G33 40 CC28
Bankfoot Dr, G52 34 BD32
Bankfoot Rd, G52 50 BD33
Bankfoot Rd, Pais. PA3 31 AR31
Bankglen Rd, G15 8 BD17
Bankhall St, G42 53 BR35
Bankhead Av, G13 20 BC23
Bankhead Dr, (Ruther.) G73 55 BW38
Bankhead Rd, (Ruther.) G73 66 BV39
Bankier St, G40 38 BU32

Name	Page	Grid
Banknock St, G32	40	CA31
Bank Rd, G32	57	CE37
Bankside Av, John. PA5	45	AH34
Bank St, G12	37	BN27
Bank St, (Camb.) G72	68	CC39
Bank St, (Barr.) G78	61	AY43
Bank St, Pais. PA1	48	AV33
Banktop Pl, John. PA5	45	AH34
Bannatyne Av, G31	39	BX30
Bannercross Av, (Baill.) G69	42	CJ32
Bannercross Dr, (Baill.) G69	42	CJ32
Bannercross Gdns, (Baill.) G69	42	CJ32
Banner Dr, G13	9	BE20
Bannerman Pl, Clyde. G81	7	AX19
Banner Rd, G13	9	BE20
Bantaskin St, G20	22	BL22
Banton Pl, G33	42	CJ30
Barassie Ct, (Both.) G71	71	CP43
Barbae Pl, (Both.) G71	71	CQ42
Barberry Av, G53	62	BD43
Barberry Gdns, G53	62	BD43
Barberry Pl, G53	63	BE43
Barbreck Rd, G42	53	BQ35
off Pollokshaws Rd		
Barcaldine Av, (Chry.) G69	28	CK21
Barclay Av, (Elder.) John. PA5	46	AK35
Barclay Sq, Renf. PA4	33	AX28
Barclay St, G21	24	BV24
off Lenzie St		
Barcraigs Dr, Pais. PA2	48	AV37
Bard Av, G13	20	BD21
Bardowie St, G22	23	BR25
Bardrain Av, (Elder.) John. PA5	46	AL35
Bardrain Rd, Pais. PA2	48	AS38
Bardrill Dr, (Bishop.) G64	12	BU20
Barfillan Dr, G52	35	BG32
Barfillan Rd, G52	51	BG33
Bargany Ct, G53	50	BC36
Bargany Pl, G53	50	BC36
Bargany Rd, G53	50	BC36
Bargaran Rd, G53	50	BD34
Bargarron Dr, Pais. PA3	33	AW30
Bargeddie St, G33	39	BZ27
Barholm Sq, G33	41	CF27
Barke Rd, (Cumb.) G67	73	DC10
Barlanark Av, G32	41	CE30
Barlanark Cres, G33	41	CF30
Barlanark Dr, G33	41	CF30
Barlanark Pl, G32	40	CD31
Barlanark Pl, G33	41	CG30
Barlanark Rd, G33	41	CF30
Barlia Dr, G45	66	BU42
Barlia St, G45	66	BU42
Barlia Ter, G45	66	BV42
Barloch St, G22	24	BS25
Barlogan Av, G52	35	BG32
Barlogan Quad, G52	35	BG32
Barmulloch Rd, G21	25	BW25
Barnard Gdns, (Bishop.) G64	13	BW17
Barnbeth Rd, G53	50	BD35
Barnes Rd, G20	23	BQ23
Barness Pl, G33	40	CC29
Barnes St, (Barr.) G78	61	AX43
Barnflat St, (Ruther.) G73	55	BX36
Barn Grn, (Kilb.) John. PA10	44	AC34
Barnhill Dr, G21	25	BW26
off Foresthall Dr		
Barnkirk Av, G15	8	BC17
Barnsford Rd, (Abbots.) Pais. PA3	31	AQ28
Barns St, Clyde. G81	19	AY21
Barnswood Pl, (Both.) G71	71	CR42
off Burleigh Rd		
Barnton St, G32	40	CA30
Barnwell Ter, G51	35	BG30
Barochan Cres, Pais. PA3	47	AQ33
Barochan Pl, G53	50	BD34
off Barochan Rd		
Barochan Rd, G53	50	BD34
Baronald Dr, G12	22	BK23
Baronald Gate, G12	22	BK23
Baronald St, (Ruther.) G73	55	BX36
Baronhill, (Cumb.) G67	73	DC8
Baron Path, (Baill.) G69	43	CP32
off Campsie Vw		
Baron Rd, Pais. PA3	33	AW31
Baronscourt Dr, Pais. PA1	47	AP33
Baronscourt Gdns, Pais. PA1	47	AP33
Baronscourt Rd, Pais. PA1	47	AP33
Barons Gate, (Both.) G71	71	CN41
Baron St, Renf. PA4	33	AY27
Barony Ct, (Baill.) G69	42	CK31
Barony Dr, (Baill.) G69	42	CK31
Barony Gdns, (Baill.) G69	42	CK32
Barony Wynd, (Baill.) G69	42	CK31
Barra Av, Renf. PA4	33	AY28
Barrachnie Av, (Baill.) G69	42	CJ31
Barrachnie Ct, (Baill.) G69	41	CH31
Barrachnie Cres, (Baill.) G69	41	CH32
Barrachnie Dr, (Baill.) G69	42	CJ31
Barrachnie Gro, (Baill.) G69	42	CJ31
Barrachnie Pl, (Baill.) G69	42	CJ31
Barrachnie Rd, (Baill.) G69	41	CH32
Barrack St, G4	5	BU31
Barra Cres, (Old Kil.) G60	6	AS16
Barra Gdns, (Old Kil.) G60	6	AS16
Barra Rd, (Old Kil.) G60	6	AS16
Barra St, G20	22	BL21
Barrbridge Rd, (Baill.) G69	59	CR33
Barr Cres, Clyde. G81	7	AX16
Barr Gro, (Udd.) G71	59	CQ37
Barrhead Rd, G43	51	BG38
Barrhead Rd, G53	62	BB39
Barrhead Rd, Pais. PA2	48	AV34
Barrhill Cres, (Kilb.) John. PA10	44	AD35
Barrie Quad, Clyde. G81	7	AW17
Barrie Rd, G52	34	BC30
Barrington Dr, G4	37	BP27
Barrisdale Rd, G20	22	BM21
Barrisdale Way, (Ruther.) G73	67	BX42
off Shieldaig Dr		
Barrland Dr, (Giff.) G46	64	BL42
Barrland St, G41	53	BQ34
Barrmill Rd, G43	64	BJ40
Barrowfield St, G40	39	BW32
Barr Pl, Pais. PA1	48	AT33
Barr St, G20	23	BQ26
Barrwood Pl, (Udd.) G71	59	CQ37
Barrwood St, G33	40	CA27
Barscube Ter, Pais. PA2	49	AW35
Barshaw Dr, Pais. PA1	33	AW31
Barshaw Pl, Pais. PA1	33	AZ32
off Kinpurnie Rd		
Barshaw Rd, G52	34	BA31
Barskiven Rd, Pais. PA1	47	AP33
Barterholm Rd, Pais. PA2	48	AU35
Bartholomew St, G40	55	BW34
Bartiebeith Rd, G33	41	CG30
Bassett Av, G13	20	BD21
Bassett Cres, G13	20	BD21
Bathgate St, G31	39	BW31
Bathgo Av, Pais. PA1	50	BA33
Bath La, G2	4	BQ29
Bath La W, G3	4	BP29
off North St		
Bath St, G2	4	BQ29
Batson St, G42	53	BR35
Battlefield Av, G42	53	BQ38
Battlefield Cres, G42	53	BQ38
off Battlefield Gdns		
Battlefield Gdns, G42	53	BQ37
Battlefield Rd, G42	53	BQ37
Battle Pl, G41	53	BP37
Battles Burn Dr, G32	56	CC35
Battles Burn Gate, G32	56	CC35
Battles Burn Vw, G32	56	CC35
Bavelaw St, G33	41	CF27
Bayfield Av, G15	8	BC18
Bayfield Ter, G15	8	BC18
Beacon Pl, G33	40	CB29
off Bellrock St		
Beaconsfield Rd, G12	22	BK24
Beard Cres, (Gart.) G69	29	CP24
Beardmore Cotts, (Inch.) Renf. PA4	18	AU23
Beardmore Pl, Clyde. G81	6	AU18
Beardmore St, Clyde. G81	6	AT18
Beardmore Way, G31	39	BX31
Beardmore Way, Clyde. G81	6	AT19
Bearford Dr, G52	34	BD32
Bearsden Rd, G13	21	BH23
Bearsden Rd, (Bears.) G61	21	BH23
Bearsden Shop Cen, (Bears.) G61	10	BJ17
Beaton Rd, G41	53	BN35
Beatson Wynd, (Udd.) G71	59	CQ36
off Macmillan Gdns		
Beattock St, G31	39	BZ32
Beatty St, Clyde. G81	6	AU18
Beaufort Av, G43	64	BL39
Beaufort Gdns, (Bishop.) G64	12	BU20
Beauly Dr, Pais. PA2	47	AN36
Beauly Pl, G20	22	BM23
Beauly Pl, (Bishop.) G64	13	BZ19
Beauly Pl, (Chry.) G69	16	CM20
Beauly Rd, (Baill.) G69	58	CJ34
Beaumont Gate, G12	22	BL26
Beckfield Cres, G33	25	BZ22
Beckfield Dr, G33	25	BZ22
Beckfield Gate, G33	25	BZ22
off Brookfield Av		
Beckfield Gro, G33	25	BZ22
Beckfield Pl, G33	25	BZ22
off Brookfield Av		
Beckfield Wk, G33	25	BZ22
off Brookfield Av		
Bedale Rd, (Baill.) G69	57	CH33
Bedford Av, Clyde. G81	7	AZ19
Bedford La, G5	37	BR32
Bedford St, G5	37	BR32
Bedlay Ct, (Chry.) G69	17	CQ18
Bedlay Vw, (Udd.) G71	59	CR36
Bedlay Wk, (Chry.) G69	17	CQ18
off Bedlay Ct		
Beech Av, G41	36	BK32
Beech Av, (Baill.) G69	42	CJ32
Beech Av, (Camb.) G72	68	CB39
Beech Av, (Ruther.) G73	67	BY41
Beech Av, (Elder.) John. PA5	46	AL35
Beech Av, Pais. PA2	49	AW36
Beech Cres, (Camb.) G72	69	CG41
Beech Dr, Clyde. G81	7	AW16
Beeches Av, Clyde. G81	6	AV15
Beeches Rd, Clyde. G81	6	AV15
Beeches Ter, Clyde. G81	7	AW15
Beech Gdns, (Baill.) G69	42	CJ32
Beechgrove, (Chry.) G69	17	CP19
Beech Gro, (Gart.) G69	29	CQ24
Beechgrove St, G40	55	BX35
Beechlands Av, G44	65	BN43
Beechmount Rd, (Lenz.) G66	15	CE17
Beech Pl, (Bishop.) G64	25	BX21
Beech Rd, (Bishop.) G64	25	BX21
Beech Rd, (Lenz.) G66	15	CE15
Beech Rd, John. PA5	45	AF36
Beechwood Av, (Ruther.) G73	67	BY39
Beechwood Ct, (Bears.) G61	9	BH18
off Drymen Rd		
Beechwood Dr, (Cumb.) G67	72	DB13
Beechwood Dr, G11	21	BH25
Beechwood Dr, Renf. PA4	33	AX28
Beechwood Gdns, (Mood.) G69	17	CP20
Beechwood Gro, (Barr.) G78	61	AY44
Beechwood La, (Bears.) G61	9	BH18
Beechwood Pl, G11	21	BH25
Beechwood Rd, (Cumb.) G67	72	DB12
Beecroft Pl, (Blan.) G72	71	CN44
Beil Dr, G13	20	BB22
Beith Rd, John. PA5	46	AJ35
Beith Rd, (How.) John. PA9	44	AD38
Beith Rd, (Millik.) John. PA10	44	AD38
Beith St, G11	36	BK28
Belgrave La, G12	23	BN26
off Kensington Rd		
Belgrave Ter, G12	23	BN26
Belhaven Cres La, G12	22	BL25
off Kensington Rd		
Belhaven Pk, (Muir.) G69	28	CL22
Belhaven Ter, G12	22	BL25
Belhaven Ter, (Ruther.) G73	67	BY39
Belhaven Ter La, G12	22	BL25
Belhaven Ter W, G12	22	BL25
Belhaven Ter W La, G12	22	BL25
Bellahouston Dr, G52	51	BG34
Bellahouston La, G52	51	BG33
Bellairs Pl, (Blan.) G72	70	CL44
Belleisle Av, (Udd.) G71	71	CN39
Belleisle Ct, (Cumb.) G68	72	DA9
Belleisle Cres, (Cumb.) G68	72	DA9
Belleisle Dr, (Cumb.) G68	72	DA9
Belleisle Gdns, (Cumb.) G68	72	DA9
Belleisle Gro, (Cumb.) G68	72	DA9
Belleisle St, G42	53	BR36
Bellevue Pl, G21	38	BV28
Bellfield Ct, (Barr.) G78	61	AX41
off Bellfield Cres		
Bellfield Cres, (Barr.) G78	61	AX41
Bellfield St, G31	39	BW31
Bellflower Av, G53	62	BD42

Name	Page	Grid
Bellflower Gdns, G53	63	BE42
Bellflower Pl, G53	63	BE42
Bellgrove St, G31	38	BV31
Bellrock Ct, G33	40	CD29
Bellrock Cres, G33	40	CC29
Bellrock Path, G33	40	CD29
off Bellrock St		
Bellrock St, G33	40	CC29
Bellscroft Av, (Ruther.) G73	54	BV38
Bellshaugh Gdns, G12	22	BL24
Bellshaugh La, G12	22	BL24
Bellshaugh Pl, G12	22	BL24
Bellshaugh Rd, G12	22	BL24
Bellshill Rd, (Udd.) G71	71	CP40
Bell St, G1	5	BT31
Bell St, G4	5	BT31
Bell St, Clyde. G81	19	AZ22
Bell St, Renf. PA4	19	AZ25
Belltrees Cres, Pais. PA3	47	AQ33
Bellview Ct, Renf. PA4	19	AZ25
Bellwood St, G41	53	BN38
Belmar Ct, (Linw.) Pais. PA3	30	AL32
off Langholm Dr		
Belmont Av, (Udd.) G71	59	CN38
Belmont Cres, G12	23	BN26
Belmont Dr, (Giff.) G46	64	BK42
Belmont Dr, (Ruther.) G73	55	BX38
Belmont Dr, (Barr.) G78	61	AZ44
Belmont La, G12	23	BN26
Belmont Rd, G21	24	BV23
Belmont Rd, (Camb.) G72	68	CA41
Belmont Rd, Pais. PA3	33	AW31
Belmont St, G12	23	BN26
Belmont St, Clyde. G81	19	AX21
Belses Dr, G52	35	BE32
Belses Gdns, G52	35	BE32
Belstane Pl, (Both.) G71	71	CQ42
Belsyde Av, G15	8	BC19
Beltane St, G3	4	BP29
off Dorset St		
Beltrees Av, G53	50	BC35
Beltrees Cres, G53	50	BC36
Beltrees Rd, G53	50	BC36
Belvidere Cres, (Bishop.) G64	13	BX19
Bemersyde, (Bishop.) G64	13	BY19
Bemersyde Av, G43	64	BK40
Bemersyde Rd, Pais. PA2	46	AM37
Ben Aigan Pl, G53	63	BE40
off Glen Moriston Rd		
Ben Alder Dr, Pais. PA2	49	AZ36
Benalder St, G11	36	BL28
Benarty Gdns, (Bishop.) G64	13	BX19
Benbow Rd, Clyde. G81	6	AV19
Ben Buie Way, Pais. PA2	49	AZ36
Bencroft Dr, G44	66	BU40
Ben Donich Pl, G53	63	BF41
off Ben Vorlich Dr		
Ben Edra Pl, G53	63	BF41
off Ben Vorlich Dr		
Bengairn St, G31	39	BY30
Bengal Pl, G43	52	BL38
off Christian St		
Bengal St, G43	52	BL38
Ben Garrisdale Pl, G53	63	BF40
off Ben Vorlich Dr		
Ben Glas Pl, G53	63	BF40
off Ben Vorlich Dr		
Benhar Pl, G33	40	CB30
Benholm St, G32	56	CB34
Ben Hope Av, Pais. PA2	49	AZ35
Ben Laga Pl, G53	63	BF41
off Ben Vorlich Dr		
Ben Lawers Dr, Pais. PA2	49	AZ35
Ben Ledi Av, Pais. PA2	49	AZ35
Ben Loyal Av, Pais. PA2	49	AZ35
Ben Lui Dr, Pais. PA2	49	AY36
Ben Lui Pl, G53	63	BF41
off Ben Vorlich Dr		
Ben Macdui Gdns, G53	63	BF41
Ben More Dr, Pais. PA2	49	AZ35
Benmore St, G21	24	BV23
Bennan Sq, G42	54	BS35
Ben Nevis Rd, Pais. PA2	49	AZ36
Benny Lynch Ct, G5	38	BS32
Ben Oss Pl, G53	63	BE41
Benston Pl, John. PA5	45	AG36
off Craigview Av		
Benaton Rd, John. PA5	45	AG36
Benthall St, G5	54	BT33
Bentinck St, G3	37	BN28
Bents Rd, (Baill.) G69	42	CK32
Ben Uird Pl, G53	63	BF41
Ben Vane Av, Pais. PA2	49	AY36
Ben Venue Way, Pais. PA2	49	AZ36
Benvie Gdns, (Bishop.) G64	13	BX19
Benview St, G20	23	BP25
Benview Ter, Pais. PA2	49	AX35
Ben Vorlich Dr, G53	63	BF41
Ben Vorlich Pl, G53	63	BF41
Ben Wyvis Dr, Pais. PA2	49	AY36
Berelands Cres, (Ruther.) G73	54	BU38
Berelands Pl, (Ruther.) G73	54	BV38
Beresford Av, G14	21	BG25
Berkeley St, G3	37	BN29
Berkeley Ter La, G3	4	BP29
off Elderslie St		
Berkley Dr, (Blan.) G72	70	CL44
Bernard Path, G40	55	BW33
Bernard St, G40	55	BW33
Bernard Ter, G40	55	BW33
Berneray St, G22	24	BS22
Berridale Av, G44	65	BQ39
Berriedale Av, (Baill.) G69	58	CJ33
Berryburn Rd, G21	25	BY25
Berryhill Dr, (Giff.) G46	64	BK43
Berryhill Rd, (Giff.) G46	64	BK44
Berryhill Rd, (Cumb.) G67	72	DA11
Berryknowe Av, (Chry.) G69	28	CL21
Berryknowes Av, G52	35	BE32
Berryknowes La, G52	35	BE32
Berryknowes Rd, G52	35	BE32
Bertram St, G41	53	BN36
Bertrohill Ter, G33	41	CE30
off Stepps Rd		
Bervie St, G51	35	BH31
Berwick Dr, G52	50	BD33
Berwick Dr, (Ruther.) G73	67	BZ39
Betula Dr, Clyde. G81	7	AW16
Bevan Gro, John. PA5	45	AF35
Beverley Rd, G43	64	BM39
Bevin Av, Clyde. G81	7	AZ20
Bideford Cres, G32	57	CF34
Biggar St, G31	39	BX31
Bigton St, G33	40	CD27
Bilsland Ct, G20	23	BR24
Bilsland Dr, G20	23	BP24
Binend Rd, G53	51	BE37
Binniehill Rd, (Cumb.) G68	72	CZ11
Binnie Pl, G40	38	BU32
Binns Rd, G33	41	CE27
Birch Cres, John. PA5	46	AJ36
Birch Dr, (Lenz.) G66	15	CF16
Birch Dr, (Camb.) G72	69	CE39
Birchend Dr, G21	39	BX27
Birchend Pl, G21	39	BW27
Birchfield Dr, G14	20	BD25
Birch Gro, (Udd.) G71	59	CR38
Birch Knowe, (Bishop.) G64	25	BX21
Birchlea Dr, (Giff.) G46	64	BM41
Birch Pl, (Camb.) G72	69	CH41
Birch Rd, Clyde. G81	7	AW17
Birch St, G5	54	BT34
off Silverfir St		
Birch Vw, (Bears.) G61	10	BJ16
Birchwood Av, G32	57	CG33
Birchwood Dr, Pais. PA2	47	AQ36
Birchwood Pl, G32	57	CG33
Birdston Rd, G21	25	BY23
Birgidale Rd, G45	66	BT43
Birgidale Ter, G45	66	BT43
Birkdale Ct, (Both.) G71	71	CP43
Birken Rd, (Lenz.) G66	15	CG17
Birkenshaw Ind Est, (Udd.) G71	59	CN35
Birkenshaw St, G31	39	BX30
Birkenshaw Way, Pais. PA3	32	AU29
Birkhall Av, G52	50	BB33
Birkhall Av, (Inch.) Renf. PA4	18	AT27
Birkhall Dr, (Bears.) G61	9	BH19
Birkhill Av, (Bishop.) G64	13	BX19
Birkhill Gdns, (Bishop.) G64	13	BX19
Birkmyre Rd, G51	35	BH31
Birks Rd, Renf. PA4	33	AX27
off Tower Dr		
Birkwood St, G40	55	BX35
off Dalmarnock Rd		
Birmingham Rd, Renf. PA4	33	AX28
Birnam Av, (Bishop.) G64	13	BX19
Birnam Cres, (Bears.) G61	10	BK16
Birnam Gdns, (Bishop.) G64	13	BX19
Birnam Rd, G31	55	BZ34
off London Rd		
Birness Dr, G43	52	BM37
Birness St, G43	52	BM38
off Pleasance St		
Birnie Ct, G21	25	BY26
Birnie Rd, G21	25	BY25
Birnock Av, Renf. PA4	34	BA28
Birsay Rd, G22	23	BR22
Bishop Gdns, (Bishop.) G64	12	BU19
Bishopmill Pl, G21	25	BY25
Bishopmill Rd, G21	25	BY24
Bishopsgate Dr, G21	24	BU22
Bishopsgate Gdns, G21	24	BU22
Bishopsgate Pl, G21	24	BU22
Bishopsgate Rd, G21	24	BU22
Bishop St, G3	4	BQ30
Bissett Cres, Clyde. G81	6	AU15
Blackburn Sq, (Barr.) G78	61	AZ44
Blackburn St, G51	36	BM31
Blackbyres Ct, (Barr.) G78	61	AZ41
Blackbyres Rd, (Barr.) G78	61	AY39
Blackcraig Av, G15	8	BC18
Blackcroft Gdns, G32	57	CF33
Blackcroft Rd, G32	57	CF33
Blackfaulds Rd, (Ruther.) G73	54	BU37
Blackford Rd, Pais. PA2	49	AW34
Blackfriars St, G1	5	BT30
Blackhall Ct, Pais. PA2	49	AX34
off Cartha Cres		
Blackhall La, Pais. PA1	48	AV34
Blackhall St, Pais. PA1	48	AV34
Blackhill Cotts, G23	11	BQ20
Blackhill Pl, G33	40	CA27
off Maxwelton Rd		
Blackhill Rd, G23	11	BN19
Blackie St, G3	36	BM29
Blackland Gro, Pais. PA2	48	AS37
Blacklands Pl, (Lenz.) G66	15	CG17
Blacklaw La, Pais. PA3	32	AU31
Blackstone Av, G53	51	BE37
Blackstone Cres, G53	51	BE36
Blackstone Rd, Pais. PA3	31	AQ29
Blackstoun Av, (Linw.) Pais. PA3	30	AK32
Blackstoun Oval, Pais. PA3	31	AR32
Blackstoun Rd, Pais. PA3	31	AQ32
Black St, G4	5	BT28
Blackthorn Av, (Kirk.) G66	14	CC16
Blackthorn Gro, (Kirk.) G66	14	CD16
Blackthorn Rd, (Cumb.) G67	73	DF9
Blackthorn St, G22	24	BU24
Blackwood Av, (Linw.) Pais. PA3	30	AJ31
Blackwoods Cres, (Mood.) G69	17	CP19
Blackwood St, G13	21	BG22
Blackwood St, (Barr.) G78	61	AX43
Blackwood Ter, John. PA5	45	AF37
Bladda La, Pais. PA1	48	AV33
Blades Ct, (Gart.) G69	29	CQ23
Bladnoch Dr, G15	9	BE19
Blaeloch Av, G45	66	BS44
Blaeloch Dr, G45	65	BR44
Blaeloch Ter, G45	65	BR44
Blairatholl Av, G11	22	BJ26
Blairatholl Gdns, G11	22	BJ26
Blairbeth Dr, G44	54	BR38
Blairbeth Pl, (Ruther.) G73	67	BW40
off Drumilaw Rd		
Blairbeth Rd, (Ruther.) G73	67	BW40
Blairbeth Ter, (Ruther.) G73	67	BY40
off Blairbeth Rd		
Blairbuie Dr, G20	22	BL22
Blair Cres, (Baill.) G69	58	CJ34
Blairdardie Rd, G13	8	BD20
Blairdardie Rd, G15	8	BD20
Blairdenan Av, (Mood.) G69	17	CP18
Blairdenon Dr, (Cumb.) G68	72	CY11
Blairgowrie Rd, G52	51	BE33
Blairhall Av, G41	53	BP37
Blairhill Av, (Kirk.) G66	16	CJ15
Blairlogie St, G33	40	CD28
Blairmore Av, Pais. PA1	33	AY32
Blair Rd, Pais. PA1	34	BA32
Blairston Av, (Both.) G71	71	CQ44
Blairston Gdns, (Both.) G71	71	CR44
Blair St, G32	40	CB32
Blairtum Dr, (Ruther.) G73	67	BX40
Blairtummock Rd, G33	41	CE29
Blake Rd, (Cumb.) G67	73	DC11

Name	No.	Grid
Blanefield Gdns, G13	21	BH21
Blane St, G4	38	BT27
Blaneview, (Stepps) G33	27	CF25
Blantyre Ferme Rd, (Udd.) G71	58	CL38
Blantyre Mill Rd, (Both.) G71	71	CP43
Blantyre Rd, (Both.) G71	71	CQ43
Blantyre St, G3	36	BM28
Blaven Ct, (Baill.) G69	58	CL33
Blawarthill St, G14	20	BB24
Bleasdale Ct, Clyde. G81	7	AX19
Blenheim Av, (Stepps) G33	27	CF23
Blenheim Ct, (Stepps) G33	27	CF23
Blenheim Ct, Pais. PA1	32	AT32
Blenheim La, (Stepps) G33	27	CG23
Blochairn Rd, G21	39	BW28
Bluebell Gdns, G45	67	BW43
Bluevale St, G31	39	BW31
Blyth Pl, G33	41	CF31
Blyth Rd, G33	41	CG31
Blythswood Av, Renf. PA4	19	AZ25
Blythswood Ct, G2	4	BQ30
off Cadogan St		
Blythswood Dr, Pais. PA3	32	AT31
Blythswood Retail Pk, Renf.PA4	19	AX25
Blythswood Rd, Renf. PA4	19	AY24
Blythswood Sq, G2	4	BQ29
off Blythswood St		
Blythswood St, G2	4	BQ30
Bobbins Gate, Pais. PA1	47	AR34
Boclair Av, (Bears.) G61	9	BH17
Boclair Cres, (Bears.) G61	10	BJ17
Boclair Cres, (Bishop.) G64	13	BW20
Boclair Rd, (Bears.) G61	10	BJ17
Boclair Rd, (Miln.) G62	10	BM15
Boclair Rd, (Bishop.) G64	13	BW19
Boclair St, G13	21	BG21
Boden Ind Est, G40	55	BX33
Boden St, G40	55	BW33
Bodmin Gdns, (Chry.) G69	17	CP18
off Gartferry Rd		
Bogany Ter, G45	66	BU43
Bogbain Rd, G34	42	CJ29
Boggknowe, (Udd.) G71	58	CM37
Boghall Rd, (Udd.) G71	58	CJ34
Boghall St, G33	40	CD28
Boghead Rd, G21	25	BW24
Boghead Rd, (Kirk.) G66	14	CC16
Bogleshole Rd, (Camb.) G72	56	CA38
Bogmoor Pl, G51	35	BE28
Bogmoor Rd, G51	35	BE29
Bogside Pl, (Baill.) G69	42	CL30
off Whamflet Av		
Bogside Rd, G33	26	CC24
Bogside St, G40	55	BX33
Bogton Av, G44	65	BP41
Bogton Av La, G44	65	BP41
Boleyn Rd, G41	53	BN35
Bolivar Ter, G42	54	BS37
Bolton Dr, G42	53	BQ37
Bon Accord Sq, Clyde. G81	19	AX21
Bonawe St, G20	23	BP25
off Kirkland St		
Boness St, G40	55	BX33
Bonhill St, G22	23	BR26
Bonnar St, G40	55	BW34
Bonnaughton Rd, (Bears.) G61	8	BD15
Bonnyholm Av, G53	50	BC34
Bonnyrigg Dr, G43	64	BJ40
Bonyton Av, G13	20	BB23
Boon Dr, G15	8	BD19
Boquhanran Pl, Clyde. G81	7	AW18
Boquhanran Rd, Clyde. G81	6	AV19
Borden La, G13	21	BG24
Borden Rd, G13	21	BG24
Boreland Dr, G13	20	BC22
Boreland Pl, G13	20	BD23
Borgie Cres, (Camb.) G72	68	CC40
Borland Rd, (Bears.) G61	10	BJ18
Borron St, G4	24	BS26
Borthwick St, G33	40	CD28
Boswell Ct, G42	53	BP38
Boswell Sq, G52	34	BB30
Botanic Cres, G20	22	BM25
Botanic Cres La, G20	22	BM25
Bothlin Dr, (Stepps) G33	27	CF23
Bothlyn Cres, (Gart.) G69	29	CN22
Bothlyn Rd, (Chry.) G69	28	CM21
Bothwell La, G2	4	BQ30
Bothwellpark Ind Est, (Udd.) G71	71	CQ40
Bothwellpark Rd, (Both.) G71	71	CR43
Bothwell Pl, Pais. PA2	47	AN37
Bothwell Rd, (Udd.) G71	71	CP40
Bothwell St, G2	4	BQ29
Bothwell St, (Camb.) G72	68	CA39
Bothwick Way, Pais. PA2	46	AM37
off Crosbie Dr		
Boundary Rd, (Ruther.) G73	54	BU35
off Rutherglen Rd		
Bourne Ct, (Inch.) Renf. PA4	18	AT22
Bourne Cres, (Inch.) Renf. PA4	18	AT22
Bourock Sq, (Barr.) G78	61	AZ44
Bouverie St, G14	20	BA23
Bouverie St, (Ruther.) G73	54	BV38
Bowden Dr, G52	34	BD31
Bower St, G12	23	BN26
Bowes Cres, (Baill.) G69	57	CH33
Bowfield Av, G52	34	BB31
Bowfield Cres, G52	34	BB31
Bowfield Dr, G52	34	BB31
Bowfield Path, G52	34	BB31
off Bowfield Av		
Bowfield Pl, G52	34	BB31
Bowfield Ter, G52	34	BB31
off Bowfield Cres		
Bowhouse Way, (Ruther.) G73	67	BW41
Bowling Grn La, G14	21	BF26
Bowling Grn Rd, G14	21	BF26
Bowling Grn Rd, G32	57	CF33
Bowling Grn Rd, G44	65	BQ40
off Clarkston Rd		
Bowling Grn Rd, (Chry.) G69	28	CM21
Bowman St, G42	53	BO35
Bowmont Gdns, G12	22	BL26
Bowmont Hill, (Bishop.) G64	13	BW17
Bowmont Pl, (Camb.) G72	69	CF40
Bowmont Ter, G12	22	BL26
Bowmore Gdns, (Udd.) G71	59	CN37
Bowmore Gdns, (Ruther.) G73	68	CA42
off Ardbeg Av		
Bowmore Rd, G52	35	BG32
Boydstone Pl, (Thornlie.) G46	63	BH40
Boydstone Rd, G43	63	BG40
Boydstone Rd, (Thornlie.) G46	63	BG39
Boydstone Rd, G53	63	BG40
Boyd St, G42	53	BR36
Boylestone Rd, (Barr.) G78	61	AW41
Boyle St, Clyde. G81	19	AZ21
Boyndie Path, G34	42	CK29
Boyndie St, G34	42	CK29
Brabloch Cres, Pais. PA3	32	AV31
Bracadale Dr, (Baill.) G69	58	CM33
Bracadale Gdns, (Baill.) G69	58	CM33
Bracadale Gro, (Baill.) G69	58	CL33
Bracadale Rd, (Baill.) G69	58	CL33
Brackenbrae Av, (Bishop.) G64	12	BU19
Brackenbrae Rd, (Bishop.) G64	12	BV20
Brackenrig Rd, (Thornlie.) G46	63	BG43
Bracken St, G22	23	BR23
Bracken Ter, (Both.) G71	71	CQ42
Brackla Av, G13	20	BA21
Brackla Av, Clyde. G81	20	BA21
Bradan Av, G13	20	BA22
Bradan Av, Clyde. G81	20	BA22
Bradda Av, (Ruther.) G73	67	BY41
Bradfield Av, G12	22	BL24
Brady Cres, (Mood.) G69	17	CQ18
Braeface Rd, (Cumb.) G67	72	DA11
Braefield Dr, (Thornlie.) G46	64	BJ42
Braefoot Cres, Pais. PA2	48	AU38
Braehead Rd, (Cumb.) G67	73	DD10
Braehead Rd, Pais. PA2	60	AS39
Braehead Shop Cen, G51	20	BC26
Braehead St, G5	54	BT34
Braemar Av, Clyde. G81	6	AV16
Braemar Ct, G44	65	BN41
Braemar Cres, (Bears.) G61	9	BH19
Braemar Cres, Pais. PA2	48	AV36
Braemar Dr, (Elder.) John. PA5	46	AK36
Braemar Rd, (Ruther.) G73	68	CA42
Braemar Rd, (Inch.) Renf. PA4	18	AT22
Braemar St, G42	53	BP38
Braemar Vw, Clyde. G81	6	AV16
Braemore Gdns, G22	24	BT25
Braemount Av, Pais. PA2	60	AS39
Braes Av, Clyde. G81	7	AZ20
Braeside Av, (Mood.) G69	17	CP19
Braeside Av, (Ruther.) G73	55	BY38
Braeside Cres, (Baill.) G69	43	CP32
Braeside Cres, (Barr.) G78	62	BA44
Braeside Dr, (Barr.) G78	61	AZ44
Braeside Pl, (Camb.) G72	68	CD41
Braeside St, G20	23	BP26
Braeview Av, Pais. PA2	47	AR38
Braeview Dr, Pais. PA2	47	AR38
Braeview Gdns, Pais. PA2	47	AR38
Braeview Rd, Pais. PA2	47	AR38
Braidbar Ct, (Giff.) G46	64	BL42
off Braidbar Rd		
Braidbar Fm Rd, (Giff.) G46	64	BM41
Braidbar Rd, (Giff.) G46	64	BL42
Braidcraft Pl, G53	51	BE37
off Braidcraft Rd		
Braidcraft Rd, G53	51	BE36
Braidcraft Ter, G53	51	BF36
off Braidcraft Rd		
Braidfauld Gdns, G32	56	CB34
Braidfauld Pl, G32	56	CB35
Braidfauld St, G32	56	CB34
Braidfield Gro, Clyde. G81	7	AX16
Braidfield Rd, Clyde. G81	7	AX16
Braidholm Cres, (Giff.) G46	64	BL42
Braidholm Rd, (Giff.) G46	64	BL42
Braidpark Dr, (Giff.) G46	64	BM42
Braids Ct, Pais. PA2	48	AU36
Braids Dr, G53	50	BB36
Braids Gait, Pais. PA2	48	AT36
Braid Sq, G4	37	BQ27
Braids Rd, Pais. PA2	48	AU36
Braid St, G4	37	BQ27
Bramley Pl, (Lenz.) G66	15	CG17
Branchock Av, (Camb.) G72	69	CF41
Brandon Gdns, (Camb.) G72	68	CA40
Brandon St, G31	38	BV31
Brand Pl, G51	36	BL31
Brand St, G51	36	BL31
Branklyn Ct, G13	21	BF23
Branklyn Cres, G13	21	BF23
Branklyn Gro, G13	21	BF23
Branklyn Pl, G13	21	BF23
Branscroft, (Kilb.) John. PA10	44	AD33
Brassey St, G20	23	BN23
Breadalbane Gdns, (Ruther.) G73	67	BZ41
Breadalbane St, G3	4	BP29
off St. Vincent St		
Brechin Rd, (Bishop.) G64	13	BY20
Brechin St, G3	37	BN29
Breck Av, Pais. PA2	46	AM37
Brediland Rd, Pais. PA2	47	AN36
Brediland Rd, (Linw.) Pais. PA3	30	AJ31
Bredisholm Dr, (Baill.) G69	58	CL33
Bredisholm Rd, (Baill.) G69	58	CL33
Bredisholm Ter, (Baill.) G69	58	CL33
Bremner Cotts, Clyde. G81	6	AV15
Brenfield Av, G44	65	BP41
Brenfield Dr, G44	65	BP41
Brenfield Rd, G44	65	BP41
Brent Av, (Thornlie.) G46	63	BH40
Brent Dr, (Thornlie.) G46	63	BH40
Brent Gdns, (Thornlie.) G46	64	BJ40
Brent Rd, (Thornlie.) G46	63	BH40
Brent Way, (Thornlie.) G46	63	BH40
Brentwood Av, G53	62	BC41
Brentwood Dr, G53	62	BC41
Brentwood Sq, G53	62	BD41
Brereton St, G42	54	BS36
Bressay Rd, G33	41	CG31
Breval Ct, (Baill.) G69	58	CL33
Brewery St, John. PA5	45	AH34
Brewster Av, Pais. PA3	33	AW30
Briarcroft Dr, G33	25	BZ22
Briarcroft Pl, G33	26	CA23
Briarcroft Rd, G33	25	BZ23
Briar Dr, Clyde. G81	7	AX17
Briar Gdns, G43	64	BM40
Briar Gro, G43	64	BM40
Briarlea Dr, (Giff.) G46	64	BL41
Briar Neuk, (Bishop.) G64	25	BX21
off Woodfield Av		
Briar Rd, G43	64	BM40
Briarwood Ct, G32	57	CG35
Briarwood Gdns, G32	57	CG35
off Woodend Rd		
Brick La, Pais. PA3	32	AV32
off Weir St		
Bridgegate, G1	5	BS31
Bridgegate Path, G1	5	BS31
off Bridgegate		

Street			Street			Street		
Bridge La, Pais. PA2	47	AR34	Broomknowe, (Cumb.) G68	72	CZ10	Buchanan Dr, (Ruther.) G73	67	BX39
off Tenters Way			Broomknowes Av, (Kirk.) G66	15	CG17	Buchanan Gdns, G32	57	CG35
Bridgend Cres, (Mood.) G69	17	CN19	Broomknowes Rd, G21	25	BW25	Buchanan Gro, (Baill.) G69	42	CK32
Bridgend Pl, (Mood.) G69	17	CN19	Broomlands Av, Ersk. PA8	18	AT21	Buchanan St, G1	4	BR30
Bridge of Weir Rd, (Linw.) Pais. PA3	30	AK32	Broomlands Cres, Ersk. PA8	18	AT21	Buchanan St, (Baill.) G69	58	CK33
			Broomlands Gdns, Ersk. PA8	18	AT21	Buchanan St, John. PA5	45	AG35
Bridge St, G5	4	BR31	Broomlands Rd, (Cumb.) G67	73	DC13	Buchan St, G5	37	BR32
Bridge St, (Camb.) G72	68	CC39	Broomlands St, Pais. PA1	48	AS33	off Norfolk St		
Bridge St, Clyde. G81	6	AU18	Broomlands Way, Ersk. PA8	18	AU21	Buchan Ter, (Camb.) G72	68	CA42
Bridge St, Pais. PA1	48	AU33	Broomlea Cres, (Inch.) Renf. PA4	18	AS22	Buchlyvie Gdns, (Bishop.) G64	24	BV21
Bridge St, (Linw.) Pais. PA3	30	AL31	Broomley Dr, (Giff.) G46	64	BL44	Buchlyvie Path, G34	42	CL30
Bridgeton Business Cen, G40	38	BV32	Broomley La, (Giff.) G46	64	BL44	Buchlyvie Rd, Pais. PA1	34	BA31
Bridgeton Cross, G40	38	BV32	Broomloan Ct, G51	36	BJ32	Buchlyvie St, G34	42	CK30
Brigham Pl, G23	23	BN21	Broomloan Pl, G51	36	BJ31	Buckingham Dr, G32	56	CD37
Brighton Pl, G51	36	BK31	Broomloan Rd, G51	36	BJ31	Buckingham Dr, (Ruther.) G73	55	BZ38
Brighton St, G51	36	BK31	Broompark Circ, G31	38	BV29	Buckingham St, G12	22	BM26
Brightside Av, (Udd.) G71	71	CP40	Broompark Dr, G31	38	BV30	Buckingham Ter, G12	22	BM26
Bright St, G21	38	BV28	Broompark Dr, (Inch.) Renf. PA4	18	AT22	Bucklaw Gdns, G52	51	BE33
Brisbane Ct, (Giff.) G46	64	BM42	Broompark La, G31	38	BV30	Bucklaw Pl, G52	51	BE33
Brisbane St, G42	53	BQ38	Broompark St, G31	38	BV30	Bucklaw Ter, G52	51	BE33
Brisbane St, Clyde. G81	6	AT17	Broompath, (Baill.) G69	57	CH34	Buckley St, G22	24	BT23
Britannia Way, Clyde. G81	7	AX19	Broom Pl, G43	64	BM40	Bucksburn Rd, G21	25	BY25
off Sutherland Rd			Broom Rd, G43	64	BM40	Buckthorne Pl, G53	62	BD42
Britannia Way, Renf. PA4	33	AY28	Broom Rd, (Cumb.) G67	73	DF8	Buddon St, G40	55	BY33
Briton St, G51	36	BK31	Broom Ter, John. PA5	46	AJ35	Budhill Av, G32	40	CD32
Broadford St, G4	38	BS27	Broomton Rd, G21	25	BY22	Bulldale Ct, G14	20	BA24
Broadholm St, G22	23	BR23	Broomward Dr, John. PA5	46	AK34	Bulldale Rd, G14	20	BA24
Broadleys Av, (Bishop.) G64	12	BV18	Brora Dr, (Giff.) G46	64	BM43	Bulldale St, G14	20	BA23
Broadlie Dr, G13	20	BC23	Brora Dr, (Bears.) G61	10	BK17	Buller Cres, (Blan.) G72	70	CL43
Broadloan, Renf. PA4	33	AY27	Brora Dr, Renf. PA4	20	BA26	Bullionslaw Dr, (Ruther.) G73	67	BZ39
Broad St, G40	38	BV32	Brora Gdns, (Bishop.) G64	13	BX20	Bulloch Av, (Giff.) G46	64	BM43
Broadwood Dr, G44	65	BR39	Brora La, G33	39	BZ28	Bullwood Av, G53	50	BB36
Brockburn Cres, G53	50	BD37	off Brora St			Bullwood Ct, G53	50	BB37
Brockburn Pl, G53	50	BC35	Brora Rd, (Bishop.) G64	13	BX20	Bullwood Dr, G53	50	BB36
Brockburn Rd, G53	50	BC35	Brora St, G33	39	BZ28	Bullwood Gdns, G53	50	BB36
Brockburn Ter, G53	51	BE37	Broughton Dr, G23	23	BN21	Bullwood Pl, G53	50	BB36
Brock Oval, G53	63	BE39	Broughton Gdns, G23	11	BP20	Bunessan St, G52	35	BH32
Brock Pl, G53	51	BE38	off Broughton Rd			Bunhouse Rd, G3	36	BL28
Brock Rd, G53	63	BE39	Broughton Rd, G23	23	BN21	Burghead Dr, G51	35	BG30
Brock Ter, G53	63	BE39	Brown Av, Clyde. G81	20	BA21	Burghead Pl, G51	35	BG29
Brockville St, G32	40	CB31	Brownhill Rd, G43	64	BK41	Burgher St, G31	39	BY32
Brock Way, (Cumb.) G67	72	DB12	Brownlie St, G42	53	BR37	Burgh Hall La, G11	36	BK27
off North Carbrain Rd			Brown Pl, (Camb.) G72	68	CC39	Burgh Hall St, G11	36	BK27
Brodick Sq, (Bishop.) G64	25	BX22	Brown Rd, (Cumb.) G67	72	DB11	Burgh La, G12	22	BM26
Brodick St, G21	39	BW28	Brownsdale Rd, (Ruther.)	54	BV38	Burleigh Rd, (Both.) G71	71	CR42
Brodie Av, Pais. PA2	48	AU35	Brownside Av, (Camb.) G72	68	CA40	Burleigh St, G51	36	BJ29
Brodie Pk Cres, Pais. PA2	48	AT35	Brownside Av, (Barr.) G78	61	AW40	Burlington Av, G12	22	BK23
Brodie Pk Gdns, Pais. PA2	48	AU35	Brownside Av, Pais. PA2	48	AS38	Burmola St, G22	23	BR25
Brodie Rd, G21	25	BZ22	Brownside Cres, (Barr.) G78	61	AW40	Burnacre Gdns, (Udd.) G71	59	CN38
Bron Way, (Cumb.) G67	73	DC12	Brownside Dr, G13	20	BB23	Burnawn Gdns, G33	25	BZ22
Brookfield Av, G33	25	BZ22	Brownside Dr, (Barr.) G78	61	AW40	off Brookfield Dr		
Brookfield Cor, G33	25	BZ22	Brownside Gro, (Barr.) G78	61	AW40	Burnawn Gro, G33	25	BZ22
Brookfield Dr, G33	25	BZ22	Brownside Ms, (Camb.) G72	68	CA40	off Brookfield Av		
Brookfield Gdns, G33	25	BZ22	Brownside Rd, (Camb.) G72	68	CA40	Burnawn Pl, G33	25	BZ22
off Brookfield Av			Brownside Rd, (Ruther.) G73	67	BZ40	off Brookfield Av		
Brookfield Gate, G33	25	BZ22	Brownsland Ct, (Gart.) G69	29	CP23	Burnbank Dr, (Barr.) G78	61	AY44
off Brookfield Av			Browns La, Pais. PA1	48	AU33	Burnbank Gdns, G20	37	BP27
Brookfield Pl, G33	25	BZ22	Brown St, G2	4	BQ30	Burnbank La, G20	37	BP27
Brookfield Rd, G33	25	BZ22	Brown St, Pais. PA1	32	AS32	off Napiershall St		
Brooklands Av, (Udd.) G71	59	CN38	Brown St, Renf. PA4	33	AX27	Burnbank Pl, G4	5	BU30
Brooklea Dr, (Giff.) G46	64	BL40	Bruce Av, John. PA5	45	AG37	off Drygate		
Brookside St, G40	39	BW32	Bruce Av, Pais. PA3	33	AW30	Burnbank Pl, G20	37	BQ27
Brook St, G40	38	BV32	Brucefield Pl, G34	42	CM39	off Burnbank Ter		
Brook St, Clyde. G81	6	AV17	Bruce Rd, G41	53	BN33	Burnbank Ter, G20	37	BP27
Broom Cres, (Barr.) G78	61	AW40	Bruce Rd, Pais. PA3	33	AW31	Burnbrae, Clyde. G81	7	AW15
Broom Dr, Clyde. G81	7	AW17	Bruce Rd, Renf. PA4	33	AW28	Burnbrae Av, (Mood.) G69	17	CQ19
Broomdyke Way, Pais. PA3	32	AT29	Bruce St, Clyde. G81	7	AX20	Burnbrae Av, (Linw.) Pais. PA3	30	AL32
Broomfield Av, (Camb.) G72	55	BZ38	Bruce Ter, (Blan.) G72	71	CN44	off Bridge St		
off Cambuslang Rd			Brunstane Rd, G34	42	CJ28	Burnbrae Dr, (Ruther.) G73	67	BZ40
Broomfield La, G21	24	BV24	Brunswick Ho, Clyde. G81	6	AT15	off East Kilbride Rd		
Broomfield Pl, G21	24	BV24	off Perth Cres			Burnbrae Dr, (Linw.) Pais. PA3	46	AM33
Broomfield Rd, G21	24	BV24	Brunswick La, G1	5	BS30	Burnbrae Rd, (Lenz.) G66	15	CG19
Broomfield Ter, (Udd.) G71	59	CP36	Brunswick St, G1	5	BS30	Burnbrae Rd, (Chry.) G69	16	CK19
Broom Gdns, (Kirk.) G66	14	CD15	Brunton St, G44	65	BQ40	Burnbrae Rd, (Linw.) Pais. PA3	46	AK33
Broomhill Av, G11	35	BH27	Brunton Ter, G44	65	BP41	Burnbrae St, G21	25	BW25
Broomhill Av, G32	56	CD37	Bruntsfield Av, G53	62	BD42	Burncleuch Av, (Camb.) G72	68	CC41
Broomhill Dr, G11	21	BH26	Bruntsfield Gdns, G53	62	BD42	Burncrooks Ct, Clyde. G81	6	AV15
Broomhill Dr, (Ruther.) G73	67	BX40	Brydson Pl, (Linw.) Pais. PA3	30	AK31	Burndyke Ct, G51	36	BK30
Broomhill Gdns, G11	21	BH26	Buccleuch Av, G52	34	BA29	Burndyke Sq, G51	36	BK30
Broomhill La, G11	21	BH26	Buccleuch La, G3	4	BQ28	Burndyke St, G51	36	BK30
Broomhill Path, G11	35	BH27	Buccleuch St, G3	4	BQ28	Burnett Rd, G33	41	CG30
Broomhill Pl, G11	21	BH26	Buchanan Business Pk, (Stepps) G33	27	CH23	Burnfield Av, (Thornlie.) G46	64	BK41
Broomhill Ter, G11	35	BH27				Burnfield Cotts, (Thornlie.) G46	64	BK41
Broomieknowe Dr, (Ruther.) G73	67	BX39	Buchanan Cres, (Bishop.) G64	25	BY22	Burnfield Dr, G43	64	BK41
Broomieknowe Gdns, (Ruther.) G73	67	BW39	Buchanan Dr, (Bears.) G61	10	BJ17	Burnfield Gdns, (Giff.) G46	64	BL41
Broomieknowe Rd, (Ruther.) G73	67	BX39	Buchanan Dr, (Bishop.) G64	25	BY21	Burnfield Rd, G43	64	BJ40
			Buchanan Dr, (Lenz.) G66	15	CF18	Burnfield Rd, (Thornlie.) G46	64	BK41
Broomielaw, G1	4	BQ31	Buchanan Dr, (Camb.) G72	68	CA39	Burnfoot Cres, (Ruther.) G73	67	BZ40
						Burnfoot Cres, Pais. PA2	48	AS38
						Burnfoot Dr, G52	34	BD32

Entry		
Burngreen Ter, (Camb.) G67	73	DD8
Burnham Rd, G14	20	BC25
Burnham Ter, G14	20	BC25
off Burnham Rd		
Burnhead Rd, G43	65	BN40
Burnhead Rd, (Cumb.) G68	72	CY11
Burnhead St, (Udd.) G71	59	CR38
Burnhill Quad, (Ruther.) G73	54	BV37
Burnhill St, (Ruther.) G73	54	BV37
Burnhouse St, G20	22	BM23
Burnmouth Ct, G33	41	CH31
off Pendeen Rd		
Burnmouth Pl, (Bears.) G61	10	BJ16
Burnmouth Rd, G33	41	CH31
Burnpark Av, (Udd.) G71	58	CM38
Burn Pl, (Camb.) G72	56	CA38
off Burn Ter		
Burns Dr, John. PA5	45	AG37
Burns Gdns, (Blan.) G72	70	CL44
Burns Gro, (Thornlie.) G46	64	BJ43
Burnside Av, (Barr.) G78	61	AX41
Burnside Ct, (Ruther.) G73	67	BY40
Burnside Ct, Clyde. G81	6	AU17
Burnside Gdns, (Millik.) John. PA10	44	AD35
Burnside Gate, (Ruther.) G73	67	BY40
off Burnside Rd		
Burnside Gro, John. PA5	45	AG35
Burnside Pl, Pais. PA3	31	AQ30
Burnside Rd, (Ruther.) G73	67	BY40
Burnside Rd, (Elder.) John. PA5	46	AL36
Burns Rd, (Cumb.) G67	73	DD10
Burns St, G4	37	BR27
Burns St, Clyde. G81	6	AU18
Burntbroom Dr, (Baill.) G69	57	CH34
Burntbroom Gdns, (Baill.) G69	57	CH34
Burntbroom St, G33	41	CF29
Burn Ter, (Camb.) G72	56	CA38
Burntshields Rd, (Kilb.) John. PA10	44	AA35
Burn Vw, (Cumb.) G67	73	DD10
Burra Gdns, (Bishop.) G64	13	BZ18
Burrells La, G4	5	BU30
Burrelton Rd, G43	65	BP39
Burton La, G42	53	BQ36
off Langside Rd		
Bushes Av, Pais. PA2	48	AT36
Busheyhill St, (Camb.) G72	68	CC40
Bute Av, Renf. PA4	33	AZ28
Bute Cres, (Old Kil.) G60	6	AS16
Bute Cres, (Bears.) G61	9	BH19
Bute Cres, Pais. PA2	48	AT38
Bute Dr, (Old Kil.) G60	6	AS15
Bute Dr, John. PA5	45	AF36
Bute Gdns, G12	36	BM27
Bute Gdns, G44	65	BP41
Bute Gdns, (Old Kil.) G60	6	AS15
Bute La, G12	36	BM27
off Great George St		
Bute Pl, (Old Kil.) G60	6	AT15
Bute Rd, (Abbots.) Pais. PA3	32	AT28
Bute Ter, (Udd.) G71	59	CR38
Bute Ter, (Ruther.) G73	67	BW40
Butterbiggins Rd, G42	53	BQ34
Butterfield Pl, G41	53	BQ34
off Pollokshaws Rd		
Byrebush Rd, G53	51	BE36
Byres Av, Pais. PA3	33	AW31
Byres Cres, Pais. PA3	33	AW31
Byres Rd, G11	36	BL27
Byres Rd, G12	36	BL27
Byres Rd, (Elder.) John. PA5	46	AM35
Byron Ct, (Both.) G71	71	CR43
Byron St, G11	35	BG27
Byron St, Clyde. G81	7	AW17
Byshot St, G22	24	BT25

C

Entry		
Cable Dep Rd, Clyde. G81	6	AV19
Cadder Ct, (Bishop.) G64	13	BX16
Cadder Gro, G20	23	BN22
off Cadder Rd		
Cadder Pl, G20	23	BN22
Cadder Rd, G20	23	BN22
Cadder Rd, G23	23	BN22
Cadder Rd, (Bishop.) G64	13	BX16
Cadder Way, (Bishop.) G64	13	BX16
Cadoc St, (Camb.) G72	68	CD40
Cadogan St, G2	4	BQ30
Cadzow Dr, (Camb.) G72	68	CB40
Cadzow St, G2	4	BQ30
Caird Dr, G11	36	BK27
Cairn Av, Renf. PA4	34	BA28
Cairnban St, G51	35	BF31
Cairnbrook Rd, G34	42	CL29
Cairncraig St, G31	55	BY33
Cairndow Av, G44	65	BP41
Cairndow Av La, G44	65	BP41
Cairndow Ct, G44	65	BP41
Cairn Dr, (Linw.) Pais. PA3	30	AK31
Cairngorm Cres, (Bears.) G61	8	BD15
Cairngorm Cres, (Barr.) G78	61	AY44
Cairngorm Cres, Pais. PA2	48	AU36
Cairngorm Rd, G43	64	BL40
Cairnhill Circ, G52	50	BB34
Cairnhill Dr, G52	50	BB34
Cairnhill Pl, G52	50	BB34
Cairnhill Rd, (Bears.) G61	9	BH20
Cairnlea Dr, G51	36	BK31
Cairns Av, (Camb.) G72	68	CD40
Cairnsmore Rd, G15	8	BA19
Cairns Rd, (Camb.) G72	68	CD41
Cairn St, G21	24	BV23
Cairnswell Av, (Camb.) G72	69	CE41
Cairnswell Pl, (Camb.) G72	69	CE41
Cairntoul Dr, G14	20	BC23
Cairntoul Pl, G14	20	BC23
Caithness St, G20	23	BP25
off Auchingill Rd		
Calcots Path, G34	42	CL28
off Auchingill Rd		
Calcots Pl, G34	42	CL28
Caldarvan St, G22	23	BR26
Calder Av, (Barr.) G78	61	AY44
Calderbank Vw, (Baill.) G69	58	CL34
Calderbraes Av, (Udd.) G71	59	CN37
Caldercuilt Rd, G20	22	BL21
Caldercuilt Rd, G23	10	BL20
Calder Dr, (Camb.) G72	68	CC40
Calder Gate, (Bishop.) G64	12	BV17
Calderglen Av, (Blan.) G72	70	CL42
Calderpark Av, (Udd.) G71	58	CK35
Calderpark Cres, (Udd.) G71	58	CK35
Calder Pl, (Baill.) G69	58	CK33
Calder Rd, (Udd.) G71	70	CK40
Calder Rd, Pais. PA3	31	AQ32
Calder St, G42	53	BR35
Calderwood Av, (Baill.) G69	58	CJ34
Calderwood Dr, (Baill.) G69	58	CJ34
Calderwood Gdns, (Baill.) G69	58	CJ34
Calderwood Rd, G43	64	BM39
Calderwood Rd, (Ruther.) G73	55	BY38
Caldwell Av, G13	20	BC23
Caledonia Av, G5	54	BS34
Caledonia Av, (Ruther.) G73	55	BX37
Caledonia Ct, Pais. PA3	32	AT31
off Mossvale St		
Caledonia Dr, (Baill.) G69	58	CK34
Caledonian Cres, G12	37	BN27
off Great Western Rd		
Caledonian Pl, (Camb.) G72	69	CG39
Caledonia Rd, G5	53	BR33
Caledonia Rd, (Baill.) G69	58	CJ34
Caledonia St, G5	54	BS34
Caledonia St, Pais. PA3	32	AT31
Caledonia Way, (Abbots.) Pais. PA3	32	AT28
Caledonia Way E, (Abbots.) Pais. PA3	32	AU28
Caledonia Way W, (Abbots.) Pais. PA3	32	AT28
Caledon La, G12	22	BL26
Caledon St, G12	22	BL26
Caley Brae, (Udd.) G71	71	CP39
Calfhill Rd, G53	50	BD34
Calfmuir Rd, (Kirk.) G66	16	CJ16
Calfmuir Rd, (Chry.) G69	16	CJ16
Calgary St, G4	5	BS28
Callaghan Wynd, (Blan.) G72	70	CL44
Callander Ct, (Cumb.) G68	72	DB9
off Callander Rd		
Callander Rd, (Cumb.) G68	72	DB9
Callander St, G20	23	BQ26
Callieburn Rd, (Bishop.) G64	13	BW20
Cally Av, G15	8	BL16
Calside, Pais. PA2	48	AU34
Calside Av, Pais. PA2	48	AT34
Calside Ct, Pais. PA2	48	AU35
Calton Entry, G40	5	BU31
off Gallowgate		
Calvay Cres, G33	41	CF30
Calvay Pl, G33	41	CG30
Calvay Rd, G33	41	CF30
Cambourne Rd, (Chry.) G69	17	CP18
Cambridge Av, Clyde. G81	7	AX18
Cambridge Rd, Renf. PA4	33	AY27
Cambridge St, G2	4	BR29
Cambridge St, G3	4	BR29
Camburn St, G32	40	CB31
Cambusdoon Rd, G33	41	CE27
Cambus Kenneth Gdns, G32	41	CF32
Cambuskenneth Pl, G33	41	CE27
Cambuslang Ind Est, G32	56	CC38
Cambuslang Rd, G32	56	CA37
Cambuslang Rd, (Camb.) G72	55	BZ38
Cambuslang Rd, (Ruther.) G73	55	BX36
Cambusmore Pl, G33	41	CE27
Cambus Pl, G33	41	CE27
Camden Ter, G5	54	BS33
Camelon St, G32	40	CB31
Cameron Cotts, Clyde. G81	7	AY15
off Glasgow Rd		
Cameron Ct, (Ruther.) G73	55	BW38
Cameron Ct, Clyde. G81	19	AY21
off Cameron St		
Cameron Dr, (Bears.) G61	10	BJ18
Cameron Dr, (Udd.) G71	59	CO37
Cameron Sq, Clyde. G81	7	AY15
Cameron St, G52	34	BA30
Cameron St, Clyde. G81	19	AY21
Camlachie St, G31	39	BX32
Campbell Cres, (Both.) G71	71	CR41
Campbell Dr, (Bears.) G61	9	BF16
Campbell Dr, (Barr.) G78	61	AY43
Campbell St, G20	22	BM22
Campbell St, John. PA5	45	AH35
Campbell St, Renf. PA4	19	AZ25
Camphill, Pais. PA1	48	AT34
Camphill Av, G41	53	BN38
Camphill Ct, Pais. PA2	48	AT34
Camp Rd, (Baill.) G69	42	CK32
Camp Rd, (Ruther.) G73	54	BV35
Camps Cres, Renf. PA4	34	BA27
Campsie Av, (Barr.) G78	61	AY44
Campsie, (Kirk.) G66	15	CE15
off Westergreens Av		
Campsie Dr, Pais. PA2	48	AT37
Campsie Dr, (Abbots.) Pais. PA3	32	AU28
Campsie Dr, Renf. PA4	33	AW29
Campsie Pl, (Chry.) G69	28	CL21
Campsie St, G21	24	BV24
Campsie Vw, (Stepps) G33	27	CF25
Campsie Vw, (Cumb.) G67	73	DD10
Campsie Vw, (Baill.) G69	43	CP32
Campsie Vw, (Chry.) G69	28	CL21
Campsie Vw, (Udd.) G71	59	CO37
Campsie Vw, (Camb.) G72	69	CG42
Campston Pl, G33	40	CD28
Camstradden Dr E, (Bears.) G61	9	BE17
Camstradden Dr W, (Bears.) G61	9	BE17
Camus Pl, G15	8	BB17
Canal Av, John. PA5	45	AH35
Canal Bk La, G22	23	BQ21
Canal Gdns, (Elder.) John. PA5	46	AM34
off Canal St		
Canal Rd, John. PA5	46	AJ35
Canal St, G4	5	BS28
Canal St, Clyde. G81	7	AX20
Canal St, John. PA5	46	AJ34
Canal St, (Elder.) John. PA5	46	AM34
Canal St, Pais. PA1	48	AT33
Canal St, Renf. PA4	19	AZ25
Canal Ter, Pais. PA1	48	AT33
Canberra Av, Clyde. G81	6	AT17
Canberra Ct, (Giff.) G46	65	BN42
Cander Rigg, (Bishop.) G64	13	BW17
Candleriggs, G1	5	BT31
Candren Rd, Pais. PA3	47	AQ33
Candren Rd, (Linw.) Pais. PA3	30	AM32
Candren Way, Pais. PA3	31	AQ32
off Ferguslie Park Av		
Canmore Pl, G31	55	BZ33
Canmore St, G31	55	BZ33
Cannich Dr, Pais. PA2	49	AX36
Canniesburn Rd, (Bears.) G61	9	BF18

Canniesburn Sq, (Bears.) G61   9   BH19
off Switchback Rd
Canniesburn Toll, (Bears.) G61   9   BH19
off Drymen Rd
Canonbie St, G34   42   CM28
Canting Way, G51   36   BL30
Capelrig St, (Thornlie.) G46   63   BH41
Caplaw Rd, Pais. PA2   60   AS39
Caplethill Rd, (Barr.) G78   48   AV38
Caplethill Rd, Pais. PA2   48   AV38
Caprington Pl, G33   40   CC28
Caprington St, G33   40   CC28
Cara Dr, G51   35   BG29
off St. Kenneth Dr
Caravelle Way, Renf. PA4   33   AZ28
off Friendship Way
Carberry Rd, G41   52   BM35
Carbeth St, G22   23   BR25
Carbisdale St, G22   24   BU24
Carbost St, G23   10   BM20
Carbrain Ind Est, (Cumb.) G67   73   DD12
Carbrook St, G21   39   BW28
Carbrook St, Pais. PA1   48   AS33
Cardarrach St, G21   25   BW24
Cardell Av, Pais. PA2   47   AQ34
Cardell Dr, Pais. PA2   47   AQ34
Cardell Rd, Pais. PA2   47   AQ34
Cardonald Dr, G52   50   BC33
Cardonald Gdns, G52   50   BC33
Cardonald Pl Rd, G52   50   BD33
Cardowan Dr, (Stepps) G33   27   CG24
Cardowan Pk, (Udd.) G71   59   CR36
Cardowan Rd, G32   40   CB31
Cardowan Rd, (Stepps) G33   27   CG23
Cardow Rd, G21   25   BY25
Cardrona St, G33   26   CD26
Cardross Ct, G31   38   BV30
Cardross St, G31   38   BV30
Cardwell St, G41   53   BQ33
off Eglinton St
Cardyke St, G21   25   BW25
Careston Pl, (Bishop.) G64   13   BZ20
Carfin St, G42   53   BR35
Carfrae St, G3   36   BL29
Cargill Sq, (Bishop.) G64   25   BY21
Carham Cres, G52   35   BE32
Carham Dr, G52   35   BE32
Carillon Rd, G51   36   BL32
Carisbrooke Cres, (Bishop.) G64   13   BX17
Carlaverock Rd, G43   64   BM39
Carleith Av, Clyde. G81   6   AV15
Carleith Quad, G51   35   BF30
Carleith Ter, Clyde. G81   6   AV15
Carleston St, G21   24   BV25
Carleton Ct, (Giff.) G46   64   BL41
Carleton Dr, (Giff.) G46   64   BL41
Carleton Gate, (Giff.) G46   64   BL41
Carlibar Av, G13   20   BB23
Carlibar Dr, (Barr.) G78   61   AY42
Carlibar Gdns, (Barr.) G78   61   AY42
Carlibar Rd, (Barr.) G78   61   AY42
Carlile Pl, Pais. PA3   32   AU31
Carlisle St, G21   24   BT25
Carlisle Ter, Pais. PA3   32   AU31
Carlock Wk, G32   41   CE31
off Croftspar Pl
Carlowrie Av, (Blan.) G72   70   CL43
Carlton Ct, G5   4   BR31
Carlton Pl, G5   4   BR31
Carlyle Av, G52   34   BB29
Carlyle St, Pais. PA3   32   AU32
Carlyle Ter, (Ruther.) G73   55   BX36
Carmaben Rd, G33   41   CG29
Carment Dr, G41   52   BM37
Carment La, G41   52   BM37
Carmichael Pl, G42   53   BP38
Carmichael St, G51   36   BK31
Carmunnock La, G44   65   BR40
off Madison Av
Carmunnock Rd, G44   53   BR38
Carmunnock Rd, G45   66   BS40
Carmunnock Rd, (Busby) G76   66   BS44
Carmyle Av, G32   56   CD34
Carna Dr, G44   66   BS40
Carnarvon St, G3   4   BP28
Carnbooth Ct, G16   66   BV43
Carnegie Rd, G52   34   BC30
Carnoch St, G23   10   BM20
off Torrin Rd

Carnock Cres, (Barr.) G78   61   AX43
Carnock Rd, G53   51   BE37
Carnoustie Ct, (Both.) G71   71   CP43
Carnoustie Cres, (Bishop.) G64   13   BY20
Carnoustie Pl, G5   37   BP32
Carnoustie St, G5   37   BP32
Carntyne Gdns, G32   40   CA30
off Abbeyhill St
Carntynehall Rd, G32   40   CB30
Carntyne Ind Est, G32   40   CA31
Carntyne Path, G32   39   BZ30
Carntyne Pl, G32   39   BZ30
Carntyne Rd, G31   39   BY31
Carntyne Rd, G32   39   BZ30
Carnwadric Rd, (Thornlie.) G46   63   BG41
Carnwath Av, G43   65   BP39
Caroline St, G31   40   CA32
Carolside Dr, G15   8   BD18
Carradale Gdns, (Bishop.) G64   13   BY20
off Thrums Av
Carradale Pl, (Linw.) Pais. PA3   30   AJ31
Carrbridge Dr, G20   22   BM23
Carresbrook Av, (Kirk.) G66   16   CK15
Carriagehill Av, Pais. PA2   48   AU35
Carriagehill Dr, Pais. PA2   48   AU36
Carrickarden Rd, (Bears.) G61   9   BH18
Carrick Cres, (Giff.) G46   64   BL44
Carrick Dr, G32   57   CG34
Carrick Dr, (Ruther.) G73   67   BW40
Carrick Gro, G32   57   CG33
Carrick Mans, G32   57   CG34
off Carrick Dr
Carrick Rd, (Bishop.) G64   13   BY20
Carrick Rd, (Cumb.) G67   73   DC9
Carrick Rd, (Ruther.) G73   67   BW40
Carrickstone Rd, (Cumb.) G68   72   DA9
Carrickstone Roundabout, (Cumb.) G68   72   DA8
Carrickstone Vw, (Cumb.) G68   72   DB8
Carrick St, G2   4   BQ31
Carrick Way, (Both.) G71   71   CQ42
Carriden Pl, G33   41   CG30
Carrington St, G4   37   BP27
Carroglen Gdns, G32   41   CF32
Carroglen Gro, G32   41   CF32
Carron Ct, (Camb.) G72   69   CF40
Carron Cres, G22   24   BT24
Carron Cres, (Bears.) G61   9   BE18
Carron Cres, (Bishop.) G64   13   BX20
Carron Cres, (Lenz.) G66   15   CG17
Carron La, Pais. PA3   33   AX30
off Kilearn Rd
Carron Pl, G22   24   BT24
Carron St, G22   24   BU24
Carron Way, (Cumb.) G67   72   DB12
off Cumbernauld Shop Cen
Carron Way, Pais. PA3   33   AW30
off Priory Av
Carrour Gdns, (Bishop.) G64   12   BV19
Carsaig Dr, G52   35   BG32
Carsegreen Av, Pais. PA2   47   AR38
Carse Vw Dr, (Bears.) G61   10   BJ15
Carstairs St, G40   55   BW35
Carswell Gdns, G41   53   BN36
Cartbank Gdns, G44   65   BQ41
off Cartbank Rd
Cartbank Gro, G44   65   BQ41
off Cartbank Rd
Cartbank Rd, G44   65   BQ41
Cartcraigs Rd, G43   64   BK39
Cartha Cres, Pais. PA2   49   AX34
Cartha St, G41   52   BM38
Cartside Av, John. PA5   45   AF36
Cartside Quad, G42   53   BQ38
Cartside St, G42   53   BP38
Cartside Ter, (Millik.) John. PA10   45   AE35
off Kilbarchan Rd
Cart St, Clyde. G81   19   AX21
Cartvale La, Pais. PA3   32   AU31
Cartvale Rd, G42   53   BP38
Caskie Dr, (Blan.) G72   71   CN44
Cassiltoun Gdns, G45   66   BT43
off Stravanan Rd
Cassley Av, Renf. PA4   34   BB27
Castle Av, (Udd.) G71   71   CN41
Castle Av, (Elder.) John. PA5   46   AK36
Castlebank St, C13   21   DG23
Castlebank Cres, G11   36   BJ28
Castlebank Gdns, G13   21   BG23
Castlebank St, G11   35   BH27

Castlebank Vil, G13   21   BG23
off Munro Pl
Castlebay Dr, G22   12   BS20
Castlebay Pl, G22   24   BS21
Castlebay St, G22   24   BS21
Castlebrae Gdns, G44   65   BR39
Castle Chimmins Av, (Camb.) G72   69   CF41
Castle Chimmins Rd, (Camb.) G72   69   CF42
Castle Cres N Ct, G1   5   BS30
off Royal Ex Sq
Castlecroft Gdns, (Udd.) G71   71   CN40
Castlefern Rd, (Ruther.) G73   67   BX42
Castlefield Ct, G33   26   CD25
Castle Gait, Pais. PA1   48   AT34
Castle Gdns, (Chry.) G69   17   CP20
Castle Gdns, Pais. PA2   47   AQ34
Castle Gate, (Udd.) G71   71   CN40
Castlehill Cres, Renf. PA4   19   AZ25
Castlehill Rd, (Bears.) G61   8   BD15
Castlelaw Gdns, G32   40   CD31
Castlelaw Pl, G32   40   CD31
Castlelaw St, G32   40   CD31
Castlemilk Arc, G45   66   BU42
Castlemilk Cres, G44   66   BU40
Castlemilk Dr, G45   66   BU43
Castlemilk Rd, G44   54   BU38
Castlemilk Ter, G45   66   BU44
off Castlemilk Dr
Castle Pl, (Udd.) G71   71   CN39
Castle Rd, (Elder.) John. PA5   46   AL34
Castle Sq, Clyde. G81   6   AU18
Castle St, G4   5   BU29
Castle St, G11   36   BL28
Castle St, (Baill.) G69   58   CJ34
Castle St, (Ruther.) G73   55   BW37
Castle St, Clyde. G81   6   AU18
Castle St, Pais. PA1   48   AS33
Castleton Av, (Bishop.) G64   24   BU22
Castleton Ct, G45   66   BV43
Castle Vw, Clyde. G81   7   AX18
off Granville St
Castleview Av, Pais. PA2   47   AQ38
Castleview Dr, Pais. PA2   47   AQ38
Castleview Pl, Pais. PA2   47   AQ38
off Castleview Av
Castle Way, (Cumb.) G67   73   DE9
Castle Way, (Baill.) G69   43   CP32
off Dukes Rd
Castle Wynd, (Both.) G71   71   CR43
Cathay St, G22   24   BS21
Cathcart Cres, Pais. PA2   49   AW34
Cathcart Pl, (Ruther.) G73   54   BV38
Cathcart Rd, G42   53   BR37
Cathcart Rd, (Ruther.) G73   54   BU38
Cathedral Sq, G4   5   BU30
Cathedral St, G1   5   BS29
Cathedral St, G4   5   BS29
Catherine Pl, G3   4   BP30
off Hydepark St
Cathkin Av, (Camb.) G72   68   CA39
Cathkin Av, (Ruther.) G73   55   BY38
Cathkin Bypass, (Ruther.) G73   67   BZ42
Cathkin Ct, G45   66   BV43
Cathkin Cres, (Cumb.) G68   72   DA9
Cathkin Gdns, (Udd.) G71   59   CN36
off Watling St
Cathkin Pl, (Camb.) G72   68   CA39
Cathkin Rd, G42   53   BP38
Cathkin Rd, (Udd.) G71   59   CN36
Cathkin Rd, (Ruther.) G73   67   BY43
Cathkin Vw, G32   56   CD37
Cathkinview Pl, G42   53   BQ38
Cathkinview Rd, G42   53   BQ38
Catrine Av, Clyde. G81   7   AZ18
Catrine Ct, G53   50   BC37
Catrine Gdns, G53   50   BC37
Catrine Pl, G53   50   BC37
Catrine Rd, G53   50   BC37
Caurnie Vw, (Kirk.) G66   16   CL15

Causewayside Cres, G32   56   CC35
Causewayside St, G32   56   CC35
Causeyside St, Pais. PA1   48   AU33
Cavendish Ct, G5   53   BR33
Cavendish Pl, G5   53   BR33
Cavendish St, G5   53   BR33
Cavin Dr, G45   66   BU41

Cavin Rd, G45 — 66 BU41
Cawder Ct, (Cumb.) G68 — 72 DA8
  off Cawder Rd
Cawder Pl, (Cumb.) G68 — 72 DA8
  off Cawder Rd
Cawder Rd, (Cumb.) G68 — 72 DA8
Cawder Vw, (Cumb.) G68 — 72 DA8
  off Cawder Rd
Cawder Way, (Cumb.) G68 — 72 DA8
  off Cawder Rd
Cayton Gdns, (Baill.) G69 — 57 CH33
Cecil St, G12 — 22 BM26
Cedar Av, Clyde. G81 — 6 AT17
Cedar Av, John. PA5 — 45 AH37
Cedar Ct, G20 — 37 BQ27
Cedar Ct, (Camb.) G72 — 69 CG41
Cedar Ct, (Kilb.) John. PA10 — 44 AC34
Cedar Dr, (Lenz.) G66 — 15 CE16
Cedar Gdns, (Ruther.) G73 — 67 BY41
Cedar Rd, (Bishop.) G64 — 25 BX21
Cedar Rd, (Cumb.) G67 — 73 DF10
Cedar St, G20 — 37 BQ27
Cedar Wk, (Bishop.) G64 — 25 BX21
Cedric Pl, G13 — 21 BF22
Cedric Rd, G13 — 21 BF22
Celtic St, G20 — 22 BL22
Cemetery Rd, G52 — 35 BF32
Centenary Ct, (Barr.) G78 — 61 AX43
Centenary Ct, Clyde. G81 — 7 AX20
Central Av, G11 — 35 BH27
  off Broomhill Ter
Central Av, G32 — 57 CF34
Central Av, (Camb.) G72 — 68 CB39
Central Av, Clyde. G81 — 7 AW19
Central Gro, G32 — 57 CF33
Central Gro, (Camb.) G72 — 68 CB39
Central Path, G32 — 57 CG34
Central Rd, Pais. PA1 — 32 AU32
Central Sta, G1 — 4 BR30
Central Way, (Cumb.) G67 — 72 DA13
Central Way, Pais. PA1 — 32 AU32
  off Central Rd
Centre, The, (Barr.) G78 — 61 AX43
Centre St, G5 — 37 BQ32
Centre Way, (Barr.) G78 — 61 AX42
  off North Park Av
Ceres Gdns, (Bishop.) G64 — 13 BZ20
Cessnock Pl, (Camb.) G72 — 69 CF40
Cessnock Rd, G33 — 26 CC24
Cessnock St, G51 — 36 BL31
Chalmers Ct, G40 — 5 BU31
Chalmers Gate, G40 — 5 BU31
  off Claythorn St
Chalmers Pl, G40 — 5 BU31
  off Claythorn St
Chalmers St, G40 — 5 BU31
Chalmers St, Clyde. G81 — 7 AX20
Chamberlain La, G13 — 21 BG24
Chamberlain Rd, G13 — 21 BG23
Chancellor St, G11 — 36 BK27
Chapel Ct, (Ruther.) G73 — 54 BV37
  off Western Av
Chapelhill Rd, Pais. PA2 — 49 AW35
Chapel Rd, Clyde. G81 — 7 AW15
Chapel St, G20 — 23 BN24
Chapel St, (Ruther.) G73 — 54 BV37
Chapel St Ind Est, G20 — 23 BN23
Chapelton Av, (Bears.) G61 — 9 BH17
Chapelton Gdns, (Bears.) G61 — 9 BH17
Chapelton St, G22 — 24 BS23
Chaplet Av, G13 — 21 BE21
Chapman St, G42 — 53 BQ35
  off Allison St
Chappell St, (Barr.) G78 — 61 AX42
Charing Cross, G2 — 4 BP28
Charing Cross La, G3 — 4 BP29
  off Granville St
Charles Av, Renf. PA4 — 19 AZ25
Charles Cres, (Lenz.) G66 — 15 CF18
Charles St, G21 — 5 BU28
Charlotte La, G1 — 5 BT31
  off London Rd
Charlotte La S, G1 — 5 BT31
  off Charlotte St
Charlotte La W, G1 — 5 BT31
  off London Rd
Charlotte Pl, Pais. PA2 — 48 AU35
Charlotte St, G1 — 5 BT31
Charnwood Av, John. PA5 — 45 AF37
Chatelherault Av, (Camb.) G72 — 68 CA40

Chatton St, G23 — 10 BM20
Cheapside St, G3 — 4 BP31
Chelmsford Dr, G12 — 22 BK24
Cherry Bk, (Kirk.) G66 — 14 CD16
Cherrybank Rd, G43 — 65 BP40
Cherry Cres, Clyde. G81 — 7 AW17
Cherry Gro, (Baill.) G69 — 43 CR31
Cherry Pl, (Bishop.) G64 — 25 BX21
Cherry Pl, John. PA5 — 46 AJ36
Cherryridge Dr, (Baill.) G69 — 43 CQ31
Cherrytree Dr, (Camb.) G72 — 69 CG41
Cherrywood Rd, (Elder.) — 46 AL34
  John. PA5
Chesterfield Av, G12 — 22 BJ24
Chesters Pl, (Ruther.) G73 — 54 BV38
Chesters Rd, (Bears.) G61 — 9 BF16
Chester St, G32 — 40 CC32
Chestnut Dr, (Kirk.) G66 — 14 CD15
Chestnut Dr, Clyde. G81 — 6 AV16
Chestnut Pl, John. PA5 — 46 AJ37
Chestnut St, G22 — 24 BT24
Chestnut Way, (Camb.) G72 — 69 CG41
Cheviot Av, (Barr.) G78 — 61 AY43
Cheviot Rd, G43 — 64 BL40
Cheviot Rd, Pais. PA2 — 48 AT36
Chirmorie Pl, G53 — 50 BC36
Chirnside Pl, G52 — 34 BC31
Chirnside Rd, G52 — 34 BC31
Chisholm St, G1 — 5 BT31
Chrighton Grn, (Udd.) G71 — 59 CQ37
Christian St, G43 — 52 BL38
Christie La, Pais. PA3 — 32 AU32
Christie Pl, (Camb.) G72 — 68 CC40
Christie St, Pais. PA1 — 32 AV32
Christopher St, G21 — 39 BW27
Chryston Business Cen, — 28 CL21
  (Chry.) G69
Chryston Rd, (Kirk.) G66 — 16 CK15
Chryston Rd, (Chry.) G69 — 28 CM21
Chryston Rd, (Mood.) G69 — 16 CM16
Church Av, (Stepps) G33 — 27 CF23
Church Av, (Ruther.) G73 — 67 BY40
Church Dr, (Kirk.) G66 — 15 CE15
Church Hill, Pais. PA1 — 32 AU32
Churchill Av, John. PA5 — 45 AE37
Churchill Cres, (Both.) G71 — 71 CR42
Churchill Dr, G11 — 22 BJ26
Churchill Pl, (Kilb.) John. — 44 AC34
  PA10
Churchill Way, (Bishop.) G64 — 12 BV20
Church Rd, (Giff.) G46 — 64 BL43
Church Rd, (Muir.) G69 — 28 CL22
Church St, G11 — 36 BL27
Church St, (Baill.) G69 — 58 CK33
Church St, (Udd.) G71 — 71 CN40
Church St, Clyde. G81 — 7 AW18
Church St, John. PA5 — 45 AH34
Church St, (Kilb.) John. PA10 — 44 AC34
Church Vw, (Camb.) G72 — 56 CC38
Circus Dr, G31 — 38 BV30
Circus Pl, G31 — 38 BV30
Circus Pl La, G31 — 38 BV29
Cityford Cres, (Ruther.) G73 — 66 BV39
Cityford Dr, (Ruther.) G73 — 54 BV38
City Link Cen, G51 — 36 BJ30
Civic St, G4 — 37 BR27
Clachan Dr, G51 — 35 BG29
  off Skipness Dr
Claddens Pl, (Lenz.) G66 — 15 CG17
Claddens Quad, G22 — 24 BS23
Claddens St, G22 — 23 BR23
Claddens Wynd, (Kirk.) G66 — 15 CG17
Clairinsh Gdns, Renf. PA4 — 33 AY28
  off Sandy Rd
Clairmont Gdns, G3 — 4 BP28
Clair Rd, (Bishop.) G64 — 13 BZ20
Claremont Pas, G3 — 4 BP28
  off Claremont Ter
Claremont Pl, G3 — 4 BP28
  off Claremont Ter
Claremont St, G3 — 4 BN29
Claremont Ter, G3 — 4 BP28
Claremont Ter La, G3 — 4 BN28
Claremount Av, (Giff.) G46 — 64 BL43
Clarence Dr, G11 — 22 BJ26
Clarence Dr, G12 — 22 BJ26
Clarence Dr, Pais. PA1 — 33 AW32
Clarence Gdns, G11 — 22 BJ26
Clarence La, G12 — 22 BK26
Clarence St, Clyde. G81 — 7 AX18

Clarence St, Pais. PA1 — 33 AW32
Clarendon La, G20 — 37 BQ27
  off Clarendon St
Clarendon Pl, G20 — 37 BQ27
Clarendon Pl, (Stepps) — 27 CF24
  G33
Clarendon St, G20 — 37 BQ27
Clare St, G21 — 39 BW27
Clarion Cres, G13 — 20 BC21
Clarion Rd, G13 — 20 BC21
Clarkston Av, G44 — 65 BP41
Clarkston Rd, G44 — 65 BP41
Clark St, Clyde. G81 — 6 AV17
Clark St, John. PA5 — 45 AH34
Clark St, Pais. PA3 — 32 AS31
Clark St, Renf. PA4 — 19 AX26
Clathic Av, (Bears.) G61 — 10 BJ17
Claude Av, (Camb.) G72 — 69 CG42
Claud Rd, Pais. PA3 — 33 AW31
Clavens Rd, G52 — 34 BA31
Claverhouse Pl, Pais. PA2 — 49 AW34
Claverhouse Rd, G52 — 34 BB30
Clavering St E, Pais. PA1 — 32 AS32
Clavering St W, Pais. PA1 — 32 AS32
  off King St
Clayhouse Rd, G33 — 27 CG25
Claypotts Pl, G33 — 40 CC28
Claypotts Rd, G33 — 40 CC28
Clayslaps Rd, G3 — 36 BM28
Claythorn Av, G40 — 38 BU32
Claythorn Circ, G40 — 5 BU31
  off Claythorn Av
Claythorn Ct, G40 — 5 BU31
  off Claythorn Pk
Claythorn Pk, G40 — 38 BU32
Claythorn St, G40 — 5 BU31
Claythorn Ter, G40 — 5 BU31
  off Claythorn Pk
Clayton Ter, G31 — 38 BV30
Cleddans Cres, Clyde. G81 — 7 AY15
Cleddans Rd, Clyde. G81 — 7 AX16
Cleddans St W, Clyde. G81 — 7 AY18
  off Kirkoswald Dr
Cleddens Ct, (Bishop.) G64 — 13 BW19
Cleeves Pl, G53 — 62 BD40
Cleeves Quad, G53 — 62 BC40
Cleeves Rd, G53 — 62 BC40
Cleghorn St, G22 — 23 BR26
Cleland La, G5 — 38 BS32
Cleland St, G5 — 38 BS32
Clelland Av, (Bishop.) G64 — 25 BW21
Clerwood St, G32 — 39 BZ31
Cleveden Cres, G12 — 22 BK24
Cleveden Cres La, G12 — 22 BK24
Cleveden Dr, G12 — 22 BK24
Cleveden Dr, (Ruther.) G73 — 67 BY39
Cleveden Dr La, G12 — 22 BL25
  off Mirrlees Dr
Cleveden Gdns, G12 — 22 BL24
Cleveden La, G12 — 22 BK23
Cleveden Pl, G12 — 22 BK23
Cleveden Rd, G12 — 22 BK23
Cleveland La, G3 — 4 BP29
  off Kent Rd
Cleveland St, G3 — 4 BP29
Clifford Gdns, G51 — 36 BK32
Clifford La, G51 — 36 BL32
Clifford Pl, G51 — 36 BM31
  off Clifford St
Clifford St, G51 — 36 BK32
Cliff Rd, G3 — 4 BP28
Clifton Pl, G3 — 37 BN28
  off Clifton St
Clifton Rd, (Giff.) G46 — 64 BK42
Clifton St, G3 — 37 BN28
Clifton Ter, (Camb.) G72 — 68 CA42
Clifton Ter, John. PA5 — 46 AJ35
Clincarthill Rd, (Ruther.) G73 — 55 BW38
Clincart Rd, G42 — 53 BR37
Cloan Av, G15 — 8 BD19
Cloan Cres, (Bishop.) G64 — 13 BX18
Cloberhill Rd, G13 — 9 BE20
Clochoderick Av, (Millik.) — 44 AD35
  John. PA10
Cloch St, G33 — 40 CC29
Clonbeith St, G33 — 41 CG27
Closeburn St, G22 — 24 BS24
Cloth St, (Barr.) G78 — 61 AY43
Clouden Rd, (Cumb.) G67 — 73 DD11
Cloudhowe Ter, (Blan.) G72 — 70 CL44

Clouston Ct, G20	23	BN25
off Fergus Dr		
Clouston La, G20	23	BN25
Clouston St, G20	22	BM25
Clova Pl, (Udd.) G71	71	CP39
Clova St, (Thornlie.) G46	63	BH41
Cloverbank St, G21	39	BW28
Clovergate, (Bishop.) G64	12	BU20
Cloverhill Pl, (Chry.) G69	28	CL21
Clunie Rd, G52	51	BG33
Cluny Av, (Bears.) G61	10	BJ19
Cluny Dr, (Bears.) G61	10	BJ19
Cluny Dr, Pais. PA3	33	AW31
Cluny Gdns, G14	21	BG25
Cluny Gdns, (Baill.) G69	58	CJ33
Cluny Vil, G14	21	BG25
off Westland Dr		
Clutha St, G51	36	BM31
off Paisley Rd W		
Clyde Av, (Both.) G71	71	CP44
Clyde Av, (Barr.) G78	61	AZ44
Clydebank Business Pk,	7	AW19
Clyde. G81		
Clydebank Ind Est, Clyde. G81	6	AT19
Clydebrae Dr, (Both.) G71	71	CR44
Clydebrae St, G51	36	BK29
Clyde Ct, Clyde. G81	6	AU16
Clydeford Dr, G32	56	CA34
Clydeford Dr, (Udd.) G71	59	CN38
Clydeford Rd, (Camb.) G72	56	CC37
Clydeholm Rd, G14	35	BF27
Clydeholm Ter, Clyde. G81	19	AZ22
Clyde Ind Cen, G3	37	BN29
Clydeneuk Dr, (Udd.) G71	58	CM38
Clyde Pl, G5	4	BQ31
Clyde Pl, (Cumb.) G67	72	DB11
off Cumbernauld Shop Cen		
Clyde Pl, (Camb.) G72	69	CF41
Clyde Pl, John. PA5	45	AE37
Clyde Rd, Pais. PA3	33	AX30
Clydesdale Av, Pais. PA3	32	AV28
Clyde Shop Cen, Clyde. G81	7	AY20
Clydeside Expressway, G3	36	BL29
Clydeside Expressway, G14	36	BL29
Clydeside Ind Est, G14	35	BF27
Clydeside Rd, (Ruther.) G73	54	BV35
Clydesmill Dr, G32	56	CC38
Clydesmill Gro, G32	56	CC38
Clydesmill Ind Est, G32	56	CC37
Clydesmill Pl, G32	56	CC37
Clydesmill Rd, G32	56	CB37
Clyde St, G4	4	BR31
Clyde St, Clyde. G81	19	AY21
Clyde St, Renf. PA4	19	AZ24
Clyde Ter, (Both.) G71	71	CQ44
Clyde Tunnel, G14	35	BG28
Clyde Tunnel, G51	35	BG28
Clydevale, (Both.) G71	71	CR44
Clyde Vw, Pais. PA2	49	AX35
Clydeview La, G11	35	BH27
off Broomhill Ter		
Clydeview Ter, G32	56	CD37
Clyde Wk, (Cumb.) G67	72	DB11
off Cumbernauld Shop Cen		
Clyde Way, (Cumb.) G67	72	DB11
off Cumbernauld Shop Cen		
Clyde Way, Pais. PA3	33	AX30
off Clyde Rd		
Clynder St, G51	36	BK31
Clyth Dr, (Giff.) G46	64	BM43
Coalburn Rd, (Both.) G71	71	CR40
Coalhill St, G31	39	BX32
Coatbridge Rd, (Baill.) G69	43	CN32
Coatbridge Rd, (Gart.) G69	29	CQ25
Coats Cres, (Baill.) G69	42	CJ32
Coats Dr, Pais. PA2	47	AR34
Coatshill Av, (Blan.) G72	70	CL44
Cobblerigg Way, (Udd.) G71	71	CN40
Cobden Rd, G21	38	BV27
Cobington Pl, G33	40	CD28
Cobinshaw St, G32	40	CC31
Coburg St, G5	37	BR32
Cochno St, Clyde. G81	19	AY21
Cochranemill Rd, John. PA5	45	AE36
Cochrane Sq, (Linw.) Pais. PA3	30	AK31
Cochrane St, G1	5	BS30
Cochrane St, (Barr.) G78	61	AX43
Cochran St, Pais. PA1	48	AV33
Cockels Ln, Renf. PA4	33	AX28
Cockenzie St, G32	40	CC32
Cockmuir St, G21	25	BW25
Cogan Pl, (Barr.) G78	61	AX43
off Cogan St		
Cogan Rd, G43	64	BL39
Cogan St, G43	52	BL38
Cogan St, (Barr.) G78	61	AX43
Colbert St, G40	54	BV34
Colbreggan Ct, Clyde. G81	7	AY15
Colbreggan Gdns, Clyde. G81	7	AY15
Colbreggan Pl, Clyde. G81	7	AY15
off Glasgow Rd		
Colchester Dr, G12	22	BJ23
Coldingham Av, G14	20	BA23
Coldstream Dr, (Ruther.) G73	67	BZ39
Coldstream Dr, Pais. PA2	47	AQ36
Coldstream Pl, G21	24	BS26
Coldstream Rd, Clyde. G81	7	AX20
Colebrooke La, G12	23	BN26
off Colebrooke St		
Colebrooke Pl, G12	23	BN26
Colebrooke St, G12	23	BN26
Colebrooke Ter, G12	23	BN26
Colebrook St, (Camb.) G72	68	CC39
Coleridge Av, (Both.) G71	71	CR42
Colfin St, G34	42	CL28
Colgrain Av, G20	23	BQ23
Colgrain Ter, G20	23	BQ23
Colgrave Cres, G32	56	CB34
Colinbar Circle, (Barr.) G78	61	AX44
Colinslee Av, Pais. PA2	48	AV36
Colinslee Cres, Pais. PA2	48	AV36
Colinslee Dr, Pais. PA2	48	AV36
Colinslie Rd, G53	51	BE37
Colinton Pl, G32	40	CD30
Colintraive Av, G33	26	CB25
Colintraive Cres, G33	26	CA26
Colla Gdns, (Bishop.) G64	13	BZ19
Coll Av, Renf. PA4	33	AZ28
College Gate, (Bears.) G61	9	BE15
College La, Pais. PA1	32	AT32
College St, G1	5	BT30
Collessie Dr, G33	41	CE27
Collier St, John. PA5	45	AH34
Collina St, G20	22	BL23
Collins St, G4	5	BU30
Coll Pl, G21	39	BX27
Collree Gdns, G34	42	CL30
off Easterhouse Rd		
Coll St, G21	39	BW27
Collylinn Rd, (Bears.) G61	9	BG17
Colmonell Av, G13	20	BB22
Colonsay Av, Renf. PA4	33	AY28
Colonsay Rd, G52	35	BG32
off Barfillan Dr		
Colonsay Rd, Pais. PA2	48	AT38
Colquhoun Av, G52	34	BC30
Colquhoun Dr, (Bears.) G61	9	BG16
Colston Av, (Bishop.) G64	24	BV22
Colston Dr, (Bishop.) G64	24	BV22
Colston Gdns, (Bishop.) G64	24	BU22
Colston Path, (Bishop.) G64	24	BU22
Colston Pl, (Bishop.) G64	24	BU22
Colston Rd, (Bishop.) G64	24	BU22
Coltmuir Av, (Bishop.) G64	24	BU21
off Coltmuir Dr		
Coltmuir Cres, (Bishop.) G64	24	BU21
Coltmuir Dr, (Bishop.) G64	24	BU21
Coltmuir Gdns, (Bishop.)	24	BU21
G64		
Coltmuir St, G22	23	BR23
Coltness La, G33	41	CE30
Coltness St, G33	41	CE29
Coltpark Av, (Bishop.) G64	24	BU21
Coltpark La, (Bishop.) G64	24	BU21
Coltsfoot Dr, G53	62	BD42
off Waukglen Dr		
Columba, Clyde. G81	7	AZ19
off Onslow Rd		
Columba St, G51	36	BK30
Colvend Dr, (Ruther.) G73	67	BX42
Colvend La, G40	54	BV34
Colvend St, G40	54	BV34
Colville Dr, (Ruther.) G73	67	BZ39
Colwood Av, G53	62	BC41
Colwood Gdns, G53	62	BC42
Colwood Path, G53	62	BC41
off Parkhouse Rd		
Colwood Pl, G53	62	BC42
Colwood Sq, G53	62	BC41
Comedie Rd, G33	27	CG25
Comelypark Pl, G31	39	BW31
off Comelypark St		
Comelypark St, G31	38	BV31
Commerce St, G5	37	BR32
Commercial Ct, G5	38	BT32
Commercial Rd, G5	54	BS33
Commercial Rd, (Barr.) G78	61	AY42
Commonhead Rd, G34	42	CM29
Commore Av, (Barr.) G78	61	AZ44
Commore Dr, G13	20	BC22
Comrie Rd, G33	27	CE24
Comrie St, G32	56	CD34
Conan Ct, (Camb.) G72	69	CF40
Cona St, (Thornlie.) G46	63	BG41
Congress Rd, G3	36	BM30
Congress Way, G3	37	BN30
Conifer Pl, (Kirk.) G66	14	CD15
Conisborough Ct, G34	42	CJ28
Conisborough Path, G34	41	CH27
off Conisborough Rd		
Conisborough Rd, G34	41	CH27
Conistone Cres, (Baill.) G69	57	CH33
Connal St, G40	55	BX34
Conniston St, G32	40	CA30
Connollys Land, Clyde. G81	7	AW15
off Dumbarton Rd		
Connor Rd, (Barr.) G78	61	AX42
Conon Av, (Bears.) G61	9	BE18
Consett La, G33	41	CE29
Consett St, G33	41	CE29
Contin Pl, G12	22	BM24
Convair Way, Renf. PA4	33	AZ28
off Lismore Av		
Conval Way, Pais. PA3	32	AT29
off Abbotsburn Way		
Cook St, G5	37	BQ32
Cooperage Ct, G14	19	AZ23
Cooperage Pl, G3	36	BL29
Coopers Well La, G11	36	BL28
off Dumbarton Rd		
Coopers Well St, G11	36	BL28
Copland Pl, G51	36	BK30
Copland Quad, G51	36	BK31
Copland Rd, G51	36	BK31
Coplaw Ct, G42	53	BQ34
Coplaw St, G42	53	BQ34
Copperfield La, (Udd.) G71	59	CQ38
Coppice, The, Ersk. PA8	18	AT21
off Newshot Dr		
Corbett Ct, G32	56	CB34
Corbett St, G32	56	CB34
Corbiston Way, (Cumb.) G67	73	DD11
Cordiner La, G44	53	BR38
Cordiner St, G44	53	BR38
Corkerhill Gdns, G52	51	BG33
Corkerhill Pl, G52	51	BF35
Corkerhill Rd, G52	51	BF35
Corlaich Av, G42	54	BU38
Corlaich Dr, G42	54	BU38
Cornaig Rd, G53	50	BD37
Cornalee Gdns, G53	50	BC37
Cornalee Pl, G53	50	BD38
Cornalee Rd, G53	50	BD37
Cornhill St, G21	25	BW24
Cornock Cres, Clyde. G81	7	AX18
Cornock St, Clyde. G81	7	AX18
Corn St, G4	37	BR27
Cornwall Av, (Ruther.) G73	67	BZ40
Cornwall St, G41	36	BM32
Cornwall St S, G41	52	BM33
Coronation, (Gart.) G69	29	CN22
Coronation Way, (Bears.) G61	9	BH19
Corpach Pl, G34	42	CM28
Corran St, G33	40	CB29
Corrie Dr, Pais. PA1	50	BA33
Corrie Gro, G44	65	BP41
Corrie Pl, (Lenz.) G66	15	CG17
Corrour Rd, G43	52	BM38
Corsebar Av, Pais. PA2	48	AS35
Corsebar Cres, Pais. PA2	48	AS36
Corsebar Dr, Pais. PA2	48	AS35
Corsebar La, Pais. PA2	47	AR36
Corsebar Rd, Pais. PA2	47	AR36
Corsebar Way, Pais. PA2	48	AS34
Corseford Av, John. PA5	45	AE37
Corsehill Path, G34	42	CL29
Corsehill Pl, G34	42	CL29
Corsehill St, G34	42	CL29
Corselet Rd, G53	62	BD42
Corse Rd, G52	34	BA31

Name	Page	Grid
Corsewall Av, G32	57	CG34
Corsford Dr, G53	63	BE39
Corsock St, G31	39	BY30
Corston St, G33	39	BZ29
Cortachy Pl, (Bishop.) G64	13	BZ20
Coruisk Way, Pais. PA2	47	AN37
off Spencer Dr		
Corunna St, G3	37	BN29
Coshneuk Rd, G33	26	CD24
Cottar St, G20	23	BN22
Cotton Av, (Linw.) Pais. PA3	30	AK32
Cotton St, G40	54	BV35
Cotton St, Pais. PA1	48	AV33
Coulin Gdns, G22	24	BT25
Countess Way, (Baill.) G69	43	CQ32
off Park Rd		
Counting Ho, The, Pais. PA1	47	AR34
off Turners Av		
County Av, (Camb.) G72	55	BZ38
County Pl, Pais. PA1	32	AU32
County Sq, Pais. PA1	32	AU32
Couper St, G4	5	BT28
Courthill, (Bears.) G61	9	BF15
Courthill Av, G44	65	BN40
Coustonhill St, G43	52	BL38
off Pleasance St		
Coustonholm Rd, G43	52	BM37
Coventry Dr, G31	39	BX29
Cowal Dr, (Linw.) Pais. PA3	30	AJ32
Cowal Rd, G20	22	BK22
Cowal St, G20	22	BL22
Cowan Cl, (Barr.) G78	61	AZ41
Cowan Cres, (Barr.) G78	61	AZ43
Cowan La, G12	37	BN27
Cowan St, G12	37	BN27
Cowan Wynd, (Udd.) G71	59	CQ37
Cowcaddens Rd, G4	4	BR28
Cowcaddens St, G2	4	BR28
off Renfield St		
Cowden Dr, (Bishop.) G64	13	BW18
Cowdenhill Circ, G13	21	BF21
Cowdenhill Pl, G13	21	BF21
Cowdenhill Rd, G13	21	BF21
Cowden St, G51	35	BF30
Cowdray Cres, Renf. PA4	19	AZ26
Cowell Vw, Clyde. G81	7	AX18
off Granville St		
Cowglen Rd, G53	51	BE38
Cowlairs Rd, G21	24	BU25
Coxhill St, G21	24	BT26
Coxton Pl, G33	41	CF28
Coylton Rd, G43	65	BN40
Craggan Dr, G14	20	BB23
Crags Av, Pais. PA2	48	AV36
Crags Cres, Pais. PA2	48	AV35
Crags Rd, Pais. PA2	48	AV36
Craigallian Av, (Camb.) G72	69	CF42
Craiganour La, G43	64	BL39
Craiganour Pl, G43	64	BL39
off Holeburn Rd		
Craigard Pl, (Ruther.) G73	67	BZ42
Craigbank Dr, G53	62	BC39
Craigbarnet Cres, G33	26	CD25
Craigbo Av, G23	22	BM21
Craigbo Ct, G23	22	BM21
off Craigbo Rd		
Craigbo Dr, G23	22	BM21
off Craigbo Rd		
Craigbog Av, John. PA5	45	AF36
Craigbo Pl, G23	22	BM21
Craigbo Rd, G23	10	BM20
Craigbo St, G23	10	BM20
off Craigbo Rd		
Craigdonald Pl, John. PA5	45	AH34
Craigellan Rd, G43	64	BM39
Craigenbay Cres, (Lenz.) G66	15	CG16
Craigenbay Rd, (Lenz.) G66	15	CF16
Craigenbay St, G21	25	BX25
Craigencart Ct, Clyde. G81	6	AV15
off Gentle Row		
Craigendmuir Rd, G33	27	CG25
Craigendmuir St, G33	39	BZ27
Craigendon Oval, Pais. PA2	60	AS39
Craigendon Rd, Pais. PA2	48	AS38
Craigend Pl, G13	21	BG23
Craigends Dr, (Kilb.) John. PA10	44	AC34
Craigend St, G13	21	BG23
Craigenfeoch Av, John. PA5	45	AF36
Craigfaulds Av, Pais. PA2	47	AR35
Craigflower Gdns, G53	62	BC41
Craigflower Rd, G53	62	BC41
Craighalbert Rd, (Cumb.) G68	72	CY10
Craighalbert Roundabout, (Cumb.) G68	72	CY9
Craighalbert Way, (Cumb.) G68	72	CY9
Craighall Rd, G4	37	BR27
Craighead Av, G33	25	BZ26
Craighead St, (Barr.) G78	61	AX43
Craighead Way, (Barr.) G78	61	AX43
Craighouse St, G33	40	CC28
Craigiebar Dr, Pais. PA2	48	AS37
Craigieburn Gdns, G20	22	BK21
Craigieburn Rd, (Cumb.) G67	72	DB12
Craigiehall Pl, G51	36	BM31
Craigiehall St, G51	36	BM31
off Craigiehall Pl		
Craigielea Ct, Renf. PA4	19	AY25
off Kirklandneuk Rd		
Craigielea Dr, Pais. PA3	31	AR31
Craigielea Pk, Renf. PA4	19	AY26
Craigielea Rd, Renf. PA4	19	AY26
Craigielea St, G31	39	BW29
Craigie Pk, (Lenz.) G66	15	CG16
Craigie St, G42	53	BQ35
Craigievar St, G33	41	CG27
Craigknowe Rd, (Blan.) G72	70	CL43
Craigleith St, G32	40	CA31
Craiglockhart St, G33	41	CF27
Craigmaddie Ter La, G3	37	BN28
off Derby St		
Craigmillar Rd, G42	53	BQ38
Craigmont Dr, G20	23	BN24
Craigmont St, G20	23	BN23
Craigmore St, G31	39	BY31
Craigmount Av, Pais. PA2	60	AS39
Craigmuir Cres, G52	34	BB31
Craigmuir Pl, G52	34	BA31
Craigmuir Rd, G52	34	BA31
Craigneil St, G33	41	CG27
Craignethan Gdns, G11	36	BK27
off Lawrie St		
Craignure Rd, (Ruther.) G73	67	BX42
Craigpark, G31	39	BW30
Craigpark Dr, G31	39	BW30
Craigpark Ter, G31	39	BW30
off Craigpark		
Craigpark Way, (Udd.) G71	59	CR38
off Newton Dr		
Craig Rd, G44	65	BQ40
Craigs Av, Clyde. G81	7	AY15
Craigston Pl, John. PA5	45	AH35
Craigston Rd, John. PA5	45	AG35
Craigton Av, (Barr.) G78	62	BA44
Craigton Dr, G51	35	BH31
Craigton Dr, (Barr.) G78	62	BA44
Craigton Pl, G51	35	BG31
Craigton Pl, (Blan.) G72	70	CM44
Craigton Rd, G51	35	BH31
Craigvicar Gdns, G32	57	CF33
Craigview Av, John. PA5	45	AF37
Craigview Ter, John. PA5	45	AF36
off Craigview Av		
Craigwell Av, (Ruther.) G73	67	BZ39
Crail St, G31	39	BZ32
Cramond Av, Renf. PA4	34	BA27
Cramond St, G5	54	BT35
Cramond Ter, G32	40	CD32
Cranberry Rd, G12	22	BJ24
Cranbrooke Dr, G20	22	BM22
Cranston St, G3	4	BP29
Cranworth La, G12	22	BM26
Cranworth St, G12	22	BM26
Crarae Av, (Bears.) G61	9	BG19
Crathes Ct, G44	65	BN41
Crathie Dr, G11	36	BJ27
Crathie La, G11	36	BJ27
off Exeter Dr		
Crawford Av, (Lenz.) G66	15	CG18
Crawford Cres, (Udd.) G71	59	CN38
Crawford Dr, G15	8	BD20
Crawford La, G11	36	BJ27
off Crawford St		
Crawford Path, G11	36	BJ27
off Crawford St		
Crawford St, G11	36	BJ27
Crawford Dr, Pais. PA3	31	AR31
Crawford Gdns, (Ruther.) G73	67	BY41
Crawford Rd, (Ruther.) G73	67	BX41
Crawriggs Av, (Kirk.) G66	15	CF15
Craw Rd, Pais. PA2	48	AS34
Crebar Dr, (Barr.) G78	61	AY43
Crebar St, (Thornlie.) G46	63	BG41
Credon Gdns, (Ruther.) G73	67	BY41
Cree Av, (Bishop.) G64	13	BZ20
Cree Gdns, G32	40	CB32
Creran Dr, Renf. PA4	19	AX25
Crescent, The, Clyde. G81	6	AU18
off Stewart St		
Crescent Ct, Clyde. G81	6	AU18
Crescent Rd, G13	20	BD24
Crescent Rd, G14	20	BD24
Cressdale Av, G45	66	BT43
Cressdale Ct, G45	66	BT43
Cressdale Dr, G45	66	BT43
Cressland Dr, G45	66	BT44
Cressland Pl, G45	66	BT44
Cresswell La, G12	22	BM26
Cresswell St, G12	22	BM26
Cressy St, G51	35	BG29
Crest Av, G13	20	BD21
Crestlea Av, Pais. PA2	48	AU37
Creswell Ter, (Udd.) G71	71	CN39
off Kylepark Dr		
Crichton Ct, G45	66	BV43
Crichton Pl, G21	24	BU25
off Crichton St		
Crichton St, G21	24	BU25
Crieff Ct, G3	4	BP29
off North St		
Criffell Gdns, G32	57	CF34
Criffell Rd, G32	57	CF33
Crimea St, G2	4	BQ30
Crinan Gdns, (Bishop.) G64	13	BY20
Crinan Rd, (Bishop.) G64	13	BY20
Crinan St, G31	39	BX29
Cripps Av, Clyde. G81	7	AZ20
Croftbank Av, (Both.) G71	71	CR44
Croftbank Cres, (Both.) G71	71	CR44
Croftbank Gate, (Both.) G71	71	CR44
Croftbank Gro, (Udd.) G71	71	CP39
Croftbank St, G21	24	BV25
Croftburn Dr, G44	66	BT41
Croftcroighn Rd, G33	40	CD28
Croftend Av, G44	66	BU39
Croftfoot Cres, G45	67	BW41
Croftfoot Dr, G45	66	BV41
Croftfoot Pl, (Gart.) G69	29	CQ23
off Inchnock Av		
Croftfoot Quad, G45	66	BU41
Croftfoot Rd, G44	66	BT41
Croftfoot Rd, G45	66	BT41
Croftfoot St, G45	67	BW41
off Tormusk Rd		
Croftfoot Ter, G45	66	BV41
Crofthead St, (Udd.) G71	71	CP40
Crofthill Av, (Udd.) G71	71	CP39
Crofthill Rd, G44	66	BU40
Crofthouse Dr, G44	66	BU41
Croftmont Av, G44	66	BU41
Croftmoraig Av, (Mood.) G69	17	CQ17
Crofton Av, G44	66	BT41
Croftpark Av, G44	66	BS41
Croft Rd, (Camb.) G72	68	CD40
Croftside Av, G44	66	BU41
Croftspar Av, G32	41	CE31
Croftspar Ct, G32	41	CF31
off Croftspar Gro		
Croftspar Dr, G32	41	CE31
Croftspar Gate, G32	41	CF31
off Croftspar Gro		
Croftspar Gro, G32	41	CE31
Croftspar Pl, G32	41	CE31
off Croftspar Gro		
Croft Way, Renf. PA4	33	AZ28
Croftwood, (Bishop.) G64	13	BW17
Croftwood Av, G44	66	BT41
Croft Wynd, (Udd.) G71	71	CQ39
Cromarty Av, G43	65	BP39
Cromarty Av, (Bishop.) G64	13	BZ19
Cromarty Gdns, (Clark.) G76	65	BQ44
Cromarty Pl, (Chry.) G69	16	CM20
Crombie Gdns, (Baill.) G69	58	CJ34
Cromdale St, G51	35	BG31
Cromer Gdns, G20	23	BP24
Cromer La, Pais. PA3	32	AT29
off Abbotsburn Way		
Cromer Way, Pais. PA3	32	AT30
off Mosslands Rd		
Crompton Av, G44	65	BR40
Cromptons Gro, Pais. PA1	47	AR34

Cromwell La, G20	37	BQ27
Cromwell St, G20	37	BQ27
Cronberry Quad, G52	50	BB34
Cronberry Ter, G52	50	BB34
Crookston Av, G52	50	BC33
Crookston Ct, G52	50	BC33
Crookston Dr, G52	50	BB33
Crookston Dr, Pais. PA1	50	BB33
Crookston Gdns, G52	50	BB33
Crookston Gro, G52	50	BC33
Crookstonhill Path, G52	50	BB33
off Ralston Pl		
Crookston Path, G52	50	BB33
off Crookston Quad		
Crookston Pl, G52	50	BB33
Crookston Quad, G52	50	BB33
Crookston Rd, G52	50	BB34
Crookston Rd, G53	50	BC37
Crosbie Dr, Pais. PA2	47	AN38
Crosbie La, G20	22	BL21
Crosbie St, G20	22	BL21
Crosbie Wd, Pais. PA2	47	AR36
Cross, The, Pais. PA1	32	AU32
Cross Arthurlie St, (Barr.) G78	61	AX42
Crossbank Av, G42	54	BU36
Crossbank Dr, G42	54	BT36
Crossbank Rd, G42	54	BT36
Crossbank Ter, G42	54	BT36
Cross Ct, (Bishop.) G64	12	BV20
off Kenmure Av		
Crossflat Cres, Pais. PA1	33	AW32
Crossford Dr, G23	11	BN20
off Broughton Rd		
Crosshill Av, G42	53	BR36
Crosshill Av, (Kirk.) G66	15	CF15
Crosshill Dr, (Ruther.) G73	67	BX39
Crosshill Rd, (Bishop.) G64	13	BY16
Crosshill Rd, (Kirk.) G66	14	CD18
Crosshill Sq, (Baill.) G69	58	CL33
off Bredisholm Rd		
Cross Hill St, Coat. ML5	59	CR33
off Aitkenhead Av		
Crosslees Ct, (Thornlie.) G46	64	BJ41
off Crosslees Dr		
Crosslees Dr, (Thornlie.) G46	63	BH42
Crosslees Pk, (Thornlie.) G46	63	BH42
Crosslees Rd, (Thornlie.) G46	63	BH43
Crosslee St, G52	35	BF32
Crossloan Rd, G51	35	BH30
Crossloan Ter, G51	35	BH30
Crossmill Av, (Barr.) G78	61	AZ41
Crossmyloof Gdns, G41	52	BM36
Crosspoint Dr, G23	11	BN20
off Invershiel Rd		
Cross Rd, Pais. PA2	47	AR35
Cross St, G32	57	CE36
Cross St, Pais. PA1	48	AS33
Crosstobs Rd, G53	50	BC36
Crossview Av, (Baill.) G69	42	CM32
Crossview Pl, (Baill.) G69	42	CM32
Crovie Rd, G53	50	BC38
Crowflats Rd, (Udd.) G71	71	CN39
off Lady Isle Cres		
Crowhall Dr, G32	41	CG31
Crowhill Rd, (Bishop.) G64	24	BV21
Crowhill St, G22	24	BS23
Crow La, G13	21	BH24
Crowlin Cres, G33	40	CD29
Crown Av, Clyde. G81	7	AW18
Crown Circ, G12	22	BL26
Crown Ct, G1	5	BS30
off Virginia St		
Crown Gdns, G12	22	BL26
Crownhall Pl, G32	41	CE32
Crownhall Rd, G32	41	CE32
Crown Mans, G11	22	BK26
off North Gardner St		
Crownpoint Rd, G40	38	BV32
Crown Rd N, G12	22	BK26
Crown Rd S, G12	22	BK26
Crown St, G5	38	BS32
Crown St, (Baill.) G69	57	CH34
Crown Ter, G12	22	BK26
Crow Rd, G11	22	BJ26
Crow Rd, G13	21	BH24
Crow Wd Rd. (Chry.) G69	28	CK22
Crow Wd Ter, (Chry.) G69	28	CK22
Croy Pl, G21	25	BY24
Croy Rd, G21	25	BY24
Cruachan Av, Pais. PA2	48	AU37
Cruachan Av, Renf. PA4	33	AY28
Cruachan Dr, (Barr.) G78	61	AY44
Cruachan Rd, (Ruther.) G73	67	BZ42
Cruachan St, (Thornlie.) G46	63	BH41
Cruachan Way, (Barr.) G78	61	AY44
Cruden St, G51	35	BH31
Crum Av, (Thornlie.) G46	64	BJ42
Crusader Av, G13	9	BF20
Cubie St, G40	38	BV32
Cuilhill Rd, (Baill.) G69	43	CP30
Cuillins, The, (Mood.) G69	17	CQ17
Cuillins, The, (Udd.) G71	59	CN36
Cuillins Rd, (Ruther.) G73	67	BZ42
Cuillin Way, (Barr.) G78	61	AY43
Culbin Dr, G13	20	BB21
Cullen Pl, (Udd.) G71	59	CQ37
Cullen St, G32	56	CC33
Culloden St, G31	39	BX29
Culrain Gdns, G32	40	CC33
Culrain St, G32	40	CC32
Culross La, G32	57	CE33
Culross St, G32	57	CE33
Culross Way, (Mood.) G69	17	CQ18
Cult Rd, (Lenz.) G66	15	CG17
Cults St, G51	35	BH31
Culzean Cres, (Baill.) G69	58	CJ33
Culzean Dr, G32	57	CF33
Cumberland Arc, G5	54	BS33
off Sandyfaulds Sq		
Cumberland Pl, G5	54	BS33
Cumberland St, G5	37	BR32
Cumbernauld Rd, G31	39	BX30
Cumbernauld Rd, G33	39	BZ28
Cumbernauld Rd, (Chry.) G69	28	CJ22
Cumbernauld Shop Cen,	72	DB11
(Cumb.) G67		
Cumbrae Ct, Clyde. G81	7	AX19
Cumbrae Rd, Pais. PA2	48	AU38
Cumbrae Rd, Renf. PA4	33	AZ28
Cumbrae St, G33	40	CC29
Cumlodden Dr, G20	22	BL22
Cumming Dr, G42	53	BR37
Cumnock Dr, (Barr.) G78	61	AZ44
Cumnock Rd, G33	26	CA23
Cunard Ct, Clyde. G81	19	AX21
Cunard St, Clyde. G81	19	AX21
Cunningham Dr, (Giff.) G46	65	BN42
Cunningham Dr, Clyde. G81	6	AV15
Cunningham Rd, (Kilb.)	44	AD34
John. PA10		
Cunningham Rd, G52	34	BB29
Cunningham Rd, (Ruther.) G73	55	BY36
Curfew Rd, G13	9	BF20
Curle St, G14	35	BG27
Curlew Pl, John. PA5	45	AE38
Curling Cres, G44	54	BS38
Currie St, G20	23	BN23
Curtis Av, G44	54	BU38
Curtis Av, (Ruther.) G73	54	BS37
Curzon St, G20	23	BN23
Custom Ho Quay, G1	5	BS31
off Clyde St		
Cut, The, (Udd.) G71	71	CP40
Cuthbertson St, G42	53	BQ35
Cuthbert St, (Udd.) G71	59	CR38
Cuthelton Dr, G31	56	CA33
Cuthelton St, G31	55	BZ33
Cuthelton Ter, G31	55	BZ33
Cypress Av, (Udd.) G71	59	CR37
Cypress Ct, (Kirk.) G66	14	CD15
Cypress St, G22	24	BT24
Cypress Way, (Camb.) G72	69	CH41
Cyprus Av, (Elder.) John. PA5	46	AK36
Cyprus Gro, (Baill.) G69	43	CR31
Cyril St, Pais. PA1	49	AW33

D

Daer Av, Renf. PA4	34	BA28
Dairsie Ct, G44	65	BP41
off Clarkston Rd		
Dairsie Gdns, (Bishop.) G64	25	BZ21
Dairsie St, G44	65	BP41
Daisy St, G42	53	BR35
Dakota Way, Renf. PA4	33	AZ28
Dalbeth Pl, G32	56	CB35
Dalbeth Rd, G32	56	CB35
Dalcharn Path, G34	42	CJ29
off Kildermorie Rd		
Dalcharn Pl, G34	42	CJ29
off Kildermorie Rd		
Dalcraig Cres, (Blan.) G72	70	CL43
Dalcross La, G11	36	BL27
off Byres Rd		
Dalcross Pas, G11	36	BL27
off Dalcross St		
Dalcross St, G11	36	BL27
Dalcruin Gdns, (Mood.) G69	17	CQ17
Daldowie Av, G32	57	CF34
Daldowie Rd, (Udd.) G71	58	CJ35
Dale Path, G40	54	BV33
Dale St, G40	54	BV33
Daleview Av, G12	22	BK23
Dale Way, (Ruther.) G73	67	BX41
Dalfoil Ct, Pais. PA1	50	BB33
Dalgarroch Av, Clyde. G81	20	BA21
Dalgleish Av, Clyde. G81	6	AU15
Dalhousie Gdns, (Bishop.) G64	12	BV19
Dalhousie La, G3	4	BQ28
Dalhousie Rd, (Millik.) John.	44	AD35
PA10		
Dalhousie St, G3	4	BQ28
Dalilea Dr, G34	42	CM28
Dalilea Pl, G34	42	CM28
Dalintober St, G5	37	BQ32
Dalkeith Av, G41	52	BK33
Dalkeith Av, (Bishop.) G64	13	BX18
Dalkeith Rd, (Bishop.) G64	13	BX17
Dalmahoy St, G32	40	CA30
Dalmally St, G20	23	BP26
Dalmarnock Br, G40	55	BX35
Dalmarnock Br, (Ruther.) G73	55	BX35
Dalmarnock Ct, G40	55	BX34
Dalmarnock Rd, G40	54	BV33
Dalmarnock Rd, (Ruther.) G73	55	BX35
Dalmarnock Rd Trd Est,	55	BX36
(Ruther.) G73		
Dalmary Dr, Pais. PA1	33	AX31
Dalmellington Dr, G53	50	BC37
Dalmellington Rd, G53	50	BC37
Dalmeny Av, (Giff.) G46	64	BL42
Dalmeny Dr, (Barr.) G78	61	AW43
Dalmeny St, G5	54	BU35
Dalmuir Ct, Clyde. G81	6	AU18
Dalnair St, G3	36	BL28
Dalness Pas, G32	56	CC33
off Ochil St		
Dalness St, G32	56	CC34
Dalreoch Av, (Baill.) G69	42	CL32
Dalreoch Path, (Baill.) G69	42	CL31
off Dalreoch Av		
Dalriada St, G40	55	BY33
Dalry Rd, (Udd.) G71	59	CR38
Dalry St, G32	56	CD33
Dalserf Ct, G31	39	BX32
Dalserf Cres, (Giff.) G46	64	BK44
Dalserf Gdns, G31	39	BX32
Dalserf St, G31	39	BX32
Dalsetter Av, G15	8	BB19
Dalsetter Pl, G15	8	BC19
Dalsholm Av, G20	22	BK21
Dalsholm Ind Est, G20	22	BK22
Dalsholm Rd, G20	22	BK22
Dalskeith Av, Pais. PA3	31	AQ32
Dalskeith Cres, Pais. PA3	31	AQ32
Dalskeith Rd, Pais. PA3	47	AQ33
Dalswinton Path, G34	42	CM29
Dalswinton Pl, G34	42	CL29
off Dalswinton St		
Dalswinton St, G34	42	CL29
Dalton Av, Clyde. G81	8	BA20
Dalton St, G31	40	CA32
Dalveen Ct, (Barr.) G78	61	AY44
Dalveen Dr, (Udd.) G71	59	CN37
Dalveen St, G32	40	CB32
Dalveen Way, (Ruther.) G73	67	BY42
Dalwhinnie Av, (Blan.) G72	70	CL43
Daly Gdns, (Blan.) G72	71	CN44
Dalziel Dr, G41	52	BL34
Dalziel Quad, G41	52	BL34
Dalziel Rd, G52	34	BB29
Damshot Cres, G53	51	BF36
Damshot Rd, G53	51	BF38
Danby Rd, (Baill.) G69	57	CH33
Danes Av, G14	21	BE25
Danes Cres, G14	20	BD24
Danes Dr, G14	20	BD24
Danes La N, G14	21	BE26
off Upland Rd		
Danes La S, G14	21	BE25
off Verona Av		

91

Dargarvel Av, G41	52	BK33
Dargarvel Path, G41	52	BJ34
off Dumbreck Av		
Darkwood Ct, Pais. PA3	31	AR31
Darkwood Cres, Pais. PA3	31	AR31
Darkwood Dr, Pais. PA3	31	AR31
off Darkwood Cres		
Darleith St, G32	40	CB32
Darley Rd, (Cumb.) G68	72	DA8
Darnaway Av, G33	41	CF27
Darnaway Dr, G33	41	CF27
Darnaway St, G33	41	CF27
Darnick St, G21	25	BX26
Darnley Cres, (Bishop.) G64	12	BV18
Darnley Gdns, G41	53	BN35
Darnley Ind Est, G53	62	BD41
Darnley Mains Rd, G53	63	BE42
Darnley Path, (Thornlie.) G46	63	BG40
off Kennisholm Av		
Darnley Pl, G41	53	BN35
off Darnley Rd		
Darnley Rd, G41	53	BN35
Darnley Rd, (Barr.) G78	61	AZ42
Darnley St, G41	53	BP35
Darroch Way, (Cumb.) G67	73	DC10
Dartford St, G22	23	BR26
Darvel Cres, Pais. PA1	33	AZ32
Darvel St, G53	62	BB39
Darwin Pl, Clyde. G81	6	AT17
Davaar Dr, Pais. PA2	48	AU38
Davaar Rd, Renf. PA4	33	AZ28
Davaar St, G40	55	BX33
Dava St, G51	36	BJ30
Daventry Dr, G12	22	BJ24
off Dorchester Pl		
David Pl, (Baill.) G69	57	CH33
David Pl, Pais. PA3	33	AX30
Davidson Gdns, G14	21	BG25
off Westland Dr		
Davidson Pl, G32	41	CE31
Davidson St, G40	55	BW35
Davidson St, Clyde. G81	20	BA21
Davidston Pl, (Kirk.) G66	15	CH17
off Netherhouse Av		
David St, G40	39	BW32
David Way, Pais. PA3	33	AX30
Davieland Rd, (Giff.) G46	64	BJ44
Davies Sq, Clyde. G81	7	AW15
Daviot St, G51	35	BF31
Dawson Pl, G4	23	BR26
Dawson Rd, G4	23	BR26
Deaconsbank Av, (Thornlie.) G46	63	BF44
Deaconsbank Cres, (Thornlie.) G46	63	BF44
Deaconsbank Gdns, (Thornlie.)	63	BG44
off Deaconsbank Av		
Deaconsbank Gro, (Thornlie.) G46	63	BG44
Deaconsbank Pl, (Thornlie.) G46	63	BF44
Dealston Rd, (Barr.) G78	61	AX41
Deanbrae St, (Udd.) G71	71	CP39
Dean Cres, (Chry.) G69	16	CM20
Deanfield Quad, G52	34	BB31
Dean Pk Dr, (Camb.) G72	69	CF41
Dean Pk Rd, Renf. PA4	34	BA27
Deans Av, (Camb.) G72	69	CF42
Deanside La, G4	5	BT30
off Rottenrow		
Deanside Rd, G52	34	BC29
Deanston Av, (Barr.) G78	61	AX44
Deanston Dr, G41	52	BM37
Deanston Gdns, (Barr.) G78	61	AX44
Deanston Pk, (Barr.) G78	61	AX44
Dean St, Clyde. G81	7	AY20
Deanwood Av, G44	65	BP42
Deanwood Rd, G44	65	BP42
Dechmont Av, (Camb.) G72	69	CF42
Dechmont Cotts, (Camb.) G72	69	CH42
Dechmont Gdns, (Udd.) G71	59	CN37
off Watling St		
Dechmont Gdns, (Blan.) G72	70	CL44
Dechmont Pl, (Camb.) G72	69	CF42
Dechmont Rd, (Udd.) G71	59	CN36
off Watling St		
Dechmont St, G31	39	BY32
Dechmont Vw, (Udd.) G71	59	CQ38
Dee Av, Pais. PA2	47	AP35
Dee Av, Renf. PA4	20	BA26
Dee Dr, Pais. PA2	47	AP36
Deepdene Rd, (Bears.) G61	9	BF18
Deepdene Rd, (Chry.) G69	17	CP19
Dee Pl, John. PA5	45	AE37
Dee St, G33	39	BZ28
Delhi Av, Clyde. G81	6	AS17
Delny Pl, G33	41	CG30
Delvin Rd, G44	65	BO39
Denbeck St, G32	40	CB32
Denbrae St, G32	40	CB32
Dene Wk, (Bishop.) G64	25	BY21
Denewood Av, Pais. PA2	48	AT37
Denham St, G22	23	BR26
Denholm Dr, (Giff.) G46	64	BL44
Denmark St, G22	24	BS25
Denmilne Gdns, G34	42	CL30
Denmilne Path, G34	42	CL30
Denmilne Pl, G34	42	CL30
Denmilne Rd, (Baill.) G69	42	CM30
Denmilne St, G34	42	CL30
Derby St, G3	37	BN29
Derby Ter La, G3	37	BN28
Derwent St, G22	23	BR25
Despard Av, G32	57	CF33
Despard Gdns, G32	57	CG33
Deveron Av, (Giff.) G46	64	BM43
Deveron Rd, (Bears.) G61	9	BE19
Deveron St, G33	39	BZ28
Devol Cres, G53	50	BD37
Devondale Av, (Blan.) G72	70	CM44
Devon Gdns, (Bishop.) G64	12	BV18
Devon Pl, G41	53	BR33
Devonshire Gdns, G12	22	BK25
Devonshire Gdns La, G12	22	BK25
off Hyndland Rd		
Devonshire Ter, G12	22	BK25
Devonshire Ter La, G12	22	BK25
Devon St, G5	53	BR33
Dewar Cl, (Udd.) G71	59	CQ36
Diana Av, G13	20	BD21
Dickens Av, Clyde. G81	6	AV17
Dick St, G20	23	BP26
Dilwara Av, G14	35	BG27
Dimity St, John. PA5	45	AH35
Dinard Dr, (Giff.) G46	64	BL41
Dinart St, G33	39	BZ28
Dinduff St, G34	42	CL28
Dinmont Av, Pais. PA2	47	AP36
Dinmont Pl, G41	53	BN36
off Norham St		
Dinmont Rd, G41	52	BM36
Dinmont Way, Pais. PA2	47	AP36
off Ivanhoe Rd		
Dinwiddie St, G21	39	BY27
Dipple Pl, G15	8	BD19
Dirleton Dr, G41	53	BN37
Dirleton Dr, Pais. PA2	47	AQ36
off Tantallon Dr		
Dirleton Gate, (Bears.) G61	9	BF19
Dirleton Pl, G41	53	BN37
Dixon Av, G42	53	BR36
Dixon Rd, G42	53	BR36
Dixons Blazes Ind Est, G5	54	BS34
Dixon St, G1	4	BR31
Dixon St, Pais. PA1	48	AV33
Dobbies Ln, G4	4	BR29
Dobbies Ln Pl, G4	5	BT29
Dochart Av, Renf. PA4	34	BA28
Dochart St, G33	40	CA27
Dock St, Clyde. G81	19	AZ22
Dodhill Pl, G13	20	BD23
Dodside Gdns, G32	57	CE33
Dodside Pl, G32	57	CE33
Dodside St, G32	57	CE33
Dolan St, (Baill.) G69	42	CK32
Dollar Ter, G20	22	BL21
Dolphin Rd, G41	52	BM35
Donaldson Dr, Renf. PA4	19	AZ26
off Ferguson St		
Donaldson Grn, (Udd.) G71	59	CR37
Donaldswood Pk, Pais. PA2	48	AS37
Donaldswood Rd, Pais. PA2	48	AS37
Donald Way, (Udd.) G71	59	CQ38
Don Av, Renf. PA4	34	BA27
Doncaster St, G20	23	BQ25
Don Dr, Pais. PA2	47	AP36
Donnies Brae, (Neil.) G78	60	AV44
Donohoe Ct, (Bishop.) G64	13	BW20
off Emerson Rd		
Don Pl, John. PA5	45	AE37
Don St, G33	39	BZ29
Doon Cres, (Bears.) G61	9	BF18
Doonfoot Rd, G43	64	BM39
Doon Side, (Cumb.) G67	73	DD11
Doon St, Clyde. G81	7	AZ18
Dora St, G40	54	BV34
Dorchester Av, G12	22	BJ23
Dorchester Ct, G12	22	BJ23
Dorchester Pl, G12	22	BJ23
Dorlin Rd, G33	27	CG24
Dormanside Ct, G53	50	BD34
off Dormanside Rd		
Dormanside Gate, G53	50	BD34
off Dormanside Rd		
Dormanside Gro, G53	50	BD34
off Dormanside Rd		
Dormanside Pl, G53	51	BE35
off Dormanside Rd		
Dormanside Rd, G53	50	BD34
Dornal Av, G13	20	BA22
Dornford Av, G32	57	CF35
Dornford Rd, G32	57	CF35
Dornie Dr, G32	56	CD37
Dornie Dr, (Thornlie.) G46	63	BG42
Dornoch Av, (Giff.) G46	64	BL44
Dornoch Pl, (Bishop.) G64	13	BY19
Dornoch Pl, (Chry.) G69	16	CM20
Dornoch Rd, (Bears.) G61	9	BF19
Dornoch St, G40	38	BV32
Dornoch Way, (Cumb.) G68	73	DC8
Dorset Sq, G3	4	BP29
off Dorset St		
Dorset St, G3	4	BP29
Dosk Av, G13	20	BA21
Dosk Pl, G13	20	BB21
Dougalston Rd, G23	11	BN20
Douglas Av, G32	56	CD37
Douglas Av, (Giff.) G46	64	BL44
Douglas Av, (Lenz.) G66	15	CF15
Douglas Av, (Ruther.) G73	67	BY40
Douglas Av, (Elder.) John. PA5	46	AK35
Douglas Ct, (Lenz.) G66	15	CF16
Douglas Cres, (Udd.) G71	59	CR37
Douglas Dr, G15	8	BB20
Douglas Dr, (Baill.) G69	41	CH32
Douglas Dr, (Both.) G71	71	CQ44
Douglas Dr, (Camb.) G72	68	CB40
Douglas Gdns, (Giff.) G46	64	BL44
Douglas Gdns, (Bears.) G61	9	BH17
Douglas Gdns, (Lenz.) G66	15	CF16
Douglas Gdns, (Udd.) G71	71	CP40
Douglas Gate, (Camb.) G72	68	CB40
Douglas La, G2	4	BQ29
Douglas Pk Cres, (Bears.) G61	10	BJ15
Douglas Pl, (Bears.) G61	9	BG16
Douglas Pl, (Kirk.) G66	15	CF16
Douglas Rd, Renf. PA4	33	AW29
Douglas St, G2	4	BQ29
Douglas St, (Udd.) G71	59	CR38
Douglas St, Pais. PA1	32	AS32
Douglas Ter, G41	53	BP34
off Glencairn Dr		
Douglas Ter, Pais. PA3	32	AU28
Dougray Pl, (Barr.) G78	61	AY43
Dougrie Dr, G45	66	BT42
Dougrie Dr La, G45	66	BT42
off Dougrie Dr		
Dougrie Gdns, G45	66	BT43
Dougrie Pl, G45	66	BU42
Dougrie Rd, G45	66	BT42
Dougrie St, G45	66	BU42
Dougrie Ter, G45	66	BT42
Doune Cres, (Bishop.) G64	13	BX17
Doune Gdns, G20	23	BN26
Doune Gdns La, G20	23	BN26
Doune Quad, G20	23	BN26
Dovecot, G43	52	BL37
Dovecothall St, (Barr.) G78	61	AZ42
Dover St, G3	37	BN29
Dove St, G53	62	BC40
Downfield Rd, (Cumb.) G67	72	CZ12
Downhill St, G11	36	BL27
Downhill St La, G12	22	BL26
Downside La, G12	22	BM26
off Byres Rd		
Downside Rd, G12	22	BL26

Downcraig Dr, G45	66	BT43
Downcraig Gro, G45	66	BT43
Downcraig Rd, G45	66	BS44
Downcraig Ter, G45	66	BT43
Downfield Gdns, (Both.) G71	71	CP43
Downfield St, G32	56	CA34
Downiebrae Rd, (Ruther.) G73	55	BX35
Downie Cl, (Udd.) G71	59	CR37
Downs St, G21	24	BV25
Dowrie Cres, G53	50	BD36
Drakemire Av, G45	66	BS41
Drakemire Dr, G44	66	BS42
Drakemire Dr, G45	66	BS42
Drake St, G40	38	BU32
Dreghorn St, G31	39	BY30
Drem Pl, G11	36	BK27
off Merkland St		
Drimnin Rd, G33	27	CH24
Drive Rd, G51	35	BG29
Drochil St, G34	42	CJ28
Drumbeg Dr, G53	62	BC39
Drumbeg Pl, G53	62	BC39
off Drumbeg Dr		
Drumbottie Rd, G21	25	BW24
Drumbowie Vw, (Cumb.) G68	72	CY10
Drumcavel Rd, (Muir.) G69	28	CM22
Drumchapel Gdns, G15	8	BC19
Drumchapel Pl, G15	8	BD19
Drumchapel Rd, G15	8	BD19
Drumchapel Shop Cen, G15	8	BB18
Drumclog Gdns, G33	26	CB23
Drumcross Pl, G53	51	BE36
Drumcross Rd, G53	51	BE36
Drumhead La, G32	56	CB36
Drumhead Pl, G32	56	CB36
Drumhead Rd, G32	56	CB36
Drumilaw Cres, (Ruther.) G73	67	BW40
off Drumilaw Rd		
Drumilaw Rd, (Ruther.) G73	67	BW40
Drumilaw Way, (Ruther.) G73	67	BW40
Drumlaken Av, G23	10	BL20
off Caldercuilt Rd		
Drumlaken Ct, G23	10	BL20
off Arrochar St		
Drumlaken Path, G23	10	BM20
off Littleton St		
Drumlaken Pl, G23	10	BM20
off Chatton St		
Drumlaken St, G23	10	BL20
Drumlanrig Av, G34	42	CL28
Drumlanrig Pl, G34	42	CM28
Drumlochy Rd, G33	40	CC28
Drummond Av, (Ruther.) G73	54	BV37
Drummond Dr, Pais. PA1	49	AZ33
Drummore Rd, G15	8	BD17
Drumover Dr, G31	56	CA33
Drumoyne Av, G51	35	BG29
Drumoyne Circ, G51	35	BG31
Drumoyne Dr, G51	35	BG30
Drumoyne Pl, G51	35	BG31
Drumoyne Quad, G51	35	BG31
Drumoyne Rd, G51	35	BG31
Drumoyne Sq, G51	35	BG30
Drumpark St, (Thornlie.) G46	63	BH41
Drumpark St, Coat. ML5	59	CR33
Drumpellier Av, (Baill.) G69	58	CK34
Drumpellier Pl, (Baill.) G69	58	CK33
Drumpellier Rd, (Baill.) G69	58	CJ34
Drumpellier St, G33	39	BZ27
Drumreoch Dr, G42	54	BU37
Drumreoch Pl, G42	54	BU37
Drumry Pl, G15	8	BA19
Drumry Rd, Clyde. G81	7	AY18
Drumry Rd E, G15	8	BA19
Drumsack Av, (Chry.) G69	28	CK21
Drumsargard Rd, (Ruther.) G73	67	BZ40
Drums Av, Pais. PA3	31	AR31
Drums Cres, Pais. PA3	32	AS31
Drumshaw Dr, G32	57	CE37
Drums Rd, G53	50	BC34
Drumvale Dr, (Chry.) G69	17	CN19
Drury St, G2	4	BR30
Dryad St, (Thornlie.) G46	63	BG40
Dryburgh Av, (Ruther.) G73	55	BX38
Dryburgh Av, Pais. PA2	47	AQ36
Dryburgh Gdns, G20	23	BP26
off Wilton St		
Dryburgh Rd, (Bears.) G61	9	BE15
Dryburgh Wk, (Mood.) G69	17	CQ18
Dryburn Av, G52	34	BC32

Drygate, G4	5	BU30
Drygrange Rd, G33	41	CE27
Drymen Pl, (Lenz.) G66	15	CF18
Drymen Rd, (Bears.) G61	9	BF15
Drymen St, G52	35	BG32
Drymen Wynd, (Bears.) G61	9	BH18
Drynoch Pl, G22	23	BR22
Drysdale St, G14	20	BB24
Duart Dr, (Elder.) John. PA5	46	AK36
Duart St, G20	22	BL21
Dubbs Rd, (Barr.) G78	62	BA42
Dubton Path, G34	42	CK28
Dubton St, G34	42	CK28
Duchall Pl, G14	20	BD25
Duchess Pl, (Ruther.) G73	55	BY37
Duchess Rd, (Ruther.) G73	55	BY36
Duchess Way, (Baill.) G69	43	CP31
off Park Rd		
Duchray Dr, Pais. PA1	50	BB33
Duchray La, G33	39	BZ28
Duchray St, G33	39	BZ28
Dudhope St, G33	41	CF27
Dudley Dr, G12	22	BJ26
Dudley La, G12	22	BJ26
Duffus Pl, G32	57	CE37
Duffus St, G34	41	CH28
Duffus Ter, G32	57	CE37
Duich Gdns, G23	11	BN19
Duisdale Rd, G32	57	CE37
Dukes Gate, (Both.) G71	71	CN41
Dukes Rd, (Baill.) G69	43	CP32
Dukes Rd, (Camb.) G72	68	CA39
Dukes Rd, (Ruther.) G73	67	BY40
Duke St, G4	5	BU30
Duke St, G31	39	BW30
Duke St, Pais. PA2	48	AU35
Duke St, (Linw.) Pais. PA3	30	AL31
Dullatur Rd, (Cumb.) G68	72	DA8
Dullatur Roundabout, (Cumb.)	72	DB8
G68		
Dulnain St, (Camb.) G72	69	CF40
Dulsie Rd, G21	25	BY23
Dumbarton Rd, G11	36	BJ27
Dumbarton Rd, G14	35	BG27
Dumbarton Rd, Clyde. G81	6	AT17
Dumbarton Rd, (Dunt.) Clyde.	6	AV15
G81		
Dumbreck Av, G41	52	BJ33
Dumbreck Ct, G41	52	BJ34
Dumbreck Path, G41	52	BJ33
off Dumbreck Av		
Dumbreck Pl, G41	52	BJ34
Dumbreck Pl, (Kirk.) G66	15	CG17
Dumbreck Rd, G41	52	BK34
Dumbreck Rd, G41	52	BJ33
Dunagoil Gdns, G45	66	BU43
Dunagoil Pl, G45	66	BU44
Dunagoil Rd, G45	66	BT43
Dunagoil St, G45	66	BU43
Dunagoil Ter, G45	66	BU44
Dunalistair Dr, G33	26	CD24
Dunan Pl, G33	41	CG30
Dunard Rd, (Ruther.) G73	55	BX38
Dunard St, G20	23	BP25
Dunard Way, Pais. PA3	32	AT30
off Mosslands Rd		
Dunaskin St, G11	36	BL28
Dunbar Av, (Ruther.) G73	55	BY38
Dunbar Av, John. PA5	45	AG37
Dunbar Rd, Pais. PA2	47	AQ36
Dunbeith Pl, G20	22	BM24
Dunblane St, G4	4	BR28
Duncan Av, G14	21	BE26
Duncan La, G14	21	BE26
off Gleneagles La N		
Duncan La N, G14	21	BE25
off Duncan Av		
Duncan La S, G14	21	BE25
off Gleneagles La N		
Duncansby Rd, G33	41	CF31
Duncan St, Clyde. G81	7	AX18
Dunchattan Pl, G31	38	BV30
Dunchattan St, G31	38	BV30
Dunchurch Rd, Pais. PA1	33	AZ32
Dunclutha Dr, (Both.) G71	71	CQ44
Dunclutha St, G40	55	BX35
Duncombe St, G20	22	BM22
Duncombe Vw, Clyde. G81	7	AY18
off Kirkoswald Dr		
Duncraig Cres, John. PA5	45	AE36

Duncrub Dr, (Bishop.) G64	12	BU20
Duncruin St, G20	22	BM22
Duncryne Av, G32	57	CF33
Duncryne Gdns, G32	57	CG33
Duncryne Pl, (Bishop.) G64	24	BU21
Dundaff Hill, (Cumb.) G68	72	CY11
Dundashill, G4	37	BR27
Dundas La, G1	5	BS29
Dundas St, G1	5	BS29
Dundasvale Ct, G4	4	BR28
off Maitland St		
Dundasvale Rd, G4	4	BR28
off Maitland St		
Dundee Dr, G52	50	BD33
Dundee Path, G52	51	BE34
Dundonald Av, John. PA5	45	AF36
Dundonald Rd, G12	22	BL25
Dundonald Rd, Pais. PA3	33	AW30
Dundrennan Rd, G42	53	BP38
Dunearn Pl, Pais. PA2	49	AW34
Dunearn St, G4	37	BP27
Dunedin Ter, Clyde. G81	19	AY21
Dunellan Av, (Mood.) G69	17	CQ19
Dunellan Ct, (Mood.) G69	17	CQ19
off Dunellan Av		
Dunellan Cres, (Mood.) G69	17	CQ19
Dunellan Gdns, (Mood.) G69	17	CQ19
off Dunellan Av		
Dunellan St, G52	35	BG32
Dungeonhill Rd, G34	42	CM29
Dunglass Av, G14	21	BE25
Dunglass La, G14	21	BE25
off Dunglass Av		
Dunglass La N, G14	21	BE25
off Verona Av		
Dunglass La S, G14	21	BE25
off Verona Av		
Dungoil Rd, (Lenz.) G66	15	CG17
Dungoyne St, G20	22	BL21
off Crosbie St		
Dunholme Pk, Clyde. G81	6	AT18
Dunira St, G32	56	CB34
Dunivaig St, G33	41	CG29
Dunkeld Av, (Ruther.) G73	55	BX38
Dunkeld Dr, (Bears.) G61	10	BK17
Dunkeld Gdns, (Bishop.) G64	13	BX19
Dunkeld La, (Chry.) G69	17	CQ19
off Burnbrae Av		
Dunkeld St, G31	55	BY33
Dunkenny Pl, G15	8	BB17
Dunkenny Rd, G15	8	BA18
Dunkenny Sq, G15	8	BB18
Dunlin, G12	22	BJ23
off Ascot Av		
Dunlop Cres, (Both.) G71	71	CQ44
Dunlop Cres, Renf. PA4	19	AZ25
off Fulbar St		
Dunlop Gro, (Udd.) G71	59	CQ36
Dunlop St, G1	5	BS31
Dunlop St, (Camb.) G72	69	CG39
Dunlop St, (Linw.) Pais. PA3	30	AL31
Dunlop St, Renf. PA4	19	AZ25
off Fulbar St		
Dunmore La, G5	37	BR32
off Norfolk St		
Dunmore St, G5	38	BS32
Dunmore St, Clyde. G81	19	AY21
Dunnachie Dr, Coat. ML5	59	CR33
Dunnachie Pl, Coat. ML5	59	CR33
off Kenmuir St		
Dunnichen Gdns, (Bishop.) G64	13	BZ20
Dunnottar St, G33	40	CD27
Dunnottar St, (Bishop.) G64	13	BZ19
Dunn St, G40	55	BW33
Dunn St, Clyde. G81	6	AU18
Dunn St, (Dunt.) Clyde. G81	6	AV15
Dunn St, Pais. PA1	33	AW32
Dunolly St, G21	39	BW28
Dunphail Dr, G34	42	CM29
Dunphail Rd, G34	42	CM29
Dunragit St, G31	39	BY30
Dunrobin Av, (Elder.) John.	46	AL36
PA5		
Dunrobin St, G31	39	BX31
Dunrod St, G32	56	CD33
Dunside Dr, G53	62	BC39
Dunskaith Pl, G34	42	CM30
Dunskaith St, G34	42	CM29
Dunsmuir St, G51	36	BK30
Dunster Gdns, (Bishop.) G64	13	BX17

Dunswin Av, Clyde. G81	6	AU18
Dunswin Ct, Clyde. G81	6	AU18
off Dunswin Av		
Dunsyre Pl, G23	11	BN20
Dunsyre St, G33	40	CA29
Duntarvie Av, G34	42	CL29
Duntarvie Cl, G34	42	CL29
Duntarvie Cres, G34	42	CL29
Duntarvie Dr, G34	42	CK29
Duntarvie Gdns, G34	42	CL29
Duntarvie Gro, G34	42	CL29
Duntarvie Pl, G34	42	CK29
Duntarvie Rd, G34	42	CK29
Dunterlie Av, G13	20	BC23
Dunterlie Ct, (Barr.) G78	61	AY42
Duntiglennan Rd, Clyde. G81	7	AW15
Duntocher Rd, (Bears.) G61	8	BC15
Duntocher Rd, Clyde. G81	6	AV18
Duntocher Rd, (Dunt.) Clyde.	7	AW15
G81		
Duntreath Av, G13	20	BA21
Duntreath Av, G15	8	BB20
Duntreath Dr, G15	8	BB20
Duntreath Gdns, G15	8	BB19
Duntreath Gro, G15	8	BB20
Duntroon St, G31	39	BX29
Dunure Dr, (Ruther.) G73	66	BV40
Dunure St, G20	22	BM22
Dunvegan Av, (Elder.) John.	46	AK36
PA5		
Dunvegan Dr, (Bishop.) G64	13	BW17
Dunvegan Pl, (Udd.) G71	58	CM37
Dunvegan Quad, Renf. PA4	19	AX25
off Kirklandneuk Rd		
Dunwan Av, G13	20	BB22
Dunwan Pl, G13	20	BB22
Durban Av, Clyde. G81	6	AS17
Durham St, G41	36	BM32
Durness Av, (Bears.) G61	10	BK16
Durno Path, G33	41	CG30
Duror St, G32	40	CC31
Durris Gdns, G32	57	CF34
Durrockstock Cres, Pais. PA2	47	AP38
Durrockstock Rd, Pais. PA2	47	AP38
Durrockstock Way, Pais. PA2	47	AP38
off Durrockstock Cres		
Durward Av, G41	52	BM36
Durward Ct, G41	52	BM36
Durward Cres, Pais. PA2	47	AP36
Durward Way, Pais. PA2	47	AP36
off Durward Cres		
Duthie Pk Gdns, G13	21	BF23
Duthie Pk Pl, G13	21	BF22
Duthil St, G51	35	BF31
Dyce La, G11	36	BJ27
Dyer's La, G1	5	BT31
Dyers Wynd, Pais. PA1	32	AU32
off Gilmour St		
Dykebar Av, G13	20	BC23
Dykebar Cres, Pais. PA2	49	AX35
Dykehead La, G33	41	CF30
Dykehead Rd, (Baill.) G69	43	CP32
Dykehead St, G33	41	CF30
Dykemuir Pl, G21	25	BX25
off Dykemuir St		
Dykemuir Quad, G21	25	BW25
off Dykemuir St		
Dykemuir St, G21	25	BW25
Dyke Pl, G13	20	BC21
Dyke Rd, G13	20	BC22
Dyke Rd, G14	20	BB23
Dyke St, (Baill.) G69	42	CL32
Dyke St, Coat. ML5	59	CR33
E		
Eagle Cres, (Bears.) G61	8	BD15
Eaglesham Ct, G51	37	BN31
off Blackburn St		
Eaglesham Pl, G51	37	BN31
Eagle St, G4	38	BS27
Earlbank Av, G14	21	BE25
Earlbank La N, G14	21	BE25
off Verona Av		
Earlbank La S, G14	21	BE25
off Verona Av		
Earl Haig Rd, G52	34	BB30
Earl La, G14	21	BE26
Earl Pl, G14	21	BE25
Earlsburn Rd, (Lenz.) G66	15	CG17
Earlscourt, (Mood.) G69	17	CP20
Earls Gate, (Both.) G71	71	CN42
Earlspark Av, G43	53	BP38
Earlston Av, G21	38	BV28
Earlston Pl, G21	5	BU28
Earl St, G14	21	BE26
Earlybraes Dr, G32	41	CG31
Earlybraes Gdns, G33	41	CF31
Earn Av, (Bears.) G61	10	BK17
Earn Av, Renf. PA4	34	BA27
off Almond Av		
Earnock St, G33	25	BZ25
Earnside St, G32	40	CD32
Earn St, G33	40	CA28
Easdale Dr, G32	56	CC33
East Av, Renf. PA4	19	AZ26
Eastbank Dr, G32	41	CE32
Eastbank Pl, G32	41	CE32
Eastbank Ri, G32	41	CE32
East Barns St, Clyde. G81	19	AZ21
East Bath La, G2	5	BS29
off Sauchiehall St		
East Buchanan St, Pais. PA1	32	AV32
Eastburn Cres, G21	25	BX23
Eastburn Pl, G21	25	BX23
off Eastburn Cres		
Eastburn Rd, G21	25	BX24
East Campbell St, G1	5	BU31
Eastcote Av, G14	21	BG26
Eastcroft, (Ruther.) G73	55	BX37
Eastcroft Ter, G21	25	BW25
Easter Av, (Udd.) G71	71	CN39
Eastercraigs, G31	39	BX29
Easter Garngaber Rd, (Lenz.)	15	CG16
G66		
Easterhill Pl, G32	56	CB34
Easterhill St, G32	56	CB34
Easterhouse Pl, G34	42	CL29
off Easterhouse Rd		
Easterhouse Quad, G34	42	CL30
Easterhouse Rd, G34	42	CL29
Easterhouse Rd, (Baill.) G69	42	CK32
Easterhouse Township Cen,	42	CJ29
G34		
Easter Ms, (Udd.) G71	71	CN39
Easter Queenslie Rd, G33	41	CG29
Eastfield Av, (Camb.) G72	68	CA39
Eastfield Rd, G21	24	BU25
Eastgate, (Gart.) G69	29	CQ24
East Greenlees Av, (Camb.)	69	CE42
G72		
East Greenlees Cres, (Camb.)	68	CD42
G72		
East Greenlees Dr, (Camb.)	69	CE42
G72		
East Greenlees Gro, (Camb.)	68	CC42
G72		
East Greenlees Rd, (Camb.)	68	CC42
G72		
Easthall Pl, G33	41	CH30
East Kilbride Rd, (Ruther.)	67	BY40
G73		
East La, Pais. PA1	49	AW33
Eastmuir St, G32	40	CD32
East Queenslie Ind Est, G33	41	CG29
East Rd, (Kilb.) John. PA10	44	AC33
East Springfield Ter, (Bishop.)	25	BX21
G64		
East Thomson St, Clyde. G81	7	AX18
Eastvale Pl, G3	36	BL29
East Wellington St, G31	39	BZ32
East Whitby St, G31	55	BY33
Eastwood Av, G41	52	BM37
Eastwood Av, (Giff.) G46	64	BL43
Eastwood Ct, (Thornlie.) G46	64	BJ41
off Crosslees Dr		
Eastwood Cres, (Thornlie.) G46	63	BH41
Eastwoodmains Rd, (Giff.) G46	64	BL44
Eastwoodmains Rd, (Clark.)	64	BL44
G76		
Eastwood Pk, (Thornlie.) G46	64	BJ43
Eastwood Pk, (Thornlie.) G46	64	BJ43
Eastwood Rd, (Mood.) G69	17	CP19
Eastwood Vw, (Camb.) G72	69	CG39
Easwald Bk, (Kilb.) John. PA10	44	AD35
Eccles St, G22	24	BU24
off Carron St		
Eckford St, G32	56	CC33
Eday St, G22	24	BT23
Edderton Pl, G34	42	CJ30
Edderton Way, G34	42	CJ30
Eddleston Pl, (Camb.) G72	69	CG40
off Montgomery St		
Eddlewood Ct, G33	42	CJ30
Eddlewood Path, G33	41	CH30
off Eddlewood Rd		
Eddlewood Pl, G33	41	CH30
Eddlewood Rd, G33	41	CH30
Edelweiss Ter, G11	36	BK27
off Gardner St		
Eden La, G33	39	BZ28
Eden Pk, (Both.) G71	71	CP43
Eden Pl, (Camb.) G72	69	CF40
Eden Pl, Renf. PA4	34	BA27
Eden St, G33	39	BZ28
Edenwood St, G31	40	CA32
Edgam Dr, G52	35	BE32
Edgefauld Av, G21	24	BV26
Edgefauld Dr, G21	24	BV25
Edgefauld Pl, G21	24	BV24
Edgefauld Rd, G21	24	BV25
Edgehill La, G11	22	BJ25
Edgehill Rd, G11	21	BH25
Edgehill Rd, (Bears.) G61	9	BG15
Edgemont St, G41	53	BN37
Edinbeg Av, G42	54	BU37
Edinbeg Pl, G42	54	BU37
Edinburgh Rd, G33	39	BZ30
Edinburgh Rd, (Baill.) G69	41	CH31
Edington Gdns, (Mood.) G69	17	CP18
Edington St, G4	37	BR27
Edison St, G52	34	BA29
Edmiston Dr, G51	35	BH31
Edmonstone Ct, Clyde. G81	19	AZ22
off Hamilton Ter		
Edrom Ct, G32	40	CB32
Edrom Path, G32	40	CC32
off Edrom St		
Edrom St, G32	40	CB32
Edward Av, Renf. PA4	20	BA25
Edward St, (Baill.) G69	43	CP32
Edward St, Clyde. G81	19	AZ22
Edwin St, G51	36	BM32
Edzell Ct, G14	35	BF27
Edzell Dr, (Elder.) John. PA5	46	AM35
Edzell Gdns, (Bishop.) G64	25	BY21
Edzell Pl, G14	21	BF26
Edzell St, G14	35	BF27
Egidia Av, (Giff.) G46	64	BL43
Egilsay Cres, G22	24	BS21
Egilsay Pl, G22	24	BS21
Egilsay St, G22	24	BS21
Egilsay Ter, G22	24	BS21
Eglinton Av, (Udd.) G71	71	CN39
off Lady Isle Cres		
Eglinton Ct, G5	37	BR32
Eglinton Dr, (Giff.) G46	64	BL43
Eglinton St, G5	37	BR32
Eider, G12	22	BJ22
off Ascot Av		
Eighth St, (Udd.) G71	59	CN36
Eildon Dr, (Barr.) G78	61	AY44
Eileen Gdns, (Bishop.) G64	13	BX19
Elba La, G31	39	BY32
Elcho St, G40	38	BV31
Elderbank, (Bears.) G61	9	BG18
Elder Cres, (Camb.) G72	69	CG41
Elder Gro, (Udd.) G71	59	CR38
Elder Gro Av, G51	35	BF30
Elder Gro Ct, G51	35	BF30
Elder Gro Pl, G51	35	BF30
Elderpark Gdns, G51	35	BH30
off Elderpark St		
Elderpark Gro, G51	35	BH30
Elderpark St, G51	35	BH30
Elderslie St, G3	4	BP28
Elder St, G51	35	BH29
Eldin Pl, (Elder.) John. PA5	46	AK35
Eldon Ct, G11	36	BK27
off Caird Dr		
Eldon Gdns, (Bishop.) G64	12	BU20
Eldon St, G3	37	BN27
Elgin St, G40	39	BW32
off Rowchester St		
Elibank St, G33	40	CC28
Elie Ct, (Cumb.) G68	72	DB8
Elie St, G11	36	BL27
Elizabethan Way, Renf. PA4	33	AY28
Elizabeth Cres, (Thornlie.) G46	64	BJ42
Elizabeth St, G51	36	BL32

Ellangowan Rd, G41 52 BL37
Ellergreen Rd, (Bears.) G61 9 BG17
Ellerslie St, John. PA5 46 AJ34
Ellesmere St, G22 23 BQ25
Ellinger Ct, Clyde. G81 6 AU17
off Scott St
Elliot Av, (Giff.) G46 64 BL43
Elliot Av, Pais. PA2 46 AM38
Elliot Dr, (Giff.) G46 64 BL42
Elliot Pl, G3 37 BN29
off Finnieston St
Elliot St, G3 37 BN30
Ellisland Av, Clyde. G81 7 AY18
Ellisland Cres, (Ruther.) G73 66 BV40
Ellisland Rd, G43 64 BM39
Ellisland Rd, (Cumb.) G67 73 DD11
Ellismuir Fm Rd, (Baill.) G69 58 CM33
off Bredisholm Ter
Ellismuir Pl, (Baill.) G69 58 CL33
Ellismuir Rd, (Baill.) G69 58 CL33
Ellismuir Way, (Udd.) G71 59 CQ36
Elliston Av, G53 63 BE40
Elliston Cres, G53 63 BE40
Elliston Dr, G53 63 BE40
Ellon Dr, (Linw.) Pais. PA3 30 AJ32
Ellon Gro, Pais. PA3 32 AV30
off Ellon Way
Ellon Way, Pais. PA3 32 AV30
Elm Av, (Lenz.) G66 15 CE15
Elm Av, Renf. PA4 19 AY25
Elm Bk, (Bishop.) G64 13 BX20
Elmbank Av, (Udd.) G71 59 CR38
Elmbank Cres, G2 4 BQ29
Elmbank La, G3 4 BP29
off North St
Elmbank St, G2 4 BQ29
Elmbank St La, G2 4 BQ29
Elm Dr, (Camb.) G72 69 CE40
Elm Dr, John. PA5 46 AJ36
Elmfoot St, G5 54 BT35
Elm Gdns, (Bears.) G61 9 BG15
Elmira Rd, (Muir.) G69 28 CM22
Elm La E, G14 21 BF26
off Westland Dr
Elm La W, G14 21 BF26
off Westland Dr
Elmore Av, G44 65 BR40
Elmore La, G44 65 BR40
Elm Rd, (Ruther.) G73 67 BX41
Elm Rd, Clyde. G81 7 AW16
Elm Rd, Pais. PA2 49 AW36
Elmslie Ct, (Baill.) G69 58 CL33
Elm St, G14 21 BF26
Elmtree Gdns, G45 66 BV41
Elmvale Row, G21 24 BU24
Elmvale Row E, G21 24 BU24
off Elmvale Row
Elmvale Row W, G21 24 BU24
off Elmvale Row
Elmvale St, G21 24 BU24
Elm Wk, (Bears.) G61 9 BG15
Elm Way, (Camb.) G72 69 CG41
Elmwood Av, G11 21 BH25
Elmwood Ct, (Both.) G71 71 CQ43
Elmwood Gdns, (Kirk.) G66 14 CC16
Elmwood La, G11 21 BH25
Elphinstone Pl, G51 36 BL30
Elphin St, G23 10 BM20
off Invershiel Rd
Elrig Rd, G44 65 BP40
Elspeth Gdns, (Bishop.) G64 13 BY19
Eltham St, G22 23 BR26
off Bonhill St
Elvan Ct, G32 40 CC32
off Edrom Ct
Elvan St, G32 40 CB32
Embo Dr, G13 20 BD23
Emerson Rd, (Bishop.) G64 13 BW20
Emerson Rd W, (Bishop.) G64 13 BW20
off Crowhill Rd
Emerson St, G20 23 BQ23
Endfield Av, G12 22 BK23
Endrick Bk, (Bishop.) G64 13 BW17
Endrick Dr, (Bears.) G61 9 BH17
Endrick Dr, Pais. PA1 33 AX31
Endrick St, G21 24 BT26
Ensay St, G22 24 BT22
Enterkin St, G32 56 CB33
Eriboll Pl, G22 23 BR22
Eriboll St, G22 23 BR22
Ericht Rd, G43 64 BL40
Eriska Av, G14 20 BC24
Eriskay Dr, (Old Kil.) G60 6 AS15
Eriskay Pl, (Old Kil.) G60 6 AS15
Erradale St, G22 23 BQ22
Errogie St, G34 42 CK29
Errol Gdns, G5 54 BS33
Erskine Av, G41 52 BK33
Erskinefauld Rd, (Linw.) Pais. PA3 30 AJ31
Erskine Sq, G52 34 BB30
Erskine Vw, Clyde. G81 7 AX18
Ervie St, G34 42 CL30
Esk Av, Renf. PA4 34 BA27
Eskbank St, G32 40 CC31
Eskbank Toll, (Giff.) G46 64 BK44
Eskdale Dr, (Ruther.) G73 55 BZ38
Eskdale Rd, (Bears.) G61 9 BF19
Eskdale St, G42 53 BR36
Esk Dr, Pais. PA2 47 AN36
Esk St, G14 20 BB24
Esk Way, Pais. PA2 47 AN36
Esmond St, G3 36 BL28
Espedair St, Pais. PA2 48 AU34
Essenside Av, G15 9 BE19
Essex Dr, G14 21 BG25
Essex La, G14 21 BF25
Esslemont Av, G14 20 BD24
Estate Quad, G32 57 CE36
Estate Rd, G32 57 CE36
Etive Av, (Bears.) G61 10 BK17
Etive Ct, Clyde. G81 7 AY16
Etive Cres, (Bishop.) G64 13 BX20
Etive Dr, (Giff.) G46 64 BM44
Etive St, G32 40 CC32
Eton La, G12 37 BN27
Ettrick Av, Renf. PA4 34 BB27
off Morriston Cres
Ettrick Ct, (Camb.) G72 69 CG41
off Gateside Av
Ettrick Cres, (Ruther.) G73 55 BY38
Ettrick Oval, Pais. PA2 47 AN37
Ettrick Pl, G43 52 BM38
Ettrick Sq, (Cumb.) G67 72 DB12
off Cumbernauld Shop Cen
Ettrick Ter, John. PA5 45 AE37
Ettrick Wk, (Cumb.) G67 72 DB12
off Cumbernauld Shop Cen
Ettrick Way, (Cumb.) G67 72 DB12
off Cumbernauld Shop Cen
Ettrick Way, Renf. PA4 34 BB27
off Morriston Cres
Evan Cres, (Giff.) G46 64 BM43
Evan Dr, (Giff.) G46 64 BM44
Evanton Dr, (Thornlie.) G46 63 BG43
Evanton Pl, (Thornlie.) G46 63 BG42
Everard Ct, G21 24 BU22
Everard Dr, G21 24 BU23
Everard Pl, G21 24 BU22
Everard Quad, G21 24 BU23
Everglades, The, (Chry.) G69 28 CK21
Eversley St, G32 56 CC34
Everton Rd, G53 51 BE35
Ewing Pl, G31 39 BY32
Ewing St, (Ruther.) G73 55 BW38
Ewing St, (Kilb.) John. PA10 44 AC34
Exchange Pl, G1 5 BS30
off Buchanan St
Exeter Dr, G11 36 BJ27
Exeter La, G11 36 BJ27
off Exeter Dr
Eynort St, G22 23 BQ22
Eyrepoint Ct, G33 40 CC29
off Sutherness Dr

F

Fagan Ct, (Blan.) G72 71 CN44
Faifley Rd, Clyde. G81 7 AX15
Fairbairn Cres, (Thornlie.) G46 64 BJ43
Fairbairn Path, G40 55 BW33
off Ruby St
Fairbairn St, G40 55 BW33
Fairburn St, G32 56 CB33
Fairfax Av, G44 66 BS40
Fairfield Dr, Renf. PA4 33 AZ28
Fairfield Gdns, G51 35 BH29
off Fairfield St
Fairfield Pl, G51 35 BH29
off Fairfield St
Fairfield Pl, (Both.) G71 71 CR43
Fairfield St, G51 35 BH29
Fairhaven Rd, G23 23 BN21
Fairhill Av, G53 51 BE38
Fairholm St, G32 56 CB33
Fairley St, G51 36 BK31
Fairlie Pk Dr, G11 36 BJ27
Fairway, (Bears.) G61 8 BD16
Fairway Av, Pais. PA2 48 AT37
Fairways Vw, Clyde. G81 7 AZ15
Fairyknowe Gdns, (Both.) G71 71 CR43
Falcon Cres, Pais. PA3 31 AR31
Falcon Rd, John. PA5 45 AF38
Falcon Ter, G20 22 BL21
Falcon Ter La, G20 22 BL21
Falfield St, G5 53 BQ33
Falkland Cres, (Bishop.) G64 25 BZ21
Falkland La, G12 22 BK26
Falkland St, G12 22 BK26
Falloch Rd, G42 53 BQ38
Falloch Rd, (Bears.) G61 9 BE19
Fallside Rd, (Both.) G71 71 CQ43
Falside Av, Pais. PA2 48 AU36
Falside Rd, G32 56 CD35
Falside Rd, Pais. PA2 48 AT36
Fara St, G23 23 BP21
Farie St, (Ruther.) G73 54 BV37
Farm Ct, (Both.) G71 71 CR41
Farme Castle Ct, (Ruther.) G73 55 BY36
Farme Castle Est, (Ruther.) G73 55 BY36
Farme Cross, (Ruther.) G73 55 BX36
Farmeloan Ind Est, (Ruther.) G73 55 BX36
Farmeloan Rd, (Ruther.) G73 55 BX37
Farmington Av, G32 41 CF32
Farmington Gdns, G32 41 CF32
Farmington Gate, G32 57 CF33
Farmington Gro, G32 41 CF32
Farm La, (Udd.) G71 71 CQ40
off Myers Cres
Farm Pk, (Lenz.) G66 15 CF17
Farm Rd, G41 36 BK32
Farm Rd, (Blan.) G72 70 CM44
Farm Rd, (Dalmuir) Clyde. G81 6 AT18
Farne Dr, G44 65 BR41
Farnell St, G4 37 BR27
Farrier Ct, John. PA5 45 AH34
Faskally Av, (Bishop.) G64 12 BU18
Faskin Cres, G53 50 BB38
Faskin Pl, G53 50 BB38
Faskin Rd, G53 50 BB38
Fasque Pl, G15 8 BA17
Fastnet St, G33 40 CC29
Fauldhouse St, G5 54 BT34
Faulds, (Baill.) G69 42 CL32
Faulds Gdns, (Baill.) G69 42 CL32
Fauldshead Rd, Renf. PA4 19 AY26
Fauldspark Cres, (Baill.) G69 42 CL31
Fauldswood Cres, Pais. PA2 47 AR35
Fauldswood Dr, Pais. PA2 47 AR35
Fearnach Pl, G20 22 BK22
off Skaethorn Rd
Fearnmore Rd, G20 22 BM22
Felton Pl, G13 20 BB22
Fendoch St, G32 56 CC33
Fenella St, G32 40 CD32
Fennsbank Av, (Ruther.) G73 67 BZ42
Fenwick Dr, (Barr.) G78 61 AZ44
Fenwick Pl, (Giff.) G46 64 BK44
Fenwick Rd, (Giff.) G46 64 BL44
Fereneze Av, (Barr.) G78 61 AX42
Fereneze Av, Renf. PA4 33 AW29
Fereneze Cres, G13 20 BC22
Fereneze Dr, Pais. PA2 48 AS37
Fereneze Gro, (Barr.) G78 61 AX41
Fergus Av, Pais. PA3 31 AQ32
Fergus Ct, G20 23 BN25
off Fergus Dr
Fergus Dr, G20 23 BN25
Fergus Dr, Pais. PA3 31 AQ32
Fergus La, G20 23 BP25
Ferguslie, Pais. PA1 47 AQ33
Ferguslie Pk Av, Pais. PA3 31 AR31
Ferguslie Pk Cres, Pais. PA3 47 AQ33
off Ferguslie Park Av
Ferguslie Wk, Pais. PA1 47 AR33
Ferguson Av, Renf. PA4 19 AZ26
Ferguson St, John. PA5 45 AG34
Ferguson St, Renf. PA4 19 AZ25
Fergusson Rd, (Cumb.) G67 72 DB11
Ferguston Rd, (Bears.) G61 9 BH17

Name	Page	Grid
Fernan St, G32	40	CB32
Fern Av, (Bishop.) G64	25	BX21
Fern Av, (Lenz.) G66	15	CE17
Fernbank Av, (Camb.) G72	69	CE41
Fernbank St, G21	24	BU24
Fernbank St, G22	24	BU24
Fernbrae Av, (Ruther.) G73	67	BY42
Fernbrae Way, (Ruther.) G73	67	BX42
Fern Cotts, G13	21	BH24
off Fern La		
Ferncroft Dr, G44	66	BT40
Ferndale Ct, G23	22	BM21
Ferndale Dr, G23	10	BM20
Ferndale Gdns, G23	22	BM21
Ferndale Pl, G23	22	BM21
Fern Dr, (Barr.) G78	61	AX41
Ferness Oval, G21	25	BY22
Ferness Pl, G21	25	BY22
Ferness Rd, G21	25	BY23
Fern Gro, (Gart.) G69	29	CQ23
off Inchnock Av		
Ferngrove Av, G12	22	BK23
Fernhill Gra, (Both.) G71	71	CQ44
Fernhill Rd, (Ruther.) G73	67	BW41
Fernie Gdns, G20	23	BN22
Fern La, G13	21	BH24
Fernlea, (Bears.) G61	9	BG18
Fernleigh Pl, (Mood.) G69	17	CP19
Fernleigh Rd, G43	64	BM40
Ferryden Ct, G14	35	BG27
off Ferryden St		
Ferryden St, G14	35	BG28
Ferry Rd, G3	36	BK28
Ferry Rd, (Both.) G71	71	CQ43
Ferry Rd, (Udd.) G71	71	CN39
Ferry Rd, Renf. PA4	19	AZ25
Fersit St, G43	64	BL39
Fetlar Dr, G44	66	BS40
Fettercairn Av, G15	8	BA18
Fettercairn Gdns, (Bishop.) G64	13	BY20
Fettes St, G33	40	CB29
Fidra St, G33	40	CB29
Fielden Pl, G40	39	BW32
Fielden St, G40	39	BW32
Fieldhead Dr, G43	64	BJ40
Fieldhead Sq, G43	64	BJ40
Fife Av, G52	50	BD33
Fife Cres, (Both.) G71	71	CQ44
Fife Way, (Bishop.) G64	25	BZ21
Fifth Av, G12	21	BH24
Fifth Av, (Stepps) G33	26	CD24
Fifth Av, (Kirk.) G66	15	CF19
Fifth Av, Renf. PA4	33	AY27
Fifty Pitches Pl, G51	34	BD30
Fifty Pitches Rd, G51	34	BD30
Finart Dr, Pais. PA2	49	AX36
Finch Dr, G13	20	BC21
Finch Pl, John. PA5	45	AF38
Findhorn Av, Pais. PA2	47	AQ36
Findhorn Av, Renf. PA4	20	BA26
off Dee Av		
Findhorn St, G33	39	BZ29
Findochty St, G33	41	CG37
Fingal La, G20	22	BL22
off Fingal St		
Fingal St, G20	22	BM22
Fingask St, G32	57	CE33
Finglas Av, Pais. PA2	49	AX36
Finglen Pl, G53	62	BD41
Fingleton Av, (Barr.) G78	61	AZ44
Finhaven St, G32	56	CA34
Finlarig St, G34	42	CL30
Finlas St, G22	24	BT25
Finlay Dr, G31	39	BW30
Finnart Sq, G40	54	BV34
Finnart St, G40	54	BV34
Finnieston Quay, G3	37	BN30
Finnieston Sq, G3	37	BN29
off Finnieston St		
Finnieston St, G3	37	BN30
Finsbay St, G51	35	BF31
Fintry Av, Pais. PA2	48	AU37
Fintry Cres, (Bishop.) G64	25	BY21
Fintry Cres, (Barr.) G78	61	AY44
Fintry Dr, G44	54	BS38
Firbank Ter, (Barr.) G78	62	BA44
Fir Ct, (Camb.) G72	69	CG41
Firdon Cres, G15	8	BA20
Fir Gro, (Udd.) G71	59	CR38
Firhill Rd, G20	23	BQ25
Firhill St, G20	23	BQ25
Firpark Pl, G31	38	BV29
off Firpark St		
Firpark Rd, (Bishop.) G64	25	BX21
Firpark St, G31	38	BV29
Firpark Ter, G31	38	BV30
Fir Pl, (Baill.) G69	58	CJ34
Fir Pl, (Camb.) G72	69	CE39
Fir Pl, John. PA5	46	AJ35
First Av, (Millerston) G33	26	CD24
First Av, G44	65	BP43
First Av, (Bears.) G61	10	BJ18
First Av, (Kirk.) G66	15	CF20
First Av, (Udd.) G71	59	CN37
First Av, Renf. PA4	33	AY27
First Gdns, G41	52	BJ33
First St, (Udd.) G71	59	CP37
First Ter, Clyde. G81	7	AW18
Firwood Dr, G44	66	BS39
Fischer Gdns, Pais. PA1	47	AP33
Fisher Av, Pais. PA1	47	AP33
Fisher Ct, G31	38	BV30
Fisher Cres, Clyde. G81	7	AX15
Fisher Dr, Pais. PA1	47	AP33
Fishers Rd, Renf. PA4	19	AY23
Fisher Way, Pais. PA1	47	AP33
Fishescoates Av, (Ruther.) G73	67	BY40
Fishescoates Gdns, (Ruther.) G73	67	BY40
Fitzalan Dr, Pais. PA3	33	AW31
Fitzalan Rd, Renf. PA4	33	AW28
Fitzroy La, G3	37	BN29
Fitzroy Pl, G3	37	BN28
off Royal Ter		
Flax Rd, (Udd.) G71	71	CQ40
Fleet Av, Renf. PA4	34	BA28
Fleet St, G32	56	CD33
Fleming Av, (Chry.) G69	28	CL22
Fleming Av, Clyde. G81	7	AZ20
Fleming Rd, (Cumb.) G67	72	DB11
Fleming St, G31	39	BX31
Fleming St, Pais. PA3	32	AU30
Flemington Ind Est, (Camb.) G72	69	CG41
Flemington Rd, (Camb.) G72	69	CH44
Flemington St, G21	24	BV26
Fleurs Av, G41	52	BK33
Fleurs Rd, G41	52	BK33
Floorsburn Cres, John. PA5	45	AG35
Floors St, John. PA5	45	AH35
Flora Gdns, (Bishop.) G64	13	BY19
Florence Dr, (Giff.) G46	64	BL43
Florence Gdns, (Ruther.) G73	67	BY41
Florence St, G5	38	BS32
Florida Av, G42	53	BR37
Florida Cres, G42	53	BR37
Florida Dr, G42	53	BQ37
Florida Gdns, (Baill.) G69	42	CJ32
Florida Sq, G42	53	BR37
Florida St, G42	53	BR37
Florish Rd, Ersk. PA8	18	AT21
Flowerdale Pl, G53	62	BD43
off Waukglen Dr		
Flures Av, Ersk. PA8	18	AU21
Flures Cres, Ersk. PA8	18	AU21
Flures Dr, Ersk. PA8	18	AU21
Flures Pl, Ersk. PA8	18	AU21
Fochabers Dr, G52	35	BE31
Fogo Pl, G20	22	BM23
Foinaven Dr, (Thornlie.) G46	63	BH39
Foinaven Gdns, (Thornlie.) G46	64	BJ39
Foinaven Way, (Thornlie.) G46	64	BJ40
Forbes Dr, G40	38	BV32
Forbes Pl, Pais. PA1	48	AU33
Forbes St, G40	38	BV31
Fordneuk St, G40	39	BW32
Fordoun St, G34	42	CM29
Ford Rd, G12	22	BM25
Fordyce St, G11	36	BK27
Forehouse Rd, (Kilb.) John. PA10	44	AA34
Foremount Ter La, G12	22	BK26
Forest Dr, (Both.) G71	71	CQ42
Forest Gdns, (Kirk.) G66	14	CC17
Foresthall Cres, G21	25	BW26
Foresthall Dr, G21	25	BW26
Forest Pl, (Kirk.) G66	14	CC17
Forest Pl, Pais. PA2	48	AU35
Fore St, G14	21	BE26
Forest Rd, (Cumb.) G67	73	DE11
Forest Vw, (Cumb.) G67	73	DE10
Forfar Av, G52	50	BD33
Forfar Cres, (Bishop.) G64	25	BY21
Forgan Gdns, (Bishop.) G64	25	BZ21
Forge, The, (Giff.) G46	64	BM42
off Braidpark Dr		
Forge Pl, G21	39	BX27
Forge Retail Pk, G31	39	BX31
Forge Shop Cen, The, G31	39	BY32
Forge St, G21	39	BX27
Forglen St, G34	42	CK28
Formby Dr, G23	10	BM20
Forres Av, (Giff.) G46	64	BL42
Forres Gate, (Giff.) G46	64	BM43
Forres St, G23	11	BN20
off Tolsta St		
Forrester Ct, (Bishop.) G64	24	BV21
Forrestfield St, G21	39	BW28
Forrest Gate, (Udd.) G71	59	CR36
Forrest St, G40	39	BW32
Fortevoit Av, (Baill.) G69	42	CL32
Forteviot Pl, (Baill.) G69	42	CL32
Forth Av, Pais. PA2	47	AN36
Forth Pl, John. PA5	45	AE37
Forth Rd, (Bears.) G61	9	BE19
Forth St, G41	53	BP34
Forth St, Clyde. G81	7	AY20
Forth Wk, (Cumb.) G67	72	DB11
off Cumbernauld Shop Cen		
Forties Ct, (Thornlie.) G46	63	BH40
Forties Cres, (Thornlie.) G46	64	BJ40
Forties Gdns, (Thornlie.) G46	64	BJ40
Forties Way, (Thornlie.) G46	64	BJ40
Fortingall Av, G12	22	BL23
Fortingall Pl, G12	22	BL23
Fortrose St, G11	36	BK27
Foswell Dr, G15	8	BB16
Foswell Pl, G15	8	BB16
Fotheringay La, G41	52	BM35
Fotheringay Rd, G41	52	BM35
Foulis La, G13	21	BH23
Foulis St, G13	21	BH23
off Crow Rd		
Foundry La, (Barr.) G78	61	AY43
Foundry St, G21	24	BV25
Fountain Dr, (Inch.) Renf. PA4	18	AS24
Fountain St, G31	5	BU31
Fountainwell Av, G21	38	BT26
Fountainwell Dr, G21	38	BT27
Fountainwell Pl, G21	38	BT27
Fountainwell Rd, G21	38	BT27
Fountainwell Sq, G21	38	BU27
Fountainwell Ter, G21	38	BU27
Fourth Av, G33	26	CD24
Fourth Av, (Kirk.) G66	15	CF20
Fourth Av, Renf. PA4	33	AY27
Fourth Gdns, G41	52	BJ33
Fourth St, (Udd.) G71	59	CP36
Foxbar Cres, Pais. PA2	47	AN38
Foxbar Dr, G13	20	BD23
Foxbar Dr, Pais. PA2	47	AN38
Foxbar Rd, (Elder.) John. PA5	46	AM38
Foxbar Rd, Pais. PA2	47	AP38
Foxes Gro, (Lenz.) G66	15	CG16
Foxglove Pl, G53	62	BD42
Foxhills Pl, G23	11	BN20
Foxley St, G32	57	CE36
Fox St, G1	4	BR31
Foyers Ter, G21	25	BW25
Francis St, G5	53	BQ33
Frankfield St, G33	27	CG24
Frankfield St, G33	39	BZ27
Frankfort St, G41	53	BN36
Franklin St, G40	54	BV34
Fraser Av, (Ruther.) G73	55	BY38
Fraser Av, John. PA5	46	AJ35
Fraser St, (Camb.) G72	68	CA39
Frazer St, G40	39	BW32
Freeland Ct, G53	63	BE39
off Freeland Cres		
Freeland Cres, G53	62	BD39
Freeland Dr, G53	62	BD39
Freeland Dr, (Inch.) Renf. PA4	18	AS23
Freelands Ct, (Old Kil.) G60	6	AS16
off Freelands Rd		
Freelands Cres, (Old Kil.) G60	6	AS16
Freelands Pl, (Old Kil.) G60	6	AS17
off Freelands Rd		
Freelands Rd, (Old Kil.) G60	6	AS16

French St, G40 — 54 BV34
French St, Clyde. G81 — 6 AU18
French St, Renf. PA4 — 33 AX27
Freuchie St, G34 — 42 CK30
Friar Av, (Bishop.) G64 — 13 BX17
Friarscourt Av, G13 — 21 BF21
Friarscourt Rd, (Chry.) G69 — 16 CK20
Friars Pl, G13 — 21 BF21
off Knightswood Rd
Friarton Rd, G43 — 65 BP39
Friendship Way, Renf. PA4 — 33 AZ28
Fruin Pl, G22 — 24 BS25
Fruin Rd, G15 — 8 BB20
Fruin St, G22 — 24 BS25
Fulbar Av, Renf. PA4 — 19 AY25
Fulbar Ct, Renf. PA4 — 19 AZ25
off Fulbar Av
Fulbar Cres, Pais. PA2 — 47 AP35
Fulbar Gdns, Pais. PA2 — 47 AP35
Fulbar La, Renf. PA4 — 19 AZ25
Fulbar Rd, G51 — 35 BE30
Fulbar Rd, Pais. PA2 — 47 AP34
Fulbar St, Renf. PA4 — 19 AZ25
Fullarton Av, G32 — 56 CC35
Fullarton Dr, G32 — 56 CC36
Fullarton La, G32 — 56 CC35
Fullarton Rd, G32 — 56 CB37
Fullarton Rd, (Cumb.) G68 — 72 DA8
Fullerton St, Pais. PA3 — 32 AT30
Fullerton Ter, Pais. PA3 — 32 AU30
Fulmar Ct, (Bishop.) G64 — 24 BV21
Fulmar Pl, John. PA5 — 45 AE38
Fulton Cres, (Kilb.) John. PA10 — 44 AC34
Fulton St, G13 — 21 BF22
Fulwood Av, G13 — 20 BC22
Fulwood Av, (Linw.) Pais. PA3 — 30 AK31
Fulwood Pl, G13 — 20 BB22
Fyvie Av, G43 — 64 BK40

G
Gadie Av, Renf. PA4 — 34 BA27
Gadie St, G33 — 39 BZ29
Gadloch Av, (Kirk.) G66 — 15 CF19
Gadloch Gdns, (Kirk.) G66 — 15 CF19
Gadloch St, G22 — 24 BS23
Gadloch Vw, (Kirk.) G66 — 15 CF19
Gadsburn Ct, G21 — 25 BY23
Gadshill St, G21 — 38 BV28
Gailes Pk, (Both.) G71 — 71 CP43
Gailes Rd, (Cumb.) G68 — 72 DB8
Gailes St, G40 — 55 BX33
Gairbraid Av, G20 — 22 BL23
Gairbraid Ct, G20 — 22 BL23
Gairbraid Pl, G20 — 22 BM23
Gairbraid Ter, (Baill.) G69 — 43 CQ32
Gala Av, Renf. PA4 — 34 BA27
Gala St, G33 — 40 CA27
Galbraith Av, G51 — 35 BG29
off Burghead Dr
Galbraith Dr, G51 — 35 BF29
off Skipness Dr
Galbraith St, G51 — 35 BF29
off Moss Rd
Galdenoch St, G33 — 40 CD27
Gallacher Av, Pais. PA2 — 47 AQ36
Gallan Av, G23 — 11 BN20
Galloway Dr, (Ruther.) G73 — 67 BX42
Galloway St, G21 — 24 BV23
Gallowflat St, (Ruther.) G73 — 55 BX37
Gallowgate, G1 — 5 BT31
Gallowgate, G4 — 5 BU31
Gallowgate, G31 — 39 BW31
Gallowgate, G40 — 5 BU31
Gallowhill Av, (Lenz.) G66 — 15 CE15
Gallowhill Ct, Pais. PA3 — 33 AW29
off Montgomery Rd
Gallowhill Rd, (Kirk.) G66 — 15 CE15
Gallowhill Rd, Pais. PA3 — 33 AW31
Galston St, G53 — 62 BB39
Gamrie Dr, G53 — 50 BC38
Gamrie Gdns, G53 — 50 BC38
Gamrie Rd, G53 — 50 BC37
Gannochy Dr, (Bishop.) G64 — 13 BY20
Gantock Cres, G33 — 40 CD29
Gardenside Av, G32 — 56 CD37
Gardenside Av, (Udd.) G71 — 71 CN39
Gardenside Cres, G32 — 56 CD37
Gardenside Gro, G32 — 50 CD37
Gardenside Pl, G32 — 56 CD37
Gardenside St, (Udd.) G71 — 71 CN39

Gardner Gro, (Udd.) G71 — 59 CQ37
Gardner St, G11 — 36 BK27
Gardyne St, G34 — 42 CJ27
off Conisborough Rd
Gareloch Av, Pais. PA2 — 47 AQ35
Garfield St, G31 — 39 BW31
Garforth Rd, (Baill.) G69 — 57 CH33
Gargrave Av, (Baill.) G69 — 57 CH33
Garion Dr, G13 — 20 BD23
Garlieston Rd, G33 — 41 CH31
Garmouth Ct, G51 — 36 BJ29
Garmouth Gdns, G51 — 36 BJ29
off Garmouth St
Garmouth St, G51 — 35 BH29
Garnet Ct, G4 — 4 BQ28
off New City Rd
Garnethill St, G3 — 4 BQ28
Garnet St, G3 — 4 BQ28
Garngaber Av, (Lenz.) G66 — 15 CF16
Garngaber Ct, (Kirk.) G66 — 15 CG16
Garnie Av, Ersk. PA8 — 6 AT20
Garnie Cres, Ersk. PA8 — 6 AT20
Garnieland Rd, Ersk. PA8 — 18 AT21
Garnie La, Ersk. PA8 — 18 AT21
Garnie Oval, Ersk. PA8 — 6 AT20
Garnie Pl, Ersk. PA8 — 6 AT20
Garnkirk La, G33 — 27 CG24
Garnkirk St, G21 — 5 BU28
Garnock St, G21 — 38 BV27
Garrell Way, (Cumb.) G67 — 72 DA11
Garrioch Cres, G20 — 22 BM24
Garrioch Dr, G20 — 22 BM24
Garrioch Gate, G20 — 23 BN24
off Garrioch Rd
Garriochmill Rd, G20 — 23 BN25
Garriochmill Way, G20 — 23 BP26
off South Woodside Rd
Garrioch Quad, G20 — 22 BM24
Garrioch Rd, G20 — 22 BM25
Garrowhill Dr, (Baill.) G69 — 57 CH33
Garry Av, (Bears.) G61 — 10 BJ18
Garry Dr, Pais. PA2 — 47 AQ35
Garry St, G44 — 53 BQ38
Garscadden Rd, G15 — 8 BC20
Garscadden Rd S, G13 — 20 BC21
Garscadden Vw, Clyde. G81 — 7 AZ18
off Kirkoswald Dr
Garscube Cross, G4 — 37 BR27
Garscube Rd, G4 — 23 BQ26
Garscube Rd, G20 — 23 BQ26
Gartartan Rd, Pais. PA1 — 34 BB32
Gartconnell Dr, (Bears.) G61 — 9 BG15
Gartconnell Gdns, (Bears.) G61 — 9 BG15
Gartconnell Rd, (Bears.) G61 — 9 BG15
Gartcosh Rd, (Gart.) G69 — 43 CQ29
Gartcraig Path, G33 — 40 CC28
off Gartcraig Pl
Gartcraig Pl, G33 — 40 CB28
Gartcraig Rd, G33 — 40 CA29
Gartferry Av, (Chry.) G69 — 17 CP19
Gartferry Rd, (Mood.) G69 — 17 CN19
Gartferry St, G21 — 24 BV25
Garthamlock Rd, G33 — 41 CG28
Garthland Dr, G31 — 39 BW30
Garthland La, Pais. PA1 — 32 AV32
Garth St, G1 — 5 BS30
off Glassford St
Gartliston Ter, (Baill.) G69 — 43 CQ32
Gartloch Cotts, (Gart.) G69 — 29 CN26
Gartloch Cotts, (Muir.) G69 — 28 CK24
Gartloch Rd, G33 — 40 CB27
Gartloch Rd, G34 — 41 CE28
Gartloch Rd, (Gart.) G69 — 28 CL26
Gartly St, G44 — 65 BP41
off Clarkston Rd
Gartmore Gdns, (Udd.) G71 — 59 CN37
Gartmore La, (Mood.) G69 — 17 CQ19
Gartmore Rd, Pais. PA1 — 49 AX33
Gartmore Ter, (Camb.) G72 — 68 CA42
Gartness St, G31 — 39 BX30
Gartocher Dr, G32 — 41 CE32
Gartocher Rd, G32 — 41 CE32
Gartocher Ter, G32 — 41 CE32
Gartons Rd, G21 — 25 BY24
Gartshore Rd, (Kirk.) G66 — 17 CQ15
Gartshore Rd, (Cumb.) G68 — 17 CQ15
Garturk St, G42 — 53 BR35
Garvald Ct, G40 — 55 BW35
off Baltic St

Garvald St, G40 — 55 BX34
Garve Av, G44 — 65 BQ41
Garvel Cres, G33 — 41 CG31
Garvel Rd, G33 — 41 CG31
Garvock Dr, G43 — 64 BJ40
Gaskin Path, G33 — 27 CG24
Gask Pl, G13 — 20 BB21
Gas St, John. PA5 — 46 AJ34
Gatehouse St, G32 — 40 CD32
Gateside Av, (Camb.) G72 — 69 CF40
Gateside Cres, (Barr.) G78 — 61 AW44
Gateside Pl, (Kilb.) John. PA10 — 44 AC34
Gateside Rd, (Barr.) G78 — 60 AV44
Gateside St, G31 — 39 BX31
Gauldry Av, G52 — 51 BE34
Gauze St, Pais. PA1 — 32 AU32
Gavins Rd, Clyde. G81 — 7 AX16
Gavinton St, G44 — 65 BP40
Gear Ter, G40 — 55 BX35
Geary St, G23 — 10 BM20
off Torrin Rd
Geddes Rd, G21 — 25 BY22
Gelston St, G32 — 56 CD33
Generals Gate, (Udd.) G71 — 71 CN39
General Terminus Quay, G51 — 4 BP31
Gentle Row, Clyde. G81 — 6 AV15
George Av, Clyde. G81 — 7 AY18
George Ct, Pais. PA1 — 48 AT33
off George St
George Cres, Clyde. G81 — 7 AY18
George Gray St, (Ruther.) G73 — 55 BY37
George La, Pais. PA1 — 48 AU33
George Mann Ter, (Ruther.) G73 — 67 BW40
George Pl, Pais. PA1 — 48 AU33
George Reith Av, G12 — 21 BH24
George Sq, G2 — 5 BS30
George St, G1 — 5 BS30
George St, (Baill.) G69 — 58 CK33
George St, (Barr.) G78 — 61 AX42
George St, John. PA5 — 45 AH34
George St, Pais. PA1 — 48 AT33
Gertrude Pl, (Barr.) G78 — 61 AW43
Gibson Cres, John. PA5 — 45 AG35
Gibson Rd, Renf. PA4 — 33 AX29
Gibson St, G12 — 37 BN27
Gibson St, G40 — 5 BU31
Giffnock Pk Av, (Giff.) G46 — 64 BL41
Gifford Dr, G52 — 34 BC32
Gifford Wynd, Pais. PA2 — 47 AP35
Gilbertfield Path, G33 — 40 CD27
off Gilbertfield St
Gilbertfield Pl, G33 — 40 CD27
Gilbertfield Rd, (Camb.) G72 — 69 CE42
Gilbertfield St, G33 — 40 CD27
Gilbert St, G3 — 36 BL29
Gilfillan Way, Pais. PA2 — 47 AN37
off Spencer Dr
Gilhill St, G20 — 22 BM22
Gilia St, (Camb.) G72 — 68 CA39
Gillies La, (Baill.) G69 — 58 CL33
Gilmerton St, G32 — 56 CC33
Gilmour Av, Clyde. G81 — 7 AX16
Gilmour Cres, (Ruther.) G73 — 54 BV37
Gilmour Pl, G5 — 54 BS33
Gilmour Pl, Clyde. G81 — 7 AY17
Gilmour St, Pais. PA1 — 32 AU32
Girdons Way, (Udd.) G71 — 71 CN39
Girthon St, G32 — 57 CE33
Girvan St, G33 — 39 BZ28
Gladney Av, G13 — 20 BA21
Gladsmuir Rd, G52 — 34 BD31
Gladstone Av, (Barr.) G78 — 61 AX43
Gladstone Av, John. PA5 — 45 AF38
Gladstone St, G4 — 37 BQ27
Gladstone St, Clyde. G81 — 6 AV19
Glaive Rd, G13 — 9 BF20
Glamis Av, (Elder.) John. PA5 — 46 AK36
Glamis Gdns, (Bishop.) G64 — 13 BX17
Glamis Rd, G31 — 55 BZ33
Glanderston Av, (Barr.) G78 — 62 BA43
off Aurs Rd
Glanderston Ct, G13 — 20 BC21
Glanderston Dr, G13 — 20 BC22
Glasgow Airport, (Abbots.) Pais. PA3 — 32 AS27
Glasgow and Edinburgh Rd, (Baill.) G69 — 59 CP33
Glasgow Br, G1 — 4 BR31
Glasgow Br, G5 — 4 BR31

Name	Page	Grid
Glasgow Business Pk, (Baill.) G69	42	CK30
Glasgow Cross, G1	5	BT31
Glasgow E Investment Pk, G32	56	CB36
Glasgow Grn, G1	38	BT32
Glasgow Grn, G40	38	BT32
Glasgow Rd, G53	61	AZ41
Glasgow Rd, (Cumb.V.) G67	73	DD9
Glasgow Rd, (Baill.) G69	57	CH33
Glasgow Rd, (Udd.) G71	59	CN38
Glasgow Rd, (Blan.) G72	70	CL44
Glasgow Rd, (Camb.) G72	68	CA39
Glasgow Rd, (Turnlaw) G72	68	CB44
Glasgow Rd, (Ruther.) G73	54	BV35
Glasgow Rd, (Barr.) G78	61	AZ41
Glasgow Rd, Clyde. G81	19	AX21
Glasgow Rd, (Hardgate) Clyde. G81	7	AY15
Glasgow Rd, Pais. PA1	33	AW32
Glasgow Rd, Renf. PA4	20	BA26
Glasgow St, G12	23	BN26
Glassel Rd, G34	42	CM28
Glasserton Pl, G43	65	BP40
Glasserton Rd, G43	65	BP40
Glassford St, G1	5	BS30
Glaudhall Av, (Gart.) G69	29	CN22
Glebe, The, (Both.) G71	71	CR43
Glebe Av, (Both.) G71	71	CR43
Glebe Ct, G4	5	BT29
Glebe Hollow, (Both.) G71	71	CR43
Glebe Pl, (Camb.) G72	68	CD40
Glebe Pl, (Ruther.) G73	54	BV37
Glebe St, G4	5	BT28
Glebe St, Renf. PA4	19	AZ26
Glebe Wynd, (Both.) G71	71	CR43
Gleddoch Rd, G52	34	BA31
Glenacre Cres, (Udd.) G71	59	CN37
Glenacre Dr, G45	66	BT42
Glenacre Gro, G45	66	BU41
Glenacre Rd, (Cumb.) G67	72	DB13
Glenacre St, G45	66	BT42
Glenacre Ter, G45	66	BT42
Glenallan Way, Pais. PA2	46	AM38
Glenalmond Rd, (Ruther.) G73	67	BZ42
off Fennsbank Av		
Glenalmond St, G32	56	CC33
Glenapp Av, Pais. PA2	49	AX36
Glenapp Pl, (Mood.) G69	17	CP18
off Whithorn Cres		
Glenapp Rd, Pais. PA2	49	AX36
Glenapp St, G41	53	BP34
Glenarklet Dr, Pais. PA2	49	AW36
Glenartney Rd, (Chry.) G69	16	CL20
Glenashdale Way, Pais. PA2	49	AW36
Glen Av, G32	40	CD31
Glen Av, (Chry.) G69	17	CP19
Glenavon Rd, G20	22	BM22
Glenbank Av, (Lenz.) G66	15	CE17
Glenbank Ct, (Thornlie.) G46	63	BH43
off Glenbank Dr		
Glenbank Dr, (Thornlie.) G46	63	BH43
Glenbank Rd, (Lenz.) G66	15	CE17
Glenbarr St, G21	38	BV28
Glenbervie Cres, (Cumb.) G68	72	DB9
off Lansdowne Dr		
Glenbervie Pl, G23	11	BN20
off Hollinwell Rd		
Glenboig Rd, (Gart.) G69	29	CR21
Glenbrittle Dr, Pais. PA2	49	AW36
Glenbrittle Way, Pais. PA2	49	AW36
Glenbuck Av, G33	26	CB23
Glenbuck Dr, G33	26	CB23
Glenburn Av, (Baill.) G69	42	CL32
Glenburn Av, (Chry.) G69	17	CP19
Glenburn Av, (Camb.) G72	67	BZ40
Glenburn Cres, Pais. PA2	48	AT37
Glenburn Gdns, (Bishop.) G64	12	BV19
Glenburnie Pl, G34	42	CJ30
Glenburn La, G20	23	BN22
off Thornton St		
Glenburn Rd, (Giff.) G46	64	BK44
Glenburn Rd, (Bears.) G61	9	BG16
Glenburn Rd, Pais. PA2	47	AR37
Glenburn St, G20	23	BN22
Glenburn Wk, (Baill.) G69	42	CL32
off Glenburn Av		
Glencairn Dr, Pais. PA3	33	AX29
off Montgomery Rd		
Glencairn Dr, G41	52	BM35
Glencairn Dr, (Chry.) G69	17	CN19
Glencairn Dr, (Ruther.) G73	54	BV37
Glencairn Gdns, G41	53	BN35
Glencairn Gdns, (Camb.) G72	69	CF40
Glencairn La, G41	53	BP35
Glencairn Path, G32	41	CE31
off Hallhill Rd		
Glencairn Rd, (Cumb.) G67	73	DE11
Glencairn Rd, Pais. PA3	33	AW29
Glencally Av, Pais. PA2	49	AX36
Glencart Gro, (Millik.) John. PA10	45	AE36
off Milliken Pk Rd		
Glenclora Dr, Pais. PA2	49	AW36
Glen Clova Dr, (Cumb.) G68	72	CY9
Glencloy St, G20	22	BL22
Glen Clunie Dr, G53	63	BE41
Glen Clunie Pl, G53	63	BE41
off Glen Clunie Dr		
Glencoats Dr, Pais. PA3	31	AQ32
Glencoe Pl, G13	21	BG22
Glencoe Rd, (Ruther.) G73	67	BZ42
Glencoe St, G13	21	BH22
Glen Cona Dr, G53	63	BE40
Glencorse Rd, Pais. PA2	48	AS35
Glencorse St, G32	40	CA30
Glen Cres, G13	20	BA22
Glencroft Av, (Udd.) G71	59	CN37
Glencroft Rd, G44	66	BT40
Glencryan Rd, (Cumb.) G67	73	DD12
Glendale Cres, (Bishop.) G64	25	BY21
Glendale Dr, (Bishop.) G64	25	BY21
Glendale Pl, G31	39	BX31
Glendale Pl, (Bishop.) G64	25	BY22
Glendale St, G31	39	BX31
Glendaruel Av, (Bears.) G61	10	BK17
Glendaruel Rd, (Ruther.) G73	68	CA43
Glendarvel Gdns, G22	24	BT25
Glendee Gdns, Renf. PA4	33	AZ27
Glendee Rd, Renf. PA4	33	AZ27
Glen Dene Way, G53	63	BE41
Glendevon Pl, Clyde. G81	6	AV18
Glendevon Sq, G33	40	CD27
Glen Dewar Pl, G53	63	BE41
Glendinning Rd, G13	9	BG20
Glendore St, G14	35	BG27
Glen Douglas Dr, (Cumb.) G68	72	CY9
Glendower Way, Pais. PA2	47	AN37
Glenduffhill Rd, (Baill.) G69	41	CH32
Gleneagles Av, (Cumb.) G68	73	DC8
Gleneagles Dr, (Bishop.) G64	13	BW18
Gleneagles Gdns, (Bishop.) G64	12	BV18
Gleneagles La N, G14	21	BE25
Gleneagles La S, G14	21	BE25
Gleneagles Pk, (Both.) G71	71	CP43
Glenelg Quad, G34	42	CM28
Glen Esk Cres, G53	63	BE41
Glen Esk Dr, G53	63	BE41
Glen Esk Pl, G53	63	BE41
off Kennishead Rd		
Glen Etive Pl, (Ruther.) G73	68	CA43
Glenfarg Cres, (Bears.) G61	10	BK17
Glenfarg Rd, (Ruther.) G73	67	BX41
Glenfarg St, G20	37	BQ27
Glenfield Av, Pais. PA2	48	AT38
Glenfield Cres, Pais. PA2	60	AT39
Glenfield Gdns, Pais. PA2	60	AT39
Glenfield Gra, Pais. PA2	60	AU39
Glenfield Gro, Pais. PA2	60	AT39
Glenfield Rd, Pais. PA2	48	AS38
Glenfinnan Dr, G20	22	BM23
Glenfinnan Dr, (Bears.) G61	10	BK18
Glenfinnan Pl, G20	22	BM23
off Glenfinnan Rd		
Glenfinnan Rd, G20	22	BM23
Glenfruin Cres, Pais. PA2	49	AX36
Glen Gdns, (Elder.) John. PA5	46	AL34
Glengarry Dr, G52	35	BE32
Glengavel Cres, G33	26	CB23
Glengyre St, G34	42	CL28
Glenhead Cres, G22	24	BS23
Glenhead Rd, (Lenz.) G66	15	CE17
Glenhead Rd, Clyde. G81	6	AV16
Glenhead St, G22	24	BS23
Glenholme Av, Pais. PA2	47	AR36
off Corsebar Rd		
Glenhove Rd, (Cumb.) G67	73	DC11
Gleniffer Av, G13	20	BC23
Gleniffer Ct, Pais. PA2	47	AR38
Gleniffer Cres, (Elder.) John. PA5	46	AL36
Gleniffer Dr, (Barr.) G78	61	AW40
Gleniffer Rd, Pais. PA2	47	AR38
Gleniffer Rd, Renf. PA4	33	AX29
Gleniffer Vw, Clyde. G81	7	AZ18
off Kirkoswald Dr		
Glenisla Av, (Mood.) G69	17	CQ17
Glenisla St, G31	55	BZ34
Glenkirk Dr, G15	8	BD19
Glen Kyle Dr, G53	63	BE41
Glen La, Pais. PA3	32	AU32
Glenlee Cres, G52	50	BB34
Glen Livet Pl, G53	63	BE41
off Glen Moriston Rd		
Glenlora Dr, G53	50	BC38
Glenlora Ter, G53	50	BD38
Glen Loy Pl, G53	63	BE41
Glenluce Dr, G32	57	CF34
Glenluce Gdns, (Mood.) G69	17	CQ19
off Brady Cres		
Glenlui Av, (Ruther.) G73	67	BX40
Glen Luss Pl, G53	63	BE41
Glen Lyon Pl, (Ruther.) G73	67	BY42
Glenmalloch Pl, (Elder.) John. PA5	46	AL34
Glenmanor Av, (Mood.) G69	17	CN19
Glenmanor Rd, (Chry.) G69	17	CN19
Glenmavis St, G4	4	BR28
Glenmore Av, G42	54	BU37
Glen Moriston Rd, G53	63	BE41
Glenmuir Dr, G53	62	BD40
Glen Nevis Pl, (Ruther.) G73	67	BY43
Glen Ogle St, G32	57	CF33
Glen Orchy Dr, G53	63	BE41
Glen Orchy Gro, G53	63	BE41
Glen Orchy Pl, G53	63	BF41
off Glen Orchy Dr		
Glen Orchy Way, G53	63	BE42
Glenpark Av, (Thornlie.) G46	63	BH43
Glenpark Gdns, (Camb.) G72	56	CA38
off Glenpark Ter		
Glenpark Rd, G31	39	BX31
Glenpark St, G31	39	BX31
Glenpark Ter, (Camb.) G72	56	CA38
Glenpatrick Bldgs, (Elder.) John. PA5	46	AL36
Glenpatrick Rd, (Elder.) John. PA5	46	AM35
Glenraith Path, G33	26	CD26
Glenraith Rd, G33	26	CD26
Glenraith Sq, G33	26	CD26
Glenraith Wk, G33	26	CD26
Glen Rd, G32	40	CD30
Glen Sannox Gro, (Cumb.) G68	72	CY9
Glen Sannox Ln, (Cumb.) G68	72	CY9
Glen Sannox Way, (Cumb.) G68	72	CY9
Glen Sannox Wynd, (Cumb.) G68	72	CY9
Glen Sax Dr, Renf. PA4	34	BA28
Glenshee Ct, G31	55	BZ34
Glenshee Gdns, G31	56	CA34
Glenshee St, G31	55	BZ33
Glenshiel Av, Pais. PA2	49	AW36
Glenshira Av, Pais. PA2	49	AW36
Glenside Av, G53	50	BD35
Glenside Dr, (Ruther.) G73	67	BZ39
Glenspean Pl, G43	52	BM38
off Glenspean St		
Glenspean St, G43	52	BL39
Glen St, (Camb.) G72	69	CF41
Glen St, (Barr.) G78	61	AY42
Glen St, Pais. PA3	32	AT32
Glentanar Dr, (Mood.) G69	17	CQ19
Glentanar Pl, G22	24	BS21
Glentanar Rd, G22	23	BR21
Glentarbert Rd, (Ruther.) G73	67	BZ42
Glentrool Gdns, G22	24	BS25
Glentrool Gdns, (Mood.) G69	17	CQ18
Glenturret St, G32	56	CC33
Glentyan Av, (Kilb.) John. PA10	44	AC33
Glentyan Dr, G53	50	BC38
Glentyan Pl, G53	50	BC38
Glen Vw, (Cumb.) G67	73	DE10
Glenview Cres, (Mood.) G69	17	CP18
Glenview Pl, (Blan.) G72	70	CM44
Glenville Av, (Giff.) G46	64	BK42
Glenwood Business Pk, G45	66	BU42
Glenwood Ct, (Kirk.) G66	14	CC16
Glenwood Dr, (Thornlie.) G46	63	BH43

Glenwood Gdns, (Kirk.) G66   14   CC16
Glenwood Path, G45   66   BU42
Glenwood Pl, G45   66   BU42
Glenwood Pl, (Kirk.) G66   14   CC16
Glenwood Rd, (Kirk.) G66   14   CC16
Gloucester Av, (Ruther.) G73   67   BZ40
Gloucester St, G5   37   BQ32
Gockston Rd, Pais. PA3   32   AT30
Gogar Pl, G33   40   CA29
Gogar St, G33   40   CA29
Goldberry Av, G14   20   BD24
Goldie Rd, (Udd.) G71   71   CQ41
Golf Ct, G44   65   BN43
Golf Dr, G15   8   BB20
Golf Dr, Pais. PA1   49   AY33
Golfhill Dr, G31   39   BW29
Golfhill Ter, G31   38   BV29
  off Firpark St
Golf Rd, (Ruther.) G73   67   BX41
Golf Vw, (Bears.) G61   8   BD16
Golf Vw, Clyde. G81   6   AV17
Golspie St, G51   36   BJ29
Goosedubbs, G1   5   BS31
  off Stockwell St
Gopher Av, (Udd.) G71   59   CR37
Gorbals Cross, G5   38   BS32
Gorbals La, G5   4   BR31
  off Oxford St
Gorbals St, G5   53   BR33
Gordon Av, G44   65   BN43
Gordon Av, G52   34   BA29
Gordon Av, (Baill.) G69   41   CH32
Gordon Dr, G44   65   BN42
Gordon La, G1   4   BR30
  off Mitchell St
Gordon Rd, G44   65   BN43
Gordon St, G1   4   BR30
Gordon St, Pais. PA1   48   AU33
Gordon Ter, (Blan.) G72   70   CL43
Gorebridge St, G32   40   CA30
Gorget Av, G13   9   BE20
Gorget Pl, G13   9   BE20
Gorget Quad, G13   8   BD20
Gorse Dr, (Barr.) G78   61   AX41
Gorse Pl, (Udd.) G71   59   CR37
Gorsewood, (Bishop.) G64   12   BU20
Gorstan Pl, G20   22   BL24
  off Wyndford Rd
Gorstan St, G23   22   BM21
Gosford La, G14   20   BC25
Goudie St, Pais. PA3   32   AS30
Gough St, G33   39   BZ29
Gourlay Path, G21   24   BT26
  off Endrick St
Gourlay St, G21   24   BT26
Gourock St, G5   53   BQ33
  off Eglinton St
Govan Cross, G51   36   BJ29
  off Govan Rd
Govan Cross Shop Cen, G51   36   BJ29
Govanhill St, G42   53   BR35
Govan Rd, G51   36   BL31
Gowanbank Gdns, John. PA5   45   AG35
  off Floors St
Gowan Brae, (Kirk.) G66   15   CE15
  off Marguerite Av
Gowanlea Av, G15   8   BC20
Gowanlea Dr, (Giff.) G46   64   BM41
Gowanlea Ter, (Udd.) G71   59   CR38
Gower La, G51   36   BM32
  off North Gower St
Gower St, G41   52   BL33
Gower St, G51   52   BL33
Gower Ter, G41   36   BL32
Goyle Av, G15   9   BE18
Grace Av, (Baill.) G69   43   CP32
Grace St, G3   4   BP30
Graffham Av, (Giff.) G46   64   BM42
Grafton Pl, G1   5   BS29
Graham Av, (Camb.) G72   69   CF40
Graham Av, Clyde. G81   7   AX18
Graham Sq, G31   38   BV31
Grahamston Ct, Pais. PA2   49   AY37
Grahamston Cres, Pais. PA2   49   AY37
Grahamston Pk, (Barr.) G78   61   AX40
Grahamston Pl, Pais. PA2   49   AY37
Grahamston Rd, (Barr.) G78   61   AX39
Grahamston Rd, Pais. PA2   61   AX39
Graham St, (Barr.) G78   61   AX42
Graham St, John. PA5   45   AG35

Graham Ter, (Bishop.) G64   25   BX22
Graignestock Pl, G40   38   BU32
  off London Rd
Graignestock St, G40   38   BU32
Grainger Rd, (Bishop.) G64   13   BZ20
Grampian Av, Pais. PA2   48   AT33
Grampian Cres, G32   56   CD33
Grampian Pl, G32   56   CD33
Grampian St, G32   56   CD33
Grampian Way, (Barr.) G78   61   AY44
Granby La, G12   22   BM26
Grandtully Dr, G12   22   BL23
Grange Gdns, (Both.) G71   71   CR44
  off Blairston Av
Grangeneuk Gdns, (Cumb.)   72   CY12
  G68
Grange Rd, G42   53   BQ37
Grange Rd, (Bears.) G61   9   BH16
Gran St, Clyde. G81   20   BA21
Grantlea Gro, G32   57   CF33
Grantlea Ter, G32   57   CF33
Grantley Gdns, G41   52   BM37
Grantley St, G41   52   BM37
Granton St, G5   54   BU35
Grants Av, Pais. PA2   48   AS36
Grants Cres, Pais. PA2   48   AT37
Grants Pl, Pais. PA2   48   AS37
Grant St, G3   4   BP28
Grants Way, Pais. PA2   48   AS36
Granville St, G3   4   BP29
Granville St, Clyde. G81   7   AX18
Gray Dr, (Bears.) G61   9   BH18
Gray's Rd, (Udd.) G71   71   CR40
Gray St, G3   37   BN28
Great Dovehill, G1   5   BT31
Great George St, G12   22   BM26
Great Hamilton St, Pais. PA2   48   AU35
Great Kelvin La, G12   37   BN27
  off Glasgow St
Great Western Retail Pk, G15   8   BB20
Great Western Rd, G4   23   BN26
Great Western Rd, G12   22   BK25
Great Western Rd, G13   8   BB20
Great Western Rd, G15   8   BB20
Great Western Ter, G12   22   BL25
Great Western Ter La, G12   22   BL25
Green, The, G40   38   BU32
Greenacres Ct, G53   63   BE41
Greenacres Dr, G53   63   BE41
Greenacres Way, G53   63   BE41
Greenan Av, G42   54   BU38
Greenbank Dr, Pais. PA2   48   AT38
Greenbank Rd, (Cumb.) G68   72   CY11
Greenbank St, (Ruther.) G73   55   BW37
Greendyke St, G1   5   BT31
Greenend Av, John. PA5   45   AF36
Greenend Pl, G32   41   CE30
Greenfarm Rd, (Linw.) Pais.   30   AK31
  PA3
Greenfaulds Cres, (Cumb.) G67   73   DC13
Greenfield Av, G32   40   CD31
Greenfield Pl, G32   40   CD31
Greenfield Rd, G32   41   CE30
Greenfield St, G51   35   BH30
Greengairs Av, G51   35   BF29
Greenhead Rd, (Bears.) G61   9   BH17
Greenhead Rd, (Inch.) Renf.   18   AS22
  PA4
Greenhead St, G40   54   BU33
Greenhill, (Bishop.) G64   25   BY21
Greenhill Av, (Giff.) G46   64   BK44
Greenhill Av, (Gart.) G69   29   CN22
Greenhill Business Pk, Pais.   32   AS31
  PA3
Greenhill Ct, (Ruther.) G73   55   BW37
Greenhill Cres, (Elder.) John.   46   AM35
  PA5
Greenhill Cres, (Linw.) Pais.   30   AK31
  PA3
Greenhill Dr, (Linw.) Pais. PA3   30   AL31
Greenhill Rd, (Ruther.) G73   55   BW37
Greenhill Rd, Pais. PA3   32   AS31
Greenhill St, (Ruther.) G73   55   BW38
Greenholm Av, (Udd.) G71   59   CN38
Greenholme St, G44   65   BQ39
Greenknowe Rd, G43   64   BK39
Greenlaw Av, Pais. PA1   33   AW31
Greenlaw Cres, Pais. PA1   33   AW31
Greenlaw Dr, Pais. PA1   33   AW32
Greenlaw Rd, G14   19   AZ23

Greenlea Rd, (Chry.) G69   28   CK21
Greenlea St, G13   21   BG23
Greenlees Gdns, (Camb.) G72   68   CB42
Greenlees Pk, (Camb.) G72   68   CC42
Greenlees Rd, (Camb.) G72   68   CC40
Greenloan Av, G51   35   BF29
Greenlodge Ter, G40   54   BU33
  off Greenhead St
Greenmount, G22   23   BQ22
Greenock Av, G44   65   BR40
Greenock Rd, Pais. PA3   32   AS29
Green Pl, (Both.) G71   71   CR43
Greenrig, (Udd.) G71   71   CP39
Greenrigg Rd, (Cumb.) G67   73   DC12
Greenrig St, G33   25   BZ26
Greenrig St, (Udd.) G71   71   CP39
Green Rd, (Ruther.) G73   55   BW37
Green Rd, Pais. PA2   47   AP34
Greenshields Rd, (Baill.) G69   42   CK32
Greenside Cres, G33   26   CA26
Greenside St, G33   26   CA26
Green St, G40   38   BU32
Green St, (Both.) G71   71   CR43
Green St, Clyde. G81   7   AW18
Greentree Dr, (Baill.) G69   57   CH34
Greenview St, G43   52   BL37
Greenways Av, Pais. PA2   47   AQ35
Greenways Ct, Pais. PA2   47   AQ35
Greenwood Av, (Chry.) G69   17   CP19
Greenwood Av, (Camb.) G72   69   CG39
Greenwood Dr, (Bears.) G61   10   BJ17
Greenwood Dr, John. PA5   45   AG37
Greenwood Quad, Clyde. G81   7   AZ20
Greer Quad, Clyde. G81   7   AX17
Grenville Dr, (Camb.) G72   68   CB41
Gretna St, G40   55   BX33
Greyfriars Rd, (Udd.) G71   58   CL37
Greyfriars St, G32   40   CB30
Greystone Av, (Ruther.) G73   67   BY39
Greywood St, G13   21   BG22
Grier Path, G31   39   BZ32
  off Crail St
Grierson La, G33   39   BZ29
  off Lomax St
Grierson St, G33   39   BZ29
Grieve Cft, (Both.) G71   71   CP44
Grieve Rd, (Cumb.) G67   73   DC10
Griffin Av, Pais. PA1   31   AN32
Griqua Ter, (Both.) G71   71   CR43
Grogarry Rd, G15   8   BC17
Grosvenor Cres, G12   22   BM26
Grosvenor Cres La, G12   22   BM26
  off Byres Rd
Grosvenor La, G12   22   BM26
Grosvenor Ter, G12   22   BM26
Grove, The, (Kilb.) John. PA10   44   AC33
Groveburn Av, (Thornlie.) G46   64   BJ41
Grove Pk, (Lenz.) G66   15   CF17
Grovepark Ct, G20   37   BQ27
Grovepark Gdns, G20   37   BQ27
Grovepark Pl, G20   23   BQ26
Grovepark St, G20   23   BQ26
Groves, The, (Bishop.) G64   25   BY22
  off Woodhill Gro
Grudie St, G34   42   CJ29
Gryffe Av, Renf. PA4   19   AX24
Gryffe Cres, Pais. PA2   47   AP35
Gryffe St, G44   53   BQ38
Guildford St, G33   41   CE28
Gullane St, G11   36   BK28
  off Anderson St
Guthrie Dr, (Udd.) G71   59   CQ36
Guthrie St, G20   22   BM23

H
Haberlea Av, G53   63   BE42
Haberlea Gdns, G53   63   BE43
  off Haberlea Av
Haddow Gro, (Udd.) G71   59   CQ37
Hagg Cres, John. PA5   45   AG34
Hagg Pl, John. PA5   45   AG34
Hagg Rd, John. PA5   45   AG35
Haggs Rd, G41   52   BL36
Haggswood Av, G41   52   BL35
Haghill Rd, G31   39   BY31
Haig Dr, (Baill.) G69   57   CH33
Haig St, G21   24   BV25
Hailes Av, G32   41   CF32
Haining, The, Renf. PA4   33   AZ27
Haining Rd, Renf. PA4   19   AY26

Name		
Hairst St, Renf. PA4	19	AZ25
Halbeath Av, G15	8	BB18
Halbert St, G41	53	BN36
Haldane La, G14	21	BF26
off Victoria Park St		
Haldane St, G14	21	BF26
Halgreen Av, G15	8	BA19
Halifax Way, Renf. PA4	33	AY28
off Britannia Way		
Hallbrae St, G33	40	CA27
Halley Dr, G13	20	BA23
Halley Pl, G13	20	BA23
Halley Sq, G13	20	BA23
Halley St, G13	20	BA22
Hallforest St, G33	40	CD27
off Gartloch Rd		
Hallhill Cres, G33	41	CG31
Hallhill Rd, G32	41	CE31
Hallhill Rd, G33	41	CG31
Hallhill Rd, John. PA5	45	AE38
Halliburton Cres, G34	42	CJ30
off Ware Rd		
Halliburton Rd, G34	41	CH30
Halliburton Ter, G34	42	CJ30
Hallidale Cres, Renf. PA4	34	BB27
Hallrule Dr, G52	35	BE32
Hallside Av, (Camb.) G72	69	CG40
Hallside Boul, (Camb.) G72	69	CH42
Hallside Cres, (Camb.) G72	69	CG40
Hallside Dr, (Camb.) G72	69	CG40
Hallside Pl, G5	54	BS33
Hallside Rd, (Camb.) G72	69	CH41
Hall St, Clyde. G81	7	AW20
Hallydown Dr, G13	21	BE24
Halton Gdns, (Baill.) G69	57	CH33
Hamilton Av, G41	52	BM34
Hamilton Ct, Pais. PA2	48	AU35
Hamilton Cres, (Camb.) G72	69	CE41
Hamilton Cres, Renf. PA4	19	AZ24
Hamilton Dr, G12	23	BN26
Hamilton Dr, (Giff.) G46	64	BM43
Hamilton Dr, (Both.) G71	71	CR44
Hamilton Dr, (Camb.) G72	68	CB40
Hamiltonhill Cres, G22	23	BR25
off Hamiltonhill Rd		
Hamiltonhill Rd, G22	23	BR26
Hamilton Pk Av, G12	23	BN26
Hamilton Rd, G32	57	CF35
Hamilton Rd, (Both.) G71	71	CR44
Hamilton Rd, (Udd.) G71	58	CJ35
Hamilton Rd, (Camb.) G72	68	CD40
Hamilton Rd, (Ruther.) G73	55	BX37
Hamilton St, G42	54	BS36
Hamilton St, Clyde. G81	19	AZ22
Hamilton St, Pais. PA3	32	AV31
Hamilton Ter, Clyde. G81	19	AZ22
Hamilton Vw, (Udd.) G71	59	CQ38
Hampden Dr, G42	53	BR38
Hampden La, G42	53	BR37
Hampden Pk, G42	54	BS38
Hampden Ter, G42	53	BR37
Hampden Way, Renf. PA4	33	AZ28
off Lewis Av		
Handel Pl, G5	54	BS33
Hangingshaw Pl, G42	54	BS37
Hanover Cl, G42	53	BQ37
off Battlefield Gdns		
Hanover Ct, Pais. PA1	33	AW32
off Kelburne Gdns		
Hanover Gdns, Pais. PA1	48	AS33
Hanover St, G1	5	BS30
Hanson St, G31	38	BV29
Hapland Av, G53	51	BE35
Hapland Rd, G53	51	BE35
Harbour La, Pais. PA3	32	AU32
Harbour Rd, Pais. PA3	32	AU31
Harburn Pl, G23	11	BN19
Harbury Pl, G14	20	BB23
Harcourt Dr, G31	39	BX29
Hardgate Dr, G51	35	BE29
Hardgate Gdns, G51	35	BE29
Hardgate Path, G51	35	BE29
off Hardgate Dr		
Hardgate Pl, G51	35	BE29
off Hardgate Dr		
Hardgate Rd, G51	35	BE29
Hardie Av, (Ruther.) G73	55	BY37
Hardridge Pl, G52	51	BG35
Hardridge Rd, G52	51	BF35
Harefield Dr, G14	20	BD24
Harelaw Av, G44	65	BP41
Harelaw Av, (Barr.) G78	61	AZ44
Harelaw Cres, Pais. PA2	48	AS38
Harfield Dr, G32	41	CG31
Harfield Gdns, G32	41	CG31
Harhill St, G51	35	BH30
Harland Cotts, G14	21	BE26
off South St		
Harland St, G14	21	BE26
Harlaw Gdns, (Bishop.) G64	13	BZ19
Harley St, G51	36	BL32
Harmetray St, G22	24	BT23
Harmony Ct, G52	36	BJ30
Harmony Pl, G51	36	BJ30
Harmony Row, G51	36	BJ30
Harmony Sq, G51	36	BJ30
off Harmony Row		
Harmsworth St, G11	35	BG27
Harport St, (Thornlie.) G46	63	BG40
Harriet Pl, G43	64	BK39
Harriet St, (Ruther.) G73	55	BW37
Harris Gdns, (Old Kil.) G60	6	AS16
Harrison Dr, G51	36	BK31
off Copland Rd		
Harris Rd, G23	10	BM20
Harrow Ct, G15	8	BB18
off Linkwood Dr		
Harrow Pl, G15	8	BB18
Hartfield Ter, Pais. PA2	48	AV35
Hartlaw Cres, G52	34	BC31
Hartree Av, G13	20	BA21
Hartstone Pl, G53	50	BD38
Hartstone Rd, G53	50	BD38
Hartstone Ter, G53	50	BD38
Hart St, G31	40	CA32
Hart St, (Linw.) Pais. PA3	30	AK32
Harvey St, G4	38	BS27
Harvie St, G51	36	BM31
Harwood Gdns, (Mood.) G69	17	CQ18
off Dryburgh Wk		
Harwood St, G32	40	CA30
Hastie St, G3	36	BM28
Hatfield Dr, G12	21	BH24
Hathaway Dr, (Giff.) G46	64	BK43
Hathaway La, G20	23	BN24
Hathaway St, G20	23	BN24
Hathersage Av, (Baill.) G69	42	CK32
Hathersage Dr, (Baill.) G69	42	CK32
Hathersage Gdns, (Baill.) G69	42	CK32
Hatton Dr, G52	50	BC33
Hatton Gdns, G52	50	BC33
Hatton Path, G52	50	BC33
off Haughburn Rd		
Haugh Rd, G3	36	BM29
Havelock La, G11	36	BL27
Havelock St, G11	36	BL27
Hawick Av, Pais. PA2	47	AR36
Hawick St, G13	20	BA22
Hawkhead Av, Pais. PA2	49	AX35
Hawkhead Rd, Pais. PA1	49	AX33
Hawkhead Rd, Pais. PA2	49	AY36
Hawthorn Av, (Bishop.) G64	25	BX21
Hawthorn Av, (Lenz.) G66	15	CE16
Hawthorn Av, Ersk. PA8	18	AU21
Hawthorn Av, John. PA5	46	AJ36
Hawthorn Cres, Ersk. PA8	18	AU21
Hawthornden Gdns, G23	11	BN19
Hawthorn Gdns, (Camb.) G72	69	CG41
Hawthorn Quad, G22	24	BS24
Hawthorn Rd, Ersk. PA8	18	AU21
Hawthorn St, G22	24	BS24
Hawthorn St, Clyde. G81	7	AW17
Hawthorn Ter, (Udd.) G71	59	CR38
Hawthorn Wk, (Camb.) G72	67	BZ40
Hawthorn Way, Ersk. PA8	18	AU21
Hayburn Ct, G11	36	BK27
off Hayburn St		
Hayburn Cres, G11	22	BJ26
Hayburn Gate, G11	36	BK27
Hayburn La, G11	22	BJ26
Hayburn Pl, G11	36	BK27
off Hayburn Wk		
Hayburn St, G11	36	BK28
Hay Dr, John. PA5	46	AK34
Hayfield Ct, G5	54	BT33
Hayfield St, G5	54	BT33
Hayle Gdns, (Chry.) G69	17	CP18
Haylynn St, G14	35	BG27
Haymarket St, G32	40	CA30
Haystack Pl, (Lenz.) G66	15	CF17
Hayston Cres, G22	23	BR24
Hayston Rd, (Cumb.) G68	72	DA9
Hayston St, G22	23	BR24
Haywood St, G22	23	BR23
Hazel Av, G44	65	BP41
Hazel Av, (Lenz.) G66	15	CF15
Hazel Av, John. PA5	46	AJ36
Hazel Av La, G44	65	BP41
off Hazel Av		
Hazel Dene, (Bishop.) G64	13	BX20
Hazelden Gdns, G44	65	BN41
Hazel Gro, (Kirk.) G66	15	CF15
Hazellea Dr, (Giff.) G46	64	BM41
Hazel Rd, (Cumb.) G67	73	DF10
Hazel Ter, (Udd.) G71	59	CR38
Hazelwood Av, Pais. PA2	47	AN38
Hazelwood Gdns, (Ruther.) G73	67	BY41
Hazelwood Rd, G41	52	BL33
Hazlitt Gdns, G20	23	BQ23
off Bilsland Dr		
Hazlitt Pl, G20	23	BR23
off Hazlitt St		
Hazlitt St, G20	23	BR23
Heath Av, (Bishop.) G64	25	BX21
Heath Av, (Lenz.) G66	15	CE17
Heathcliff Av, (Blan.) G72	70	CL44
Heathcot Av, G15	8	BA19
Heathcot Pl, G15	7	AZ19
off Heathcot Av		
Heather Av, (Barr.) G78	61	AW40
Heatherbrae, (Bishop.) G64	12	BU20
Heather Dr, (Kirk.) G66	14	CC16
Heather Gdns, (Kirk.) G66	14	CC17
Heather Pl, (Kirk.) G66	14	CC16
Heather Pl, John. PA5	46	AJ35
Heatheryknowe Rd, (Baill.) G69	43	CN29
Heathfield Av, (Mood.) G69	17	CQ19
Heathfield St, G33	41	CE29
Heathside Rd, (Giff.) G46	64	BM42
Heathwood Dr, (Thornlie.) G46	64	BJ42
Hecla Av, G15	8	BB18
Hecla Pl, G15	8	BB18
Hecla Sq, G15	8	BB19
Hector Rd, G41	52	BM37
Heddle Pl, G2	4	BQ30
off Cadogan St		
Helena Ter, Clyde. G81	7	AW15
off Chapel Rd		
Helensburgh Dr, G13	21	BF23
Helenslea, (Camb.) G72	69	CF41
Helen St, G51	36	BJ30
Helen St, G52	35	BH32
Helenvale Ct, G31	55	BZ33
Helenvale St, G31	55	BY33
Helmsdale Av, (Blan.) G72	70	CL42
Helmsdale Ct, (Camb.) G72	69	CF40
Helmsdale Dr, Pais. PA2	47	AP35
Hemlock St, G13	21	BG22
Henderland Dr, (Bears.) G61	9	BG19
Henderland Rd, (Bears.) G61	9	BG19
Henderson Av, (Camb.) G72	69	CF39
Henderson St, G20	23	BP26
Henderson St, Clyde. G81	20	BA21
Henderson St, Pais. PA1	32	AT32
Henrietta St, G14	21	BE26
Henry St, (Barr.) G78	61	AX42
Hepburn Rd, G52	34	BD30
Herald Av, G13	9	BF20
Herald Way, Renf. PA4	33	AY28
off Viscount Av		
Herbertson Gro, (Blan.) G72	70	CL44
Herbert St, G20	23	BP26
Hercules Way, Renf. PA4	33	AZ28
Heriot Av, Pais. PA2	47	AN37
Heriot Ct, Pais. PA2	47	AP37
off Heriot Av		
Heriot Cres, (Bishop.) G64	13	BW18
Heriot Rd, (Lenz.) G66	15	CE18
Heriot Way, Pais. PA2	47	AN37
off Heriot Av		
Herma St, G23	23	BN21
Hermiston Av, G32	40	CD31
Hermiston Pl, G32	41	CE31
Hermiston Rd, G32	40	CD30
Hermitage Av, G13	21	BE22
Heron Ct, Clyde. G81	7	AX16
Heron Pl, John. PA5	45	AF38

Heron St, G40 54 BV33
Heron Way, Renf. PA4 33 AY28
off Britannia Way
Herries Rd, G41 52 BL35
Herriet St, G41 53 BP34
Hertford Av, G12 22 BK23
Hexham Gdns, G41 52 BM36
Heys St, (Barr.) G78 61 AY43
Hickman St, G42 54 BS35
Hickman Ter, G42 54 BS35
Hickory St, G22 24 BU24
High Barholm, (Kilb.) John. 44 AC34
PA10
Highburgh Dr, (Ruther.) G73 67 BX40
Highburgh Rd, G12 22 BL26
High Calside, Pais. PA2 48 AT34
Highcraig Av, John. PA5 45 AF36
High Craighall Rd, G4 37 BR27
Highcroft Av, G44 66 BT40
Highfield Av, Pais. PA2 48 AS38
Highfield Cres, Pais. PA2 48 AT38
Highfield Dr, G12 22 BK23
Highfield Dr, (Ruther.) G73 67 BY42
Highfield Pl, G12 22 BK23
Highkirk Vw, John. PA5 45 AH35
Highland La, G51 36 BL29
High Mair, Renf. PA4 33 AY27
High Parksail, Ersk. PA8 18 AS21
High Rd, (Castlehead) Pais. 48 AS34
PA2
High Row, (Bishop.) G64 13 BX16
High St, G1 5 BT31
High St, G4 5 BT31
High St, (Ruther.) G73 55 BW37
High St, John. PA5 45 AH34
High St, Pais. PA1 48 AT33
High St, Renf. PA4 19 AZ25
Hilary Dr, (Baill.) G69 41 CH32
Hilda Cres, G33 26 CA25
Hillary Av, (Ruther.) G73 67 BZ39
Hillcrest, (Chry.) G69 28 CM21
Hillcrest Av, G32 56 CD37
Hillcrest Av, G44 65 BN41
Hillcrest Av, (Cumb.) G67 72 DB12
off North Carbrain Rd
Hillcrest Av, Pais. PA2 60 AS39
Hillcrest Ct, (Cumb.) G67 72 DB12
Hillcrest Rd, G32 57 CE37
Hillcrest Rd, (Bears.) G61 9 BH17
Hillcrest Rd, (Udd.) G71 59 CQ38
Hillcrest Ter, (Both.) G71 71 CR42
Hillcroft Ter, (Bishop.) G64 24 BV21
Hillend Cres, Clyde. G81 6 AV15
Hillend Rd, G22 23 BQ22
Hillend Rd, (Ruther.) G73 67 BX40
Hillfoot Av, (Bears.) G61 9 BH16
Hillfoot Av, (Ruther.) G73 55 BW38
Hillfoot Dr, (Bears.) G61 9 BH16
Hillfoot Gdns, (Udd.) G71 59 CN37
Hillfoot St, G31 39 BW30
Hillhead Av, (Chry.) G69 17 CP19
Hillhead Av, (Ruther.) G73 67 BX41
Hillhead Pl, G12 37 BN27
off Bank St
Hillhead Pl, (Ruther.) G73 67 BX41
Hillhead Rd, G21 25 BZ22
Hillhead St, G12 36 BM27
Hillhouse St, G21 25 BW25
Hillington Gdns, G52 51 BE33
Hillington Ind Est, G52 34 BB29
Hillington Pk Circ, G52 35 BE32
Hillington Quad, G52 34 BC32
Hillington Rd, G52 34 BB27
Hillington Rd S, G52 34 BC32
Hillington Shop Cen, 34 BB29
(Hillington Ind. Est.) G52
Hillington Ter, G52 34 BC32
Hillkirk Pl, G21 24 BU25
off Hillkirk St
Hillkirk St, G21 24 BU25
Hillkirk St La, G21 24 BV25
off Hillkirk St
Hillneuk Av, (Bears.) G61 9 BH16
Hillneuk Dr, (Bears.) G61 10 BJ16
Hillpark Av, Pais. PA2 48 AT36
Hillpark Dr, G43 64 BL39
Hill Path, G52 34 BC32
Hill Pl, G52 34 BC32
Hill Rd, (Cumb.) G67 72 DA11
Hillsborough Rd, (Baill.) G69 41 CH32

Hillsborough Ter, G12 23 BN26
off Bower St
Hillside Av, (Bears.) G61 9 BH16
Hillside Ct, (Thornlie.) G46 63 BH42
Hillside Dr, (Bears.) G61 10 BJ16
Hillside Dr, (Bishop.) G64 13 BW19
Hillside Gdns, G41 61 AW42
Hillside Gdns La, G11 22 BK26
off North Gardner St
Hillside Gro, (Barr.) G78 61 AW42
Hillside Pk, Clyde. G81 7 AX15
Hillside Quad, G43 64 BK40
Hillside Rd, G43 64 BK40
Hillside Rd, (Barr.) G78 61 AW42
Hillside Rd, Pais. PA2 49 AW35
Hill St, G3 4 BQ28
Hill St, G14 20 BC24
Hillsview, (Chry.) G69 28 CL21
Hillswick Cres, G22 23 BR21
Hilltop Rd, (Mood.) G69 17 CP19
Hillview Dr, (Blan.) G72 70 CM43
Hillview Cres, (Udd.) G71 59 CN37
Hillview Rd, (Elder.) John. PA5 46 AL35
Hillview St, G32 40 CB32
Hilton Gdns, G13 21 BH22
Hilton Pk, (Bishop.) G64 12 BV17
Hilton Rd, (Bishop.) G64 12 BV18
Hilton Ter, G13 21 BG22
Hilton Ter, (Bishop.) G64 12 BV17
Hilton Ter, (Camb.) G72 68 CA42
Hinshaw St, G20 23 BQ26
Hinshelwood Dr, G51 36 BJ31
Hirsel Pl, (Both.) G71 71 CR42
Hobart Cres, Clyde. G81 6 AT16
Hobart St, G22 23 BR25
Hobden St, G21 25 BW26
Hoddam Av, G45 66 BV42
Hoddam Ter, G45 67 BW42
Hogan Ct, Clyde. G81 6 AV15
Hogarth Av, G32 39 BZ30
Hogarth Cres, G32 39 BZ30
Hogarth Dr, G32 39 BZ30
Hogarth Gdns, G32 39 BZ30
Hogganfield Ct, G33 39 BZ27
Hogganfield St, G33 39 BZ27
Hogg Av, John. PA5 45 AG36
Holeburn La, G43 64 BL39
Holeburn Rd, G43 64 BL39
Holehouse Dr, G13 20 BC23
Holland St, G2 4 BQ29
Hollinwell Rd, G23 22 BM21
Hollowglen Rd, G32 40 CD31
Hollows Av, Pais. PA2 47 AP38
Hollows Cres, Pais. PA2 47 AP38
Hollybank Pl, (Camb.) G72 68 CD41
Hollybank St, G21 39 BW28
Hollybrook Pl, G42 54 BS35
off Hollybrook St
Hollybrook St, G42 54 BS35
Hollybush Av, Pais. PA2 47 AR38
Hollybush Rd, G52 34 BB32
Holly Dr, G21 25 BW26
Hollymount, (Bears.) G61 9 BH19
Holly Pl, John. PA5 46 AJ37
Holly St, Clyde. G81 7 AW17
Holm Av, (Udd.) G71 71 CN39
Holm Av, Pais. PA2 48 AV35
Holmbank Av, G41 53 BN38
Holmbrae Av, (Udd.) G71 59 CP38
Holmbrae Rd, (Udd.) G71 59 CP38
Holmbyre Ct, G45 65 BR44
Holmbyre Rd, G45 66 BS44
Holmbyre Ter, G45 66 BS43
Holmes Av, Renf. PA4 33 AY28
Holmfauldhead Dr, G51 35 BG29
Holmfauldhead Pl, G51 35 BG28
off Govan Rd
Holmfauld Rd, G51 35 BG28
Holmhead Cres, G44 65 BQ39
Holmhead Pl, G44 65 BQ39
Holmhead Rd, G44 65 BQ40
Holmhill Av, (Camb.) G72 68 CC41
Holmhills Dr, (Camb.) G72 68 CB42
Holmhills Gdns, (Camb.) G72 68 CB41
Holmhills Gro, (Camb.) G72 68 CB41
Holmhills Pl, (Camb.) G72 68 CB41
Holmhills Rd, (Camb.) G72 68 CB42
Holmhills Ter, (Camb.) G72 68 CB41
Holmlea Rd, G44 53 BQ38

Holm Pl, (Linw.) Pais. PA3 30 AK30
Holms Pl, (Gart.) G69 29 CN22
Holm St, G2 4 BQ30
Holmwood Av, (Udd.) G71 59 CP38
Holmwood Gdns, (Udd.) G71 71 CP39
Holmwood Gro, G44 65 BQ41
Holyrood Cres, G20 37 BP27
Holyrood Quad, G20 37 BP27
Holywell St, G31 39 BX32
Homeston Av, (Both.) G71 71 CQ42
Honeybog Rd, G52 34 BA30
Hood St, Clyde. G81 7 AY19
Hopefield Av, G12 22 BL24
Hopehill Gdns, G20 23 BQ26
Hopehill Rd, G20 23 BQ26
Hopeman Av, (Thornlie.) G46 63 BG41
Hopeman Dr, (Thornlie.) G46 63 BG41
Hopeman Path, (Thornlie.) G46 63 BG40
off Kennishead Pl
Hopeman Rd, (Thornlie.) G46 63 BG41
Hopeman St, (Thornlie.) G46 63 BG41
Hope St, G2 4 BR30
Hopetoun Pl, G23 11 BN19
off Broughton Rd
Hopetoun Ter, G21 25 BW26
Hornal Rd, (Udd.) G71 71 CP41
Hornbeam Dr, Clyde. G81 6 AV17
Hornbeam Rd, (Udd.) G71 59 CR37
Hornden Ct, (Bishop.) G64 13 BW17
Horndean Cres, G33 41 CF29
Horne St, G22 24 BU24
off Hawthorn St
Hornshill Fm Rd, (Stepps) G33 27 CG22
Hornshill St, G21 25 BW25
Horsburgh St, G33 41 CF27
off Dudhope St
Horselethill Rd, G12 22 BL25
Horseshoe La, (Bears.) G61 9 BG17
Horseshoe Rd, (Bears.) G61 9 BG16
Hospital St, G5 38 BS32
Hotspur St, G20 23 BN24
Houldsworth La, G3 37 BN29
Houldsworth St, G3 37 BN29
Househillmuir Cres, G53 63 BE39
Househillmuir La, G53 51 BE38
off Househillmuir Rd
Househillmuir Pl, G53 51 BE38
Househillmuir Rd, G53 63 BD39
Househillwood Cres, G53 50 BD38
Househillwood Rd, G53 62 BD39
Housel Av, G13 20 BD23
Houston Pl, G5 4 BP31
Houston Pl, (Elder.) John. PA5 46 AL35
Houston St, G5 37 BP32
Houston St, Renf. PA4 19 AZ25
Houstoun Ct, John. PA5 45 AH34
off William St
Houstoun Sq, John. PA5 45 AH34
Howard St, G1 4 BR31
Howard St, Pais. PA1 33 AW32
Howat St, G51 36 BJ29
Howcraigs Ct, Clyde. G81 19 AZ22
off Mill Rd
Howden Dr, (Linw.) Pais. PA3 30 AJ32
Howe Gdns, (Udd.) G71 59 CQ38
Howford Rd, G52 50 BD33
Howgate Av, G15 8 BB18
Howieshill Av, (Camb.) G72 68 CC40
Howieshill Rd, (Camb.) 69 CE40
G72
Howth Dr, G13 21 BH21
Howth Ter, G13 21 BH21
Hoxley Pl, G20 23 BP23
Hoylake Pk, (Both.) G71 71 CP43
Hoylake Pl, G23 11 BN20
Hozier Cres, (Udd.) G71 59 CP37
Hozier Pl, (Both.) G71 71 CR42
Hughenden Dr, G12 22 BK25
Hughenden Gdns, G12 22 BJ25
Hughenden La, G12 22 BK25
Hughenden Rd, G12 22 BK25
Hughenden Ter, G12 22 BK25
off Hughenden Rd
Hugh Murray Gro, (Camb.) G72 69 CE40
Hugo St, G20 23 BP24
Hume Dr, (Both.) G71 71 CQ42
Hume Dr, (Udd.) G71 59 CN38
Hume Rd, (Cumb.) G67 73 DC10
Hume St, Clyde. G81 7 AX20
Hunterfield Dr, (Camb.) G72 68 CA40

Name	Page	Grid
Hunterhill Av, Pais. PA2	48	AV34
Hunterhill Rd, Pais. PA2	48	AV34
Hunter Pl, (Kilb.) John. PA10	44	AC35
Hunter Rd, (Ruther.) G73	55	BY36
Huntersfield Rd, John. PA5	45	AE36
Hunters Hill Ct, G21	24	BV23
off Belmont Rd		
Huntershill Rd, (Bishop.) G64	25	BW21
Huntershill St, G21	24	BV23
off Springburn Rd		
Huntershill Way, (Bishop.) G64	24	BV22
Hunter St, G4	5	BU31
Hunter St, Pais. PA1	32	AU32
Huntingdon Rd, G21	38	BU27
Huntingdon Sq, G21	38	BU27
Huntingtower Rd, (Baill.) G69	57	CH33
Huntley Rd, G52	34	BB29
Huntly Av, (Giff.) G46	64	BM43
Huntly Ct, (Bishop.) G64	25	BW21
Huntly Dr, (Camb.) G72	68	CD41
Huntly Gdns, G12	22	BL26
Huntly Path, (Chry.) G69	17	CP19
off Burnbrae Av		
Huntly Rd, G12	22	BL26
Huntly Ter, Pais. PA2	49	AW36
Hurlethill Ct, G53	50	BB38
Hurlet Rd, G53	49	AY37
Hurlet Rd, Pais. PA2	49	AY37
Hurlford Av, G13	20	BB22
Hurly Hawkin, (Bishop.) G64	25	BZ21
Hutcheson Rd, (Thornlie.) G46	64	BJ43
Hutcheson St, G1	5	BS30
Hutchinson Pl, (Camb.) G72	69	CG42
Hutchinsontown Ct, G5	54	BS33
Hutchison Ct, (Giff.) G46	64	BL44
off Berryhill Rd		
Hutchison Dr, (Bears.) G61	10	BJ19
Hutton, G12	22	BJ23
off Ascot Av		
Hutton Dr, G12	35	BG29
Hydepark St, G3	4	BP30
Hyndal Av, G53	50	BD36
Hyndland Av, G11	36	BK27
Hyndland Rd, G12	22	BK25
Hyndland St, G11	36	BL27
Hyndlee Dr, G52	35	BE32
Hyslop Pl, Clyde. G81	7	AW18
I		
Iain Dr, (Bears.) G61	9	BE15
Iain Rd, (Bears.) G61	9	BE15
Ian Smith Ct, Clyde. G81	19	AZ21
Ibroxholm Av, G51	36	BK32
Ibroxholm Oval, G51	36	BK32
Ibroxholm Pl, G51	36	BK32
off Paisley Rd W		
Ibrox Ind Est, G51	36	BL31
Ibrox St, G51	36	BL31
Ibrox Ter, G51	36	BK31
Ibrox Ter La, G51	36	BK31
Ilay Av, (Bears.) G61	21	BH21
Ilay Ct, (Bears.) G61	22	BJ21
Ilay Rd, (Bears.) G61	22	BJ21
Inchbrae Rd, G52	51	BE33
Inchcolm Gdns, (Mood.) G69	17	CQ18
off Culross Way		
Inchcruin Pl, G15	8	BA17
Inchfad Cres, G15	8	BA18
Inchfad Dr, G15	8	BA18
Inchfad Pl, G15	8	BA18
Inchholm La, G11	35	BG27
off Byron St		
Inchholm St, G11	35	BG27
Inchinnan Business Pk,	18	AS25
(Inch.) Renf. PA4		
Inchinnan Dr, (Inch.) Renf. PA4	18	AS25
Inchinnan Rd, Pais. PA3	32	AU30
Inchinnan Rd, Renf. PA4	19	AX25
Inchkeith Pl, G32	40	CD30
Inchlaggan Pl, G15	8	BA17
Inchlee St, G14	35	BG27
Inch Meadow, Ersk. PA8	18	AT21
off Newshot Dr		
Inchmoan Pl, G15	8	BB17
Inchmurrin Dr, (Ruther.) G73	67	BZ43
Inchmurrin Gdns, (Ruther.) G73	67	BZ43
Inchmurrin Pl, (Ruther.) G73	67	BZ43
Inchnock Av, (Gart.) G69	29	CP23
Inchoch St, G33	41	CG27
Inchrory Pl, G15	8	BA17
Incle St, Pais. PA1	32	AV32
India Dr, (Inch.) Renf. PA4	18	AS23
India St, G2	4	BQ29
Inga St, G20	23	BN22
Ingerbreck Av, (Ruther.) G73	67	BZ41
Ingleby Dr, G31	39	BW30
Inglefield St, G42	53	BR34
Ingleneuk Av, G33	26	CD24
Ingleside, (Lenz.) G66	15	CE15
Inglestone Av, (Thornlie.) G46	64	BJ43
Inglewood Cres, Pais. PA2	47	AN35
Inglis St, G31	39	BW31
Ingram St, G1	5	BS30
Inishail Rd, G33	41	CE28
Inkerman Rd, G52	34	BB32
Innellan Gdns, G20	22	BK22
Innellan Pl, G20	22	BK22
Innerwick Dr, G52	34	BD32
Inveraray Dr, (Bishop.) G64	13	BX17
Invercanny Dr, G15	8	BC18
Invercanny Pl, G15	8	BC17
Inverclyde Gdns, (Ruther.) G73	67	BZ42
Inveresk Quad, G32	40	CC31
Inveresk St, G32	40	CC31
Inverewe Av, (Thornlie.) G46	63	BF42
Inverewe Dr, (Thornlie.) G46	63	BF43
Inverewe Gdns, (Thornlie.) G46	63	BF43
Inverewe Pl, (Thornlie.) G46	63	BF42
Invergarry Av, (Thornlie.) G46	63	BF44
Invergarry Ct, (Thornlie.) G46	63	BG44
Invergarry Dr, (Thornlie.) G46	63	BF43
Invergarry Gdns, (Thornlie.) G46	63	BF44
Invergarry Gro, (Thornlie.) G46	63	BF43
Invergarry Pl, (Thornlie.) G46	63	BG43
off Invergarry Dr		
Invergarry Quad, (Thornlie.) G46	63	BG43
Invergarry Vw, (Thornlie.) G46	63	BG43
Inverglas Av, Renf. PA4	34	BB28
off Morriston Cres		
Invergordon Av, G43	53	BP38
Invergyle Dr, G52	34	BD32
Inverkar Dr, Pais. PA2	47	AQ35
Inverlair Av, G43	65	BP39
Inverlair Av, G44	65	BP39
Inverleith St, G32	39	BZ31
Inverlochy St, G33	41	CF28
Inverness St, G51	35	BF31
Inveroran Dr, (Bears.) G61	10	BK17
Inver Rd, G33	41	CG30
Invershiel Rd, G23	10	BM20
Invershin Dr, G20	22	BM24
Inverurie St, G21	24	BT26
Inzievar Ter, G32	56	CD36
Iona Cres, (Old Kil.) G60	6	AT16
Iona Dr, (Old Kil.) G60	6	AS16
Iona Dr, Pais. PA2	48	AT38
Iona Gdns, (Old Kil.) G60	6	AS16
Iona La, (Mood.) G69	17	CQ19
Iona Pl, (Old Kil.) G60	6	AS16
Iona Rd, (Ruther.) G73	68	CA42
Iona Rd, Renf. PA4	33	AY28
Iona St, G51	36	BK30
Iona Way, (Stepps) G33	27	CF25
Iris Av, G45	67	BW42
Irongray St, G31	39	BY30
Irvine St, G40	55	BX34
Irving Av, Clyde. G81	7	AX16
Irving Ct, Clyde. G81	7	AX15
off Stewart Dr		
Irving Quad, Clyde. G81	7	AX15
Iser La, G41	53	BP37
Island Rd, (Cumb.) G67	72	CZ13
Islay Av, (Ruther.) G73	68	CA42
Islay Cres, (Old Kil.) G60	6	AS16
Islay Cres, Pais. PA2	48	AT38
Islay Dr, (Old Kil.) G60	6	AS16
Ivanhoe Rd, G13	21	BF21
Ivanhoe Rd, (Cumb.) G67	72	DA13
Ivanhoe Rd, Pais. PA2	47	AP36
Ivanhoe Way, Pais. PA2	47	AP36
off Ivanhoe Rd		
Ivybank Av, (Camb.) G72	69	CE41
J		
Jackson Dr, G33	27	CH24
Jacks Rd, (Udd.) G71	71	CQ41
Jagger Gdns, (Baill.) G69	57	CH33
Jamaica St, G1	4	BR30
James Dunlop Gdns,	25	BX22
(Bishop.) G64		
James Gray St, G41	53	BN36
James Morrison St, G1	5	BT31
off St. Andrews Sq		
James Nisbet St, G21	5	BU29
James St, G40	54	BU33
James Watt La, G2	4	BQ30
off James Watt St		
James Watt St, G2	4	BQ30
Jamieson Ct, G42	53	BR35
Jamieson Path, G42	53	BR35
off Jamieson St		
Jamieson St, G42	53	BR35
Janebank Av, (Camb.) G72	69	CE41
Janefield Av, John. PA5	45	AG35
Janefield St, G31	39	BX32
Jane Rae Gdns, Clyde. G81	19	AZ21
Jane's Brae, (Cumb.) G67	72	DB13
Janetta St, Clyde. G81	7	AW17
Jardine St, G20	23	BP26
Jardine Ter, (Gart.) G69	29	CP24
off Raeberry St		
Jarvie Way, Pais. PA2	47	AN37
Jean Armour Dr, Clyde. G81	7	AY18
Jean Maclean Pl, (Bishop.) G64	13	BX17
Jedburgh Av, (Ruther.) G73	55	BX38
Jedburgh Dr, Pais. PA2	47	AQ36
Jedburgh Gdns, G20	23	BP26
off Wilton St		
Jedworth Av, G15	8	BD18
Jedworth Ct, G15	8	BD18
off Tallant Rd		
Jedworth Pl, G15	9	BE18
off Tallant Rd		
Jedworth Rd, G15	8	BD18
Jellicoe St, Clyde. G81	6	AU18
Jenny's Well Ct, Pais. PA2	49	AY35
Jenny's Well Rd, Pais. PA2	49	AX35
Jerviston Rd, G33	41	CE27
Jessie St, G42	54	BT35
Jessiman Sq, Renf. PA4	33	AX28
Jocelyn Sq, G1	5	BS31
John Brown Pl, (Chry.) G69	28	CL21
John Hendry Rd, (Udd.) G71	71	CQ41
John Knox La, G4	5	BU30
off Drygate		
John Knox St, G4	5	BU30
John Knox St, Clyde. G81	19	AY21
John Lang St, John. PA5	46	AJ34
John Marshall Dr, (Bishop.)	24	BU22
G64		
Johnsburn Dr, G53	62	BD39
Johnsburn Rd, G53	62	BD39
Johnshaven St, G43	52	BL38
off Bengal St		
John Smith Gate, (Barr.) G78	61	AY41
Johnson Dr, (Camb.) G72	68	CC40
Johnston Av, Clyde. G81	19	AZ21
Johnstone Av, G52	34	BD31
Johnstone Dr, (Ruther.) G73	55	BW38
Johnston Rd, (Gart.) G69	29	CQ23
Johnston St, Pais. PA1	48	AU33
John St, G1	5	BS30
John St, (Barr.) G78	61	AX42
John St, Pais. PA1	48	AS33
off Broomlands St		
Joppa St, G33	40	CA30
Jordanhill Cres, G13	21	BF24
Jordanhill Dr, G13	21	BE24
Jordanhill La, G13	21	BG24
Jordan St, G14	35	BF27
Jordanvale Av, G14	35	BF27
Jowitt Av, Clyde. G81	7	AZ20
Jubilee Bk, (Kirk.) G66	15	CE18
off Heriot Rd		
Jubilee Ct, G52	34	BB30
Jubilee Gdns, (Bears.) G61	9	BH17
Jubilee Path, (Bears.) G61	9	BH17
off Jubilee Gdns		
Jubilee Ter, John. PA5	45	AF35
Julian Av, G12	22	BL25
Julian La, G12	22	BL25
Juniper Ct, (Kirk.) G66	14	CD16
Juniper Pl, G32	57	CH33
Juniper Pl, John. PA5	46	AJ37
Juniper Ter, G32	57	CG33
Jura Av, Renf. PA4	33	AZ28
Jura Ct, G52	35	BG32
Jura Dr, (Old Kil.) G60	6	AS16
Jura Dr, (Blan.) G72	70	CL42
Jura Gdns, (Old Kil.) G60	6	AS16

Jura Pl, (Old Kil.) G60 | 6 | AS16
Jura Rd, (Old Kil.) G60 | 6 | AS16
Jura Rd, Pais. PA2 | 48 | AT38
Jura St, G52 | 35 | BH32

K
Kaim Dr, G53 | 63 | BE39
Karol Path, G4 | 37 | BQ27
off St. Peters St
Kashmir Av, Pais. PA3 | 30 | AK32
Katewell Av, G15 | 8 | BA17
Katewell Pl, G15 | 8 | BA17
Katrine Av, (Bishop.) G64 | 13 | BX20
Katrine Dr, Pais. PA2 | 47 | AP35
Katrine Pl, (Camb.) G72 | 68 | CC39
Katrine Way, (Both.) G71 | 71 | CQ42
off Belstane Pl
Kaystone Rd, G15 | 8 | BC20
Kay St, G21 | 24 | BV25
Keal Av, G15 | 20 | BC21
Keal Cres, G15 | 20 | BC21
Keal Dr, G15 | 20 | BC21
Keal Pl, G15 | 20 | BC21
Kearn Av, G15 | 8 | BD20
Kearn Pl, G15 | 8 | BD20
Keats Pk, (Both.) G71 | 71 | CR42
Keir Dr, (Bishop.) G64 | 12 | BV19
Keir Hardie Ct, (Bishop.) G64 | 13 | BW20
Keir St, G41 | 53 | BP34
Keirs Wk, (Camb.) G72 | 68 | CC39
Keith Av, (Giff.) G46 | 64 | BM42
Keith Ct, G11 | 36 | BL28
Keith St, G11 | 36 | BL27
Kelbourne St, G20 | 23 | BN25
Kelburne Dr, Pais. PA1 | 33 | AX32
Kelburne Gdns, (Baill.) G69 | 58 | CJ34
Kelburne Gdns, Pais. PA1 | 33 | AW32
Kelburne Oval, Pais. PA1 | 33 | AW32
Kelburn St, (Barr.) G78 | 61 | AW44
Kelhead Av, G52 | 34 | BB32
Kelhead Dr, G52 | 34 | BB32
Kelhead Path, G52 | 34 | BB32
Kelhead Pl, G52 | 34 | BB32
Kellas St, G51 | 36 | BJ30
Kells Pl, G15 | 8 | BA17
Kelso Av, (Ruther.) G73 | 55 | BX38
Kelso Av, Pais. PA2 | 47 | AQ36
Kelso Gdns, (Mood.) G69 | 17 | CP18
off Whithorn Cres
Kelso Pl, G14 | 20 | BA23
Kelso St, G13 | 20 | BB21
Kelso St, G14 | 20 | BA23
Kelton St, G32 | 56 | CD33
Kelty Pl, G5 | 37 | BR32
off Bedford St
Kelvin Av, G52 | 34 | BB29
Kelvin Ct, G12 | 21 | BH23
Kelvin Cres, (Bears.) G61 | 9 | BH19
Kelvindale Bldgs, G12 | 22 | BL24
off Kelvindale Rd
Kelvindale Gdns, G20 | 22 | BL23
Kelvindale Pl, G20 | 22 | BM23
off Kelvindale Rd
Kelvindale Rd, G12 | 22 | BK23
Kelvindale Rd, G20 | 22 | BM23
Kelvin Dr, G20 | 22 | BM25
Kelvin Dr, (Bishop.) G64 | 13 | BW19
Kelvin Dr, (Chry.) G69 | 17 | CN19
Kelvin Dr, (Barr.) G78 | 61 | AZ44
Kelvingrove St, G3 | 37 | BN29
Kelvinhaugh Gate, G3 | 36 | BM29
off Kelvinhaugh St
Kelvinhaugh Pl, G3 | 36 | BM29
off Kelvinhaugh St
Kelvinhaugh St, G3 | 36 | BL29
Kelvin Rd, (Cumb.) G67 | 73 | DC13
Kelvin Rd, (Udd.) G71 | 59 | CN38
Kelvin Rd N, (Cumb.) G67 | 73 | DC13
Kelvinside Av, G20 | 23 | BN25
Kelvinside Dr, G20 | 23 | BP25
Kelvinside Gdns, G20 | 23 | BN25
Kelvinside Gdns E, G20 | 23 | BP26
Kelvinside Gdns La, G20 | 23 | BN25
Kelvinside Ter S, G20 | 23 | BN26
Kelvinside Ter W, G20 | 23 | BN26
Kelvin Way, G3 | 36 | BM28
Kelvin Way, (Both.) G71 | 71 | CQ42
Kemp Av, Pais. PA3 | 33 | AW28
Kempock St, G31 | 55 | BY33
Kempsthorn Cres, G53 | 50 | BC36

Kempsthorn Path, G53 | 50 | BD36
off Kempsthorn Rd
Kempsthorn Pl, G53 | 50 | BD36
Kempsthorn Rd, G53 | 50 | BC36
Kemp St, G21 | 24 | BU25
Kendal Av, G12 | 22 | BJ23
off Ripon Dr
Kendal Av, (Giff.) G46 | 64 | BL42
Kendal Dr, G12 | 22 | BJ23
Kendoon Av, G15 | 8 | BA18
Kenilworth Av, G41 | 52 | BM37
Kenilworth Av, Pais. PA2 | 47 | AP37
Kenilworth Ct, (Cumb.) G67 | 72 | DA13
Kenilworth Cres, (Bears.) G61 | 9 | BE15
Kenilworth Way, Pais. PA2 | 47 | AP37
off Kenilworth Av
Kenmar Gdns, (Udd.) G71 | 59 | CN37
Kenmore Gdns, (Bears.) G61 | 10 | BK16
off Methven Av
Kenmore Rd, (Cumb.) G67 | 73 | DD11
Kenmore St, G32 | 40 | CC32
Kenmuir Av, G32 | 57 | CG34
Kenmuirhill Gdns, G32 | 57 | CF35
Kenmuirhill Gate, G32 | 57 | CF35
Kenmuirhill Rd, G32 | 57 | CF35
Kenmuir Rd, G32 | 57 | CE37
Kenmuir St, Coat. ML5 | 59 | CR33
Kenmure Av, (Bishop.) G64 | 12 | BU20
Kenmure Cres, (Bishop.) G64 | 12 | BV20
Kenmure Dr, (Bishop.) G64 | 12 | BV20
Kenmure Gdns, (Bishop.) G64 | 12 | BU20
Kenmure La, (Bishop.) G64 | 12 | BV20
Kenmure Row, G22 | 11 | BR20
off Castlebay St
Kenmure St, G41 | 53 | BP35
Kenmure Way, (Ruther.) G73 | 67 | BX42
Kennedar Dr, G51 | 35 | BG29
Kennedy Ct, (Giff.) G46 | 64 | BL41
Kennedy Path, G4 | 5 | BT29
off St. Mungo Pl
Kennedy St, G4 | 5 | BT28
Kennet St, G21 | 39 | BW28
Kennishead Av, (Thornlie.) G46 | 63 | BG40
Kennishead Path, (Thornlie.) | 63 | BG40
G46
off Kennishead Pl
Kennishead Rd, (Thornlie.) G46 | 63 | BG40
Kennishead Rd, G43 | 63 | BH40
Kennishead Rd, (Thornlie.) G46 | 63 | BG40
Kennishead Rd, G53 | 62 | BD41
Kennisholm Av, (Thornlie.) G46 | 63 | BG40
Kennisholm Path, (Thornlie.) | 63 | BG40
G46
off Kennisholm Av
Kennisholm Pl, (Thornlie.) G46 | 63 | BG40
Kennoway Dr, G11 | 35 | BH27
Kennyhill Sq, G31 | 39 | BX29
Kensington Dr, (Giff.) G46 | 64 | BM44
off Kilearn Rd
Kensington Gate, G12 | 22 | BL25
off Kensington Rd
Kensington Gate La, G12 | 22 | BL25
Kensington Rd, G12 | 22 | BL25
Kensington Sq, (Bears.) G61 | 10 | BK18
Kentallen Rd, G33 | 41 | CG31
Kent Dr, (Ruther.) G73 | 67 | BZ40
Kentigern Ter, (Bishop.) G64 | 25 | BW21
Kent Rd, G3 | 37 | BN29
Kent St, G40 | 5 | BU31
Keppel Dr, G44 | 54 | BU38
Keppochhill Dr, G21 | 24 | BT26
Keppochhill Pl, G21 | 38 | BT27
Keppochhill Rd, G21 | 24 | BT26
Keppochhill Rd, G22 | 24 | BS26
Keppochhill Way, G21 | 38 | BT27
Keppoch St, G21 | 24 | BT26
Kerfield La, G15 | 8 | BA17
Kerfield Pl, G15 | 8 | BA17
Kerr Dr, G40 | 38 | BV32
Kerrera Pl, G33 | 41 | CF31
Kerrera Rd, G33 | 41 | CF31
Kerr Gdns, (Udd.) G71 | 59 | CO37
Kerr Pl, G40 | 38 | BV32
Kerr St, G40 | 38 | BV32
Kerr St, (Barr.) G78 | 61 | AW43
Kerr St, Pais. PA3 | 32 | AT32
Kerrycroy Av, G42 | 54 | BT38
Kerrycroy Pl, G42 | 54 | BT37
off Kerrycroy Av
Kerrycroy St, G42 | 54 | BT37
Kerrydale St, G40 | 55 | BX33

Kerrylamont Av, G42 | 54 | BU38
Kerry Pl, G15 | 8 | BA18
Kersland La, G12 | 22 | BM26
Kersland St, G12 | 22 | BM26
Kessington Dr, (Bears.) G61 | 10 | BJ17
Kessington Rd, (Bears.) G61 | 10 | BJ18
Kessock Dr, G22 | 23 | BR26
Kessock Pl, G22 | 23 | BR26
Kestrel Ct, Clyde. G81 | 7 | AW16
Kestrel Pl, John. PA5 | 45 | AF38
Kestrel Rd, G13 | 21 | BE23
Kew Gdns, G12 | 22 | BM26
off Ruthven St
Kew Gdns, (Udd.) G71 | 59 | CR38
Kew La, G12 | 22 | BM26
Kew Ter, G12 | 22 | BM26
Kibbleston Rd, (Kilb.) John. | 44 | AC34
PA10
Kidston Pl, G5 | 54 | BS33
Kidston Ter, G5 | 54 | BS33
Kierhill Rd, (Cumb.) G68 | 72 | CY11
Kilbarchan Rd, John. PA5 | 45 | AF35
Kilbarchan Rd, (Millik.) John. | 45 | AF35
PA10
Kilbarchan St, G5 | 37 | BR32
off Bedford St
Kilbeg Ter, (Thornlie.) G46 | 63 | BF42
Kilberry St, G21 | 39 | BW28
Kilbirnie Pl, G5 | 53 | BQ33
Kilbirnie St, G5 | 53 | BQ33
Kilbowie Ct, Clyde. G81 | 7 | AX18
off Crown Av
Kilbowie Retail Pk, Clyde. G81 | 7 | AY19
Kilbowie Rd, (Cumb.) G67 | 73 | DC13
Kilbowie Rd, Clyde. G81 | 7 | AX15
Kilbowie Roundabout, Clyde. | 7 | AX16
G81
Kilbrennan Rd, (Linw.) Pais. | 30 | AK31
PA3
Kilbride St, G5 | 54 | BT35
Kilbride Vw, (Udd.) G71 | 59 | CQ38
Kilburn Gro, (Blan.) G72 | 70 | CM44
Kilburn Pl, G13 | 20 | BD23
Kilchattan Dr, G44 | 54 | BS38
Kilchoan Rd, G33 | 41 | CE27
Kilcloy Av, G15 | 8 | BC17
Kildale Way, (Ruther.) G73 | 54 | BV37
Kildary Av, G44 | 65 | BQ40
Kildary Rd, G44 | 65 | BQ40
Kildermorie Path, G34 | 42 | CJ29
off Kildermorie Rd
Kildermorie Rd, G34 | 42 | CJ29
Kildonan Dr, G11 | 36 | BJ27
Kildrostan St, G41 | 53 | BP35
Kildrum Rd, (Cumb.) G67 | 73 | DD10
Kilearn Rd, Pais. PA3 | 33 | AX30
Kilearn Sq, Pais. PA3 | 33 | AX30
off Kilearn Rd
Kilearn Way, Pais. PA3 | 33 | AX30
Kilfinan St, G22 | 23 | BR22
Kilgarth St, Coat. ML5 | 59 | CR33
Kilkerran Dr, G33 | 26 | CB23
Killearn Dr, Pais. PA1 | 50 | BB33
Killearn St, G22 | 23 | BR25
Killermont Av, (Bears.) G61 | 10 | BJ19
Killermont Ct, (Bears.) G61 | 10 | BK18
Killermont Meadows, (Both.) | 71 | CN43
G71
Killermont Rd, (Bears.) G61 | 10 | BJ18
Killermont St, G2 | 5 | BS29
Killermont Vw, G20 | 10 | BJ19
Killiegrew Rd, G41 | 52 | BM35
Killin St, G32 | 56 | CD34
Killoch Av, Pais. PA3 | 31 | AQ32
Killoch Dr, G13 | 20 | BC22
Killoch Dr, (Barr.) G78 | 61 | AZ44
Killoch La, Pais. PA3 | 31 | AQ32
off Killoch Av
Killoch Rd, Pais. PA3 | 31 | AQ32
Killoch Way, Pais. PA3 | 31 | AQ32
off Killoch Av
Kilmailing Rd, G44 | 65 | BR40
Kilmair Pl, G20 | 22 | BM24
Kilmaluag Ter, (Thornlie.) G46 | 63 | BG42
off Kyleakin Rd
Kilmany Dr, G32 | 40 | CB32
Kilmany Gdns, G32 | 40 | CB32
Kilmardinny Av, (Bears.) G61 | 9 | BH15
Kilmardinny Cres, (Bears.) G61 | 9 | BH15
Kilmardinny Dr, (Bears.) G61 | 9 | BH15

Kilmardinny Gate, (Bears.) G61	9	BH15	Kingsdale Av, G44	54	BS38	Kirkhill Dr, G20	23	BN24
off Kilmardinny Av			King's Dr, G40	54	BU33	Kirkhill Gdns, (Camb.) G72	68	CC42
Kilmardinny Gro, (Bears.) G61	9	BH15	Kingsdyke Av, G44	54	BS38	Kirkhill Gro, (Camb.) G72	68	CC42
Kilmari Gdns, G15	8	BA17	Kingsford Av, G44	65	BN41	Kirkhill Pl, G20	22	BM24
Kilmarnock Rd, G41	64	BM39	Kingsheath Av, (Ruther.) G73	66	BU39	off Kirkhill Dr		
Kilmarnock Rd, G43	64	BM39	Kingshill Dr, G44	66	BS39	Kirkhill Rd, (Gart.) G69	29	CP24
Kilmartin Pl, (Thornlie.) G46	63	BG41	Kingshouse Av, G44	54	BS38	Kirkhill Rd, (Udd.) G71	59	CN37
Kilmartin Pl, (Udd.) G71	59	CQ36	Kingshurst Av, G44	54	BS38	Kirkhill Ter, (Camb.) G72	68	CC42
Kilmaurs Dr, (Giff.) G46	65	BN42	Kings Inch Dr, G51	34	BD28	Kirkhope Dr, G15	8	BD19
Kilmaurs St, G51	35	BH31	Kings Inch Pl, Renf. PA4	34	BB27	Kirkinner Rd, G32	57	CF34
Kilmore Cres, G15	8	BA17	Kings Inch Rd, G51	20	BA25	Kirkintilloch Rd, (Bishop.) G64	24	BV21
Kilmorie Dr, (Ruther.) G73	54	BU38	Kings Inch Rd, Renf. PA4	20	BA25	Kirkintilloch Rd, (Kirk.) G66	15	CE16
Kilmory Av, (Udd.) G71	59	CQ38	Kingsknowe Dr, (Ruther.) G73	66	BU39	Kirkland Gro, John. PA5	45	AH34
Kilmuir Cres, (Thornlie.) G46	63	BF41	Kingsland Cres, G52	34	BD31	Kirklandneuk Cres, Renf. PA4	19	AW25
Kilmuir Dr, (Thornlie.) G46	63	BG41	Kingsland Dr, G52	34	BD31	off Kirklandneuk Rd		
Kilmuir Rd, (Thornlie.) G46	63	BG41	Kingsland La, G52	35	BE32	Kirklandneuk Rd, Renf. PA4	19	AX25
Kilmuir Rd, (Udd.) G71	59	CP36	off Berryknowes Rd			Kirklands Cres, (Both.) G71	71	CQ42
Kilmun St, G20	22	BM22	Kings La W, Renf. PA4	19	AZ25	Kirkland St, G20	23	BP26
Kilncroft La, Pais. PA2	48	AU35	off Bell St			Kirk La, G43	52	BL38
Kilnside Rd, Pais. PA1	32	AV32	Kingsley Av, G42	53	BR36	off Riverbank St		
Kiloran St, (Thornlie.) G46	63	BH41	Kingsley Ct, (Udd.) G71	59	CQ38	Kirk La, (Bears.) G61	9	BG16
Kilpatrick Av, Pais. PA2	47	AR35	Kingslynn Dr, G44	66	BT39	Kirklea Av, Pais. PA3	31	AQ31
Kilpatrick Cres, Pais. PA2	48	AT36	Kingslynn La, G44	66	BT39	off Blackstone Rd		
Kilpatrick Dr, Renf. PA4	33	AX29	off Kingslynn Dr			Kirklea Gdns, Pais. PA3	31	AQ32
Kilpatrick Way, (Udd.) G71	59	CQ37	Kingsmuir Dr, (Ruther.) G73	66	BU39	Kirklee Circ, G12	22	BL25
Kiltearn Rd, G33	41	CH30	off King's Park Av			Kirklee Gdns, G12	22	BL24
Kilvaxter Dr, (Thornlie.) G46	63	BG41	King's Pk Av, G44	66	BS39	Kirklee Gdns La, G12	22	BM25
Kilwynet Way, Pais. PA3	33	AW30	King's Pk Av, (Ruther.) G73	66	BU39	Kirklee Gate, G12	22	BM26
Kimberley St, Clyde. G81	6	AT16	Kings Pk Rd, G44	53	BR38	Kirklee Pl, G12	22	BM25
Kinalty Rd, G44	65	BQ40	Kings Pl, G22	23	BR22	Kirklee Quad, G12	22	BM25
Kinarvie Cres, G53	50	BB38	Kings Rd, John. PA5	46	AK35	Kirklee Quad La, G12	22	BM25
Kinarvie Gdns, G53	50	BB38	Kingston Av, (Udd.) G71	59	CQ37	off Kirklee Quad		
Kinarvie Pl, G53	50	BB38	Kingston Br, G3	4	BQ31	Kirklee Rd, G12	22	BL25
Kinarvie Rd, G53	50	BB38	Kingston Br, G5	4	BQ31	Kirklee Ter, G12	22	BL25
Kinarvie Ter, G53	50	BB38	Kingston Ind Est, G5	37	BP32	Kirklee Ter La, G12	22	BL25
Kinbuck St, G22	24	BT25	Kingston Pl, Clyde. G81	6	AT17	Kirkliston St, G32	40	CB31
Kincaid Gdns, (Camb.) G72	56	CC38	Kingston St, G5	4	BQ31	Kirk Ms, (Camb.) G72	68	CC40
Kincardine Dr, (Bishop.) G64	25	BX21	King St, G1	5	BS31	Kirkmichael Av, G11	22	BJ26
Kincardine Pl, (Bishop.) G64	25	BY22	King St, (Ruther.) G73	55	BX37	off Blairatholl Av		
off Kincardine Dr			King St, Clyde. G81	19	AZ21	Kirkmichael Gdns, G11	22	BJ26
Kincardine Sq, G33	41	CF27	King St, Pais. PA1	32	AS32	off Blairatholl Av		
Kincath Av, (Ruther.) G73	67	BZ42	King's Vw, (Ruther.) G73	54	BV38	Kirkmuir Dr, (Ruther.) G73	67	BX42
Kinclaven Av, G15	8	BC18	Kingsway, G14	20	BC24	Kirknewton St, G32	40	CC31
Kincraig St, G51	35	BF31	Kingsway Ct, G14	20	BD24	Kirkoswald Dr, Clyde. G81	7	AY18
Kinellan Rd, (Bears.) G61	9	BH20	Kingswood Dr, G44	66	BS39	Kirkoswald Rd, G43	64	BM39
Kinellar Dr, G14	20	BC23	Kingussie Dr, G44	66	BS39	Kirkpatrick St, G40	39	BW32
Kinfauns Dr, G15	8	BB18	Kiniver Dr, G15	8	BC20	Kirk Pl, (Bears.) G61	9	BG16
Kingarth La, G42	53	BD35	Kinloch Av, (Camb.) G72	68	CD41	Kirk Pl, (Udd.) G71	71	CN40
Kingarth St, G42	53	BD35	Kinloch Av, (Linw.) Pais. PA3	30	AJ31	Kirkriggs Av, (Ruther.) G73	67	BX40
King Edward La, G13	21	BG24	Kinloch Rd, Renf. PA4	33	AX29	Kirkriggs Gdns, (Ruther.) G73	67	BX40
off King Edward Rd			Kinloch St, G40	55	BY33	Kirkriggs Vw, (Ruther.) G73	67	BX40
King Edward Rd, G13	21	BH24	Kinmount Av, G44	53	BR38	off Kirkriggs Av		
Kingfisher Dr, G13	20	BB22	Kinnaird Cres, (Bears.) G61	10	BK17	Kirkriggs Way, (Ruther.) G73	67	BX40
Kingfisher Gdns, G13	20	BC22	Kinnaird Dr, (Linw.) Pais. PA3	30	AK30	off Kirkriggs Gdns		
King George Ct, Renf. PA4	34	BA28	Kinnaird Pl, (Bishop.) G64	25	BX21	Kirk Rd, (Bears.) G61	9	BG16
off King George Park Av			Kinnear Rd, G40	55	BX34	Kirkstall Gdns, (Bishop.) G64	13	BX17
King George V Br, G1	4	BR31	Kinnell Av, G52	51	BE34	Kirkton Av, G13	20	BC23
King George V Br, G5	4	BR31	Kinnell Cres, G52	51	BE34	Kirkton Av, (Barr.) G78	61	AX43
King George V Dock, G51	34	BD27	Kinnell Path, G52	51	BE34	Kirkton Cres, G13	20	BC23
King George Gdns, Renf. PA4	34	BA27	off Kinnell Cres			Kirkton Rd, (Camb.) G72	68	CD40
King George Pk Av, Renf. PA4	34	BA28	Kinnell Pl, G52	51	BF34	Kirktonside, (Barr.) G78	61	AX44
King George Pl, Renf. PA4	34	BA28	off Mosspark Dr			Kirkview Gdns, (Udd.) G71	59	CN37
off King George Park Av			Kinnell Sq, G52	51	BE34	Kirkville Pl, G15	8	BD20
King George Way, Renf. PA4	34	BA28	Kinning Pk Ind Est, G5	37	BP32	Kirkwall, (Cumb.) G67	73	DC8
off King George Park Av			Kinnoul La, G12	22	BL26	Kirkwall Av, (Blan.) G72	70	CL43
Kinghorn Dr, G44	66	BS39	off Dowanside Rd			Kirkwell Rd, G44	65	BR40
Kinglass Rd, (Bears.) G61	9	BE19	Kinpurnie Rd, Pais. PA1	33	AZ32	Kirkwood Av, G33	27	CH24
King Pl, (Baill.) G69	43	CQ32	Kinross Av, G52	50	BD33	Kirkwood Av, Clyde. G81	7	AZ20
Kingsacre Rd, G44	54	BT38	Kinsail Dr, G52	34	BB31	Kirkwood Quad, Clyde. G81	7	AZ20
Kingsacre Rd, (Ruther.) G73	54	BU38	Kinstone Av, G14	20	BC24	off Kirkwood Av		
Kingsbarns Dr, G44	53	BR38	Kintessack Pl, (Bishop.) G64	13	BZ19	Kirkwood Rd, (Udd.) G71	59	CQ37
Kingsborough Gdns, G12	22	BK26	Kintillo Dr, G13	20	BD23	Kirkwood St, G51	36	BL32
Kingsborough Gate, G12	22	BK26	Kintore Rd, G43	65	BP39	Kirkwood St, (Ruther.) G73	55	BW37
off Prince Albert Rd			Kintra St, G51	36	BK30	Kirn St, G20	22	BL21
Kingsborough La, G12	22	BK26	Kintyre Av, (Linw.) Pais. PA3	30	AJ32	Kirriemuir Av, G52	51	BE34
Kingsborough La E, G12	22	BK26	Kintyre St, G21	39	BW28	Kirriemuir Gdns, (Bishop.) G64	13	BY19
Kingsbrae Av, G44	54	BS38	Kippen St, G22	24	BT23	Kirriemuir Pl, G52	51	BE33
King's Br, G5	54	BT33	Kippford St, G32	57	CE33	Kirriemuir Rd, (Bishop.) G64	13	BY20
King's Br, G40	54	BT33	Kirkaig Av, Renf. PA4	34	BB27	Kirtle Dr, Renf. PA4	34	BA27
Kingsbridge Cres, G44	66	BT39	Kirkbean Av, (Ruther.) G73	67	BW41	Kishorn Pl, G33	41	CE28
Kingsbridge Dr, G44	66	BT39	Kirkburn Av, (Camb.) G72	68	CC41	Knapdale St, G22	23	BQ22
Kingsbridge Dr, (Ruther.) G73	66	BU39	Kirkcaldy Rd, G41	52	BM35	Knightsbridge St, G13	21	BF22
Kingsburgh Dr, Pais. PA1	33	AX31	Kirkconnel Av, G13	20	BB22	Knightscliffe Av, G13	21	BF21
Kingsburn Dr, (Ruther.) G73	67	BW39	Kirkconnel Dr, (Ruther.) G73	66	BV40	Knights Gate, (Both.) G71	71	CN40
Kingsburn Gro, (Ruther.) G73	67	BW39	Kirkdale Dr, G52	51	BG33	Knightswood Ct, G13	21	BF23
Kingscliffe Av, G44	66	BS39	Kirkfield Rd, (Both.) G71	71	CQ42	off Knightswood Rd		
Kingscourt Av, G44	54	BT38	Kirkford Rd, (Chry.) G69	17	CN19	Knightswood Cross, G13	21	BF22
Kings Cres, (Camb.) G72	68	CD40	off Bridgeburn Dr			Knightswood Rd, G13	9	BE20
Kings Cres, (Elder.) John. PA5	46	AL34	Kirkhill Av, (Camb.) G72	68	CC42	Knightswood Ter, (Blan.) G72	71	CN44
Kings Cross, G31	38	BV30						

105

Knockburnie Rd, (Both.) G71 71 CQ41
Knockhall St, G33 41 CF27
Knockhill Dr, G44 53 BR38
Knockhill Rd, Renf. PA4 33 AW28
Knockside Av, Pais. PA2 48 AT38
Knock Way, Pais. PA3 33 AW30
Knowehead Dr, (Udd.) G71 71 CN39
Knowehead Gdns, G41 53 BN34
  off Knowehead Ter
Knowehead Gdns, (Udd.) G71 71 CN39
Knowehead Ter, G41 53 BN34
Knowe Rd, (Chry.) G69 28 CL21
Knowe Rd, Pais. PA3 33 AX30
Knowetap St, G20 23 BN22
Knox St, Pais. PA1 47 AR33
Kyleakin Dr, (Blan.) G72 70 CK44
  off Dalcraig Cres
Kyleakin Rd, (Thornlie.) G46 63 BF42
Kyleakin Ter, (Thornlie.) G46 63 BF42
Kyle Ct, (Camb.) G72 68 CC39
Kyle Dr, (Giff.) G46 65 BN42
Kylepark Av, (Udd.) G71 70 CM39
Kylepark Cres, (Udd.) G71 58 CM38
Kylepark Dr, (Udd.) G71 58 CM38
Kylerhea Rd, (Thornlie.) G46 63 BF42
Kyle Rd, (Cumb.) G67 73 DD11
Kyle Sq, (Ruther.) G73 66 BV40
Kyle St, G4 5 BS28

L
La Belle Allee, G3 37 BN28
La Belle Pl, G3 37 BN28
Laburnum Gdns, (Kirk.) G66 14 CD16
  off Laburnum Gro
Laburnum Gro, (Kirk.) G66 14 CD16
Laburnum Pl, John. PA5 46 AJ37
Laburnum Rd, G41 52 BL33
Laburnum Rd, (Cumb.) G67 73 DF11
La Crosse Ter, G12 23 BN26
Lacy St, Pais. PA1 33 AW32
Ladeside Dr, John. PA5 45 AF35
Lade Ter, G52 50 BC33
Ladhope Pl, G13 20 BA21
Ladyacres, (Inch.) Renf. PA4 18 AT23
Ladyacres Way, (Inch.) Renf. PA4 18 AT23
Lady Anne St, G14 20 BB23
  off Speirshall Cl
Ladybank Dr, G52 51 BG33
Ladyburn St, Pais. PA1 49 AW33
Ladyhill Dr, (Baill.) G69 58 CJ33
Lady Isle Cres, (Udd.) G71 71 CN39
Lady Jane Gate, (Both.) G71 71 CN41
Ladykirk Cres, G52 34 BD31
Ladykirk Cres, Pais. PA2 48 AV34
Ladykirk Dr, G52 34 BD31
Lady La, Pais. PA1 48 AT33
Ladyloan Av, G15 8 BA17
Ladyloan Ct, G15 8 BB17
Ladyloan Gdns, G15 8 BB17
Ladyloan Pl, G15 8 BA17
Ladymuir Cres, G53 51 BE35
Ladysmith Av, (Millik.) John. PA10 44 AD35
Ladywell St, G4 5 BU30
Laggan Rd, G43 65 BN40
Laggan Rd, (Bishop.) G64 13 BX20
Laggan Ter, Renf. PA4 19 AX25
Laidlaw Gdns, (Udd.) G71 59 CP36
Laidlaw St, G5 37 BQ32
Laighcartside St, John. PA5 46 AJ34
Laighlands Rd, (Both.) G71 71 CR43
Laighmuir St, (Udd.) G71 71 CP40
Laighpark Harbour, Pais. PA3 32 AU30
Laighpark Vw, Pais. PA3 32 AU30
Lainshaw Dr, G45 65 BQ43
Laird Gro, (Udd.) G71 59 CQ37
Laird Pl, G40 54 BV33
Lairds Gate, (Udd.) G71 70 CM40
Lairds Hill, (Cumb.) G67 72 DA11
Lairg Dr, (Blan.) G72 70 CL43
Lamberton Dr, G52 34 BD31
Lambhill Quad, G41 37 BN32
Lambhill St, G41 36 BM32
Lamb St, G22 23 RR23
Lamerton Rd, (Cumb.) G67 73 DE11
Lamington Rd, G52 50 BD33
Lamlash Cres, G33 40 CD29
Lamlash Pl, G33 40 CD29
  off Lamlash Cres

Lamlash Sq, G33 41 CE29
Lammermoor Av, G52 51 BE33
Lammermuir Ct, Pais. PA2 48 AU37
Lammermuir Dr, Pais. PA2 48 AT37
Lamont Rd, G21 25 BX23
Lanark St, G1 5 BT31
Lancaster Cres, G12 22 BL25
Lancaster Cres La, G12 22 BL25
Lancaster Rd, (Bishop.) G64 13 BX17
Lancaster Ter, G12 22 BL25
Lancaster Ter La, G12 22 BL25
  off Westbourne Gdns W
Lancaster Way, Renf. PA4 33 AY28
  off Tiree Av
Lancefield Quay, G3 37 BN30
Lancefield St, G3 4 BP30
Landemer Dr, (Ruther.) G73 66 BV39
Landressy Pl, G40 54 BU33
Landressy St, G40 54 BV33
Lane Gdns, G11 22 BK26
  off North Gardner St
Lanfine Rd, Pais. PA1 33 AX32
Langa St, G20 23 BN22
Lang Av, Renf. PA4 33 AY28
Langbank St, G5 37 BR32
  off Eglinton St
Langbar Cres, G33 41 CG30
Langbar Path, G33 41 CF30
  off Bartiebeith Rd
Langcraigs Dr, Pais. PA2 60 AS39
Langcraigs Ter, Pais. PA2 60 AS39
  off Langcraigs Dr
Langcroft Dr, (Camb.) G72 69 CE41
Langcroft Pl, G51 35 BE30
Langcroft Rd, G51 35 BF30
Langcroft Ter, G51 35 BF30
  off Langcroft Rd
Langdale Av, G33 26 CA26
Langdale Rd, (Chry.) G69 17 CP19
Langdale's Av, (Cumb.) G68 72 CY11
Langdale St, G33 26 CA26
Langford Dr, G53 62 BC42
Langford Pl, G53 62 BD42
Langhaul Rd, G53 50 BB36
Langhill Dr, (Cumb.) G68 72 CZ10
Langholm Ct, (Chry.) G69 17 CP19
  off Heathfield Av
Langholm Dr, (Linw.) Pais. PA3 30 AL32
Langlands Av, G51 35 BF29
Langlands Ct, G51 35 BH29
  off Langlands Rd
Langlands Dr, G51 35 BF30
Langlands Rd, G51 35 BF30
Langlands-Seafar Interchange, (Cumb.) G67 72 DA13
Langlea Av, (Camb.) G72 67 BZ41
Langlea Ct, (Camb.) G72 68 CA41
Langlea Dr, (Camb.) G72 68 CA40
Langlea Gdns, (Camb.) G72 68 CA40
Langlea Gro, (Camb.) G72 68 CA41
Langlea Rd, (Camb.) G72 68 CA41
Langlea Way, (Camb.) G72 68 CA40
Langley Av, G13 20 BD21
Langmuirhead Rd, (Kirk.) G66 26 CC21
Langmuir Rd, (Baill.) G69 43 CQ32
Langmuir Way, (Baill.) G69 43 CQ32
Langness Rd, G33 40 CD29
Lang Pl, John. PA5 45 AG34
Langshot St, G51 36 BM32
Langside Av, G41 53 BN36
Langside Ct, (Both.) G71 71 CR44
Langside Dr, G43 65 BN40
Langside Dr, (Kilb.) John. PA10 44 AC35
Langside Gdns, G42 53 BQ38
Langside La, G42 53 BQ36
Langside Pk, (Kilb.) John. PA10 44 AC35
Langside Pl, G41 53 BP37
Langside Rd, G42 53 BQ36
Langside Rd, (Both.) G71 71 CR44
Langside St, Clyde. G81 8 BA15
Langstile Pl, G52 34 BB32
Langstile Rd, G52 34 BB32
Lang St, Pais. PA1 49 AW33
Langton Cres, G53 51 BE36
Langton Cres, (Barr.) G78 61 AZ44
Langton Gdns, (Baill.) G69 57 CH33

Langton Rd, G53 51 BE37
Langtree Av, (Giff.) G46 64 BJ44
Lanrig Pl, (Chry.) G69 28 CL21
Lanrig Rd, (Chry.) G69 28 CL21
Lansbury Gdns, Pais. PA3 32 AT30
Lansdowne Cres, G20 37 BP27
Lansdowne Cres La, G20 37 BP27
Lansdowne Dr, (Cumb.) G68 72 DB8
Lanton Dr, G52 34 BD32
Lanton Rd, G43 65 BN40
Lappin St, Clyde. G81 19 AZ21
Larbert St, G4 4 BR28
Larch Av, (Bishop.) G64 25 BX31
Larch Av, (Lenz.) G66 15 CE15
Larch Cres, (Kirk.) G66 15 CE15
Larch Dr, (Lenz.) G66 15 CE15
Larches, The, (Mood.) G69 17 CQ17
Larchfield Av, G14 20 BD25
Larchfield Dr, (Ruther.) G73 67 BY41
Larchfield Pl, G14 20 BD25
Larchfield Rd, (Bears.) G61 9 BH20
Larchfield Rd, (Mood.) G69 17 CP19
Larchgrove Av, G32 41 CE31
Larchgrove Pl, G32 41 CE30
  off Larchgrove Rd
Larchgrove Rd, G32 41 CE30
Larch Pl, John. PA5 45 AH37
Larch Rd, G41 36 BK32
Larch Rd, (Cumb.) G67 73 DF9
Largie Rd, G43 65 BP40
Largo Pl, G51 35 BG30
Largs St, G31 39 BX30
Larkfield Rd, (Lenz.) G66 15 CG16
Larkin Gdns, Pais. PA3 32 AT30
Lasswade St, G14 20 BA23
Latherton Dr, G20 22 BM24
Latherton Pl, G20 22 BM24
  off Latherton Dr
Latimer Gdns, G52 50 BC33
Latimer Path, G52 50 BC33
  off Paisley Rd W
Laudedale La, G12 22 BK26
Lauderdale Gdns, G12 22 BK26
Lauder Dr, (Ruther.) G73 67 BZ39
Lauder Dr, (Linw.) Pais. PA3 30 AK32
Lauder Gdns, (Blan.) G72 70 CL43
Laundry La, G33 27 CE24
Laurel Av, (Lenz.) G66 15 CF15
Laurel Av, Clyde. G81 6 AT17
Laurelbank Rd, (Chry.) G69 28 CK22
Laurel Gdns, (Udd.) G71 59 CP37
Laurel Pk Cl, G13 21 BE24
Laurel Pk Gdns, G13 21 BE24
Laurel Pl, G11 22 BJ26
Laurel St, G11 36 BJ27
Laurel Wk, (Ruther.) G73 67 BY42
Laurel Way, (Barr.) G78 61 AX42
Laurence Ct, G15 8 BA18
  off Laurence Dr
Laurence Dr, G15 8 BA18
Laurence Dr, (Bears.) G61 9 BF15
Laurence Gdns, G15 8 BA18
  off Laurence Dr
Lauren Way, Pais. PA2 47 AP36
Laurie Ct, (Udd.) G71 59 CQ38
Laurieston Rd, G5 53 BR33
Laurieston Way, (Ruther.) G73 67 BX41
Laverockhall St, G21 24 BV26
Laverock Rd, (Chry.) G69 17 CP20
Lawers Dr, (Bears.) G61 9 BE15
Lawers Rd, G43 64 BK40
Lawers Rd, Renf. PA4 33 AX28
Lawhill Av, G44 66 BT41
  off Croftfoot Rd
Lawmoor Av, G5 54 BS34
Lawmoor Pl, G5 54 BS35
Lawmoor Rd, G5 54 BS34
Lawmoor St, G5 54 BS34
Lawn St, Pais. PA1 32 AV32
Lawrence Av, (Giff.) G46 64 BL44
Lawrence St, G11 36 BL27
Law St, G40 39 BW32
Laxford Av, G44 65 BQ41
Laxton Dr, (Lenz.) G66 15 CG17
Leabank Av, Pais. PA2 48 AU37
Leadburn Rd, G21 25 BY25
Leadburn St, G32 40 CA30
Leader St, G33 39 BZ28
Leander Cres, Renf. PA4 34 BA27
Leckie St, G43 52 BL37

Ledaig Pl, G31	39	BY30	Leven St, G41	53	BP34	Linacre Gdns, G32	41	CF32
Ledaig St, G31	39	BY30	Leven Vw, Clyde. G81	7	AX18	Linburn Pl, G52	34	BC31
Ledard Rd, G42	53	BP37	*off Crown Av*			Linburn Rd, G52	34	BA30
Ledcameroch Cres, (Bears.)	9	BF17	Leven Way, (Cumb.) G67	72	DB12	Linclive Link Rd, (Linw.) Pais.	31	AN31
G61			*off Cumbernauld Shop Cen*			PA3		
Ledcameroch Pk, (Bears.) G61	9	BF17	Leven Way, Pais. PA2	47	AN36	Linclive Ter, (Linw.) Pais. PA3	30	AM32
Ledcameroch Rd, (Bears.) G61	9	BF17	Levern Br Ct, G53	50	BB38	*off Candren Rd*		
Ledgowan Pl, G20	22	BM21	Levern Br Gro, G53	50	BB38	Lincluden Path, G41	53	BP33
Ledi Rd, G43	64	BL40	Levern Br Pl, G53	62	BB39	*off McCulloch St*		
Ledmore Dr, G15	8	BB17	Levern Br Rd, G53	62	BB39	Lincoln Av, G13	21	BE23
Lednock Rd, (Stepps) G33	27	CE24	Levern Br Way, G53	62	BB39	Lincoln Av, (Udd.) G71	59	CP36
Lednock Rd, G52	34	BC32	Levern Cres, (Barr.) G78	61	AX44	Lincuan Av, (Giff.) G46	64	BL44
Lee Av, G33	40	CA28	Leverndale Ct, G53	50	BB36	Lindams, (Udd.) G71	71	CP40
Leebank Dr, G44	65	BP44	Leverndale Ind Cen, G53	50	BB37	Linden Ct, Clyde. G81	7	AW15
Lee Cres, (Bishop.) G64	25	BW21	Leverndale Rd, G53	50	BB36	*off Linden Dr*		
Leefield Dr, G44	65	BP43	Levern Gdns, (Barr.) G78	61	AX42	Linden Dr, Clyde. G81	7	AW15
Leehill Rd, G21	24	BU22	Levernside Av, G53	51	BE37	Linden Pl, G13	21	BH22
Leeside Rd, G21	24	BU22	*off Levernside Cres*			Linden St, G13	21	BH22
Leesland, (Udd.) G71	59	CQ37	Levernside Av, (Barr.) G78	61	AW43	Linden Way, G13	21	BH22
Leewood Dr, G44	65	BQ43	Levernside Cres, G53	50	BD36	*off Linden St*		
Leggatston Dr, G53	63	BE42	Levernside Rd, G53	51	BE36	Lindores Av, (Ruther.) G73	55	BX38
Leggatston Rd, G53	63	BE43	Lewis Av, Renf. PA4	33	AZ28	Lindores St, G42	53	BR38
Leglen Wd Cres, G21	25	BZ23	Lewis Cres, (Millik.) John.	45	AE35	*off Somerville Dr*		
Leglen Wd Dr, G21	25	BZ23	PA10			Lindrick Dr, G23	11	BN20
Leglen Wd Pl, G21	25	BZ23	Lewis Gdns, (Old Kil.) G60	6	AS16	Lindsaybeg Ct, (Chry.) G69	28	CL21
Leglen Wd Rd, G21	25	BZ23	Lewis Gdns, (Bears.) G61	8	BD15	Lindsaybeg Rd, (Lenz.) G66	15	CH17
Leicester Av, G12	22	BK24	Lewis Gro, (Old Kil.) G60	6	AS16	Lindsaybeg Rd, (Chry.) G69	16	CK20
Leighton St, G20	23	BN23	Lewis Pl, (Old Kil.) G60	6	AS16	Lindsay Dr, G12	22	BK23
Leitchland Rd, (Elder.) John.	46	AM37	Lewiston Dr, G23	10	BM20	Lindsay Pl, G12	22	BK23
PA5			*off Lewiston Rd*			Lindsay Pl, (Lenz.) G66	15	CF18
Leitchland Rd, Pais. PA2	46	AM37	Lewiston Pl, G23	10	BM20	Lindsay Pl, John. PA5	46	AJ34
Leithland Av, G53	50	BD36	*off Lewiston Rd*			*off Thorn Brae*		
Leithland Rd, G53	50	BD36	Lewiston Rd, G23	10	BM20	Linfern Rd, G12	22	BL26
Leith St, G33	39	BZ29	Lexwell Av, (Elder.) John. PA5	46	AM34	Links Rd, G32	57	CF34
Lendale La, (Bishop.) G64	13	BW18	Leyden Ct, G20	23	BN24	Links Rd, G44	66	BS41
Lendel Pl, G51	36	BM32	Leyden Gdns, G20	23	BN24	Linkwood Av, G15	8	BB18
off Paisley Rd W			Leyden St, G20	23	BN24	Linkwood Cres, G15	8	BC18
Lenihall Dr, G45	66	BU43	Leys, The, (Bishop.) G64	13	BW20	Linkwood Dr, G15	8	BC18
Lenihall Ter, G45	66	BU43	Liberton St, G33	39	BZ29	Linkwood Gdns, G15	8	BD18
Lennox Av, G14	21	BE26	Liberty Av, (Baill.) G69	43	CQ32	Linkwood Pl, G15	8	BB18
Lennox Cres, (Bishop.) G64	24	BV21	Libo Av, G53	51	BF36	Linn Brae, John. PA5	45	AH35
Lennox Dr, (Bears.) G61	9	BH15	Library Gdns, (Camb.) G72	68	CB39	Linn Cres, Pais. PA2	48	AS38
Lennox Gdns, G14	21	BF25	Liddells Ct, (Bishop.) G64	25	BW21	Linn Dr, G44	65	BP42
Lennox La E, G14	21	BF26	Liddell St, G32	57	CE36	Linnet Av, John. PA5	45	AE38
Lennox La W, G14	21	BF25	Liddel Rd, (Cumb.) G67	72	DA12	Linnet Pl, G13	20	BB22
off Lennox Av			Liddesdale Av, Pais. PA2	46	AM38	Linnhead Dr, G53	62	BD39
Lennox Pl, G14	21	BE26	Liddesdale Pl, G22	24	BU21	Linnhead Pl, G14	20	BD25
off Scotstoun St			Liddesdale Rd, G22	24	BS22	Linnhe Av, G44	65	BQ41
Lennox Pl, Clyde. G81	6	AU18	Liddesdale Sq, G22	24	BU22	Linnhe Av, (Bishop.) G64	13	BX20
Lennox Rd, (Cumb.) G67	72	DB11	Liddesdale Ter, G22	24	BU22	Linnhe Dr, (Barr.) G78	61	AX40
Lennox St, G20	22	BL22	Liddoch Way, (Ruther.) G73	54	BV37	Linnhe Pl, (Blan.) G72	70	CL43
off Maryhill Rd			Liff Gdns, (Bishop.) G64	25	BZ21	Linn Pk, G44	65	BR42
Lennox Ter, Pais. PA3	33	AW29	Liff Pl, G34	42	CL28	Linnpark Av, G44	65	BP43
Lennox Vw, Clyde. G81	7	AX18	Lightburn Pl, G32	40	CD30	Linnpark Ct, G44	65	BP43
off Granville St			Lightburn Rd, G31	39	BY31	Linn Pk Gdns, John. PA5	45	AH35
Lentran St, G34	42	CM30	Lightburn Rd, (Camb.) G72	69	CF41	Linn Pk Ind Est, G45	65	BR43
Leny St, G20	23	BP25	Lilac Av, Clyde. G81	6	AT16	Linn Valley Vw, G45	66	BT42
Lenziemill Ind Est, (Cumb.) G67	73	DC13	Lilac Cres, (Udd.) G71	59	CR37	Linnwell Cres, Pais. PA2	48	AT37
Lenziemill Rd, (Cumb.) G67	73	DD13	Lilac Gdns, (Bishop.) G64	25	BX21	Linnwood Ct, G44	65	BQ40
Lenzie Pl, G21	24	BV23	Lilac Pl, John. PA5	46	AJ36	Linside Av, Pais. PA1	49	AW33
Lenzie Rd, (Stepps) G33	27	CF23	*off Spruce Av*			Lintfield Ln, (Udd.) G71	71	CQ40
Lenzie Rd, (Kirk.) G66	15	CF15	Lilac Wynd, (Camb.) G72	69	CG41	*off Myers Cres*		
Lenzie St, G21	24	BV24	Lillyburn Pl, G15	8	BA16	Linthaugh Rd, G53	50	BC35
Lenzie Ter, G21	24	BV24	Lilybank Av, (Muir.) G69	28	CL22	Linthaugh Ter, G53	51	BF36
Lenzie Way, G21	24	BV23	Lilybank Av, (Camb.) G72	69	CE41	*off Linthaugh Rd*		
Leslie Rd, G41	53	BN34	Lilybank Gdns, G12	36	BM27	Linthouse Bldgs, G51	35	BG29
Leslie St, G41	53	BP34	Lilybank Gdns La, G12	36	BM27	Linthouse Rd, G51	35	BG28
Lesmuir Dr, G14	20	BB24	Lilybank La, G12	36	BM27	Lintlaw, (Blan.) G72	70	CM44
Lesmuir Pl, G14	20	BB24	*off Lilybank Gdns*			Lintlaw Dr, G52	34	BD31
Letham Ct, G43	65	BN40	Lilybank Ter, G12	36	BM27	Linton St, G33	40	CA29
Letham Dr, G43	65	BN40	*off Great George St*			Linwood Ind Est, (Linw.) Pais.	46	AL33
Letham Dr, (Bishop.) G64	25	BY21	Lily St, G40	55	BX34	PA3		
Letham Gra, (Cumb.) G68	72	DB9	Limecraigs Av, Pais. PA2	48	AS38	Linwood Rd, Pais. PA1	30	AM32
Lethamhill Cres, G33	40	CB28	Limecraigs Cres, Pais. PA2	48	AS38	Linwood Rd, (Linw.) Pais. PA3	30	AL32
Lethamhill Pl, G33	40	CA28	Limecraigs Rd, Pais. PA2	47	AR38	Lismore Av, Renf. PA4	33	AZ28
Lethamhill Rd, G33	40	CA28	Lime Gro, (Lenz.) G66	15	CF16	Lismore Dr, Pais. PA2	48	AT38
Letham Oval, (Bishop.) G64	25	BZ21	Lime Gro, (Blan.) G72	70	CL44	Lismore Gdns, (Millik.) John.	45	AE35
Letherby Dr, G42	53	BR38	Lime La, G14	21	BF26	PA10		
Letherby Dr, G44	53	BR38	*off Westland Dr*			Lismore Pl, (Mood.) G69	17	CQ18
Lethington Av, G41	53	BN37	Limeside Av, (Ruther.) G73	55	BX38	*off Altnacreag Gdns*		
Lethington Pl, G41	53	BN37	Limeside Gdns, (Ruther.) G73	55	BY38	Lismore Rd, G12	22	BK24
Letterfearn Dr, G23	11	BN20	Lime St, G14	21	BF26	Lister Pl, G52	34	BC30
Letterickhills Cres, (Camb.)	69	CG42	Limetree Av, (Udd.) G71	59	CR37	*off Lister Rd*		
G72			Limetree Dr, Clyde. G81	7	AW17	Lister Rd, G52	34	BC30
Lettoch St, G51	36	BJ30	Limeview Av, Pais. PA2	47	AR38	Lister St, G4	5	BT28
Leven Av, (Bishop.) G64	13	BX20	Limeview Cres, Pais. PA2	47	AR38	Lithgow Cres, Pais. PA2	49	AW35
Leven Ct, (Barr.) G78	61	AX40	Limeview Rd, Pais. PA2	47	AR38	Little Dovehill, G1	5	BT31
off Linnhe Dr			Limeview Way, Pais. PA2	47	AR38	*off Gallowgate*		
Leven Dr, (Bears.) G61	9	BH17	*off Limeview Av*			Littleholm Pl, Clyde. G81	6	AU17
Leven Sq, Renf. PA4	19	AX25	Linacre Dr, G32	41	CE32			

Littlemill Cres, G53	50	BC37	Lochleven Rd, G42	53	BQ38	Lorne Cres, (Bishop.) G64	13	BZ19
Littlemill Dr, G53	50	BC37	Lochlibo Av, G13	20	BB23	Lorne Dr, (Linw.) Pais. PA3	30	AJ32
Littlemill Gdns, G53	50	BC37	Lochlibo Cres, (Barr.) G78	61	AW44	Lorne Rd, G52	34	BB29
Little St, G3	4	BP30	Lochlibo Ter, (Barr.) G78	61	AW44	Lorne St, G51	36	BM31
off McIntyre St			Lochmaben Rd, G52	50	BB33	Lorne Ter, (Camb.) G72	68	CB42
Littleton Dr, G23	10	BL20	Lochmaddy Av, G44	65	BQ40	Lorraine Gdns, G12	22	BL25
off Littleton St			Lochore Av, Pais. PA3	32	AV30	*off Kensington Rd*		
Littleton St, G23	10	BM20	Loch Rd, (Stepps) G33	27	CF24	Lorraine Gdns La, G12	22	BL25
Livingstone Av, G52	34	BC29	Lochside, (Bears.) G61	9	BH18	*off Westbourne Gdns La*		
Livingstone Cres, (Blan.) G72	70	CM44	Lochside, (Gart.) G69	29	CP23	Lorraine Rd, G12	22	BL25
Livingstone La, (Both.) G71	71	CQ42	Lochside St, G41	53	BN36	*off Kensington Rd*		
off Appledore Cres			*off Minard Rd*			Loskin Dr, G22	24	BS22
Livingstone St, Clyde. G81	7	AY20	Lochview Cotts, (Gart.) G69	29	CN26	Lossie Cres, Renf. PA4	34	BB27
Lloyd Av, G32	56	CC35	Lochview Cres, G33	26	CB26	Lossie St, G33	39	BZ28
Lloyd St, G31	39	BW29	Lochview Dr, G33	26	CB26	Lothian Cres, Pais. PA2	48	AT36
Lloyd St, (Ruther.) G73	55	BX36	Lochview Gdns, G33	26	CB26	Lothian Gdns, G20	23	BN26
Loanbank Quad, G51	35	BH30	Lochview Pl, G33	26	CB26	*off Wilton St*		
Loancroft Av, (Baill.) G69	58	CL34	Lochview Rd, (Bears.) G61	9	BG18	Lothian St, G52	34	BA29
Loancroft Gdns, (Udd.) G71	71	CN40	Lochview Ter, (Gart.) G69	29	CP24	Louden Hill Dr, G33	26	CA23
Loancroft Gate, (Udd.) G71	71	CN40	Loch Voil St, G32	57	CF33	*off Louden Hill Rd*		
Loancroft Pl, (Baill.) G69	58	CK34	Lochwood Ln, (Mood.) G69	17	CQ18	Louden Hill Gdns, G33	26	CA23
Loanend Cotts, (Camb.) G72	69	CH44	Lochwood St, G33	40	CA27	*off Louden Hill Rd*		
Loanfoot Av, G13	20	BC22	Lochy Av, Renf. PA4	34	BB28	Louden Hill Pl, G33	26	CA23
Loanhead Av, (Linw.) Pais.	30	AJ31	Lochy Gdns, (Bishop.) G64	13	BX20	*off Louden Hill Rd*		
PA3			Lockerbie Av, G43	65	BP39	Louden Hill Rd, G33	26	CA23
Loanhead Av, Renf. PA4	19	AZ26	Lockhart Av, (Camb.) G72	69	CF39	Louden Hill Way, G33	25	BZ23
Loanhead La, (Linw.) Pais. PA3	30	AJ31	Lockhart Dr, (Camb.) G72	69	CF39	*off Louden Hill Rd*		
Loanhead Rd, (Linw.) Pais.	30	AJ31	Lockhart St, G21	39	BX27	Loudon Gdns, John. PA5	46	AJ34
PA3			Locksley Av, G13	21	BE21	Loudon Rd, G33	26	CD24
Loanhead St, G32	40	CB30	Locksley Rd, Pais. PA2	47	AP36	Loudon Ter, G12	22	BM26
Loaning, The, (Bears.) G61	9	BG16	Locksley Way, Pais. PA2	47	AP36	*off Observatory Rd*		
off Manse Rd			*off Locksley Rd*			Lounsdale Av, Pais. PA2	47	AR34
Lobnitz Av, Renf. PA4	19	AZ26	Logan Dr, (Cumb.) G68	72	CZ10	Lounsdale Cres, Pais. PA2	47	AQ35
Lochaber Dr, (Ruther.) G73	67	BZ41	Logan Dr, Pais. PA3	32	AS31	Lounsdale Dr, Pais. PA2	47	AR35
Lochaber Rd, (Bears.) G61	10	BJ19	Logan St, G5	54	BT34	Lounsdale Gro, Pais. PA2	47	AR34
Loch Achray Gdns, G32	57	CE33	Loganswell Dr, (Thornlie.) G46	63	BG43	Lounsdale Ho, Pais. PA2	47	AQ36
Loch Achray St, G32	57	CE33	Loganswell Gdns, (Thornlie.)	63	BG43	Lounsdale Pl, G14	20	BD25
Lochaline Av, Pais. PA2	47	AQ35	G46			Lounsdale Rd, Pais. PA2	47	AR35
Lochaline Dr, G44	65	BQ41	Loganswell Pl, (Thornlie.) G46	63	BG43	Lounsdale Way, Pais. PA2	47	AR34
Lochalsh Dr, Pais. PA2	47	AP35	Loganswell Rd, (Thornlie.) G46	63	BG43	Lourdes Av, G52	51	BF33
Lochalsh Pl, (Blan.) G72	70	CK43	Logan Twr, (Camb.) G72	69	CG41	Lourdes Ct, G52	51	BF33
Lochar Cres, G53	51	BF35	*off Claude Av*			Lovat Pl, G52	34	BA30
Lochard Dr, Pais. PA2	47	AQ35	Lomax St, G33	39	BZ29	Lovat Pl, (Ruther.) G73	67	BZ41
Lochay St, G32	57	CE33	Lomond Av, Renf. PA4	33	AX28	Lovat St, G4	38	BS27
Lochbrae Dr, (Ruther.) G73	67	BZ41	Lomond Ct, (Barr.) G78	61	AY43	*off Borron St*		
Lochbridge Rd, G34	42	CJ30	*off Eildon Dr*			Love St, Pais. PA3	32	AU30
Lochbroom Dr, Pais. PA2	47	AQ35	Lomond Cres, Pais. PA2	48	AT37	Low Barholm, (Kilb.) John.	44	AD35
Lochburn Cres, G20	23	BN22	Lomond Dr, (Bishop.) G64	12	BV18	PA10		
Lochburn Gro, G20	23	BN22	Lomond Dr, (Both.) G71	71	CR42	Low Cres, Clyde. G81	19	AZ21
off Cadder Rd			Lomond Dr, (Barr.) G78	61	AX41	Lower Bourtree Dr, (Ruther.)	67	BY41
Lochburn Pas, G20	23	BN22	Lomond Gdns, (Elder.) John.	46	AL35	G73		
Lochburn Rd, G20	22	BM23	PA5			Lower Millgate, (Udd.) G71	71	CP39
Lochdochart Path, G34	42	CL30	Lomond Pl, (Stepps) G33	27	CG25	Low Moss Ind Est, (Bishop.)	13	BX17
off Lochdochart Rd			Lomond Rd, (Bears.) G61	9	BG19	G64		
Lochdochart Rd, G34	42	CL30	Lomond Rd, (Lenz.) G66	15	CF16	Lowndes St, (Barr.) G78	61	AY43
Lochearn Cres, Pais. PA2	47	AQ35	Lomond Rd, (Udd.) G71	59	CP36	Low Parksail, Ersk. PA8	18	AS21
Lochearnhead Rd, G33	26	CD24	Lomond St, G22	23	BR24	Low Rd, (Castlehead) Pais.	48	AS34
Lochend Av, (Gart.) G69	29	CN23	Lomond Vw, Clyde. G81	7	AX18	PA2		
Lochend Cres, (Bears.) G61	9	BF18	*off Granville St*			Lowther Ter, G12	22	BL25
Lochend Dr, (Bears.) G61	9	BF18	London Arc, G1	5	BT31	*off Redlands La*		
Lochend Path, G34	42	CK28	*off London Rd*			Loyne Dr, Renf. PA4	34	BB27
off Dubton St			London La, G1	5	BT31	Luath St, G51	36	BJ29
Lochend Rd, G34	42	CK28	*off London Rd*			Lubas Av, G42	54	BT38
Lochend Rd, (Bears.) G61	9	BG18	London Rd, G1	5	BT31	Lubas Pl, G42	54	BT38
Lochend Rd, G69	43	CN27	London Rd, G31	55	BX33	Lubnaig Rd, G43	65	BN39
Lochend Rd, (Gart.) G69	29	CP24	London Rd, G32	56	CA35	Luckingsford Av, (Inch.) Renf.	18	AT22
Lochend Rd, Coat. ML5	43	CN27	London Rd, G40	38	BU32	PA4		
Lochfauld Rd, G23	11	BQ19	London St, Renf. PA4	19	AZ24	Luckingsford Dr, (Inch.) Renf.	18	AS22
Lochfield Cres, Pais. PA2	48	AV36	Lonend, Pais. PA1	48	AV33	PA4		
Lochfield Dr, Pais. PA2	49	AW36	Longay Pl, G22	24	BS21	Luckingsford Rd, (Inch.) Renf.	18	AS22
Lochfield Gdns, G34	42	CL28	Longay St, G22	24	BS21	PA4		
Lochfield Rd, Pais. PA2	48	AV36	Longcroft Dr, Renf. PA4	19	AY25	Lucy Brae, (Udd.) G71	59	CN37
Lochgilp St, G20	22	BL22	Longden St, Clyde. G81	19	AZ21	Ludovic Sq, John. PA5	45	AH34
Lochgoin Av, G15	8	BA17	Longford St, G33	39	BZ29	Luffness Gdns, G32	56	CD35
Lochgreen St, G33	25	BZ26	Longlee, (Baill.) G69	58	CK33	Lugar Dr, G52	51	BG33
Lochhead Av, (Linw.) Pais.	30	AK32	Longmeadow, John. PA5	45	AE36	Lugar Pl, G44	66	BU40
PA3			Long Row, (Baill.) G69	42	CL31	Luggiebank Pl, (Baill.) G69	59	CQ33
Lochiel La, (Ruther.) G73	67	BZ41	Longstone Pl, G33	40	CD29	Luing Rd, G52	35	BG32
Lochiel Rd, (Thornlie.) G46	63	BH41	*off Longstone Rd*			Luma Gdns, G51	35	BE30
Lochinver Cres, Pais. PA2	47	AQ35	Longstone Rd, G33	40	CD29	Lumloch St, G21	25	BW25
Lochinver Dr, G44	65	BQ41	Longwill Ter, (Cumb.) G67	73	DD9	Lumsden St, G3	36	BM29
Lochinver Gro, (Camb.) G72	68	CD40	Lonmay Rd, G33	41	CF29	Lunan Dr, (Bishop.) G64	25	BY21
off Andrew Sillars Av			Lonsdale Av, (Giff.) G46	64	BL42	Lunan Pl, G51	35	BG30
Loch Katrine St, G32	57	CE33	Loom Wk, (Kilb.) John. PA10	44	AC34	Luncarty Pl, G32	56	CC34
Loch Laidon St, G32	57	CF33	Lora Dr, G52	51	BG33	Luncarty St, G32	56	CC34
Lochlea Av, Clyde. G81	7	AY18	Lord Way, (Baill.) G69	43	CP32	Lunderston Cl, G53	62	BD39
Lochlea Rd, G43	64	BM39	*off Dukes Rd*			Lunderston Dr, G53	50	BC38
Lochlea Rd, (Cumb.) G67	73	DD10	Loretto Pl, G33	40	CB29	Lunderston Gdns, G53	62	BD39
Lochlea Rd, (Ruther.) G73	66	BV40	Loretto St, G33	40	CB29	Lundie Gdns, (Bishop.) G64	25	BZ21
Lochleven La, G42	53	BQ38	Lorn Av, (Chry.) G69	28	CM21	Lundie St, G32	56	CA34

Name		
Lusset Vw, Clyde. G81	7	AX18
off Granville St		
Lusshill Ter, (Udd.) G71	58	CK35
Luss Rd, G51	35	BH30
Lybster Cres, (Ruther.) G73	67	BZ42
Lye Brae, (Cumb.) G67	73	DD11
Lyle Pl, Pais. PA2	48	AV35
Lylesland Ct, Pais. PA2	48	AU35
Lymburn St, G3	36	BM28
Lyndale Pl, G20	22	BM21
Lyndale Rd, G20	22	BM21
Lyndhurst Gdns, G20	23	BP26
Lyndhurst Gdns La, G20	23	BN25
Lyne Cft, (Bishop.) G64	13	BW17
Lynedoch Cres, G3	4	BP28
Lynedoch Cres La, G3	4	BP28
Lynedoch Pl, G3	4	BP28
Lynedoch Pl, G3	4	BP28
Lynedoch St, G3	4	BP28
Lynedoch Ter, G3	4	BP28
Lyne Dr, G23	11	BN20
Lynnhurst, (Udd.) G71	59	CP38
Lynn Wk, (Udd.) G71	71	CQ40
off Flax Rd		
Lynton Av, (Giff.) G46	64	BJ44
Lyoncross Av, (Barr.) G78	61	AZ43
Lyoncross Cres, (Barr.) G78	61	AZ42
off Lyoncross Av		
Lyoncross Rd, G53	50	BD35
Lyon Rd, Pais. PA2	47	AP36
Lyon Rd, (Linw.) Pais. PA3	46	AK33
Lysander Way, Renf. PA4	33	AZ28
Lytham Dr, G23	11	BN20
Lytham Meadows, (Both.) G71	71	CN43

M

Name		
McAlpine St, G2	4	BQ30
McArthur St, G43	52	BL37
off Pleasance St		
Macarthur Wynd, (Camb.) G72	69	CE40
McAslin Ct, G4	5	BT29
McAslin St, G4	5	BU29
Macbeth Pl, G31	55	BZ33
Macbeth St, G31	55	BZ33
McCallum Av, (Ruther.) G73	55	BX38
Maccallum Dr, (Camb.) G72	69	CE40
McClue Av, Renf. PA4	19	AX25
McClue Rd, Renf. PA4	19	AY25
McCracken Av, Renf. PA4	33	AX27
McCreery St, Clyde. G81	19	AZ21
McCrorie Pl, (Kilb.) John. PA10	44	AC34
McCulloch St, G41	53	BP33
McDonald Av, John. PA5	45	AG36
McDonald Cres, Clyde. G81	19	AZ21
Macdonald St, (Ruther.) G73	55	BW38
off Greenhill Rd		
Macdougall Dr, (Camb.) G72	69	CE40
Macdougall St, G43	52	BL38
Macdowall St, John. PA5	45	AH34
Macdowall St, Pais. PA3	32	AT31
Macduff Pl, G31	55	BZ33
Macduff St, G31	55	BZ33
Mace Rd, G13	9	BE20
Macfarlane Cres, (Camb.) G72	69	CE40
Macfarlane Rd, (Bears.) G61	9	BH18
McFarlane St, G4	5	BU31
McFarlane St, Pais. PA3	32	AS30
McGhee St, Clyde. G81	7	AX17
McGown St, Pais. PA3	32	AT31
McGregor Av, Renf. PA4	33	AX27
Macgregor Ct, (Camb.) G72	69	CE40
off Macarthur Wynd		
McGregor Rd, (Cumb.) G67	72	DA12
McGregor St, G51	35	BH31
McGregor St, Clyde. G81	19	AZ21
Machrie Dr, G45	66	BV41
Machrie Rd, G45	66	BV41
Machrie St, G45	66	BV41
McIntosh Ct, G31	38	BV30
McIntosh St, G31	38	BV30
McIntyre Pl, Pais. PA2	48	AU35
McIntyre St, G3	4	BP30
McIntyre Ter, (Camb.) G72	68	CC39
off Keirs Wk		
McIver St, (Camb.) G72	69	CF39
McKay Cres, John. PA5	46	AJ35
Mackean St, Pais. PA3	32	AS31
McKechnie St, G51	36	BJ29
Mackeith St, G40	54	BV33

Name		
McKenzie Av, Clyde. G81	7	AX17
Mackenzie Dr, (Millik.) John. PA10	44	AD36
McKenzie St, Pais. PA3	32	AS32
McKerrell St, Pais. PA1	33	AW32
Mackiesmill Rd, (Elder.) John. PA5	46	AM37
Mackie St, G4	38	BS27
off Borron St		
Mackinlay St, G5	53	BR33
McLaren Av, Renf. PA4	33	AY28
McLaren Ct, (Giff.) G46	64	BK44
off Fenwick Pl		
McLaren Cres, G20	23	BN22
McLaren Gdns, G20	23	BN22
Maclaren Pl, G44	65	BP43
off Clarkston Rd		
McLaurin Cres, John. PA5	45	AF36
Maclay Av, (Kilb.) John. PA10	44	AC35
McLean Pl, Pais. PA3	32	AT30
off Gockston Rd		
Maclean Sq, G51	36	BM31
Maclean St, G51	36	BM31
Maclean St, Clyde. G81	20	BA21
Maclehose Rd, (Cumb.) G67	73	DE10
Maclellan St, G41	36	BL32
McLennan St, G42	53	BQ37
Macleod St, G4	5	BU29
Macleod Way, (Camb.) G72	69	CE40
Macmillan Gdns, (Udd.) G71	59	CQ37
McNair St, G32	40	CC32
McNeil Gdns, G5	54	BT33
McNeill Av, Clyde. G81	8	BA20
McNeil St, G5	54	BT33
McPhail St, G40	54	BU33
McPhater St, G4	4	BR28
McPherson Dr, (Both.) G71	71	CR42
Mactaggart Rd, (Cumb.) G67	72	DA13
Madison Av, G44	65	BR40
Madras Pl, G40	54	BV34
Madras St, G40	54	BV34
Mafeking St, G51	36	BK31
Magdalen Way, Pais. PA2	46	AM38
Magnolia Dr, (Camb.) G72	69	CH42
Magnus Cres, G44	65	BR41
Mahon Ct, (Mood.) G69	17	CP20
Maidland Rd, G53	51	BE37
Mailerbeg Gdns, (Mood.) G69	17	CP18
Mailing Av, (Bishop.) G64	13	BY19
Mainhead Ter, (Cumb.) G67	73	DD8
off Roadside		
Mainhill Av, (Baill.) G69	42	CM32
Mainhill Dr, (Baill.) G69	42	CL32
Mainhill Pl, (Baill.) G69	42	CL32
Mainhill Rd, (Baill.) G69	43	CP32
Main Rd, (Elder.) John. PA5	46	AL34
Main Rd, (Millarston) Pais. PA1	47	AN34
Main Rd, (Castlehead) Pais. PA2	48	AT33
Mains Av, (Giff.) G46	64	BK44
Mainscroft, Ersk. PA8	6	AS20
Mains Dr, Ersk. PA8	6	AS20
Mains River, Ersk. PA8	6	AS20
Main St, G40	54	BV34
Main St, (Thornlie.) G46	63	BH42
Main St, (Cumb.) G67	73	DD8
Main St, (Baill.) G69	58	CL33
Main St, (Chry.) G69	16	CM20
Main St, (Both.) G71	71	CQ43
Main St, (Udd.) G71	71	CP39
Main St, (Camb.) G72	68	CC39
Main St, (Ruther.) G73	55	BW37
Main St, (Barr.) G78	61	AX43
Mains Wd, Ersk. PA8	6	AT20
Mair St, G51	37	BN31
Maitland Pl, Renf. PA4	33	AX27
Maitland St, G4	4	BR28
Malin Pl, G33	40	CB29
Mallaig Path, G51	35	BF30
off Moss Rd		
Mallaig Pl, G51	35	BF30
off Mallaig Rd		
Mallaig Rd, G51	35	BF30
Mallard La, (Both.) G71	71	CR42
off Fallside Rd		
Mallard Rd, Clyde. G81	7	AX16
Malloch Cres, (Elder.) John. PA5	46	AK35
Malloch St, G20	23	BN24

Name		
Malta Ter, G5	53	BR33
Maltbarns St, G20	23	BQ26
Malvern Ct, G31	39	BW31
Malvern Way, Pais. PA3	32	AT29
Mambeg Dr, G51	35	BG29
off St. Kenneth Dr		
Mamore Pl, G43	64	BL39
Mamore St, G43	64	BL39
Manchester Dr, G12	22	BJ23
Mannering Ct, G41	52	BL37
Mannering Rd, G41	52	BL37
Mannering Rd, Pais. PA2	47	AN37
Mannering Way, Pais. PA2	47	AN37
off Brediland Rd		
Mannofield, (Bears.) G61	9	BE17
Manor Pk Av, Pais. PA2	47	AR36
Manor Rd, G14	21	BG25
Manor Rd, G15	8	BB20
Manor Rd, (Gart.) G69	29	CP24
Manor Rd, Pais. PA2	47	AP36
Manor Way, (Ruther.) G73	67	BY41
Manresa Pl, G4	37	BR27
Manse Av, (Bears.) G61	9	BH16
Manse Av, (Both.) G71	71	CQ43
Manse Brae, G44	65	BR39
Manse Brae, (Camb.) G72	70	CJ40
Manse Ct, (Barr.) G78	61	AZ42
Mansefield Av, (Camb.) G72	68	CC41
Manse Gdns, G32	57	CF33
Mansel St, G21	24	BV24
Manse Rd, G32	57	CF33
Manse Rd, (Bears.) G61	9	BG16
Manse Rd, (Baill.) G69	43	CN31
Manse Rd, Renf. PA4	19	AZ25
Mansewood Rd, G43	64	BK39
Mansfield Dr, (Udd.) G71	71	CP39
Mansfield Rd, G52	34	BB30
Mansfield St, G11	36	BL27
Mansion Ct, (Camb.) G72	68	CC39
Mansionhouse Av, G32	57	CE37
Mansionhouse Dr, G32	41	CE31
Mansionhouse Gdns, G41	53	BN38
Mansionhouse Gro, G32	57	CG34
Mansionhouse Rd, G32	57	CG33
Mansionhouse Rd, G41	53	BN38
Mansionhouse Rd, Pais. PA1	33	AW32
Mansion St, G22	24	BS24
Mansion St, (Camb.) G72	68	CC39
Maple Cres, (Camb.) G72	69	CH42
Maple Dr, (Kirk.) G66	14	CC16
Maple Dr, Clyde. G81	6	AV16
Maple Dr, John. PA5	45	AH37
Maple Rd, G41	52	BK33
Marchbank Gdns, Pais. PA1	49	AZ33
Marchfield, (Bishop.) G64	12	BU18
Marchfield Av, Pais. PA3	32	AT29
Marchglen Pl, G51	35	BF30
off Mallaig Rd		
March La, G41	53	BP35
off Nithsdale Dr		
Marchmont Gdns, (Bishop.) G64	12	BV18
Marchmont Ter, G12	22	BL26
off Observatory Rd		
March St, G41	53	BP35
Maree Dr, G52	51	BG33
Maree Gdns, (Bishop.) G64	13	BX20
Maree Rd, Pais. PA2	47	AQ35
Marfield St, G32	40	CA30
Mar Gdns, (Ruther.) G73	67	BZ41
Margaretta Bldgs, G44	65	BQ39
off Clarkston Rd		
Marguerite Av, (Lenz.) G66	15	CE15
Marguerite Dr, (Kirk.) G66	15	CE15
Marguerite Gdns, (Kirk.) G66	15	CE15
Marguerite Gdns, (Both.) G71	71	CR43
Marguerite Gro, (Kirk.) G66	15	CE15
Marine Cres, G51	37	BN31
Marine Gdns, G51	4	BP31
off Mavisbank Gdns		
Mariscat Rd, G41	53	BN35
Marjory Dr, Pais. PA3	33	AW30
Marjory Rd, Renf. PA4	33	AW28
Markdow Av, G53	50	BC36
Marlach Pl, G53	50	BC36
Marlborough Av, G11	21	BH26
Marlborough La N, G11	21	BH26
Marlborough La S, G11	21	BH26
Marldon La, G11	21	BH26
Marlow St, G41	53	BN33

Name	Map	Grid
Marmion Ct, Pais. PA2	47	AP37
off Heriot Av		
Marmion Rd, Pais. PA2	47	AN37
Marne St, G31	39	BX30
Marnoch Way, (Mood.) G69	17	CQ19
off Braeside Av		
Marnock Ter, Pais. PA2	49	AW34
Marquis Gate, (Udd.) G71	71	CN40
Marshall's La, Pais. PA1	48	AU33
Martha St, G1	5	BS29
Martin Cres, (Baill.) G69	42	CL32
Martin St, G40	54	BV34
Martlet Dr, John. PA5	45	AE38
Mart St, G1	5	BS31
off Bridgegate		
Martyrs Pl, (Bishop.) G64	25	BW21
Marwick St, G31	39	BX30
Maryhill Rd, G20	23	BP26
Maryhill Rd, (Bears.) G61	10	BJ19
Maryhill Shop Cen, G20	23	BN24
Maryland Dr, G52	51	BG33
Maryland Gdns, G52	35	BG32
Mary Sq, (Baill.) G69	43	CP32
Maryston Pl, G33	39	BZ27
Maryston St, G33	39	BZ27
Mary St, G4	37	BR27
Mary St, John. PA5	46	AJ34
Mary St, Pais. PA2	48	AU35
Maryville Av, (Giff.) G46	64	BL43
Maryville Gdns, (Giff.) G46	64	BL43
Maryville Vw, (Udd.) G71	58	CM36
Marywood Sq, G41	53	BP35
Masonfield Av, (Cumb.) G68	72	CZ11
Masterton St, G21	24	BS26
Masterton Way, (Udd.) G71	59	CR36
Mathieson Rd, (Ruther.) G73	55	BY36
Mathieson St, G5	54	BT33
Mathieson St, Pais. PA1	33	AX32
Matilda Rd, G41	53	BN34
Mauchline St, G5	53	BQ33
Maukinfauld Ct, G32	55	BZ34
Maukinfauld Gdns, G31	56	CA33
Maukinfauld Rd, G32	56	CA34
Mauldslie St, G40	55	BX33
Maule Dr, G11	36	BJ27
Mavis Bk, (Bishop.) G64	24	BV31
Mavisbank Gdns, G51	37	BN31
Mavisbank Ter, John. PA5	45	AH35
off Campbell St		
Mavisbank Ter, Pais. PA1	48	AV34
Maxton Av, (Barr.) G78	61	AW42
Maxton Gro, (Barr.) G78	61	AW43
Maxton Ter, (Camb.) G72	68	CB42
Maxwell Av, G41	53	BN33
Maxwell Av, (Bears.) G61	9	BG18
Maxwell Av, (Baill.) G69	58	CJ33
Maxwell Ct, G41	53	BN33
off St. John's Rd		
Maxwell Dr, G41	52	BL33
Maxwell Dr, (Baill.) G69	42	CJ32
Maxwell Gdns, G41	52	BM33
Maxwell Gro, G41	52	BM33
Maxwell La, G41	53	BN33
off Maxwell Dr		
Maxwell Oval, G41	53	BP33
Maxwell Pl, G41	53	BQ34
Maxwell Pl, (Udd.) G71	71	CQ39
off North British Rd		
Maxwell Rd, G41	53	BP33
Maxwell St, G1	5	BS31
Maxwell St, (Baill.) G69	58	CK33
Maxwell St, Clyde. G81	6	AV17
Maxwell St, Pais. PA3	32	AU32
Maxwell Ter, G41	53	BN33
Maxwellton Ct, Pais. PA1	48	AS33
Maxwellton Rd, Pais. PA1	47	AR33
Maxwellton St, Pais. PA1	48	AS34
Maxwelton Rd, G33	39	BZ27
Maybank La, G42	53	BQ36
Maybank St, G42	53	BQ36
off Albert Av		
Mayberry Cres, G32	41	CF32
Mayberry Gdns, G32	41	CF32
Mayberry Gro, G32	41	CF32
Maybole St, G53	62	BB39
Mayfield St, G20	23	BP23
May Rd, Pais. PA2	48	AU38
May Ter, G42	53	BR37
May Ter, (Giff.) G46	64	BL42
Meadowbank La, (Udd.) G71	71	CN39
Meadowburn, (Bishop.) G64	12	BV17
Meadowburn Av, (Lenz.) G66	15	CG16
Meadowhead Av, (Chry.) G69	17	CP19
Meadow La, (Both.) G71	71	CR43
Meadow La, Renf. PA4	19	AZ24
Meadowpark St, G31	39	BX30
Meadow Rd, G11	36	BJ27
Meadows Av, Ersk. PA8	6	AS20
Meadows Dr, Ersk. PA8	6	AS20
Meadowside Av, (Elder.)	46	AL35
John. PA5		
Meadowside Ind Est, Renf.	19	AZ23
PA4		
Meadowside Quay, G11	35	BG28
Meadowside St, G11	36	BJ28
Meadowside St, Renf. PA4	19	AZ24
Meadow Vw, (Cumb.) G67	73	DE10
Meadowwell St, G32	40	CD32
Mearns Way, (Bishop.) G64	13	BZ19
Medlar Ct, (Camb.) G72	69	CH42
off Maple Cres		
Medlar Rd, (Cumb.) G67	73	DF10
Medwin St, (Camb.) G72	69	CF40
Medwyn St, G14	21	BF26
Meek Pl, (Camb.) G72	68	CD40
Meetinghouse La, Pais.	32	AU32
PA1		
off Moss St		
Megan Gate, G40	54	BV33
off Megan St		
Megan St, G40	54	BV33
Meikle Av, Renf. PA4	33	AY27
Meiklerig Cres, G53	51	BE35
Meikleriggs Dr, Pais. PA2	47	AQ36
Meikle Rd, G53	51	BE37
Meiklewood Rd, G51	35	BF31
Melbourne Av, Clyde. G81	6	AT16
Melbourne Ct, (Giff.) G46	64	BM42
Melbourne St, G31	38	BV31
Meldon Pl, G51	35	BG30
off Mallaig Rd		
Meldrum Gdns, G41	52	BM35
Meldrum St, Clyde. G81	19	AZ21
Melford Av, (Giff.) G46	64	BM43
Melford Way, Pais. PA3	33	AW30
off Knock Way		
Melfort Av, G41	52	BK33
Melfort Av, Clyde. G81	7	AX18
Melfort Ct, Clyde. G81	7	AY19
Melfort Gdns, (Millik.) John.	45	AE36
PA10		
off Milliken Park Rd		
Mellerstain Dr, G14	20	BA23
Mellerstain Gro, G14	20	BB23
off Mellerstain Dr		
Melness Pl, G51	35	BF30
off Mallaig Rd		
Melrose Av, Pais. PA2	47	AQ36
Melrose Av, (Linw.) Pais. PA3	30	AK32
Melrose Ct, (Ruther.) G73	55	BX38
Melrose Gdns, G20	23	BP26
Melrose Gdns, (Udd.) G71	59	CP36
Melrose Pl, (Blan.) G72	70	CL44
Melrose St, G4	37	BP27
off Queens Cres		
Melvaig Pl, G20	22	BM24
Melvick Pl, G51	35	BF30
off Mallaig Rd		
Melville Ct, G1	5	BT31
off Brunswick St		
Melville Gdns, (Bishop.) G64	13	BW19
Melville St, G41	53	BP34
Memel St, G21	24	BU24
Memus Av, G52	51	BE33
Mennock Dr, (Bishop.) G64	13	BW17
Menock Rd, G44	65	BR39
Menteith Av, (Bishop.) G64	13	BX20
Menteith Dr, (Ruther.) G73	67	BZ43
Menteith Pl, (Ruther.) G73	67	BZ43
Menzies Dr, G21	25	BW24
Menzies Pl, G21	25	BW24
Menzies Rd, G21	25	BW24
Merchant La, G1	5	BS31
Merchants Cl, (Kilb.) John.	44	AC34
PA10		
Merchiston St, G32	40	CA30
Merkland Ct, G11	36	BK28
off Vine St		
Merkland St, G11	36	BK27
Merksworth Way, Pais. PA3	32	AU30
off Mosslands Rd		
Merlewood Av, (Both.) G71	71	CR41
Merlinford Av, Renf. PA4	20	BA26
Merlinford Cres, Renf. PA4	20	BA26
Merlinford Dr, Renf. PA4	20	BA26
Merlinford Way, Renf. PA4	20	BA26
Merlin Way, Pais. PA3	33	AX30
Merrick Gdns, G51	36	BK32
Merrick Path, G51	36	BK32
off Merrick Gdns		
Merrick Ter, (Udd.) G71	59	CR38
Merrick Way, (Ruther.) G73	67	BX42
Merryburn Av, (Giff.) G46	64	BM40
Merrycrest Av, (Giff.) G46	64	BM41
Merrycroft Av, (Giff.) G46	64	BM41
Merryland Pl, G51	36	BK30
Merryland St, G51	36	BK30
Merrylee Cres, (Giff.) G46	64	BL40
Merrylee Pk Av, (Giff.) G46	64	BM41
Merrylee Pk La, (Giff.) G46	64	BL41
Merrylee Pk Ms, (Giff.) G46	64	BM40
Merrylee Rd, G43	64	BM40
Merrylee Rd, G44	65	BN40
Merryton Av, G15	8	BD18
Merryton Av, (Giff.) G46	64	BL41
Merryton Pl, G15	8	BD18
Merryvale Av, (Giff.) G46	64	BM41
Merryvale Pl, (Giff.) G46	64	BL40
Merton Dr, G52	34	BC32
Meryon Gdns, G32	57	CF35
Meryon Rd, G32	57	CF34
off Dornford Av		
Methil St, G14	21	BE26
Methuen Rd, Pais. PA3	32	AV28
Methven Av, (Bears.) G61	10	BK16
Methven St, G31	55	BZ34
Methven St, Clyde. G81	6	AV17
Metropole La, G1	5	BS31
off Clyde St		
Mews La, Pais. PA3	32	AV30
Micklehouse Oval, (Baill.) G69	42	CK31
Micklehouse Pl, (Baill.) G69	42	CK31
Micklehouse Rd, (Baill.) G69	42	CK31
Micklehouse Wynd, (Baill.) G69	42	CK31
Mid Cotts, (Gart.) G69	28	CL26
Midcroft, (Bishop.) G64	12	BU18
Midcroft Av, G44	66	BT40
Middlemuir Av, (Kirk.) G66	15	CF15
Middlemuir Rd, (Lenz.) G66	15	CF15
Middle Pk, Pais. PA2	48	AT35
Middlerigg Rd, (Cumb.) G68	72	CZ11
Middlesex Gdns, G41	37	BN31
Middlesex St, G41	37	BN32
Middleton Cres, Pais. PA3	31	AR31
Middleton Rd, Pais. PA3	31	AR31
Middleton Rd, (Linw.) Pais.	30	AM30
PA3		
Middleton St, G51	36	BL31
Midfaulds Av, Renf. PA4	34	BA27
off King George Park Av		
Midland St, G1	4	BR30
Midlem Dr, G52	35	BE32
Midlem Oval, G52	35	BE32
Midlock St, G51	36	BL32
Midlothian Dr, G41	52	BM36
Midton Cotts, (Mood.) G69	17	CQ20
Midton St, G21	24	BV26
Midwharf St, G4	38	BS27
Migvie Pl, G20	22	BM24
off Wyndford Rd		
Milan St, G41	53	BQ34
Milford St, G33	40	CC29
Millands Av, (Blan.) G72	70	CL44
Millbank Av, G21	24	BU25
Millarston Av, Pais. PA1	47	AQ33
Millarston Ct, Pais. PA1	47	AR33
Millarston Dr, Pais. PA1	47	AQ33
Millarston Ind Est, Pais. PA1	47	AQ34
Millar St, Pais. PA1	32	AV32
off Christie St		
Millar Ter, (Ruther.) G73	55	BX36
Millbeg Cres, G33	41	CH31
Millbeg Pl, G33	41	CG32

<table>
Name	No.	Code
Millbrae Av, (Chry.) G69	28	CM21
Millbrae Ct, G42	53	BP38
Millbrae Cres, G42	53	BN38
Millbrae Cres, Clyde. G81	19	AZ22
Millbrae Gdns, G42	53	BP38
Millbrae Rd, G42	53	BN38
Millbrix Av, G14	20	BC24
Millburn Av, (Ruther.) G73	67	BW39
Millburn Av, Clyde. G81	20	BA21
Millburn Av, Renf. PA4	19	AZ26
Millburn Dr, Renf. PA4	20	BA26
Millburn Rd, Renf. PA4	19	AZ26
Millburn St, G21	38	BV28
Millburn Way, Renf. PA4	20	BA26
Mill Ct, (Ruther.) G73	55	BW37
Mill Cres, G40	54	BV34
Millcroft Rd, (Cumb.) G67	73	DD12
Millcroft Rd, (Ruther.) G73	54	BV35
Millennium Ct, G34	42	CL29
Millennium Gdns, G34	42	CL30
Millerfield Pl, G40	55	BX34
Millerfield Rd, G40	55	BX34
Miller La, Clyde. G81	7	AX20
Millersneuk Av, (Lenz.) G66	15	CF18
Millersneuk Cres, G33	26	CC24
Millersneuk Dr, (Lenz.) G66	15	CF17
Millersneuk Rd, (Kirk.) G66	15	CF17
Millers Pl, (Lenz.) G66	15	CF17
Millerston St, G31	39	BW31
Miller St, G1	5	BS30
Miller St, (Baill.) G69	58	CK33
Miller St, Clyde. G81	7	AX20
Miller St, John. PA5	46	AK34
Millford Dr, (Linw.) Pais. PA3	30	AK32
Millgate, (Udd.) G71	59	CP37
Millgate Av, (Udd.) G71	59	CP37
Millgate Ct, (Udd.) G71	59	CP38
Millholm Rd, G44	65	BR41
Millhouse Cres, G20	22	BL22
Millhouse Dr, G20	22	BL22
Millichen Rd, G23	10	BM16
Milliken Dr, (Millik.) John. PA10	45	AE35
Milliken Pk Rd, (Millik.) John. PA10	45	AE36
Milliken Rd, (Millik.) John. PA10	45	AE35
Mill Pl, (Linw.) Pais. PA3	30	AJ31
Millport Av, G44	54	BS38
Mill Ri, (Lenz.) G66	15	CF17
Mill Rd, (Both.) G71	71	CQ44
Mill Rd, (Camb.) G72	69	CF40
Mill Rd, Clyde. G81	19	AZ22
Millroad Dr, G40	5	BU31
Millroad Gdns, G40	38	BV31
Millroad St, G40	5	BU31
Millstream Ct, Pais. PA1	48	AV33
Mill St, G40	54	BV34
Mill St, (Ruther.) G73	55	BW37
Mill St, Pais. PA1	48	AV33
Millview, (Barr.) G78	61	AZ42
Millview Pl, G53	62	BD41
Millwood St, G41	53	BN37
Milnbank St, G31	39	BW29
Milncroft Pl, G33	40	CC28
Milncroft Rd, G33	40	CC28
Milner La, G13	21	BG24
Milner Rd, G13	21	BG24
Milngavie Rd, (Bears.) G61	9	BH18
Milnpark Gdns, G41	36	BM32
Milnpark St, G41	37	BN32
Milovaig Av, G23	10	BM20
Milovaig St, G23	10	BM20
Milrig Rd, (Ruther.) G73	54	BV38
Milton Av, (Camb.) G72	68	CA40
Milton Douglas Rd, Clyde. G81	7	AW15
Milton Dr, (Bishop.) G64	24	BU22
Milton Gdns, (Udd.) G71	59	CN37
Milton Mains Rd, Clyde. G81	7	AW16
Milton St, G4	5	BS28
Milverton Av, (Bears.) G61	9	BE15
Milverton Rd, (Giff.) G46	64	BJ44
Minard Rd, G41	53	BN36
Minard Way, (Udd.) G71	59	CQ38
off Newton Dr		
Minerva St, G3	37	BN29
Minerva Way, G3	37	BN29
Mingarry La, G20	23	BN25
off Clouston St		
Mingarry St, G20	23	BN25
Mingulay Cres, G22	24	BT21
Mingulay Pl, G22	24	BU21
Mingulay St, G22	24	BT21
Minister Wk, (Baill.) G69	43	CP32
off Dukes Rd		
Minmoir Rd, G53	50	BB38
Minstrel Rd, G13	9	BF20
Minto Av, (Ruther.) G73	67	BZ41
Minto Cres, G52	35	BH32
Minto St, G52	35	BH32
Mireton St, G22	23	BR24
Mirrlees Dr, G12	22	BL25
Mirrlees La, G12	22	BL25
Mitchell Arc, (Ruther.) G73	55	BX37
off Stonelaw Rd		
Mitchell Av, (Camb.) G72	69	CG39
Mitchell Av, Renf. PA4	33	AX27
Mitchell Dr, (Ruther.) G73	67	BX39
Mitchellhill Rd, G45	66	BV43
Mitchell La, G1	4	BR30
Mitchell Rd, (Cumb.) G67	72	DB11
Mitchell St, G1	4	BR30
Mitchell St, Coat. ML5	43	CR32
Mitchison Rd, (Cumb.) G67	73	DC10
Mitre Ct, G11	21	BH25
Mitre Gate, G11	21	BH25
Mitre La, G14	21	BF25
Mitre La W, G14	21	BF25
Mitre Rd, G11	21	BH25
Mitre Rd, G14	21	BG25
Moat Av, G13	21	BE22
Mochrum Rd, G43	65	BN39
Moffat Pl, (Blan.) G72	70	CM44
Moffat St, G5	54	BT33
Mogarth Av, Pais. PA2	47	AP37
Moidart Av, Renf. PA4	19	AX25
Moidart Ct, (Barr.) G78	61	AX40
Moidart Cres, G52	35	BG32
Moidart Pl, G52	35	BG32
Moidart Rd, G52	35	BG32
Moir St, G1	5	BT31
Molendinar Cl, G33	40	CA27
Molendinar Gdns, G33	39	BZ27
Molendinar St, G1	5	BT31
Mollinsburn St, G21	24	BU26
Monach Rd, G33	41	CE29
Monar Dr, G22	23	BR26
off Monar St		
Monar Pl, G22	23	BR26
off Monar St		
Monart Pl, G20	23	BP24
Moncrieff Av, (Lenz.) G66	15	CE16
Moncrieff Gdns, (Kirk.) G66	15	CF16
off Moncrieff Av		
Moncrieff St, Pais. PA3	32	AU32
off Back Sneddon St		
Moncur St, G40	5	BU31
Moness Dr, G52	51	BG33
Monifieth Av, G52	51	BF34
Monikie Gdns, (Bishop.) G64	13	BZ20
Monkcastle Dr, (Camb.) G72	68	CC39
Monkland Vw, (Udd.) G71	59	CQ36
off Lincoln Av		
Monkland Vw Cres, (Baill.) G69	43	CP32
Monksbridge Av, G13	9	BE20
Monkscroft Av, G11	22	BJ26
Monkscroft Ct, G11	36	BJ27
off Crow Rd		
Monkscroft Gdns, G11	22	BJ26
off Monkscroft Av		
Monkton Dr, G15	8	BD19
Monmouth Av, G12	22	BJ23
Monreith Av, (Bears.) G61	9	BG19
Monreith Rd, G43	65	BN39
Monreith Rd E, G44	65	BQ40
Monroe Dr, (Udd.) G71	59	CP36
Monroe Pl, (Udd.) G71	59	CP36
Montague La, G12	22	BK25
Montague St, G4	37	BP27
Montclair Pl, (Linw.) Pais. PA3	30	AJ31
Monteith Pl, G40	38	BU32
Monteith Row, G40	38	BU32
Monteith Row La, G40	38	BU32
off Monteith Pl		
Montford Av, G44	54	BT38
Montford Av, (Ruther.) G73	54	BU38
Montgomery Av, Pais. PA3	33	AX29
Montgomery Ct, Pais. PA3	33	AX30
off Montgomery Av		
Montgomery Dr, (Giff.) G46	64	BL44
Montgomery Dr, (Kilb.) John. PA10	44	AC33
off Meadside Av		
Montgomery Rd, Pais. PA3	33	AW29
Montgomery St, G40	55	BW33
Montgomery St, (Camb.) G72	69	CG40
Montraive St, (Ruther.) G73	55	BY36
Montrave Path, G52	51	BF33
off Montrave St		
Montrave St, G52	51	BF33
Montreal Ho, Clyde. G81	6	AT15
off Perth Cres		
Montrose Av, G32	57	CE36
Montrose Av, G52	34	BB29
Montrose Ct, Pais. PA2	47	AP37
off Montrose Rd		
Montrose Gdns, (Blan.) G72	70	CL43
Montrose Pl, (Linw.) Pais. PA3	30	AJ31
Montrose Rd, Pais. PA2	47	AP37
Montrose St, G1	5	BT30
Montrose St, G4	5	BT29
Montrose St, Clyde. G81	7	AX19
Montrose Ter, (Bishop.) G64	25	BY22
Monument Dr, G33	26	CA24
Monymusk Gdns, (Bishop.) G64	13	BZ19
Monymusk Pl, G15	8	BA16
Moodiesburn St, G33	39	BZ27
Moorburn Av, (Giff.) G46	64	BK42
Moore Dr, (Bears.) G61	9	BH18
Moore St, G31	38	BV31
off Gallowgate		
Moorfoot, (Bishop.) G64	13	BY19
Moorfoot Av, (Thornlie.) G46	64	BJ42
Moorfoot Av, Pais. PA2	48	AT36
Moorfoot Path, Pais. PA2	48	AT37
off Moorfoot Av		
Moorfoot St, G32	40	CA31
Moorhouse Av, Pais. PA2	47	AR35
Moorhouse St, (Barr.) G78	61	AY43
Moorings, The, Pais. PA2	47	AR34
Moorpark Av, G52	34	BB31
Moorpark Av, (Muir.) G69	28	CL22
Moorpark Dr, G52	34	BC31
Moorpark Pl, G52	34	BB31
Moorpark Sq, Renf. PA4	33	AX27
Morag Av, (Blan.) G72	70	CL44
Moraine Av, G15	8	BD20
Moraine Circ, G15	8	BC20
Moraine Dr, G15	8	BC20
Moraine Pl, G15	8	BD20
off Moraine Av		
Morar Av, Clyde. G81	7	AX17
Morar Ct, Clyde. G81	7	AX17
Morar Cres, (Bishop.) G64	12	BV19
Morar Cres, Clyde. G81	7	AX17
Morar Dr, (Bears.) G61	10	BK18
Morar Dr, (Ruther.) G73	67	BX42
Morar Dr, Clyde. G81	7	AX17
Morar Dr, Pais. PA2	47	AP35
Morar Dr, (Linw.) Pais. PA3	30	AJ32
Morar Pl, Clyde. G81	7	AX17
Morar Pl, Renf. PA4	19	AX25
Morar Rd, G52	35	BG32
Morar Rd, Clyde. G81	7	AX17
Morar Ter, (Udd.) G71	59	CR38
Morar Ter, (Ruther.) G73	67	BZ42
Moravia Av, (Both.) G71	71	CQ42
Moray Ct, (Ruther.) G73	55	BW37
Moray Gdns, (Cumb.) G68	72	DB8
Moray Gdns, (Udd.) G71	59	CP37
Moray Gate, (Both.) G71	71	CN41
Moray Pl, G41	53	BN35
Moray Pl, (Bishop.) G64	13	BY20
Moray Pl, (Chry.) G69	28	CM21
Moray Pl, (Linw.) Pais. PA3	30	AJ31
Mordaunt St, G40	55	BW34
Moredun Cres, G32	41	CE30
Moredun Dr, Pais. PA2	47	AR36
Moredun Rd, Pais. PA2	47	AR36
Moredun St, G32	41	CE30
Morefield Rd, G51	35	BF30
Morgan Ms, G42	53	BR34
Morina Gdns, G53	63	BE43
off Waukglen Cres		
Morion Rd, G13	21	BF21
Morley St, G42	53	BQ38
</table>

Name		
Morna Pl, G14	35	BG27
off Victoria Pk Dr S		
Morningside St, G33	39	BZ29
Morrin Path, G21	24	BU25
off Crichton St		
Morrin Sq, G4	5	BU29
off Collins St		
Morrin St, G21	24	BU25
Morrison Quad, Clyde. G81	8	BA19
Morrison St, G5	4	BQ31
Morrison St, Clyde. G81	6	AV15
Morriston Cres, Renf. PA4	34	BB28
Morriston Pk Dr, (Camb.) G72	68	CC39
Morriston St, (Camb.) G72	68	CC39
Morton Gdns, G41	52	BL36
Morven Av, (Bishop.) G64	13	BY20
Morven Av, (Blan.) G72	70	CL44
Morven Av, Pais. PA2	48	AT37
Morven Dr, (Linw.) Pais. PA3	30	AJ32
Morven Gait, Ersk. PA8	18	AU21
Morven Gdns, (Udd.) G71	59	CP37
Morven La, (Blan.) G72	70	CL44
Morven Rd, (Bears.) G61	9	BG15
Morven Rd, (Camb.) G72	68	CB42
Morven St, G52	35	BG32
Morven Way, (Both.) G71	71	CR42
Mosesfield St, G21	24	BV24
Mosque Av, G5	38	BS32
Moss Av, (Linw.) Pais. PA3	30	AK31
Mossbank Av, G33	26	CB25
Mossbank Dr, G33	26	CB25
Mosscastle Rd, G33	41	CE27
off Mossvale Rd		
Moss Dr, (Barr.) G78	61	AW40
Mossedge Ind Est, (Linw.)	30	AL31
Pais. PA3		
Mossend La, G33	41	CF29
Mossend St, G33	41	CF30
Mossgiel Av, (Ruther.) G73	67	BW40
Mossgiel Dr, Clyde. G81	7	AY18
Mossgiel Gdns, (Udd.) G71	59	CN37
Mossgiel Pl, (Ruther.) G73	67	BW40
Mossgiel Rd, G43	52	BM38
Mossgiel Rd, (Cumb.) G67	73	DD10
Mossgiel Ter, (Blan.) G72	70	CL43
Moss Hts Av, G52	35	BF32
Moss Knowe, (Cumb.) G67	73	DE11
Mossland Rd, G52	34	BA29
Mosslands Rd, Pais. PA3	32	AT29
Mossneuk Dr, Pais. PA2	48	AS37
Mosspark Av, G52	51	BH34
Mosspark Boul, G52	51	BG33
Mosspark Dr, G52	51	BE33
Mosspark La, G52	51	BG34
off Mosspark Dr		
Mosspark Oval, G52	51	BG34
Mosspark Sq, G52	51	BG34
Moss Path, (Baill.) G69	57	CH34
Moss Rd, G51	35	BE31
Moss Rd, (Kirk.) G66	14	CD15
Moss Rd, (Muir.) G69	28	CL22
Moss Rd, (Hous.) John. PA6	30	AK27
Moss Rd, (Linw.) Pais. PA3	30	AL31
Moss-Side Rd, G41	52	BM36
Moss St, Pais. PA1	32	AU32
Mossvale Cres, G33	41	CE27
Mossvale La, Pais. PA3	32	AT31
Mossvale Path, G33	27	CE26
Mossvale Rd, G33	26	CD26
Mossvale Sq, G33	26	CD26
Mossvale Sq, Pais. PA3	32	AT31
Mossvale St, Pais. PA3	32	AT30
Mossvale Ter, (Chry.) G69	17	CQ18
Mossvale Wk, G33	41	CE27
Mossvale Way, G33	27	CE26
off Mossvale Rd		
Mossview Quad, G52	35	BE32
Mossview Rd, G33	27	CG24
Mote Hill Rd, Pais. PA3	33	AW31
Moulin Circ, G52	50	BC33
Moulin Pl, G52	50	BC33
Moulin Rd, G52	50	BC33
Moulin Ter, G52	50	BC33
Mountainblue St, G31	39	BW32
Mount Annan Dr, G44	53	BR38
Mountblow Ho, Clyde. G81	6	AT16
off Melbourne Av		
Mountblow Rd, Clyde. G81	6	AU15
Mountgarrie Path, G51	35	BF30
off Mountgarrie Rd		
Mountgarrie Rd, G51	35	BF30
Mount Harriet Av, (Stepps) G33	27	CG23
Mount Harriet Dr, (Stepps) G33	27	CF23
Mount Lockhart, (Udd.) G71	58	CK35
Mount Lockhart Gdns, (Udd.)	58	CK35
G71		
off Mount Lockhart		
Mount Lockhart Pl, (Udd.) G71	58	CK35
off Mount Lockhart		
Mount St, G20	23	BP26
Mount Stuart St, G41	53	BN37
Mount Vernon Av, G32	57	CG34
Mowbray Av, (Gart.) G69	29	CP24
Moyne Rd, G53	50	BC35
Moy St, G11	36	BL27
off Church St		
Muckcroft Rd, (Mood.) G69	16	CL17
Muirbank Av, (Ruther.) G73	54	BV38
Muirbank Gdns, (Ruther.) G73	54	BV38
Muirbrae Rd, (Ruther.) G73	67	BX41
Muirbrae Way, (Ruther.) G73	67	BX41
off Muirbrae Rd		
Muirburn Av, G44	65	BN41
Muir Ct, G44	65	BP43
off Strathdon Av		
Muirdrum Av, G52	51	BF34
Muirdykes Av, G52	34	BC32
Muirdykes Cres, Pais. PA3	31	AR31
Muirdykes Rd, G52	34	BC32
Muirdykes Rd, Pais. PA3	31	AR31
Muiredge Ct, (Udd.) G71	71	CP39
Muiredge Ter, (Baill.) G69	58	CK33
Muirend Av, G44	65	BN40
Muirend Rd, G44	65	BN41
Muirfield Ct, G44	65	BN41
off Muirend Rd		
Muirfield Cres, G23	11	BN20
Muirfield Meadows, (Both.)	71	CN43
G71		
Muirfield Rd, (Cumb.) G68	73	DC8
Muirhead-Braehead	73	DD10
Roundabout, (Cumb.) G67		
Muirhead Ct, (Baill.) G69	58	CL33
Muirhead Dr, (Linw.) Pais. PA3	30	AJ32
Muirhead Gdns, (Baill.) G69	58	CL33
Muirhead Gate, (Udd.) G71	59	CR37
Muirhead Gro, (Baill.) G69	58	CL33
Muirhead Rd, (Baill.) G69	58	CK34
Muirhead St, G11	36	BK27
off Purdon St		
Muirhead Way, (Bishop.) G64	13	BZ20
Muirhill Av, G44	65	BN41
Muirhill Cres, G13	20	BC22
Muirkirk Dr, G13	21	BH22
Muirpark Av, Renf. PA4	33	AY27
Muirpark Dr, (Bishop.) G64	25	BW21
Muirpark St, G11	36	BK27
off Gardner St		
Muir Pk Ter, (Bishop.) G64	24	BV21
Muirshiel Av, G53	63	BE39
Muirshiel Cres, G53	63	BE39
Muirside Av, G32	57	CG34
Muirside Rd, (Baill.) G69	58	CK33
Muirside St, (Baill.) G69	58	CK33
Muirskeith Cres, G43	65	BP39
Muirskeith Pl, G43	65	BP39
Muirskeith Rd, G43	65	BP39
Muir St, (Bishop.) G64	13	BW20
Muir St, Renf. PA4	19	AZ25
Muirton Dr, (Bishop.) G64	12	BV18
Muiryfauld Dr, G31	56	CA33
Mulben Cres, G53	50	BB38
Mulben Pl, G53	50	BB38
Mulben Ter, G53	50	BB38
Mulberry Rd, G43	64	BM40
Mulberry Wynd, (Camb.) G72	69	CH42
Mullardoch St, G23	10	BM20
Mull Av, Pais. PA2	48	AT38
Mull Av, Renf. PA4	33	AY28
Mull St, G21	39	BX27
Mungo Pl, (Udd.) G71	59	CQ36
off Lincoln Av		
Munlochy Rd, G51	35	BF30
Munro Ct, Clyde. G81	6	AV15
Munro La, G13	21	BG24
Munro La E, G13	21	BG24
Munro Pl, G13	21	BG24
Munro Rd, G13	21	BG24
Murano St, G20	23	BP25
Murchison, G12	21	BH23
off Ascot Av		
Murdoch St, G21	24	BV24
off Lenzie St		
Muriel St, (Barr.) G78	61	AY42
Muriel St Ind Est, (Barr.) G78	61	AY41
Murray Business Area, Pais.	32	AT31
PA3		
Murrayfield, (Bishop.) G64	13	BW18
Murrayfield Dr, (Bears.) G61	9	BG20
Murrayfield St, G32	40	CA30
Murray Path, (Udd.) G71	71	CN39
Murray Pl, (Barr.) G78	61	AZ41
Murray Rd, (Both.) G71	71	CQ42
Murray St, Pais. PA3	32	AS31
Murray St, Renf. PA4	19	AY26
Murrin Av, (Bishop.) G64	13	BZ20
Murroes Rd, G51	35	BF30
Muslin St, G40	54	BV33
Mybster Pl, G51	35	BF30
off Mallaig Rd		
Mybster Rd, G51	35	BF30
Myers Cres, (Udd.) G71	71	CQ40
Myreside Pl, G32	39	BZ31
Myreside St, G32	39	BZ31
Myres Rd, G53	51	BF37
Myrie Gdns, (Bishop.) G64	13	BX19
Myroch Pl, G34	42	CL28
Myrtle Av, (Lenz.) G66	15	CE16
Myrtle Hill La, G42	54	BS37
Myrtle Pk, G42	53	BR36
Myrtle Pl, G42	54	BS36
Myrtle Rd, (Udd.) G71	59	CR37
Myrtle Rd, Clyde. G81	6	AT17
Myrtle Sq, (Bishop.) G64	25	BW21
Myrtle St, (Blan.) G72	70	CM44
Myrtle Vw Rd, G42	54	BS37
Myrtle Wk, (Camb.) G72	68	CB39
N		
Naburn Gate, G5	54	BS33
Nairn Av, (Blan.) G72	70	CL43
Nairn Pl, Clyde. G81	6	AV18
Nairnside Rd, G21	25	BY22
Nairn St, G3	36	BM28
Nairn St, Clyde. G81	6	AV18
Nairn Way, (Cumb.) G68	73	DC8
Naismith St, G32	57	CE36
Nansen St, G20	23	BQ26
Napier Ct, (Old Kil.) G60	6	AS16
off Freelands Rd		
Napier Dr, G51	36	BK29
Napier Gdns, (Linw.) Pais. PA3	30	AL31
Napier Pl, G51	36	BK29
Napier Pl, (Old Kil.) G60	6	AS16
Napier Rd, G51	36	BK29
Napier Rd, G52	34	BB28
Napiershall La, G20	37	BP27
Napiershall Pl, G20	37	BP27
off Napiershall St		
Napiershall St, G20	37	BP27
Napier St, G51	36	BK29
Napier St, John. PA5	45	AG34
Napier St, (Linw.) Pais. PA3	30	AL31
Napier Ter, G51	36	BK29
Naseby Av, G11	21	BH26
Naseby La, G11	21	BH26
Nasmyth Pl, G52	34	BC30
Nasmyth Rd, G52	34	BC30
Nasmyth Rd N, G52	34	BC30
Nasmyth Rd S, G52	34	BC30
Navar Pl, Pais. PA2	49	AW35
Naver St, G33	40	CA28
Neidpath, (Baill.) G69	58	CJ33
Neilsland Oval, G53	51	BF37
Neilsland Sq, G53	51	BF36
Neilston Av, G53	63	BE40
Neilston Rd, Pais. PA2	48	AU34
Neil St, Pais. PA1	48	AS33
Neilvaig Dr, (Ruther.) G73	67	BY42
Neistpoint Dr, G33	40	CC29
Nelson Mandela Pl, G2	5	BS29
Nelson Pl, (Baill.) G69	58	CK33
Nelson St, G5	4	BQ31
Nelson St, (Baill.) G69	58	CK33
Neptune St, G51	36	BK30
Ness Av, John. PA5	45	AE37

Name	Col1	Col2
Ness Dr, (Blan.) G72	71	CN44
Ness Gdns, (Bishop.) G64	13	BX20
off Wester Cleddens Rd		
Ness Rd, Renf. PA4	19	AX25
Ness St, G51	36	BJ29
Ness St, G33	40	CA28
Nethan St, G51	36	BJ29
Nether Auldhouse Rd, G43	52	BK38
Netherburn Av, G44	65	BP43
Netherby Dr, G41	52	BM33
Nethercairn Rd, G43	64	BL41
Nethercliffe Av, G44	65	BP43
Nethercommon Harbour,	32	AU30
Pais. PA3		
Nethercraigs Ct, Pais. PA2	47	AR38
Nethercraigs Dr, Pais. PA2	48	AS37
Nethercraigs Rd, Pais. PA2	47	AR38
Netherdale Dr, Pais. PA1	50	BB34
Netherfield St, G31	39	BY31
Nethergreen Cres, Renf. PA4	19	AX26
Nethergreen Rd, Renf. PA4	19	AX26
Nethergreen Wynd, Renf. PA4	19	AX26
Netherhill Av, G44	65	BP44
Netherhill Cotts, Pais. PA3	33	AX30
off Netherhill Rd		
Netherhill Cres, Pais. PA3	33	AW31
Netherhill Rd, (Mood.) G69	17	CP20
Netherhill Rd, Pais. PA3	32	AV31
Netherhill Way, Pais. PA3	33	AX30
Netherhouse Av, (Lenz.) G66	15	CG17
Netherhouse Pl, G34	43	CN29
Netherhouse Rd, (Baill.) G69	42	CM30
Netherlee Pl, G44	65	BQ41
Netherlee Rd, G44	65	BP42
Netherpark Av, G44	65	BP44
Netherplace Cres, G53	50	BD37
Netherplace Rd, G53	50	BD37
Netherton Ct, G45	66	BV43
Netherton Dr, (Barr.) G78	61	AZ43
Netherton Rd, G13	21	BG21
Netherton St, G13	21	BH22
Nethervale Av, G44	65	BP44
Netherview Rd, G44	65	BQ44
Netherway, G44	65	BP44
Nethy Way, Renf. PA4	34	BB28
off Teith Av		
Neuk Av, (Muir.) G69	28	CL22
Neuk Way, G32	57	CE37
Nevis Ct, (Barr.) G78	61	AY44
Nevis Rd, G43	64	BK40
Nevis Rd, Renf. PA4	33	AX28
Nevis Way, (Abbots.) Pais. PA3	32	AU28
Newark Dr, G41	52	BM34
Newark Dr, Pais. PA2	48	AS37
Newbank Ct, G31	56	CA33
Newbank Gdns, G31	55	BZ33
Newbank Rd, G31	56	CA33
Newbattle Ct, G32	56	CD35
Newbattle Gdns, G32	56	CD35
Newbattle Pl, G32	56	CD35
Newbattle Rd, G32	56	CC36
Newbold Av, G21	24	BU22
Newburgh St, G43	52	BM38
Newcastleton Dr, G23	11	BN20
off Broughton Rd		
New City Rd, G4	4	BR28
Newcroft Dr, G44	66	BT40
New Edinburgh Rd, (Udd.) G71	59	CP38
New Edinburgh Rd, Bell. ML4	59	CP38
Newfield La, (Both.) G71	71	CR42
Newfield Pl, (Thornlie.) G46	63	BH43
Newfield Pl, (Ruther.) G73	54	BU38
Newfield Sq, G53	62	BC39
Newgrove Gdns, (Camb.) G72	68	CC39
Newhall St, G40	54	BU34
Newhaven Rd, G33	40	CD29
Newhaven St, G32	40	CC30
Newhills Rd, G33	41	CG30
New Inchinnan Rd, Pais. PA3	32	AU30
Newington St, G32	40	CB31
New Kirk Pl, (Bears.) G61	9	BG16
off New Kirk Rd		
New Kirk Rd, (Bears.) G61	9	BG16
Newlandsfield Rd, G43	52	BM38
Newlands Gdns, (Elder.)	46	AL36
John. PA5		
Newlands Rd, G43	65	BN39
Newlands Rd, G43	65	BQ39
Newlands Rd, (Udd.) G71	59	CP37
New Luce Dr, G32	57	CF34
Newmains Rd, Renf. PA4	33	AX27

Name	Col1	Col2
Newmill Rd, G21	25	BY24
Newnham Rd, Pais. PA1	49	AZ33
Newpark Cres, (Camb.) G72	56	CC38
off Morriston Pk Dr		
New Rd, (Camb.) G72	69	CG41
Newshot Ct, Clyde. G81	19	AZ22
off Clydeholm Ter		
Newshot Dr, Ersk. PA8	18	AS22
New Sneddon St, Pais. PA3	32	AU32
Newstead Gdns, G23	11	BN20
New St, Clyde. G81	7	AW15
New St, (Kilb.) John. PA10	44	AC34
New St, Pais. PA1	48	AU33
Newton Av, (Camb.) G72	69	CF39
Newton Av, (Barr.) G78	61	AY44
Newton Av, (Elder.) John. PA5	47	AN34
Newton Brae, (Camb.) G72	69	CG39
Newton Dr, (Udd.) G71	59	CQ38
Newton Dr, (Elder.) John. PA5	47	AN34
Newton Fm Rd, (Camb.) G72	57	CH38
Newtongrange Av, G32	56	CD34
Newtongrange Gdns, G32	56	CD35
Newton Pl, G3	4	BP28
Newton Rd, (Lenz.) G66	15	CG17
Newton Sta Rd, (Camb.) G72	69	CG41
Newton St, G3	4	BQ29
off Argyle St		
Newton St, Pais. PA1	48	AS33
Newton Ter, G3	4	BP29
off Sauchiehall St		
Newton Ter, Pais. PA1	47	AP34
Newton Ter La, G3	4	BP29
Newton Way, Pais. PA3	33	AX30
off Merlin Way		
Newtyle Dr, G53	50	BB36
Newtyle Pl, G53	50	BB36
Newtyle Pl, (Bishop.) G64	13	BZ20
Newtyle Rd, Pais. PA1	49	AX33
New Wynd, G1	5	BS31
Niamh Ct, (Inch.) Renf. PA4	18	AS22
Nicholas St, G1	5	BT30
Nicholson La, G5	4	BR31
off Nicholson St		
Nicholson St, G5	4	BR31
Nicolson Ct, (Stepps) G33	27	CG24
Niddrie Rd, G42	53	BP35
Niddrie Sq, G42	53	BP35
Niddry St, Pais. PA3	32	AV32
Nigel Gdns, G41	52	BM36
Nigg Pl, G34	42	CJ29
Nimmo Dr, G51	35	BG30
Nisbet St, G31	39	BZ32
Nith Av, Pais. PA2	47	AP35
off Don Dr		
Nith Dr, Renf. PA4	34	BA27
Nith Pl, John. PA5	45	AE37
Nithsdale Cres, (Bears.) G61	9	BE15
Nithsdale Dr, G41	53	BP35
Nithsdale Pl, G41	53	BP34
off Nithsdale Rd		
Nithsdale Rd, G41	53	BP35
Nithsdale St, G41	53	BP35
Nith St, G33	39	BZ28
Nitshill Rd, (Thornlie.) G46	63	BF42
Nitshill Rd, G53	62	BB39
Niven St, G20	22	BL23
Noldrum Av, G32	57	CE37
Noldrum Gdns, G32	57	CE37
off Park Rd		
Norbreck Dr, (Giff.) G46	64	BL41
Norby Rd, G11	21	BH26
Norfield Dr, G44	53	BR38
Norfolk Ct, G5	37	BR32
Norfolk Cres, (Bishop.) G64	12	BU18
Norfolk La, G5	37	BR32
off Norfolk St		
Norfolk St, G5	38	BS32
Norham St, G41	53	BN36
Norman St, G40	54	BV34
Norse La N, G14	21	BE25
off Verona Av		
Norse La S, G14	21	BE25
off Verona Av		
Norse Pl, G14	21	BE25
Norse Rd, G14	21	BE25
Northampton Dr, G12	22	BK23
Northampton La, G12	22	BK23
North Av, (Camb.) G72	68	CB39
North Av, Clyde. G81	7	AW19
Northbank Av, (Camb.) G72	69	CF39

Name	Col1	Col2
North Bk Pl, Clyde. G81	19	AY21
Northbank St, (Camb.) G72	69	CF39
off Westburn Rd		
North Bk St, Clyde. G81	19	AY21
North Berwick Av, (Cumb.)	72	DB8
G68		
North Berwick Gdns, (Cumb.)	72	DB8
G68		
North Brae Pl, G13	20	BD22
North British Rd, (Udd.) G71	71	CP39
North Calder Gro, (Udd.) G71	58	CK35
North Calder Pl, (Udd.) G71	58	CK35
North Canal Bk, G4	38	BS27
North Canal Bk St, G4	38	BS27
North Carbrain Rd, (Cumb.)	72	DB13
G67		
North Claremont St, G3	37	BN28
off Royal Ter		
North Corsebar Rd, Pais.	48	AS35
PA2		
North Ct, G1	5	BS30
off St. Vincent Pl		
North Ct La, G1	5	BS30
Northcroft Rd, G21	24	BV25
Northcroft Rd, (Chry.) G69	17	CN19
North Cft St, Pais. PA3	32	AV32
North Dean Pk Av, (Both.) G71	71	CQ42
North Douglas St, Clyde. G81	19	AY21
North Dr, (Linw.) Pais. PA3	30	AK31
North Elgin Pl, Clyde. G81	19	AY22
North Elgin St, Clyde. G81	19	AY22
North Erskine Pk, (Bears.) G61	9	BF16
North Frederick St, G1	5	BS30
North Gardner St, G11	36	BK27
Northgate Quad, G21	25	BY23
Northgate Rd, G21	25	BY22
North Gower St, G51	36	BL32
North Gra Rd, (Bears.) G61	9	BG15
North Hanover Pl, G4	5	BS29
off North Hanover St		
North Hanover St, G1	5	BS29
Northinch Ct, G14	35	BF27
off Northinch St		
Northinch St, G14	35	BF27
North Iverton Pk Rd, John.	46	AK34
PA5		
Northland Av, G14	21	BE24
Northland Dr, G14	21	BE24
Northland Gdns, G14	21	BE24
off Northland Dr		
Northland La, G14	21	BE25
off Northland Dr		
North La, (Linw.) Pais. PA3	30	AL31
North Lo Rd, Renf. PA4	19	AY25
North Moraine La, G15	9	BE19
off Moraine Av		
Northmuir Rd, G15	8	BD17
North Pk Av, (Thornlie.) G46	63	BH41
North Pk Av, (Barr.) G78	61	AX42
Northpark St, G20	23	BP25
North Pk Vil, (Thornlie.) G46	63	BH41
off North Park Av		
North Pl, G3	4	BP29
off North St		
North Portland St, G1	5	BT30
North Rd, John. PA5	45	AH35
North St, G3	4	BP29
North St, Pais. PA3	32	AU31
Northumberland St, G20	23	BN25
North Vw, (Bears.) G61	9	BF19
North Wallace St, G4	5	BT28
Northway, (Blan.) G72	70	CL44
North Woodside Rd, G20	23	BP26
Norval St, G11	36	BJ27
Norwich Dr, G12	22	BK24
Norwood Dr, (Giff.) G46	64	BJ44
Norwood Pk, (Bears.) G61	9	BH19
Norwood Ter, (Udd.) G71	59	CQ38
Nottingham Av, G12	22	BJ23
off Northampton Dr		
Nottingham La, G12	22	BK23
off Northampton Dr		
Novar Dr, G12	22	BJ25
Novar Gdns, (Bishop.) G64	12	BU19
Nuneaton St, G40	55	BW34
Nuneaton St Ind Est, G40	55	BW34
Nurseries Rd, (Baill.) G69	41	CH31
Nursery La, G41	53	BP35
Nursery St, G41	53	BQ34
off Pollokshaws Rd		

Nutberry Ct, G42 — 53 BR36

O
Oakbank Ind Est, G20 — 23 BR26
Oak Cres, (Baill.) G69 — 58 CJ33
Oakdene Av, (Udd.) G71 — 59 CR38
Oak Dr, (Kirk.) G66 — 14 CD16
Oak Dr, (Camb.) G72 — 69 CE41
Oakfield Av, G12 — 37 BN27
Oakfield La, G12 — 37 BN27
Oakhill Av, (Baill.) G69 — 57 CH34
Oakley Dr, G44 — 65 BP42
Oakley Ter, G31 — 38 BV30
Oak Pk, (Bishop.) G64 — 13 BX20
Oakridge Cres, Pais. PA3 — 31 AR32
Oakridge Rd, (Baill.) G69 — 43 CQ31
Oak Rd, Clyde. G81 — 6 AV16
Oaks, The, John. PA5 — 45 AG35
Oakshaw Brae, Pais. PA1 — 32 AT32
Oakshawhead, Pais. PA1 — 32 AT32
Oakshaw St E, Pais. PA1 — 32 AT32
Oakshaw St W, Pais. PA1 — 32 AT32
Oak St, G2 — 4 BQ30
Oaktree Gdns, G45 — 66 BV41
Oakwood Av, Pais. PA2 — 47 AR36
Oakwood Cres, G34 — 42 CM28
Oakwood Dr, G34 — 42 CM29
Oak Wynd, (Camb.) G72 — 69 CH42
Oatfield St, G21 — 25 BX25
Oban Ct, G20 — 23 BN25
off Kelvinside Gdns
Oban Dr, G20 — 23 BN25
Oban La, G20 — 23 BN25
Observatory La, G12 — 22 BM26
off Observatory Rd
Observatory Rd, G12 — 22 BL26
Ochil Dr, (Barr.) G78 — 61 AX44
Ochil Dr, Pais. PA2 — 48 AU37
Ochil Pl, G32 — 56 CC33
Ochil Rd, (Bishop.) G64 — 13 BY20
Ochil Rd, Renf. PA4 — 33 AX28
Ochil St, G32 — 56 CC33
Ochiltree Av, G13 — 21 BH22
Ochil Vw, (Udd.) G71 — 59 CQ37
Ogilvie Pl, G31 — 55 BZ33
Ogilvie St, G31 — 55 BZ33
Old Bothwell Rd, (Both.) G71 — 71 CR44
Old Castle Gdns, G44 — 65 BR39
Old Castle Rd, G44 — 65 BR39
Old Ch Gdns, (Baill.) G69 — 43 CQ32
Old Cotts, Pais. PA2 — 49 AY37
off Grahamston Rd
Old Dalmarnock Rd, G40 — 54 BV33
Old Dumbarton Rd, G3 — 36 BL28
Old Edinburgh Rd, (Udd.) G71 — 59 CN36
Old Edinburgh Rd, Bell. ML4 — 59 CQ38
Old Fm Rd, Pais. PA2 — 49 AZ36
Old Gartloch Rd, (Gart.) G69 — 29 CP25
Old Glasgow Rd, (Udd.) G71 — 58 CM37
Old Govan Rd, Renf. PA4 — 20 BB26
Old Greenock Rd, (Inch.) — 18 AT22
Renf. PA4
Oldhall Rd, Pais. PA1 — 33 AY32
Old Manse Rd, G32 — 57 CF33
Old Mill Ct, (Dunt.) Clyde. G81 — 7 AW16
Old Mill Rd, (Both.) G71 — 71 CQ44
Old Mill Rd, (Udd.) G71 — 71 CP40
Old Mill Rd, (Camb.) G72 — 69 CF39
Old Mill Rd, Clyde. G81 — 7 AW15
Old Mill Rd, Pais. PA2 — 47 AR34
Old Rd, (Elder.) John. PA5 — 46 AL34
Old Rutherglen Rd, G5 — 54 BS33
Old Shettleston Rd, G32 — 40 CC32
Old Sneddon St, Pais. PA3 — 32 AU32
Old Sta Ct, (Both.) G71 — 71 CQ43
Old St, Clyde. G81 — 6 AV15
Old Wd Rd, (Baill.) G69 — 58 CJ34
Old Wynd, G1 — 5 BS31
Olifard Av, (Both.) G71 — 71 CR42
off Heriot Av
Oliphant Cres, Pais. PA2 — 47 AN37
Oliphant Oval, Pais. PA2 — 47 AN37
off Bothwell Pl
Olive St, G33 — 25 BZ25
Olympia St, G40 — 38 BV32
O'Neill Av, (Bishop.) G64 — 25 BX21
Onslow Dr, G31 — 39 BW30
Onslow Rd, Clyde. G81 — 7 AY19

Onslow Sq, G31 — 39 BW30
Oran Gdns, G20 — 23 BN24
Oran Gate, G20 — 23 BN24
Oran Pl, G20 — 23 BN25
Oran St, G20 — 23 BN24
Orbiston Gdns, G32 — 40 CC32
Orcades Dr, G44 — 65 BR41
Orchard Av, (Both.) G71 — 71 CR44
Orchard Brae, (Lenz.) G66 — 15 CG17
off Lindsaybeg Rd
Orchard Ct, G32 — 56 CD37
Orchard Ct, (Thornlie.) G46 — 64 BJ42
Orchard Dr, (Giff.) G46 — 64 BK42
Orchard Dr, (Ruther.) G73 — 54 BV37
Orchardfield, (Lenz.) G66 — 15 CG17
Orchard Gro, (Giff.) G46 — 64 BK41
Orchard Pk, (Giff.) G46 — 64 BL42
Orchard Pk Av, (Giff.) G46 — 64 BJ41
Orchard St, (Baill.) G69 — 57 CH34
Orchard St, Pais. PA1 — 48 AU33
Orchard St, Renf. PA4 — 19 AZ25
Orchy Av, (Clark.) G76 — 65 BP44
Orchy Ct, Clyde. G81 — 7 AY16
Orchy Cres, (Bears.) G61 — 9 BF19
Orchy Cres, Pais. PA2 — 47 AP36
Orchy Dr, (Clark.) G76 — 65 BP44
Orchy Gdns, (Clark.) G76 — 65 BP44
Orchy St, G44 — 65 BQ39
Oregon Pl, G5 — 54 BS33
Orion Way, (Camb.) G72 — 68 CC39
Orkney Pl, G51 — 36 BJ30
off Orkney St
Orkney St, G51 — 36 BK30
Orleans Av, G14 — 21 BG26
Orleans La, G14 — 21 BG26
Ormiston Av, G14 — 21 BE25
Ormiston La, G14 — 21 BE25
off Ormiston Av
Ormiston La N, G14 — 21 BE25
off Ormiston Av
Ormiston La S, G14 — 21 BE25
off Ormiston Av
Ormonde Av, G44 — 65 BP42
Ormonde Ct, G44 — 65 BN42
Ormonde Cres, G44 — 65 BP42
Ormonde Dr, G44 — 65 BP42
Ornsay St, G22 — 24 BT22
Oronsay Ct, (Old Kil.) G60 — 6 AS15
Oronsay Cres, (Old Kil.) G60 — 6 AS15
Oronsay Cres, (Bears.) G61 — 10 BK18
Oronsay Gdns, (Old Kil.) G60 — 6 AS15
Oronsay Pl, (Old Kil.) G60 — 6 AS15
Oronsay Sq, (Old Kil.) G60 — 6 AS15
Orr Pl, G40 — 38 BV31
Orr Sq, Pais. PA1 — 32 AU32
Orr St, G40 — 38 BV32
Orr St, Pais. PA1 — 32 AT32
Orr St, Pais. PA2 — 48 AU34
Osborne St, G1 — 5 BS31
Osborne St, Clyde. G81 — 7 AW18
Osborne Vil, G44 — 65 BQ40
off Holmhead Rd
Osprey Dr, (Udd.) G71 — 59 CQ38
Ossian Av, Pais. PA1 — 34 BB32
Ossian Rd, G43 — 65 BN39
Oswald St, G1 — 4 BR30
Otago La, G12 — 37 BN27
Otago La N, G12 — 37 BN27
Otago St, G12 — 37 BN27
Ottawa Cres, Clyde. G81 — 6 AT17
Otterburn Dr, (Giff.) G46 — 64 BL43
Otterswick Pl, G33 — 41 CE27
Oval, The, (Clark.) G76 — 65 BP44
Overbrae Gdns, G15 — 8 BB16
Overbrae Pl, G15 — 8 BB16
Overdale Av, G42 — 53 BP37
Overdale Gdns, G42 — 53 BP37
Overdale St, G42 — 53 BP37
Overdale Vil, G42 — 53 BP37
off Overdale St
Overlea Av, (Ruther.) G73 — 67 BZ39
Overnewton Pl, G3 — 36 BM29
off Kelvinhaugh St
Overnewton Sq, G3 — 36 BM28
off Blackie St
Overnewton St, G3 — 36 BM28
Overton Cres, John. PA5 — 46 AK35
Overton Rd, (Camb.) G72 — 69 CF41
Overton Rd, John. PA5 — 46 AJ35
Overton St, (Camb.) G72 — 69 CF41

Overtoun Ct, Clyde. G81 — 6 AU18
off Dunswin Av
Overtoun Dr, (Ruther.) G73 — 55 BW38
Overtoun Dr, Clyde. G81 — 6 AV17
Overtoun Rd, Clyde. G81 — 6 AU17
Overtown Av, G53 — 62 BC39
Overtown Pl, G21 — 39 BW32
Overtown St, G31 — 39 BW32
Overwood Dr, G44 — 66 BS39
Oxford Dr, (Linw.) Pais. PA3 — 30 AK31
Oxford La, G5 — 37 BR32
Oxford La, Renf. PA4 — 19 AY26
Oxford Rd, Renf. PA4 — 19 AY26
Oxford St, G5 — 4 BR31
Oxton Dr, G52 — 34 BD32

P
Pacific Dr, G51 — 36 BL31
Pacific Quay, G51 — 36 BM30
Paisley Rd, G5 — 4 BQ31
Paisley Rd, (Barr.) G78 — 61 AX40
Paisley Rd, Renf. PA4 — 33 AX28
Paisley Rd W, G51 — 36 BL32
Paisley Rd W, G52 — 36 BJ32
Paladin Av, G13 — 20 BD21
Palermo St, G21 — 24 BU25
off Atlas Rd
Palladium Pl, G14 — 21 BF26
off Dumbarton Rd
Palmer Av, G13 — 9 BF20
Palmerston Pl, G3 — 36 BM29
off Kelvinhaugh St
Palmerston Pl, John. PA5 — 45 AE38
Palm Pl, (Udd.) G71 — 59 CR36
Pandora Way, (Udd.) G71 — 59 CQ38
Panmure St, G20 — 23 BQ25
Park Av, G3 — 37 BP27
Park Av, (Bishop.) G64 — 13 BW18
Park Av, (Barr.) G78 — 61 AX44
Park Av, (Elder.) John. PA5 — 46 AL35
Park Av, Pais. PA2 — 48 AS36
Park Brae, Ersk. PA8 — 18 AS21
Parkbrae Gdns, G20 — 23 BQ23
Parkbrae Pl, G20 — 23 BQ23
Park Circ, G3 — 37 BN28
Park Circ La, G3 — 37 BN28
Park Circ Pl, G3 — 4 BP28
Park Ct, (Giff.) G46 — 64 BL43
Park Ct, (Bishop.) G64 — 13 BX18
Park Ct, Clyde. G81 — 6 AU17
Park Cres, (Bears.) G61 — 8 BD16
Park Cres, (Bishop.) G64 — 13 BW18
Park Cres, (Inch.) Renf. PA4 — 18 AS22
Park Dr, G3 — 37 BN27
Park Dr, (Ruther.) G73 — 55 BW38
Park Dr, Ersk. PA8 — 18 AS21
Parker St, G14 — 35 BG27
off Dumbarton Rd
Park Gdns, G3 — 37 BN28
Park Gdns, (Kilb.) John. PA10 — 44 AD33
Park Gdns La, G3 — 37 BN28
Park Gate, G3 — 37 BN28
Park Gro, Ersk. PA8 — 18 AS21
Parkgrove Av, (Giff.) G46 — 64 BM42
Parkgrove Ct, (Giff.) G46 — 64 BM42
Parkgrove Ter, G3 — 37 BN28
Parkgrove Ter La, G3 — 37 BN28
off Derby St
Parkhall Rd, Clyde. G81 — 6 AV17
Parkhall Ter, Clyde. G81 — 6 AV16
Parkhead Cross, G31 — 39 BZ32
Parkhill Dr, (Ruther.) G73 — 55 BW38
Parkhill Rd, G43 — 52 BM37
Parkhouse Path, G53 — 62 BD41
Parkhouse Rd, G53 — 62 BB41
Parkhouse Rd, (Barr.) G78 — 62 BB41
Parkinch, Ersk. PA8 — 18 AS21
Parklands Rd, G44 — 65 BP42
Parklands Vw, G53 — 50 BB35
Parklea, (Bishop.) G64 — 12 BU18
off Westfields
Parkneuk Rd, G43 — 64 BL41
Park Pl, John. PA5 — 45 AH35
off Park Rd
Park Quad, G3 — 37 BN28
Park Ridge, Ersk. PA8 — 6 AS20
Park Rd, G4 — 37 BN27
Park Rd, G32 — 57 CE37
Park Rd, (Giff.) G46 — 64 BL43

Park Rd, (Bishop.) G64	13	BW19	Penrith Dr, G12	22	BJ23	Plantation Sq, G51	37	BN31
Park Rd, (Baill.) G69	43	CP32	Penryn Gdns, G32	57	CF34	Plant St, G31	39	BY31
Park Rd, (Muir.) G69	28	CL21	Penston Rd, G33	41	CF29	Playfair St, G40	55	BW34
Park Rd, Clyde. G81	6	AV17	Pentland Av, (Linw.) Pais. PA3	30	AJ31	Pleaknowe Cres, (Chry.) G69	17	CN19
Park Rd, John. PA5	45	AH35	Pentland Ct, (Barr.) G78	61	AX44	Pleamuir Pl, (Cumb.) G68	72	CY12
Park Rd, Pais. PA2	48	AT36	*off Pentland Dr*			Plean St, G14	20	BC24
Parksail, Ersk. PA8	18	AS22	Pentland Cres, Pais. PA2	48	AT37	Pleasance La, G43	52	BL38
Parksail Dr, Ersk. PA8	18	AS21	Pentland Dr, (Bishop.) G64	13	BZ19	*off Pleasance St*		
Parkside Gdns, G20	23	BQ23	Pentland Dr, (Barr.) G78	61	AX44	Pleasance St, G43	52	BL37
Parkside Pl, G20	23	BQ23	Pentland Dr, Renf. PA4	33	AX29	Plover Pl, John. PA5	45	AE38
Park St S, G3	37	BN28	Pentland Rd, G43	64	BL40	Pointhouse Rd, G3	37	BN30
Park Ter, G3	37	BN28	Pentland Rd, (Chry.) G69	16	CM20	Pollock Rd, (Bears.) G61	10	BJ18
Park Ter, (Giff.) G46	64	BL43	Penzance Way, (Chry.) G69	17	CN18	Pollok Av, G43	52	BK37
Park Ter E La, G3	37	BN28	Peockland Gdns, John. PA5	46	AJ34	Pollok Dr, (Bishop.) G64	12	BU20
Park Ter La, G3	37	BN28	Peockland Pl, John. PA5	46	AJ34	Pollokshaws Rd, G41	53	BQ35
Park Top, Ersk. PA8	6	AS20	*off Thorn Brae*			Pollokshaws Rd, G43	52	BK38
Parkvale Av, Ersk. PA8	6	AT20	Percy Dr, (Giff.) G46	64	BL44	Pollokshields Sq, G41	53	BP35
Parkvale Cres, Ersk. PA8	18	AT21	Percy Rd, Renf. PA4	33	AW29	*off Glencairn Dr*		
Parkvale Dr, Ersk. PA8	18	AT21	Percy St, G51	36	BM31	Pollok Shop Cen, G53	51	BE38
Parkvale Gdns, Ersk. PA8	6	AT20	*off Clifford St*			Polmadie Av, G5	54	BT35
Parkvale Pl, Ersk. PA8	6	AT20	Perran Gdns, (Chry.) G69	17	CN19	Polmadie Ind Est, G5	54	BU35
Parkvale Way, Ersk. PA8	18	AT21	Perth Cres, Clyde. G81	6	AT16	Polmadie Rd, G5	54	BU34
Park Vw, (Kilb.) John. PA10	44	AC33	Perth St, G3	4	BP30	Polmadie Rd, G42	54	BS36
Park Vw, Pais. PA2	48	AT35	*off Argyle St*			Polmadie St, G42	54	BS36
Parkview Dr, (Stepps) G33	27	CG23	Petershill Ct, G21	25	BY25	Polnoon Av, G13	20	BC23
Park Way, G32	57	CE37	Petershill Dr, G21	25	BX25	Polquhap Ct, G53	50	BC37
off Park Rd			Petershill Pl, G21	25	BX25	Polquhap Gdns, G53	50	BC37
Park Way, (Cumb.) G67	73	DD9	Petershill Rd, G21	24	BV26	Polquhap Pl, G53	50	BC37
Park Winding, Ersk. PA8	18	AS21	Peterson Dr, G13	20	BA21	Polquhap Rd, G53	50	BC37
Park Wd, Ersk. PA8	6	AS20	Peterson Gdns, G13	20	BA21	Polson Dr, John. PA5	45	AG35
Parnie St, G1	5	BS31	Petition Pl, (Udd.) G71	71	CQ40	Polsons Cres, Pais. PA2	48	AT35
Parsonage Row, G1	5	BT30	Pettigrew St, G32	40	CC32	Polwarth La, G12	22	BK25
Parsonage Sq, G4	5	BT30	Peveril Av, G41	52	BM36	Polwarth St, G12	22	BK26
Parson St, G4	5	BU30	Peveril Av, (Ruther.) G73	67	BY40	Poplar Av, G11	21	BH25
Partick Br St, G11	36	BL27	Peveril Ct, (Ruther.) G73	67	BY40	*off Crow Rd*		
Partickhill Av, G11	36	BK27	*off Crow Rd*			Poplar Av, John. PA5	45	AH36
Partickhill Ct, G11	22	BK26	Pharonhill St, G31	40	CA32	Poplar Dr, (Kirk.) G66	14	CC16
Partickhill Rd, G11	22	BK26	*off Quarrybrae St*			Poplar Dr, Clyde. G81	6	AV16
Paterson St, G5	37	BQ32	Phoenix Business Pk, The,	31	AN32	Poplar Pl, (Blan.) G72	70	CL44
Pathhead Gdns, G33	26	CB23	Pais. PA1			Poplar Rd, G41	36	BK32
Patna St, G40	55	BX34	Phoenix Ind Est, Pais. PA3	32	AU29	*off Urrdale Rd*		
Paton St, G31	39	BX30	Phoenix Pk Ter, G4	37	BR27	Poplar Way, (Camb.) G72	69	CH42
Patrick St, Pais. PA2	48	AV34	*off Corn St*			Poplin St, G40	54	BV34
Patterton Dr, (Barr.) G78	61	AZ43	Phoenix Pl, (Elder.) John. PA5	46	AM34	Porchester St, G33	41	CF27
Pattison St, Clyde. G81	6	AU17	Phoenix Retail Pk, The, Pais.	47	AN33	Portal Rd, G13	21	BE21
Payne St, G4	38	BS27	PA1			Port Dundas Ind Est, G4	38	BS27
Peacock Av, Pais. PA2	47	AP35	Phoenix Rd, G4	4	BQ28	Port Dundas Pl, G2	5	BS29
Peacock Dr, Pais. PA2	47	AP34	*off Great Western Rd*			Port Dundas Rd, G4	4	BR28
Pearce La, G51	36	BJ29	Piccadilly St, G3	4	BP30	Port Dundas Trd Centres, G4	38	BS27
off Pearce St			Piershill St, G32	40	CB30	Porterfield Rd, Renf. PA4	19	AX26
Pearce St, G51	36	BJ29	Pikeman Rd, G13	21	BE23	Porter St, G51	36	BL32
Pearson Dr, Renf. PA4	33	AZ27	Pilmuir Av, G44	65	BP41	*off Clifford St*		
Pearson Pl, (Linw.) Pais. PA3	30	AK32	Pilrig St, G32	40	CA30	Porters Well, (Udd.) G71	71	CN40
Peathill Av, (Chry.) G69	16	CK20	Pilton Rd, G15	8	BC17	Portland Rd, (Cumb.) G68	72	DB8
Peathill St, G21	24	BS26	Pine Av, (Camb.) G72	69	CH42	Portland St, Pais. PA2	49	AX34
Peat Pl, G53	62	BC40	Pine Cres, John. PA5	46	AJ36	Portman Pl, G12	37	BN27
off Peat Rd			Pine Gro, (Baill.) G69	43	CQ31	*off Cowan St*		
Peat Rd, G53	62	BD39	Pine Gro, (Udd.) G71	59	CR37	Portman St, G41	37	BN32
Peebles Dr, (Ruther.) G73	55	BZ38	Pinelands, (Bishop.) G64	13	BW17	Portmarnock Dr, G23	23	BN21
Peel Glen Gdns, G15	8	BC16	Pine Pl, G5	54	BS33	*off Fairhaven Rd*		
Peel Glen Rd, G15	8	BC17	Pine Rd, Clyde. G81	6	AT17	Portreath Rd, (Chry.) G69	17	CP18
Peel Glen Rd, (Bears.) G61	8	BC15	Pine St, Pais. PA2	49	AW35	Portree Pl, G15	8	BA17
Peel La, G11	36	BK27	Pinewood Av, (Kirk.) G66	14	CC16	Portsoy Av, G13	20	BB21
Peel Pl, (Both.) G71	71	CQ42	Pinewood Ct, (Kirk.) G66	14	CC16	*off Wyvis Av*		
Peel St, G11	36	BK27	Pinewood Pl, (Kirk.) G66	14	CC16	Portsoy Pl, G13	20	BA21
Peel Vw, Clyde. G81	7	AZ18	Pinewood Sq, G15	8	BD17	Port St, G3	4	BP29
off Kirkoswald Dr			Pinkerton Av, (Ruther.) G73	54	BU37	Portugal La, G5	37	BR32
Pegasus Rd, Pais. PA1	30	AM32	Pinkerton La, Renf. PA4	33	AZ28	*off Bedford St*		
Peinchorran, Ersk. PA8	18	AS22	Pinkston Dr, G21	38	BU27	Portugal St, G5	37	BR32
Pembroke St, G3	4	BP29	Pinkston Rd, G4	24	BT26	Possil Cross, G22	24	BS26
Pencaitland Dr, G32	56	CC34	Pinkston Rd, G21	24	BT26	Possil Rd, G4	23	BR26
Pencaitland Gro, G32	56	CC35	Pinmore Path, G53	62	BB40	Potassels Rd, (Muir.) G69	28	CL22
Pencaitland Pl, G23	11	BN20	*off Seamill St*			Potter Cl, G32	56	CA34
Pendale Ri, G45	66	BT42	Pinmore Pl, G53	62	BB39	Potter Gro, G32	56	CA34
Pendeen Cres, G33	41	CG32	Pinmore St, G53	62	BB39	Potterhill Av, Pais. PA2	48	AU37
Pendeen Pl, G33	41	CH31	Pinwherry Dr, G33	26	CB23	Potterhill Rd, G53	50	BD35
Pendeen Rd, G33	41	CG32	Pinwherry Pl, (Both.) G71	71	CQ42	Potter Path, G32	56	CA34
Pendicle Cres, (Bears.) G61	9	BF18	Pitcairn St, G31	56	CA33	*off Rattray St*		
Pendicle Rd, (Bears.) G61	9	BF18	Pitcaple Dr, G43	64	BK39	Potter Pl, G32	56	CA34
Pendle Ct, (Gart.) G69	29	CP23	Pitlochry Dr, G52	50	BD33	Potter St, G32	56	CA34
Penicuik St, G32	39	BZ31	Pitmedden Rd, (Bishop.) G64	13	BZ19	Powburn Cres, (Udd.) G71	58	CM38
Penilee Rd, G52	33	AZ29	Pitmilly Rd, G15	9	BE17	Powfoot St, G31	39	BZ32
Penilee Rd, Pais. PA1	34	BA31	Pitreavie Pl, G33	41	CE27	Powrie St, G33	27	CE26
Penilee Ter, G52	34	BA31	Pitt St, G2	4	BQ30	Prentice La, (Udd.) G71	59	CQ37
Peninver Dr, G51	35	BF29	Pladda Rd, Renf. PA4	33	AZ28	Preston Pl, G42	53	BR35
Penman Av, (Ruther.) G73	54	BV37	Plaintrees Ct, Pais. PA2	48	AU35	Preston St, G42	53	BR35
Pennan Pl, G14	20	BC24	Plane Pl, (Udd.) G71	59	CR36	Prestwick Ct, (Cumb.) G68	72	DB9
Penneld Rd, G52	34	BB32	Planetree Pl, John. PA5	46	AJ36	Prestwick St, G53	62	BC39
Penrith Av, (Giff.) G46	64	BL42	Planetree Rd, Clyde. G81	7	AW17	Priesthill Av, G53	63	BE39
			Plantation Pk Gdns, G51	36	BM32	Priesthill Cres, G53	63	BE39
			off Clifford La					

Priesthill Rd, G53 — 62 BD39
Primrose Ct, G14 — 21 BE26
  off Dumbarton Rd
Primrose St, G14 — 21 BE26
Prince Albert Rd, G12 — 22 BK26
Prince Edward St, G42 — 53 BQ35
Prince of Wales Gdns, G20 — 22 BL21
  off Crosbie St
Prince's Dock, G51 — 36 BL30
Princes Gdns, G12 — 22 BK26
Princes Gate, (Both.) G71 — 71 CN41
Princes Gate, (Ruther.) G73 — 55 BW37
Princes Pl, G12 — 22 BL26
Princess Cres, Pais. PA1 — 33 AX32
Princess Dr, (Baill.) G69 — 43 CQ32
Princes Sq, G1 — 5 BS30
  off Buchanan St
Princes Sq, (Barr.) G78 — 61 AZ42
Princes Sq, (Ruther.) G73 — 55 BW37
Princes Ter, G12 — 22 BL26
Priorwood Ct, G13 — 21 BF23
Priorwood Gdns, G13 — 21 BF23
Priorwood Pl, G13 — 21 BF23
Priory Av, Pais. PA3 — 33 AW30
Priory Dr, (Udd.) G71 — 58 CM38
Priory Pl, G13 — 21 BF22
Priory Rd, G13 — 21 BF22
Prosen St, G32 — 56 CB34
Prospect Av, (Udd.) G71 — 71 CN39
Prospect Av, (Camb.) G72 — 68 CB39
Prospecthill Circ, G42 — 54 BT36
Prospecthill Cres, G42 — 54 BU37
Prospecthill Dr, G42 — 54 BS37
Prospecthill Pl, G42 — 54 BU37
Prospecthill Rd, G42 — 53 BQ37
Prospecthill Sq, G42 — 54 BT37
Prospect Rd, G43 — 52 BM37
Provand Hall Cres, (Baill.) G69 — 58 CK34
Provanhill St, G21 — 38 BV28
Provanmill Pl, G33 — 25 BZ26
  off Provanmill Rd
Provanmill Rd, G33 — 25 BZ26
Provan Rd, G33 — 39 BY28
Provost Cl, John. PA5 — 45 AH34
  off High St
Provost Driver Ct, Renf. PA4 — 33 AZ27
Purdon St, G11 — 36 BK27

Q
Quadrant Rd, G43 — 65 BN40
Quarrelton Rd, John. PA5 — 45 AG35
Quarry Av, (Camb.) G72 — 69 CG42
Quarrybank, (Kilb.) John. PA10 — 45 AE35
Quarrybrae St, G31 — 39 BZ32
Quarryknowe, (Ruther.) G73 — 54 BV38
Quarryknowe St, G31 — 40 CA32
Quarry Pl, (Camb.) G72 — 68 CA39
Quarry Rd, (Barr.) G78 — 61 AX41
Quarry Rd, Pais. PA2 — 48 AV36
Quarry St, John. PA5 — 45 AH34
Quarrywood Av, G21 — 25 BY25
Quarrywood Rd, G21 — 25 BZ25
Quay Rd, (Ruther.) G73 — 55 BW36
Quay Rd N, (Ruther.) G73 — 55 BW36
Quebec Ho, Clyde. G81 — 6 AT15
  off Perth Cres
Quebec Wynd, G32 — 57 CE37
Queen Elizabeth Av, G52 — 34 BA30
Queen Elizabeth Ct, Clyde. G81 — 7 AW18
Queen Elizabeth Sq, G5 — 54 BT33
Queen Margaret Ct, G20 — 23 BN25
  off Fergus Dr
Queen Margaret Dr, G12 — 22 BM26
Queen Margaret Dr, G20 — 22 BM26
Queen Margaret Rd, G20 — 23 BN25
Queen Mary Av, G42 — 53 BR36
Queen Mary Av, Clyde. G81 — 7 AZ19
Queen Mary Gdns, Clyde. G81 — 7 AW18
Queen Mary St, G40 — 54 BV33
Queens Av, (Camb.) G72 — 68 CD39
Queensbank Av, (Gart.) G69 — 29 CN22
Queensborough Gdns, G12 — 22 BJ25
Queensby Av, (Baill.) G69 — 42 CK31
Queensby Dr, (Baill.) G69 — 42 CK31
Queensby Pl, (Baill.) G69 — 42 CL31
Queensby Rd, (Baill.) G69 — 42 CK31
Queens Cres, G4 — 37 BQ27
Queen's Cres, (Baill.) G69 — 43 CP32
Queens Dr, G42 — 53 BP35
Queens Dr La, G42 — 53 BR36

Queensferry St, G5 — 54 BU35
Queens Gdns, G12 — 22 BL26
  off Victoria Cres Rd
Queens Gate La, G12 — 22 BL26
  off Victoria Cres Rd
Queensland Ct, G52 — 35 BE31
Queensland Dr, G52 — 35 BE31
Queensland Gdns, G52 — 35 BE31
Queensland La E, G52 — 35 BE31
Queensland La W, G52 — 35 BE31
Queenslie Ind Est, G33 — 41 CE29
Queenslie St, G33 — 39 BZ27
Queens Pk Av, G42 — 53 BR36
Queens Pl, G12 — 22 BL26
Queen Sq, G41 — 53 BP35
Queens Rd, (Elder.) John. PA5 — 46 AL35
Queen St, G1 — 5 BS30
Queen St, (Ruther.) G73 — 55 BW37
Queen St, Pais. PA1 — 48 AS33
Queen St, Renf. PA4 — 19 AZ26
Queen Victoria Ct, G14 — 21 BE25
  off Queen Victoria Dr
Queen Victoria Dr, G13 — 21 BE24
Queen Victoria Dr, G14 — 21 BE25
Queen Victoria Gate, G13 — 21 BE24
Quendale Dr, G32 — 56 CB34
Quentin St, G41 — 53 BN36
Quinton Gdns, (Baill.) G69 — 42 CJ32

R
Raasay Dr, Pais. PA2 — 48 AT38
Raasay Pl, G22 — 24 BS21
Raasay St, G22 — 24 BS21
Radnor St, G3 — 36 BM28
  off Argyle St
Radnor St, Clyde. G81 — 7 AW18
Raeberry St, G20 — 23 BP26
Raeswood Dr, G53 — 50 BB37
Raeswood Gdns, G53 — 50 BB37
Raeswood Pl, G53 — 50 BC37
Raeswood Rd, G53 — 50 BB37
Rafford St, G51 — 36 BJ30
Raglan St, G4 — 37 BQ27
Raith Av, G45 — 66 BT41
  off Croftfoot Rd
Raithburn Av, G45 — 66 BS42
Raithburn Rd, G45 — 66 BS42
Ralston Av, G52 — 50 BB33
Ralston Av, Pais. PA1 — 50 BB34
Ralston Ct, G52 — 50 BB33
Ralston Dr, G52 — 50 BB33
Ralston Path, G52 — 50 BB33
Ralston Pl, G52 — 50 BB33
Ralston Rd, (Bears.) G61 — 9 BG16
Ralston Rd, (Barr.) G78 — 61 AY43
Ralston St, Pais. PA1 — 49 AW33
Ramillies Ct, Clyde. G81 — 7 AY19
Rampart Av, G13 — 20 BC21
Ramsay Av, John. PA5 — 45 AG36
Ramsay Cres, (Millik.) John. PA10 — 44 AD35
Ramsay Pl, John. PA5 — 45 AG36
Ramsay St, Clyde. G81 — 6 AV18
Ram St, G32 — 40 CB32
Ranald Gdns, (Ruther.) G73 — 67 BZ42
Randolph Av, (Clark.) G76 — 65 BQ44
Randolph Dr, (Clark.) G76 — 65 BP44
Randolph Gdns, (Clark.) G76 — 65 BP44
Randolph Gate, G11 — 21 BH25
  off Randolph Rd
Randolph La, G11 — 21 BH26
Randolph Rd, G11 — 21 BH25
Ranfurly Dr, (Cumb.) G68 — 72 DA9
Ranfurly Rd, G52 — 34 BB32
Rankine Pl, John. PA5 — 45 AH34
Rankines La, Renf. PA4 — 19 AZ25
  off Manse St
Rankine St, John. PA5 — 45 AH34
Rankin Way, (Barr.) G78 — 61 AZ42
Rannoch Av, (Bishop.) G64 — 13 BX20
Rannoch Dr, (Bears.) G61 — 10 BJ19
Rannoch Dr, Renf. PA4 — 19 AY25
Rannoch Gdns, (Bishop.) G64 — 13 BY19
Rannoch La, (Chry.) G69 — 17 CQ19
  off Heathfield Av
Rannoch Pl, Pais. PA2 — 49 AW34
Rannoch Rd, (Udd.) G71 — 59 CN36
Rannoch Rd, John. PA5 — 45 AH36
Rannoch St, G44 — 65 BQ39

Rannoch Way, (Both.) G71 — 71 CQ42
  off Appledore Cres
Raploch Av, G14 — 20 BD25
Raploch La, G14 — 20 BD25
Rathlin St, G51 — 36 BJ29
Ratho Dr, G21 — 24 BU24
Ratho Dr, (Cumb.) G68 — 72 DA8
Rattray St, G32 — 56 CA34
Ravel Row, G31 — 39 BZ32
Ravelston Rd, (Bears.) G61 — 9 BG19
Ravelston St, G32 — 39 BZ31
Ravel Wynd, (Udd.) G71 — 59 CQ37
Ravenscliffe Dr, (Giff.) G46 — 64 BK42
Ravens Ct, (Bishop.) G64 — 24 BV21
  off Lennox Cres
Ravenscraig Av, Pais. PA2 — 48 AS35
Ravenscraig Dr, G53 — 62 BD39
Ravenscraig Ter, G53 — 63 BE40
  off Ravenscraig Dr
Ravenshall Rd, G41 — 52 BL37
Ravenstone Dr, (Giff.) G46 — 64 BL40
Ravenswood Av, Pais. PA2 — 47 AN38
Ravenswood Dr, G41 — 52 BM36
Ravenswood Rd, (Baill.) G69 — 58 CL33
Rayne Pl, G15 — 8 BD17
Redan St, G40 — 38 BV32
Redcastle Sq, G33 — 41 CF28
Redford St, G33 — 39 BZ29
Redgate Pl, G14 — 20 BD25
Redhill Rd, (Cumb.) G68 — 72 CZ10
Redhurst Cres, Pais. PA2 — 47 AR38
Redhurst La, Pais. PA2 — 47 AR38
Redhurst Way, Pais. PA2 — 47 AR38
Redlands La, G12 — 22 BL25
Redlands Rd, G12 — 22 BL25
Redlands Ter, G12 — 22 BL25
  off Julian Av
Redlands Ter La, G12 — 22 BL25
Redlawood Pl, (Camb.) G72 — 70 CJ39
Redlawood Rd, (Camb.) G72 — 70 CJ39
Redmoss St, G22 — 23 BR24
Rednock St, G22 — 24 BS25
Redpath Dr, G52 — 35 BE32
Red Rd, G21 — 25 BX25
Red Rd Ct, G21 — 25 BX26
Redwood Cres, (Camb.) G72 — 69 CH42
Redwood Dr, G21 — 25 BW26
Redwood Pl, (Kirk.) G66 — 14 CD16
  off Almond Dr
Redwood Rd, (Cumb.) G67 — 73 DF11
Reelick Av, G13 — 20 BA21
Reelick Quad, G13 — 20 BA21
Reen Pl, (Both.) G71 — 71 CR41
Regent Dr, (Ruther.) G73 — 55 BW37
  off King St
Regent Moray St, G3 — 36 BM28
Regent Pk Sq, G41 — 53 BP35
Regent Pl, Clyde. G81 — 6 AU17
Regents Gate, (Both.) G71 — 70 CM41
Regent Sq, (Lenz.) G66 — 15 CE17
Regent St, Clyde. G81 — 6 AU17
Regent St, Pais. PA1 — 33 AX32
Regwood St, G41 — 52 BM37
Reid Av, (Bears.) G61 — 10 BJ15
Reid Av, (Linw.) Pais. PA3 — 30 AK32
Reidhouse St, G21 — 24 BV25
Reid Pl, G40 — 54 BV33
Reid St, G40 — 54 BV34
Reid St, (Ruther.) G73 — 55 BX37
Reidvale St, G31 — 38 BV31
Renfield La, G2 — 4 BR30
Renfield St, G2 — 4 BR30
Renfield St, Renf. PA4 — 19 AZ25
Renfrew Ct, G2 — 4 BR29
Renfrew La, G2 — 4 BR29
  off Hope St
Renfrew Rd, G51 — 34 BD29
Renfrew Rd, Pais. PA3 — 32 AV32
Renfrew Rd, Renf. PA4 — 34 BC28
Renfrew St, G2 — 4 BR29
Renfrew St, G3 — 4 BQ28
Rennies Rd, (Inch.) Renf. PA4 — 18 AS22
Renshaw Dr, G52 — 34 BD31
Renshaw Rd, (Elder.) John. PA5 — 46 AL35
Renton St, G4 — 5 BS28
Resipol Rd, (Stepps) G33 — 27 CG24
Reston Dr, G52 — 34 BD31
Reuther Av, (Ruther.) G73 — 55 BX38
Revoch Dr, G13 — 20 BC22

Rhannan Rd, G44	65	BQ40
Rhannan Ter, G44	65	BQ40
Rhindhouse Pl, (Baill.) G69	42	CM32
Rhindhouse Rd, (Baill.) G69	42	CM32
Rhindmuir Av, (Baill.) G69	42	CL32
Rhindmuir Ct, (Baill.) G69	42	CL31
Rhindmuir Cres, (Baill.) G69	42	CM31
Rhindmuir Dr, (Baill.) G69	42	CL31
Rhindmuir Gdns, (Baill.) G69	42	CL31
Rhindmuir Gro, (Baill.) G69	42	CM31
Rhindmuir Path, (Baill.) G69	42	CM31
Rhindmuir Pl, (Baill.) G69	42	CM31
Rhindmuir Rd, (Baill.) G69	42	CL31
Rhindmuir Vw, (Baill.) G69	42	CM31
Rhindmuir Wynd, (Baill.) G69	42	CM31
Rhinds St, Coat. ML5	59	CR33
Rhinsdale Cres, (Baill.) G69	42	CL32
Rhumhor Gdns, (Millik.)	44	AD35
John. PA10		
off Ladysmith Av		
Rhymer St, G21	5	BU28
Rhymie Rd, G32	57	CF34
Rhynie Dr, G51	36	BK32
Riccarton St, G42	54	BS35
Riccartsbar Av, Pais. PA2	48	AS34
Richard St, G2	4	BQ30
off Cadzow St		
Richard St, Renf. PA4	19	AZ25
Richmond Ct, (Ruther.) G73	55	BY37
Richmond Dr, (Bishop.) G64	13	BX17
Richmond Dr, (Camb.) G72	68	CA40
Richmond Dr, (Ruther.) G73	55	BY38
Richmond Dr, (Linw.) Pais.	30	AJ30
PA3		
Richmond Gdns, (Chry.) G69	16	CK20
Richmond Gro, (Ruther.) G73	55	BY38
Richmond Pl, (Ruther.) G73	55	BY37
Richmond St, G1	5	BT30
Richmond St, Clyde. G81	7	AY20
Riddell St, Clyde. G81	7	AY18
Riddon Av, G13	20	BA21
Riddon Av, Clyde. G81	20	BA21
Riddon Pl, G13	20	BA21
Riddrie Cres, G33	40	CA29
Riddrie Knowes, G33	40	CA29
Riddrievale Ct, G33	40	CA28
Riddrievale St, G33	40	CA28
Rigby St, G32	40	CA31
Rigghead Av, (Cumb.) G67	73	DD8
Rigg Pl, G33	41	CG30
Riggside Rd, G33	41	CE27
Riglands Way, Renf. PA4	19	AY25
Riglaw Pl, G13	20	BC22
Rigmuir Rd, G51	35	BE30
Rimsdale St, G40	39	BW32
Ringford St, G21	24	BV26
Ripon Dr, G12	22	BJ23
Risk St, G40	38	BU32
Risk St, Clyde. G81	6	AV17
Ristol Rd, G13	20	BD24
off Anniesland Rd		
Ritchie Cres, (Elder.) John.	46	AL34
PA5		
Ritchie Pk, John. PA5	46	AK34
Ritchie St, G5	53	BQ33
Riverbank St, G43	52	BL38
River Cart Wk, Pais. PA1	48	AU33
off Marshall's La		
River Dr, (Inch.) Renf. PA4	18	AS24
Riverford Rd, G43	52	BL38
Riverford Rd, (Ruther.) G73	55	BY36
River Rd, G32	57	CE37
River Rd, G41	53	BP37
off Mansionhouse Rd		
Riversdale La, G14	20	BC25
Riverside Ct, G44	65	BP43
Riverside Ind Est, Clyde. G81	7	AW20
Riverside Pk, G44	65	BQ42
Riverside Pl, (Camb.) G72	69	CG39
Riverside Rd, G43	53	BN38
Riverview Dr, G5	4	BQ31
Riverview Gdns, G5	4	BQ31
Riverview Pl, G5	4	BQ31
Roaden Av, Pais. PA2	47	AP38
Roaden Rd, Pais. PA2	47	AP38
Roadside, (Cumb.) G67	73	DD8
Robb Ter, (Kirk.) G66	16	CJ15
Robert Burns Av, Clyde. G81	7	AY18
Robert Dr, G51	36	BJ29
Roberton Av, G41	52	BL35

Robertson Av, Renf. PA4	19	AX26
Robertson Cl, Renf. PA4	19	AY26
Robertson Dr, Renf. PA4	19	AX26
Robertson La, G2	4	BQ30
Robertson St, G2	4	BR30
Robertson St, (Barr.) G78	61	AX42
Robertson Ter, (Baill.) G69	42	CL32
off Edinburgh Rd		
Roberts St, Clyde. G81	6	AU18
Robert St, G51	36	BJ29
Robert Templeton Dr, (Camb.)	68	CD40
G72		
Robin Way, G32	57	CE37
Robroyston Av, G33	26	CA26
Robroyston Dr, G33	26	CA25
Robroyston Rd, G33	26	CA23
Robroyston Rd, (Bishop.) G64	14	CB30
Robslee Cres, (Giff.) G46	64	BJ42
Robslee Dr, (Giff.) G46	64	BK42
Robslee Rd, (Thornlie.) G46	64	BJ43
Robson Gro, G42	53	BR34
Rockall Dr, G44	66	BS41
Rockbank Pl, G40	39	BW32
Rockbank Pl, Clyde. G81	7	AY15
off Glasgow Rd		
Rockbank St, G40	39	BW32
Rockcliffe St, G40	54	BV34
Rock Dr, (Kilb.) John. PA10	44	AD35
Rockfield Pl, G21	25	BY24
Rockfield Rd, G21	25	BY24
Rockmount Av, (Thornlie.) G46	64	BJ41
Rockmount Av, (Barr.) G78	61	AZ44
Rock St, G4	23	BR26
Rockwell Av, Pais. PA2	48	AS37
Rodger Dr, (Ruther.) G73	67	BW39
Rodger Pl, (Ruther.) G73	67	BW39
Rodil Av, G44	66	BS41
Rodney St, G4	37	BR27
Roebank Dr, (Barr.) G78	61	AY44
Roebank St, G31	39	BX29
Roffey Pk Rd, Pais. PA1	33	AZ32
Rogart St, G40	38	BV32
Rogerfield Rd, (Baill.) G69	42	CL30
Roman Av, G15	8	BC20
Roman Av, (Bears.) G61	9	BH16
Roman Ct, (Bears.) G61	9	BH16
Roman Dr, (Bears.) G61	9	BH16
Roman Gdns, (Bears.) G61	9	BH16
Roman Rd, (Bears.) G61	9	BG16
Roman Rd, Clyde. G81	7	AW15
Romney Av, G44	66	BS40
Ronaldsay Dr, (Bishop.) G64	13	BZ19
Ronaldsay Pas, G22	24	BT22
off Scalpay St		
Ronaldsay Pl, (Cumb.) G67	72	CZ13
Ronaldsay St, G22	24	BS22
Rona St, G21	39	BX27
Rona Ter, (Camb.) G72	68	CB42
Ronay St, G22	24	BT21
Rooksdell Av, Pais. PA2	48	AS36
Ropework La, G1	5	BS31
off Clyde St		
Rosebank Av, (Blan.) G72	71	CN44
Rosebank Dr, (Camb.) G72	69	CE41
Rosebank Gdns, (Udd.) G71	58	CK35
Rosebank La, (Both.) G71	71	CR42
off Lomond Dr		
Rosebank Rd, (Udd.) G71	58	CK35
Rosebank Ter, (Baill.) G69	59	CP33
Roseberry St, G5	54	BU34
Rosedale, (Bishop.) G64	25	BX21
off Woodfield Av		
Rosedale Av, Pais. PA2	46	AM38
Rosedale Dr, (Baill.) G69	58	CJ33
Rosedale Gdns, G20	22	BL21
Rosefield Gdns, (Udd.) G71	59	CN38
Rose Knowe Rd, G42	54	BT36
Roseland Brae, Ersk. PA8	18	AT21
off Newshot Dr		
Roselea Gdns, G13	21	BH22
Roselea Pl, (Blan.) G72	70	CL44
Rosemount, (Cumb.) G68	72	DB8
Rosemount Cres, G21	38	BV29
Rosemount Meadows, (Both.)	71	CP43
G71		
Rosemount St, G21	38	BV28
Roseness Pl, G33	40	CC29
Rose St, G3	4	BR29
Rosevale Rd, (Bears.) G61	9	BG17
Rosevale St, G11	36	BJ27

Rosewood Av, Pais. PA2	47	AR36
Rosewood St, G13	21	BG22
Roslea Dr, G31	39	BW30
Roslin Twr, (Camb.) G72	68	CA42
Roslyn Dr, (Baill.) G69	43	CP32
Rosneath St, G51	36	BJ29
Ross Av, Renf. PA4	33	AW28
Rossendale Ct, G43	52	BL37
Rossendale Rd, G41	52	BL37
Rossendale Rd, G43	52	BL37
Rosshall Av, Pais. PA1	49	AY33
Ross Hall Pl, Renf. PA4	19	AZ26
Rosshill Av, G52	34	BB32
Rosshill Rd, G52	34	BB32
Rossie Cres, (Bishop.) G64	25	BY21
Rosslea Dr, (Giff.) G46	64	BL43
Rosslyn Av, (Ruther.) G73	55	BY38
Rosslyn Rd, (Bears.) G61	8	BD15
Rosslyn Ter, G12	22	BL25
Ross Pl, (Ruther.) G73	67	BZ41
Ross St, G40	5	BT31
Ross St, Pais. PA1	48	AV34
Rostan Rd, G43	64	BL40
Rosyth Rd, G5	54	BU35
Rosyth St, G5	54	BU35
Rotherwick Dr, Pais. PA1	50	BA33
Rotherwood Av, G13	9	BE20
Rotherwood Av, Pais. PA2	47	AP37
Rotherwood La, G13	9	BE19
Rotherwood Pl, G13	21	BG21
Rotherwood Way, Pais. PA2	47	AP37
off Rotherwood Av		
Rothes Dr, G23	10	BM20
Rothes Pl, G23	10	BL20
off Rothes Dr		
Rottenrow, G4	5	BT29
Rottenrow E, G4	5	BT30
Roukenburn St, (Thornlie.) G46	63	BG41
Rouken Glen Pk, (Thornlie.)	63	BH44
G46		
Rouken Glen Rd, (Thornlie.)	63	BH43
G46		
Roundhill Dr, (Elder.) John.	47	AN34
PA5		
Roundknowe Rd, (Udd.) G71	58	CL36
Rowallan Gdns, G11	22	BJ26
Rowallan La, G11	21	BH26
Rowallan La E, G11	22	BJ26
Rowallan Rd, (Thornlie.)	63	BH43
G46		
Rowallan Ter, G33	26	CD25
Rowan Av, Renf. PA4	19	AY25
Rowan Ct, Pais. PA2	48	AU35
Rowan Cres, (Lenz.) G66	15	CE16
Rowandale Av, (Baill.) G69	58	CJ33
Rowand Av, (Giff.) G46	64	BL43
Rowan Dr, Clyde. G81	6	AV17
Rowan Gdns, G41	52	BK33
Rowan Gate, Pais. PA2	48	AV35
Rowanlea Av, Pais. PA2	46	AM38
Rowanlea Dr, (Giff.) G46	64	BM41
Rowanpark Dr, (Barr.) G78	61	AW40
Rowan Pl, (Camb.) G72	69	CE39
Rowan Rd, G41	52	BK33
Rowan Rd, (Cumb.) G67	73	DF10
Rowans, The, (Bishop.) G64	12	BV19
Rowans Gdns, (Both.) G71	71	CR41
Rowan St, Pais. PA2	48	AU35
Rowantree Av, (Ruther.) G73	67	BX40
Rowantree Gdns, (Ruther.) G73	67	BX40
Rowantree Pl, John. PA5	45	AH36
off Rowantree Rd		
Rowantree Rd, John. PA5	45	AH36
Rowchester St, G40	39	BW32
Rowena Av, G13	9	BF20
Roxburgh La, G12	22	BM26
off Saltoun St		
Roxburgh Rd, Pais. PA2	46	AM38
Roxburgh St, G12	22	BM26
Royal Bk Pl, G1	5	BS30
off Buchanan St		
Royal Cres, G3	37	BN29
Royal Cres, G42	53	BQ36
off Queens Dr		
Royal Ex Bldgs, G1	5	BS30
off Royal Ex Sq		
Royal Ex Sq, G1	5	BS30
Royal Gdns, (Both.) G71	71	CN43
Royal Inch Cres, Renf. PA4	19	AZ24
off Campbell St		

Name	Page	Grid
Royal Ter, G3	37	BN28
Royal Ter La, G3	37	BN28
Roystonhill, G21	38	BV28
Royston Rd, G21	5	BU28
Royston Rd, G33	26	CA26
Royston Sq, G21	5	BU28
Roy St, G21	24	BT26
Rozelle Av, G15	8	BD18
Rubislaw Dr, (Bears.) G61	9	BG17
Ruby St, G40	55	BW33
Ruchazie Pl, G33	40	CB29
Ruchazie Rd, G32	40	CB30
Ruchazie Rd, G33	40	CB30
Ruchill Pl, G20	23	BP24
off Ruchill St		
Ruchill St, G20	23	BN24
Ruel St, G44	53	BQ38
Rufflees Av, (Barr.) G78	61	AZ41
Rugby Av, G13	20	BD21
Rullion Pl, G33	40	CB29
Rumford St, G40	54	BV34
Rupert St, G4	37	BP27
Rushyhill St, G21	25	BW25
Ruskin La, G12	23	BN26
Ruskin Pl, G12	23	BN26
off Great Western Rd		
Ruskin Sq, (Bishop.) G64	13	BW20
Ruskin Ter, G12	23	BN26
Ruskin Ter, (Ruther.) G73	55	BX37
Russell Cres, (Baill.) G69	58	CM33
Russell Dr, (Bears.) G61	9	BG15
Russell Gdns, (Udd.) G71	59	CQ38
off Kingston Av		
Russell St, G11	36	BK27
off Vine St		
Russell St, John. PA5	46	AJ34
Russell St, Pais. PA3	32	AT30
Rutherford Av, (Kirk.) G66	16	CK15
Rutherford Gra, (Kirk.) G66	15	CE15
Rutherglen Br, G40	54	BV34
Rutherglen Br, G42	54	BV34
Rutherglen Ind Est, (Ruther.) G73	55	BW36
Rutherglen Rd, G5	54	BT34
Rutherglen Rd, (Ruther.) G73	54	BT34
Ruthven Av, (Giff.) G46	64	BM44
Ruthven La, G12	22	BM26
Ruthven Pl, (Bishop.) G64	25	BY21
Ruthven St, G12	22	BM26
Rutland Ct, G51	37	BN31
off Govan Rd		
Rutland Cres, G51	37	BN31
Rutland Pl, G51	37	BN31
Ryan Rd, (Bishop.) G64	13	BX20
Ryan Way, (Ruther.) G73	67	BY42
Ryebank Rd, G21	25	BY24
Rye Cres, G21	25	BX24
Ryecroft Dr, (Baill.) G69	42	CK32
Ryedale Pl, G15	8	BC17
Ryefield Av, John. PA5	45	AF36
Ryefield Pl, John. PA5	45	AF36
Ryefield Rd, G21	25	BX24
Ryehill Pl, G21	25	BY24
Ryehill Rd, G21	25	BY24
Ryemount Rd, G21	25	BY24
Rye Rd, G21	25	BX24
Ryeside Rd, G21	25	BX24
Rye Way, Pais. PA2	47	AN36
Ryewraes Rd, (Linw.) Pais. PA3	30	AK32
Rylands Dr, G32	57	CF33
Rylands Gdns, G32	57	CG33
Rylees Cres, G52	34	BA31
Rylees Pl, G52	34	BA31
Rylees Rd, G52	34	BA31
Ryvra Rd, G13	21	BF23

S

Name	Page	Grid
Sackville Av, G13	21	BH24
Sackville La, G13	21	BH23
Saddell Rd, G15	8	BD17
St. Abbs Dr, Pais. PA2	47	AQ36
St. Andrews Av, (Bishop.) G64	12	BU19
St. Andrew's Av, (Both.) G71	71	CQ44
St. Andrews Cres, G41	53	BN33
St. Andrews Cres, Pais. PA3	32	AS28
St. Andrews Cross, G41	53	BQ34
St. Andrews Dr, G41	53	BN33
St. Andrews Dr, (Abbots.) Pais. PA3	32	AT29
St. Andrews Dr W, (Abbots.) Pais. PA3	32	AS28
St. Andrews La, G1	5	BT31
off Gallowgate		
St. Andrews Rd, G41	53	BP33
St. Andrews Rd, Renf. PA4	19	AY26
St. Andrews Sq, G1	5	BT31
St. Andrews St, G1	5	BT31
St. Annes Av, Ersk. PA8	18	AT21
off St. Annes Wynd		
St. Annes Wynd, Ersk. PA8	18	AS21
St. Anns Dr, (Giff.) G46	64	BL43
St. Barchan's Rd, (Millik.) John. PA10	44	AD35
off Easwald Bk		
St. Blanes Dr, (Ruther.) G73	66	BU39
St. Boswell's Cres, Pais. PA2	47	AQ36
St. Brides Rd, G43	64	BM39
St. Brides Way, (Both.) G71	71	CQ41
St. Catherines Rd, (Giff.) G46	64	BL43
St. Clair Av, (Giff.) G46	64	BL42
St. Clair St, G20	37	BP27
off North Woodside Rd		
St. Cyrus Gdns, (Bishop.) G64	13	BY20
St. Cyrus Rd, (Bishop.) G64	13	BY20
St. Enoch Pl, G1	4	BR31
off Howard St		
St. Enoch Shop Cen, G1	5	BS31
St. Enoch Sq, G1	4	BR31
St. Fillans Rd, G33	27	CE24
St. Georges Pl, G20	4	BQ28
off St. Georges Rd		
St. Georges Rd, G3	37	BQ27
St. Germains, (Bears.) G61	9	BG17
St. Helena Cres, Clyde. G81	7	AY15
St. Ives Rd, (Mood.) G69	17	CP18
St. James Av, Pais. PA3	31	AR30
St. James Business Cen, (Linw.) Pais. PA3	47	AN33
St. James Rd, G4	5	BT29
St. James St, Pais. PA3	32	AU32
St. John's Ct, G41	53	BN33
St. John's Quad, G41	53	BN33
St. John's Rd, G41	53	BN34
St. Joseph's Ct, G21	38	BV28
St. Joseph's Pl, G21	38	BV28
St. Joseph's Vw, G21	38	BV28
St. Kenneth Dr, G51	35	BF29
St. Kilda Dr, G14	21	BG25
St. Leonards Dr, (Giff.) G46	64	BL42
St. Luke's Pl, G5	38	BS32
St. Luke's Ter, G5	38	BS32
St. Margarets Pl, G1	5	BS31
off Bridgegate		
St. Mark Gdns, G32	40	CB32
St. Mark St, G32	40	CA32
St. Marnock St, G40	39	BW32
St. Mary's Cres, (Barr.) G78	61	AY43
St. Mary's Gdns, (Barr.) G78	61	AZ43
off Heys St		
St. Marys La, G2	4	BR30
off West Nile St		
St. Marys Rd, (Bishop.) G64	12	BU19
St. Michael's Ct, G31	39	BY32
off St. Michael's La		
St. Michael's La, G31	39	BY32
St. Mirren St, Pais. PA1	32	AU32
St. Monance St, G21	24	BV24
St. Mungo Av, G4	5	BS29
St. Mungo Pl, G4	5	BT29
St. Mungo's Rd, (Cumb.) G67	72	DB11
St. Mungo St, (Bishop.) G64	24	BV21
St. Mungos Wk, (Cumb.) G67	72	DB12
off Cumbernauld Shop Cen		
St. Ninians Cres, Pais. PA2	48	AV35
St. Ninians Rd, Pais. PA2	48	AV35
St. Ninian Ter, G5	38	BS32
off Ballater St		
St. Peters La, G2	4	BQ30
St. Peter's Path, G4	37	BQ27
off Braid St		
St. Peters St, G4	37	BQ27
St. Rollox Brae, G21	38	BU27
St. Ronans Dr, G41	52	BM36
St. Ronans Dr, (Ruther.) G73	67	BY39
St. Stephens Av, (Ruther.) G73	67	BZ42
St. Stephens Cres, (Ruther.) G73	68	CA42
St. Vincent Cres, G3	36	BM29
St. Vincent Cres La, G3	36	BM29
St. Vincent La, G2	4	BQ29
St. Vincent Pl, G1	5	BS30
St. Vincent St, G2	4	BQ29
St. Vincent St, G3	4	BP29
St. Vincent Ter, G3	4	BP29
Salamanca St, G31	39	BZ32
Salasaig Ct, G33	40	CC30
off Sutherness Dr		
Salen St, G52	35	BH32
Salisbury Pl, Clyde. G81	6	AT16
Salisbury St, G5	53	BR33
Salkeld St, G5	53	BR33
Salmona St, G22	23	BR25
Saltaire Av, (Udd.) G71	71	CQ40
Salterland Rd, G53	62	BA40
Salterland Rd, (Barr.) G78	62	BA40
Saltmarket, G1	5	BS31
Saltmarket Pl, G1	5	BS31
off Bridgegate		
Saltoun Gdns, G12	22	BM26
off Roxburgh St		
Saltoun La, G12	22	BM26
Saltoun St, G12	22	BL26
Salvia St, (Camb.) G72	68	CB39
Sandaig Rd, G33	41	CG31
Sanda St, G20	23	BN25
Sandbank Av, G20	22	BM22
Sandbank Cres, G20	22	BM23
Sandbank Dr, G20	22	BM22
Sandbank St, G20	22	BM23
Sandbank Ter, G20	22	BM22
Sandend Rd, G53	50	BC38
Sanderling Rd, Pais. PA3	32	AT29
Sandfield St, G20	23	BN24
Sandford Gdns, (Baill.) G69	42	CK32
off Scott St		
Sandgate Av, G32	57	CF34
Sandhaven Pl, G53	50	BC38
off Sandhaven Rd		
Sandhaven Rd, G53	50	BC38
Sandholes St, Pais. PA1	48	AS33
Sandholm Pl, G14	20	BB24
Sandholm Ter, G14	20	BB24
Sandiefield Rd, G5	54	BS33
Sandielands Av, Ersk. PA8	18	AT22
Sandilands St, G32	40	CD32
Sandmill St, G21	39	BW28
Sandra Rd, (Bishop.) G64	13	BY19
Sandringham Dr, (Elder.) John. PA5	46	AK36
off Glamis Av		
Sandringham La, G12	22	BM26
off Kersland St		
Sandwood Cres, G52	34	BC32
Sandwood Path, G52	34	BC32
off Hillington Rd S		
Sandwood Rd, G52	50	BC33
Sandyfaulds Sq, G5	54	BS33
Sandyfaulds St, G5	54	BT33
Sandyford Pl, G3	4	BP29
off Sauchiehall St		
Sandyford Pl La, G3	37	BN29
Sandyford Rd, Pais. PA3	32	AV29
Sandyford St, G3	36	BL29
Sandyhills Cres, G32	56	CD34
Sandyhills Dr, G32	56	CD34
Sandyhills Gro, G32	57	CE35
Sandyhills Pl, G32	56	CD34
Sandyhills Rd, G32	56	CD34
Sandyknowes Rd, (Cumb.) G67	72	DB13
Sandy La, G11	36	BJ27
off Crawford St		
Sandy Rd, G11	36	BJ28
Sandy Rd, Renf. PA4	33	AY28
Sannox Gdns, G31	39	BX29
Sanquhar Dr, G53	50	BC37
Sanquhar Gdns, G53	50	BC37
Sanquhar Gdns, (Blan.) G72	70	CK43
Sanquhar Pl, G53	50	BC37
Sanquhar Rd, G53	50	BC37
Saracen Head La, G1	5	BU31
off Gallowgate		
Saracen St, G22	24	BS26
Sardinia La, G12	22	BM26
Sardinia Ter, G12	22	BM26
off Cecil St		
Saturn Av, Pais. PA1	47	AN33
Saucelhill Ter, Pais. PA2	48	AV34
Saucel St, Pais. PA1	48	AU33
Sauchiehall Rd, (Kirk.) G66	17	CN16

Name	Page	Grid
Sauchiehall La, G2	4	BQ29
Sauchiehall St, G2	4	BQ29
Sauchiehall St, G3	36	BM28
Saughs Av, G33	26	CB23
Saughs Dr, G33	26	CB23
Saughs Gate, G33	26	CB23
Saughs Pl, G33	26	CB23
Saughs Rd, G33	26	CA24
Saughton St, G32	40	CA30
Saunders Ct, (Barr.) G78	61	AX42
off John St		
Savoy St, G40	54	BV33
Sawmillfield St, G4	37	BR27
Sawmill Rd, G11	35	BH27
off South St		
Saxon Rd, G13	21	BF22
Scadlock Rd, Pais. PA3	31	AR31
Scalpay Pas, G22	24	BT22
Scalpay Pl, G22	24	BT22
Scalpay St, G22	24	BS22
Scapa St, G23	23	BN21
Scaraway Dr, G22	24	BT21
Scaraway Pl, G22	24	BT21
Scaraway St, G22	24	BS21
Scaraway Ter, G22	24	BT21
Scarba Dr, G43	64	BK40
Scarrel Dr, G45	67	BW41
Scarrel Gdns, G45	67	BW41
Scarrel Rd, G45	67	BW41
Scarrel Ter, G45	67	BW41
Scavaig Cres, G15	8	BA17
Schaw Ct, (Bears.) G61	9	BG15
Schaw Dr, (Bears.) G61	9	BG15
Schaw Rd, Pais. PA3	33	AW31
Schipka Pas, G1	5	BT31
off Gallowgate		
School Av, (Camb.) G72	68	CD40
School Rd, (Stepps) G33	27	CG23
School Rd, Pais. PA1	34	BA32
School Wynd, Pais. PA1	32	AU32
Scioncroft Av, (Ruther.) G73	55	BY38
Scone St, G21	24	BS26
Scone Wk, (Baill.) G69	58	CJ34
Sconser St, G23	11	BN20
Scorton Gdns, (Baill.) G69	57	CG33
off Danby Rd		
Scotland St, G5	37	BP32
Scotland St W, G41	37	BN32
Scotsburn Rd, G21	25	BY25
Scotstoun Mill Rd, G11	36	BL28
off Partick Bridge St		
Scotstoun Pl, G14	21	BE26
off Scotstoun St		
Scotstoun St, G14	21	BE26
Scott Av, John. PA5	45	AG37
Scott Dr, (Bears.) G61	9	BE15
Scott Pl, John. PA5	45	AG37
Scott Rd, G52	34	BB29
Scotts Rd, Pais. PA2	49	AY34
Scott St, G3	4	BQ29
Scott St, (Baill.) G69	58	CK33
Scott St, Clyde. G81	6	AU17
Seafar Rd, (Cumb.) G67	72	DA13
Seafield Dr, (Ruther.) G73	67	BZ42
Seaforth Cres, (Barr.) G78	61	AX40
Seaforth La, (Mood.) G69	17	CQ19
off Burnbrae Av		
Seaforth Rd, G52	34	BC30
Seaforth Rd, Clyde. G81	7	AX20
Seaforth Rd N, G52	34	BC30
Seaforth Rd S, G52	34	BC30
Seagrove St, G32	39	BZ31
Seamill Path, G53	62	BB40
off Seamill St		
Seamill St, G53	62	BB40
Seamore St, G20	37	BP27
Seath Rd, (Ruther.) G73	55	BW36
Seath St, G42	54	BS35
Seaward La, G41	37	BN31
Seaward Pl, G41	53	BN33
Seaward St, G41	37	BP32
Second Av, (Millerston) G33	26	CD24
Second Av, G44	65	BR39
Second Av, (Bears.) G61	10	BJ18
Second Av, (Kirk.) G66	15	CE20
Second Av, (Udd.) G71	59	CN36
Second Av, Clyde. G81	6	AV18
Second Av, Renf. PA4	33	AY27
Second Gdns, G41	52	BJ33
Second St, (Udd.) G71	59	CP37
Seedhill, Pais. PA1	48	AV33
Seedhill Rd, Pais. PA1	48	AV33
Seggielea La, G13	21	BF24
off Helensburgh Dr		
Seggielea Rd, G13	21	BF23
Seil Dr, G44	65	BR41
Selborne Pl, G13	21	BG24
off Selborne Rd		
Selborne Pl La, G13	21	BG24
Selborne Rd, G13	21	BG24
Selby Gdns, G32	41	CF32
off Hailes Av		
Selkirk Av, G52	51	BE33
Selkirk Av, Pais. PA2	47	AQ36
Selkirk Dr, (Ruther.) G73	55	BY38
Sella Rd, (Bishop.) G64	13	BZ19
Selvieland Rd, G52	34	BB32
Semple Pl, (Linw.) Pais. PA3	30	AK30
Seton Ter, G31	38	BV30
Settle Gdns, (Baill.) G69	57	CH33
off Danby Rd		
Seven Sisters, (Kirk.) G66	15	CG16
Seventh Av, (Udd.) G71	59	CP37
Seyton Av, (Giff.) G46	64	BL44
Shaftesbury St, G3	4	BP29
Shaftesbury St, Clyde. G81	6	AV19
Shafton Pl, G13	21	BG21
Shafton Rd, G13	21	BG21
Shakespeare Av, Clyde. G81	6	AV17
Shakespeare St, G20	23	BN24
Shamrock St, G4	4	BQ28
Shandwick Sq, G34	42	CJ29
off Bogbain Rd		
Shandwick St, G34	42	CJ29
Shanks Av, (Barr.) G78	61	AY43
Shanks Cres, John. PA5	45	AG35
Shanks Ind Pk, (Barr.) G78	61	AY40
Shanks St, G20	23	BN24
Shanks Way, (Barr.) G78	61	AY41
off Blackbyres Rd		
Shannon St, G20	23	BP24
Shapinsay St, G22	24	BT21
Shawbridge Arc, G43	52	BL37
off Ashtree Rd		
Shawbridge St, G43	52	BK38
Shawfield Dr, G5	54	BU35
Shawfield Ind Est, (Ruther.) G73	54	BV35
Shawfield Rd, G5	54	BV34
Shawhill Rd, G41	52	BL37
Shawhill Rd, G43	52	BL37
Shawholm Cres, G43	52	BK38
Shawlands Arc, G41	53	BN37
Shawlands Sq, G41	52	BM37
Shawmoss Rd, G41	52	BL36
Shawpark St, G20	23	BN23
Shaw Pl, (Linw.) Pais. PA3	30	AK32
Shaw St, G51	36	BJ29
Shearers La, Renf. PA4	19	AZ26
off Fauldshead Rd		
Shearer St, G5	4	BP31
off Paisley Rd		
Sheddens Pl, G32	40	CB32
Sheepburn Rd, (Udd.) G71	59	CN38
Sheila St, G33	26	CA25
Shelley Ct, G12	22	BJ24
Shelley Dr, (Both.) G71	71	CR42
Shelley Dr, Clyde. G81	7	AW17
Shelley Rd, G12	21	BH24
Sheppard St, G21	24	BU25
off Cowlairs Rd		
Sherbrooke Av, G41	52	BL34
Sherbrooke Dr, G41	52	BL33
Sherbrooke Gdns, G41	52	BL34
Sherburn Gdns, (Baill.) G69	57	CH33
Sheriff Pk Av, (Ruther.) G73	55	BW38
Sherry Hts, (Camb.) G72	68	CC39
Sherwood Av, (Udd.) G71	71	CQ40
Sherwood Av, Pais. PA1	33	AW31
Sherwood Dr, (Thornlie.) G46	64	BJ42
Sherwood Pl, G15	8	BD18
Shetland Dr, G44	65	BR41
Shettleston Rd, G31	39	BY31
Shettleston Rd, G32	40	CC32
Shettleston Sheddings, G31	40	CA32
Shieldbridge Gdns, G23	11	BN19
Shiel Ct, (Barr.) G78	61	AX40
Shieldaig Dr, (Ruther.) G73	67	BX41
Shieldaig Rd, G22	23	BR21
Shieldburn Rd, G51	35	BE30
Shieldhall Gdns, G51	35	BE30
Shieldhall Rd, G51	34	BD29
Shields Rd, G41	37	BP32
Shiel Rd, (Bishop.) G64	13	BX20
Shilford Av, G13	20	BC22
Shillay St, G22	24	BU21
Shilton Dr, G53	63	BE40
Shinwell Av, Clyde. G81	7	AZ20
Shipbank La, G1	5	BS31
off Clyde St		
Shiskine Dr, G20	22	BL22
Shiskine Pl, G20	22	BL21
Shiskine St, G20	22	BL21
Shore St, G40	54	BV35
Shortridge St, G20	23	BN24
Shortroods Av, Pais. PA3	32	AT30
Shortroods Cres, Pais. PA3	32	AT30
Shortroods Rd, Pais. PA3	32	AT30
Shotts St, G33	41	CF29
Showcase Leisure Pk, (Baill.) G69	59	CR33
Shuna Pl, G20	23	BN24
Shuna St, G20	23	BN23
Shuttle La, G1	5	BT30
off George St		
Shuttle St, G1	5	BT30
Shuttle St, (Kilb.) John. PA10	44	AC33
Shuttle St, Pais. PA1	48	AU33
Sidland Rd, G21	25	BY24
Sidlaw Av, (Barr.) G78	61	AY44
off Ochil Dr		
Sidlaw Rd, (Bears.) G61	8	BD15
Sielga Pl, G34	42	CJ29
Siemens Pl, G21	39	BX27
Siemens St, G21	39	BX27
Sievewright St, (Ruther.) G73	55	BY36
off Hunter Rd		
Silk St, Pais. PA1	32	AV32
Silver Birch Dr, G51	35	BF30
Silver Birch Gdns, G51	35	BF30
Silverburn St, G33	40	CA29
Silverdale St, G31	55	BY33
Silverfir Ct, G5	54	BT34
off Silverfir St		
Silverfir Pl, G5	54	BT34
Silverfir St, G5	54	BT34
Silvergrove St, G40	38	BU32
Silverwells, (Both.) G71	71	CR44
Silverwells Ct, (Both.) G71	71	CQ44
Silverwells Cres, (Both.) G71	71	CQ44
Simons Cres, Renf. PA4	19	AZ24
Simpson Ct, (Udd.) G71	71	CP39
Simpson Ct, Clyde. G81	7	AW19
Simpson Gdns, (Barr.) G78	61	AX43
Simpson St, G20	23	BP26
Simshill Rd, G44	65	BR42
Sinclair Av, (Bears.) G61	9	BG15
Sinclair Dr, G42	53	BP38
Sinclair Gdns, (Bishop.) G64	25	BW21
Sinclair St, Clyde. G81	19	AZ21
Singer Rd, Clyde. G81	6	AV18
Singer St, Clyde. G81	7	AX18
Sir Michael Pl, Pais. PA1	48	AT33
Sixth Av, Renf. PA4	33	AY28
Sixth St, (Udd.) G71	59	CN36
Skaethorn Rd, G20	22	BK22
Skaterigg Dr, G13	21	BH24
Skaterigg Gdns, G13	21	BH24
Skaterigg La, G13	21	BG24
Skelbo Path, G34	42	CM28
off Auchingill Rd		
Skelbo Pl, G34	42	CM28
Skene Rd, G51	36	BK32
Skerray Quad, G22	24	BS21
Skerray St, G22	24	BS21
Skerryvore Pl, G33	40	CD29
Skerryvore Rd, G33	40	CD29
Skibo Dr, (Thornlie.) G46	63	BG42
Skibo La, (Thornlie.) G46	63	BG42
Skipness Dr, G51	35	BG29
Skirsa Ct, G23	23	BQ21
off Skirsa St		
Skirsa Pl, G23	23	BP22
Skirsa Sq, G23	23	BQ22
Skirsa St, G23	23	BP21
Skirving St, G41	53	BN37
Skye Av, Renf. PA4	33	AY28
Skye Ct, (Cumb.) G67	72	CZ13

Entry	No.	Ref.
Skye Cres, (Old Kil.) G60	6	AS16
Skye Cres, Pais. PA2	48	AT38
Skye Dr, (Old Kil.) G60	6	AS16
Skye Dr, (Cumb.) G67	72	CZ13
Skye Gdns, (Bears.) G61	8	BD15
Skye Pl, (Cumb.) G67	72	CZ13
Skye Rd, (Cumb.) G67	72	CZ13
Skye Rd, (Ruther.) G73	67	BZ42
Slakiewood Av, (Gart.) G69	29	CN22
Slatefield Ct, G31	39	BW31
off Slatefield St		
Slatefield St, G31	39	BW31
Slenavon Av, (Ruther.) G73	67	BZ42
Sloy St, G22	24	BT25
Smeaton Dr, (Bishop.) G64	13	BW17
Smeaton Gro, G20	23	BP23
Smeaton St, G20	23	BP23
Smith Cres, Clyde. G81	7	AX16
Smithhills St, Pais. PA1	32	AU32
Smiths La, Pais. PA3	32	AU31
Smith St, G14	35	BG27
Smith Ter, (Ruther.) G73	55	BX36
Smithycroft Rd, G33	40	CA28
Smithyends, (Cumb.) G67	73	DD8
Snaefeld Av, (Ruther.) G73	67	BY41
Snaefeld Cres, (Ruther.) G73	67	BY40
Snowdon Pl, G5	54	BT33
off Benthall St		
Snowdon St, G5	54	BT33
off Benthall St		
Snuff Mill Rd, G44	65	BR40
Society St, G31	39	BX32
Sollas Pl, G13	20	BA21
Solway Pl, (Chry.) G69	16	CM20
Solway Rd, (Bishop.) G64	13	BZ19
Solway St, G40	54	BV35
Somerford Rd, (Bears.) G61	9	BH20
Somerled Av, Pais. PA3	32	AV28
Somerset Pl, G3	4	BP28
Somerset Pl Ms, G3	4	BP28
Somervell St, (Camb.) G72	68	CB39
Somerville Dr, G42	53	BR37
Sorby St, G31	39	BZ32
Sorley St, G11	35	BH27
off Dumbarton Rd		
Sorn St, G40	55	BX34
Southampton Dr, G12	22	BK23
Southampton La, G12	22	BK23
South Annandale St, G42	53	BR35
South Av, Clyde. G81	7	AW19
South Av, Pais. PA2	48	AV37
South Av, Renf. PA4	19	AZ26
Southbank St, G31	39	BZ32
South Bk St, Clyde. G81	19	AY22
Southbar Av, G13	20	BC22
Southbrae Dr, G13	21	BE24
Southbrae La, G13	21	BG24
off Milner Rd		
South Campbell St, Pais. PA2	48	AU34
South Carbrain Rd, (Cumb.) G67	73	DC13
South Chester St, G32	40	CC32
Southcroft Rd, (Ruther.) G73	54	BU36
Southcroft St, G51	36	BK30
South Cft St, Pais. PA1	32	AV32
off Lawn St		
South Crosshill Rd, (Bishop.) G64	13	BW20
South Dean Pk Av, (Both.) G71	71	CQ43
Southdeen Av, G15	8	BD18
Southdeen Rd, G15	8	BC18
South Douglas St, Clyde. G81	19	AY21
South Elgin Pl, Clyde. G81	19	AY22
South Elgin St, Clyde. G81	19	AY22
Southend Rd, Clyde. G81	7	AX16
Southern Av, (Ruther.) G73	67	BX40
Southerness Dr, (Cumb.) G68	73	DC8
off Letham Gra		
South Erskine Pk, (Bears.) G61	9	BF16
Southesk Av, (Bishop.) G64	12	BV18
Southesk Gdns, (Bishop.) G64	12	BV18
Southfield Av, Pais. PA2	48	AU32
Southfield Cres, G53	51	BE37
Southfield Rd, (Cumb.) G68	72	CY12
South Frederick St, G1	5	BS30
Southhill Av, (Ruther.) G73	67	BX40
Southinch Av, G14	20	BA23
Southinch La, G14	20	BA23
Southlea Av, (Thornlie.) G46	64	BJ42
South Ln, (Chry.) G69	29	CN21
Southloch Gdns, G21	24	BV26
Southloch St, G21	24	BV26
South Moraine La, G15	9	BE19
off Moraine Av		
South Muirhead Rd, (Cumb.) G67	73	DC11
Southmuir Pl, G20	22	BM24
South Nitshill Ind Est, G53	62	BC40
Southpark Av, G12	36	BM27
South Pk Av, (Barr.) G78	61	AX42
South Pk Dr, Pais. PA2	48	AU35
Southpark La, G12	37	BN27
Southpark Ter, G12	37	BN27
off Southpark Av		
South Portland St, G5	37	BR32
South Scott St, (Baill.) G69	58	CK33
Southside Cres, G5	53	BR33
South St, G11	35	BF27
South St, G14	35	BF27
South Vesalius St, G32	40	CC32
off Shettleston Rd		
South Vw, (Blan.) G72	70	CL44
South Vw, Clyde. G81	6	AV18
Southview Ct, (Bishop.) G64	24	BV22
off Southview Vw		
Southview Dr, (Bears.) G61	9	BE16
Southview Pl, (Gart.) G69	29	CN23
Southview Ter, (Bishop.) G64	24	BV22
South William St, John. PA5	45	AH35
Southwold Rd, Pais. PA1	34	BA32
Southwood Dr, G44	66	BS40
South Woodside Rd, G4	37	BN27
South Woodside Rd, G20	23	BP26
Soutra Pl, G33	40	CD29
Spateston Rd, John. PA5	45	AE38
Spean St, G44	65	BQ39
Speirsfield Ct, Pais. PA2	48	AT34
Speirsfield Gdns, Pais. PA2	48	AU34
Speirshall Ct, G14	20	BB23
Speirshall Ter, G14	20	BA23
Speirs Rd, (Bears.) G61	10	BJ18
Speirs Rd, John. PA5	46	AK34
Spencer Dr, Pais. PA2	46	AM37
Spencer St, G13	21	BH22
Spencer St, Clyde. G81	7	AW18
Spence St, G20	22	BL21
Spey Av, Pais. PA2	47	AN36
Spey Dr, Renf. PA4	34	BA27
Spey Pl, John. PA5	45	AE37
Spey Rd, (Bears.) G61	9	BE19
Spey St, G33	40	CB29
Spey Wk, (Cumb.) G67	72	DB12
off Cumbernauld Shop Cen		
Spiersbridge Av, (Thornlie.) G46	63	BH42
Spiersbridge La, (Thornlie.) G46	63	BG42
Spiersbridge Rd, (Thornlie.) G46	63	BH42
Spiersbridge Ter, (Thornlie.) G46	63	BG42
Spiersbridge Toll, (Thornlie.) G46	63	BH43
Spiers Gro, (Thornlie.) G46	63	BH42
Spiers Pl, (Linw.) Pais. PA3	30	AL30
Spiers Wf, G4	37	BR27
Spindlehowe Rd, (Udd.) G71	71	CP39
Spinners Gdns, Pais. PA2	47	AR34
Spinners Row, John. PA5	45	AF35
Spittal Rd, (Ruther.) G73	66	BV41
Spittal Ter, (Camb.) G72	70	CJ43
Spoolers Rd, Pais. PA1	48	AS34
Spoutmouth, G1	5	BT31
off Gallowgate		
Springbank Rd, Pais. PA3	32	AT30
Springbank St, G20	23	BP25
Springbank Ter, Pais. PA3	32	AT30
Springboig Av, G32	41	CE31
Springboig Rd, G32	41	CE30
Springburn Rd, G21	38	BU27
Springburn Rd, (Bishop.) G64	24	BU24
Springburn Shop Cen, G21	24	BV25
Springburn Way, G21	24	BU25
Springcroft Av, (Baill.) G69	42	CK31
Springcroft Cres, (Baill.) G69	42	CK31
Springcroft Dr, (Baill.) G69	42	CJ31
Springcroft Gdns, (Baill.) G69	42	CL31
Springcroft Gro, (Baill.) G69	42	CK31
Springcroft Rd, (Baill.) G69	42	CK31
Springcroft Wynd, (Baill.) G69	42	CK31
Springfield Av, (Bishop.) G64	25	BW21
Springfield Av, (Udd.) G71	71	CP40
Springfield Av, Pais. PA1	49	AX33
Springfield Ct, G1	5	BS30
Springfield Cres, (Bishop.) G64	25	BW21
Springfield Cres, (Udd.) G71	71	CP40
Springfield Dr, (Barr.) G78	62	BA44
Springfield Pk, John. PA5	46	AJ35
Springfield Pk Rd, (Ruther.) G73	67	BY39
Springfield Quay, G5	4	BP31
Springfield Rd, G31	55	BY33
Springfield Rd, G40	55	BX34
Springfield Rd, (Bishop.) G64	13	BW20
Springfield Rd, (Cumb.) G67	73	DC9
Springfield Sq, (Bishop.) G64	25	BW21
Springfield Wds, John. PA5	46	AJ35
off Springfield Pk		
Springhall Ct, (Ruther.) G73	67	BZ41
off Cruachan Rd		
Springhill Dr N, (Baill.) G69	42	CJ30
Springhill Dr S, (Baill.) G69	42	CJ30
Springhill Fm Gro, (Baill.) G69	42	CJ31
Springhill Fm Pl, (Baill.) G69	42	CJ31
Springhill Fm Rd, (Baill.) G69	42	CJ31
Springhill Fm Way, (Baill.) G69	42	CJ31
Springhill Gdns, G41	53	BN36
Springhill Rd, (Baill.) G69	41	CH32
Springhill Rd, (Barr.) G78	61	AX43
Springkell Av, G41	52	BL34
Springkell Dr, G41	52	BK35
Springkell Gdns, G41	52	BL35
Springkell Gate, G41	52	BM35
Spring La, G5	54	BS34
off Lawmoor St		
Springside Gdns, G15	8	BC16
Springside Pl, G15	8	BC17
Springvale Dr, Pais. PA2	47	AP35
Springvale Ter, G21	24	BU25
Spruce Av, John. PA5	46	AJ36
Spruce Dr, (Kirk.) G66	14	CC16
Spruce Rd, (Cumb.) G67	73	DF9
Spruce St, G22	24	BT24
Spruce Way, (Camb.) G72	69	CH41
Spynie Pl, (Bishop.) G64	13	BZ19
Squire St, G14	35	BF27
Stable Gro, Pais. PA1	47	AR33
Staffa Av, Renf. PA4	33	AY28
Staffa Dr, Pais. PA2	48	AU38
Staffa Rd, (Camb.) G72	68	CB42
Staffa St, G31	39	BX29
Staffa Ter, (Camb.) G72	68	CB42
Staffin Dr, G23	10	BM20
Staffin Path, G23	11	BN20
Staffin St, G23	11	BN20
Stafford St, G4	5	BT28
Stag St, G51	36	BK30
Stair St, G20	23	BP25
Stamford St, G31	39	BX32
Stamford St, G40	39	BX32
Stamperland Gdns, (Clark.) G76	65	BP44
Stanalane St, (Thornlie.) G46	63	BH41
Standburn Rd, G21	25	BY22
Stanely Av, Pais. PA2	47	AR36
Stanely Cres, Pais. PA2	47	AR37
Stanely Dr, Pais. PA2	48	AS36
Stanely Gro, Pais. PA2	47	AR37
Stanely Rd, Pais. PA2	48	AS36
Stanford St, Clyde. G81	7	AY20
Stanhope Dr, (Ruther.) G73	67	BZ40
Stanley Dr, (Bishop.) G64	13	BX19
Stanley Pl, (Blan.) G72	70	CM44
Stanley St, G41	37	BN32
Stanley St La, G41	37	BN32
Stanmore Rd, G42	53	BR37
Stark Av, Clyde. G81	6	AU15
Startpoint St, G33	40	CC29
Station Cres, Renf. PA4	19	AZ25
off Sta Rd		
Station Pk, (Baill.) G69	58	CL33
Station Rd, G20	22	BL21
Station Rd, (Millerston) G33	26	CC24
Station Rd, (Stepps) G33	27	CF24
Station Rd, (Giff.) G46	64	BL42
off Fenwick Rd		
Station Rd, (Bears.) G61	9	BE18
Station Rd, (Baill.) G69	58	CL33

Name	Pg	Grid
Station Rd, (Muir.) G69	28	CL23
Station Rd, (Both.) G71	71	CQ43
Station Rd, (Udd.) G71	71	CN39
Station Rd, G72	71	CN44
Station Rd, (Kilb.) John. PA10	44	AC35
Station Rd, Pais. PA1	47	AQ34
Station Rd, Renf. PA4	19	AZ25
Station Way, (Udd.) G71	71	CQ39
Station Wynd, (Kilb.) John. PA10	44	AD35
Staybrae Dr, G53	50	BB36
Staybrae Gro, G53	50	BB36
Steel St, G1	5	BT31
Steeple Sq, (Kilb.) John. PA10	44	AC34
off Ewing St		
Steeple St, (Kilb.) John. PA10	44	AC34
Stenhouse Av, (Muir.) G69	28	CL21
Stenton St, G32	40	CA30
Stepford Pl, G33	41	CH30
Stepford Rd, G33	41	CH30
Stephen Cres, (Baill.) G69	41	CH32
Stephenson St, G52	34	BA29
Steppshill Ter, G33	27	CE24
Stepps Rd, G33	41	CE28
Stepps Rd, (Kirk.) G66	15	CG19
Stevenson St, G40	5	BU31
Stevenson St, Clyde. G81	6	AV17
Stevenson St, Pais. PA2	48	AU34
Stewart Av, Renf. PA4	33	AX28
Stewart Ct, (Ruther.) G73	55	BY38
Stewart Ct, (Barr.) G78	61	AY41
off Stewart St		
Stewart Cres, (Barr.) G78	61	AZ41
Stewart Dr, (Baill.) G69	43	CR31
Stewart Dr, Clyde. G81	7	AX15
Stewarton Dr, (Camb.) G72	68	CA40
Stewarton Rd, (Thornlie.) G46	63	BG43
Stewart Pl, (Barr.) G78	61	AZ41
Stewart Rd, Pais. PA2	48	AV37
Stewart St, G4	4	BR28
Stewart St, (Barr.) G78	61	AZ41
Stewart St, Clyde. G81	6	AU18
Stewartville St, G11	36	BK27
Stirling Av, (Bears.) G61	9	BG19
Stirling Dr, (Bears.) G61	9	BE15
Stirling Dr, (Bishop.) G64	12	BU18
Stirling Dr, (Ruther.) G73	67	BX40
Stirling Dr, John. PA5	45	AF35
Stirlingfauld Pl, G5	37	BR32
Stirling Gdns, (Bishop.) G64	12	BU18
Stirling Rd, G4	5	BT29
Stirling St, (Cumb.) G67	73	DD9
Stirling Way, (Baill.) G69	58	CJ33
off Huntingtower Rd		
Stirling Way, Renf. PA4	33	AZ28
off York Way		
Stirrat St, G20	22	BL23
Stirrat St, Pais. PA3	31	AR30
Stobcross Rd, G3	36	BM29
Stobcross St, G3	4	BP30
Stobcross Wynd, G3	36	BL29
Stobhill Cotts, G21	25	BW22
off Stobhill Rd		
Stobhill Rd, G21	24	BV22
Stobs Dr, (Barr.) G78	61	AX40
Stobs Pl, G34	42	CL28
Stock Av, Pais. PA2	48	AU34
Stockholm Cres, Pais. PA2	48	AU34
Stock St, Pais. PA2	48	AU34
Stockwell Pl, G1	5	BS31
Stockwell St, G1	5	BS31
Stoddard Sq, (Elder.) John. PA5	46	AM34
Stonebank Gro, G45	66	BT42
Stonedyke Gro, G15	8	BD19
Stonefield Av, G12	22	BK23
Stonefield Av, Pais. PA2	48	AV36
Stonefield Cres, Pais. PA2	48	AV36
Stonefield Dr, Pais. PA2	48	AV36
Stonefield Gdns, Pais. PA2	48	AV36
Stonefield Grn, Pais. PA2	48	AU36
Stonefield Gro, Pais. PA2	48	AU36
Stonefield Pk, Pais. PA2	48	AU37
Stonelaw Dr, (Ruther.) G73	55	BX38
Stonelaw Rd, (Ruther.) G73	55	BX38
Stonelaw Twrs, (Ruther.) G73	67	BY39
Stoneside Dr, G43	64	BJ39
Stoneside Sq, G43	64	BJ39
Stoney Brae, Pais. PA1	32	AU32
Stoney Brae, Pais. PA2	48	AU37
Stoneyetts Cotts, (Chry.) G69	17	CN17
Stoneyetts Rd, (Mood.) G69	17	CP18
Stonyhurst St, G22	23	BR25
Stonylee Rd, (Cumb.) G67	73	DC12
Storie St, Pais. PA1	48	AU33
Stormyland Way, (Barr.) G78	61	AY43
Stornoway St, G22	24	BS21
Stow Brae, Pais. PA1	48	AU33
Stow St, Pais. PA1	48	AU33
Strachur St, G22	23	BQ22
Straiton St, G32	40	CA30
Stranka Av, Pais. PA2	48	AS34
Stranraer Dr, G15	9	BE19
Stratford St, G20	22	BM24
Strathallon Pl, (Ruther.) G73	67	BZ42
off Ranald Gdns		
Strathblane Gdns, G13	21	BH21
Strathbran St, G31	55	BZ33
Strathcarron Cres, Pais. PA2	49	AX36
Strathcarron Dr, Pais. PA2	49	AX36
Strathcarron Pl, G20	23	BN23
off Glenfinnan Rd		
Strathcarron Pl, Pais. PA2	49	AX36
Strathcarron Rd, Pais. PA2	49	AX37
Strathcarron Way, Pais. PA2	49	AX36
Strathclyde Dr, (Ruther.) G73	55	BW38
Strathclyde Path, (Udd.) G71	71	CN39
Strathclyde St, G40	55	BW35
Strath Clyde Vw, (Both.) G71	71	CR44
Strathcona Dr, G13	21	BH22
Strathcona Gdns, G13	22	BJ22
Strathcona Pl, (Ruther.) G73	67	BZ41
off Ross Pl		
Strathcona St, G13	21	BH22
Strathdee Av, Clyde. G81	7	AX16
Strathdee Rd, G44	65	BN43
Strathdon Av, G44	65	BP43
Strathdon Av, Pais. PA2	48	AS35
Strathdon Dr, G44	65	BP43
Strathendrick Dr, G44	65	BN41
Strathkelvin Av, (Bishop.) G64	24	BV22
off Southview Ter		
Strathkelvin Retail Pk, (Bishop.)	13	BY16
Strathmore Av, (Blan.) G72	70	CL44
Strathmore Av, Pais. PA1	49	AZ33
Strathmore Gdns, (Ruther.) G73	67	BZ41
Strathmore Rd, G22	23	BR22
Strathord Pl, (Mood.) G69	17	CQ18
Strathord St, G32	56	CC34
Strathtay Av, G44	65	BP43
Strathview Gdns, (Bears.) G61	9	BF17
Strathview Gro, G44	65	BN43
Strathview Pk, G44	65	BP43
Strathy Pl, G20	22	BM24
off Glenfinnan Rd		
Strathyre Gdns, (Bears.) G61	10	BK16
Strathyre Gdns, (Mood.) G69	17	CQ18
off Heathfield Av		
Strathyre St, G41	53	BN37
Stratton Dr, (Giff.) G46	64	BK43
Strauss Av, Clyde. G81	8	BA20
Stravaig Path, Pais. PA2	47	AQ38
Stravaig Wk, Pais. PA2	47	AQ38
Stravanan Av, G45	66	BU43
Stravanan Ct, G45	66	BU43
Stravanan Gdns, G45	66	BT43
Stravanan Rd, G45	66	BT43
Stravanan St, G45	66	BT43
Stravanan Ter, G45	66	BT43
Streamfield Gdns, G33	25	BZ22
Streamfield Gate, G33	25	BZ22
off Brookfield Dr		
Streamfield Lea, G33	25	BZ22
Streamfield Pl, G33	25	BZ22
Strenabey Av, (Ruther.) G73	67	BZ41
Striven Gdns, G20	23	BP26
Stroma St, G21	39	BX27
Stromness St, G5	53	BQ33
Stronend St, G22	23	BR24
Strone Rd, G33	40	CD30
Stronsay Pl, (Bishop.) G64	13	BZ19
Stronsay St, G21	39	BX27
Stronvar Dr, G14	20	BD25
Stronvar La, G14	20	BD25
off Larchfield Av		
Strowan Cres, G32	56	CD33
Strowan St, G32	56	CD33
Struan Av, (Giff.) G46	64	BK42
Struan Gdns, G44	65	BQ40
Struan Rd, G44	65	BQ40
Struie St, G34	42	CJ29
Stuart Av, (Ruther.) G73	67	BX40
Stuart Dr, (Bishop.) G64	24	BU21
Succoth St, G13	21	BH22
Suffolk St, G40	5	BU31
off Kent St		
Sugworth Av, (Baill.) G69	42	CK32
Suisinsh, Ersk. PA8	18	AS22
Sumburgh St, G33	40	CB29
Summerfield Cotts, G14	35	BG27
Summerfield St, G40	55	BX35
Summerhill Dr, G15	8	BD17
Summerhill Gdns, G15	8	BD17
Summerhill Pl, G15	8	BD17
Summerhill Rd, G15	8	BC17
Summerlea Rd, (Thornlie.) G46	63	BH41
Summerlee St, G33	41	CE29
Summer St, G40	38	BV32
Summertown Rd, G51	36	BK30
Sunart Av, Renf. PA4	19	AX25
Sunart Gdns, (Bishop.) G64	13	BY20
Sunart Rd, G52	35	BG32
Sunart Rd, (Bishop.) G64	13	BY20
Sunningdale Rd, G23	22	BM21
Sunningdale Wynd, (Both.) G71	71	CN42
Sunnybank St, G40	55	BX34
Sunnylaw Dr, Pais. PA2	47	AQ35
Sunnylaw St, G22	23	BR25
Sunnyside Av, (Udd.) G71	71	CP40
Sunnyside Dr, G15	8	BC20
Sunnyside Dr, (Baill.) G69	43	CP32
Sunnyside Oval, Pais. PA2	48	AU36
Sunnyside Pl, G15	8	BC20
Sunnyside Pl, (Barr.) G78	61	AX43
Sunnyside Rd, Pais. PA2	48	AT35
Surrey St, G5	53	BR33
Sussex St, G41	37	BN32
Sutcliffe Ct, G13	21	BG22
off Sutcliffe Rd		
Sutcliffe Rd, G13	21	BG22
Sutherland Av, G41	52	BK34
Sutherland Dr, (Giff.) G46	64	BM44
Sutherland La, G12	36	BL27
Sutherland Rd, Clyde. G81	7	AX19
Sutherland St, Pais. PA1	32	AT32
Sutherness Dr, G33	40	CC30
Swallow Gdns, G13	20	BB22
Swan Pl, John. PA5	45	AE38
Swanston St, G40	55	BW35
Swan St, G4	5	BS28
Swan St, Clyde. G81	6	AV18
Sween Av, G44	65	BQ41
Sweethope Gdns, (Both.) G71	71	CR43
Sweethope Pl, (Both.) G71	71	CQ42
Swift Cres, G13	20	BB22
Swift Pl, John. PA5	45	AF38
Swindon St, Clyde. G81	6	AU18
Swinton Av, (Baill.) G69	42	CL32
Swinton Cres, (Baill.) G69	42	CL32
Swinton Cres, Coat. ML5	59	CR33
Swinton Dr, G52	34	BD32
Swinton Gdns, (Baill.) G69	42	CM32
off Swinton Dr		
Swinton Path, (Baill.) G69	42	CM32
Swinton Pl, G52	34	BD32
Swinton Pl, Coat. ML5	59	CR33
off Dunnachie Dr		
Swinton Rd, (Baill.) G69	42	CL32
Swinton Vw, (Baill.) G69	42	CL32
Switchback Rd, (Bears.) G61	9	BH19
Swordale Path, G34	42	CJ29
off Swordale Pl		
Swordale Pl, G34	42	CJ29
Sword St, G31	38	BV31
Sycamore Av, (Lenz.) G66	15	CF15
Sycamore Av, John. PA5	46	AJ36
Sycamore Dr, Clyde. G81	6	AV17
Sycamore Way, (Camb.) G72	69	CH41
Sydenham La, G12	22	BK26
off Crown Rd S		
Sydenham Rd, G12	22	BL26
Sydney St, G31	5	BU31
Sydney St, Clyde. G81	6	AT17
Sylvania Way, Clyde. G81	7	AX19
Sylvania Way S, Clyde. G81	7	AX20
Symington Dr, Clyde. G81	7	AW19

Syriam Pl, G21	24	BV25
off Syriam St		
Syriam St, G21	24	BV25
T		
Tabard Pl, G13	21	BE21
Tabard Pl N, G13	21	BE21
off Tabard Rd		
Tabard Pl S, G13	21	BE21
off Tabard Rd		
Tabard Rd, G13	21	BE21
Tabernacle La, (Camb.) G72	68	CC40
Tabernacle St, (Camb.) G72	68	CC40
Tain Pl, G34	42	CM29
Tait Av, (Barr.) G78	61	AZ41
Talbot Ct, G13	20	BD24
Talbot Dr, G13	20	BD24
Talbot Pl, G13	20	BD24
Talbot Ter, G13	20	BD24
off Kintillo Dr		
Talbot Ter, (Udd.) G71	59	CN37
Talisman, Clyde. G81	7	AZ19
off Onslow Rd		
Talisman Rd, G13	21	BE23
Talisman Rd, Pais. PA2	47	AN38
Tallant Rd, G15	8	BD18
Tallant Ter, G15	9	BE18
Talla Rd, G52	34	BD32
Tambowie St, G13	21	BG22
Tamshill St, G20	23	BP23
Tamworth St, G40	39	BW32
off Rimsdale St		
Tanar Av, Renf. PA4	34	BB28
Tanar Way, Renf. PA4	34	BA28
off Afton Dr		
Tandlehill Rd, (Millik.) John.	44	AD36
PA10		
Tanera Av, G44	66	BS40
Tanfield Pl, G32	41	CE30
off Tanfield St		
Tanfield St, G32	41	CE30
Tankerland Rd, G44	65	BQ39
Tannadice Av, G52	51	BE34
Tannadice Path, G52	51	BE33
off Tannadice Av		
Tanna Dr, G52	51	BH34
Tannahill Cres, John. PA5	45	AG36
Tannahill Rd, G43	65	BP39
Tannahill Rd, Pais. PA3	31	AR31
Tannahill Ter, Pais. PA3	31	AR31
Tannochside Business Pk,	59	CQ36
(Udd.) G71		
Tannochside Dr, (Udd.) G71	59	CQ36
Tannock St, G22	23	BR25
Tantallon Dr, Pais. PA2	47	AQ36
Tantallon Rd, G41	53	BN38
Tantallon Rd, (Baill.) G69	58	CJ34
Tantallon Rd, (Both.) G71	71	CR42
off Olifard Av		
Tanzieknowe Av, (Camb.) G72	68	CD41
Tanzieknowe Dr, (Camb.) G72	68	CD42
Tanzieknowe Pl, (Camb.) G72	68	CD42
Tanzieknowe Rd, (Camb.) G72	68	CD42
Taransay Ct, G22	24	BT22
off Liddesdale Sq		
Taransay St, G51	36	BJ29
Tarbert Av, (Blan.) G72	70	CL43
Tarbolton Dr, Clyde. G81	7	AY18
Tarbolton Rd, G43	64	BM39
Tarbolton Rd, (Cumb.) G67	73	DD11
Tarbolton Sq, Clyde. G81	7	AY18
off Tarbolton Dr		
Tarfside Av, G52	51	BE33
Tarfside Gdns, G52	51	BF33
Tarfside Oval, G52	51	BF33
Tarland St, G51	35	BH31
Tarn Gro, G33	25	BZ22
Tarras Dr, Renf. PA4	34	BA28
Tarras Pl, (Camb.) G72	69	CF40
Tassie St, G41	52	BM37
Tattershall Rd, G33	41	CE27
Tavistock Dr, G43	64	BM40
Tay Av, Pais. PA2	47	AP36
off Don Dr		
Tay Av, Renf. PA4	20	BA26
Tay Ct, (Mood.) G69	17	CQ19
off Deepdene Rd		
Tay Cres, G33	40	CA28
Tay Cres, (Bishop.) G64	13	BX20
Taylor Av, (Kilb.) John. PA10	44	AB34

Taylor Pl, G4	5	BT29
Taylor St, G4	5	BT30
Taylor St, Clyde. G81	19	AY21
Taymouth St, G32	56	CD34
Taynish Dr, G44	65	BR41
Tay Pl, John. PA5	45	AE37
Tay Rd, (Bears.) G61	9	BF19
Tay Rd, (Bishop.) G64	13	BX20
Tay Wk, (Cumb.) G67	72	DB11
off Cumbernauld Shop Cen		
Teal Dr, G13	20	BC22
Tealing Av, G52	51	BE33
Tealing Cres, G52	51	BE33
Teasel Av, G53	62	BD42
Teith Av, Renf. PA4	34	BB27
Teith Dr, (Bears.) G61	9	BF18
Teith Pl, (Camb.) G72	69	CF40
Teith St, G33	40	CA28
Telephone La, G12	22	BL26
Telford Ct, Clyde. G81	7	AW19
Telford Rd, (Cumb.) G67	73	DC13
Templar Av, G13	21	BF21
Temple Gdns, G13	21	BH22
Templeland Av, G53	51	BE35
Templeland Rd, G53	51	BE35
Temple Locks Ct, G13	22	BJ22
Temple Locks Pl, G13	21	BH22
Temple Rd, G13	22	BJ22
Templetons Business Cen, G40	38	BU32
Templeton St, G40	38	BU32
Tennant Rd, Pais. PA3	31	AR31
Tennant St, Renf. PA4	19	AZ25
Tennyson Dr, G31	56	CA33
Tenters Way, Pais. PA2	47	AR34
Tern Pl, John. PA5	45	AF38
Terrace Pl, (Camb.) G72	69	CG40
Terregles Av, G41	52	BK35
Terregles Cres, G41	52	BK35
Terregles Dr, G41	52	BL35
Teviot Av, (Bishop.) G64	13	BW18
Teviot Av, Pais. PA2	47	AN37
Teviot Cres, (Bears.) G61	9	BF19
Teviot Pl, (Camb.) G72	69	CF40
Teviot Sq, (Cumb.) G67	72	DB11
Teviot St, G3	36	BL29
Teviot Ter, G20	23	BN25
off Sanda St		
Teviot Ter, John. PA5	45	AE37
Teviot Wk, (Cumb.) G67	72	DB12
off Cumbernauld Shop Cen		
Thane Rd, G13	21	BE23
Thanes Gate, (Udd.) G71	71	CN40
Tharsis St, G21	38	BV28
Third Av, (Millerston) G33	26	CD24
Third Av, G44	53	BR38
Third Av, (Kirk.) G66	15	CF20
Third Av, Renf. PA4	33	AY27
Third Gdns, G41	52	BJ33
Thirdpart Cres, G13	20	BA22
Third St, (Udd.) G71	59	CP37
Thistle Bk, (Lenz.) G66	15	CF17
Thistle St, Pais. PA2	48	AS35
Thistle Ter, G5	54	BS33
Thomas Muir Av, (Bishop.)	25	BW21
G64		
Thomas St, Pais. PA1	47	AR33
Thompson Pl, Clyde. G81	7	AY15
Thomson Av, John. PA5	45	AG34
Thomson Dr, (Bears.) G61	9	BH15
Thomson Gro, (Camb.) G72	56	CC38
off Morriston Park Dr		
Thomson St, G31	39	BW31
Thomson St, John. PA5	45	AG35
Thomson St, Renf. PA4	33	AY27
Thornbank St, G3	36	BL28
Thorn Brae, John. PA5	46	AJ34
Thornbridge Av, G12	22	BL24
off Balcarres Av		
Thornbridge Av, (Baill.) G69	42	CJ31
Thornbridge Gdns, (Baill.) G69	42	CJ32
Thornbridge Rd, (Baill.) G69	42	CJ32
Thorncliffe Gdns, G41	53	BN35
Thorncliffe La, G41	53	BN35
Thorn Ct, John. PA5	46	AK35
off Thornhill		
Thorncroft Dr, G44	66	BT41
Thorndene, (Elder.) John. PA5	46	AK35
Thornden La, G14	20	BC25
Thorn Dr, (Bears.) G61	9	BF16
Thorn Dr, (Ruther.) G73	67	BY41

Thornhill, John. PA5	46	AK35
Thornhill Av, (Elder.) John.	46	AK35
PA5		
Thornhill Dr, (Elder.) John.	46	AK35
PA5		
Thornhill La, (Both.) G71	71	CR42
off Churchill Cres		
Thornhill Path, G31	55	BZ33
off Crail St		
Thorniewood Gdns, (Udd.) G71	59	CQ38
Thorniewood Rd, (Udd.) G71	59	CP37
Thornlea Dr, (Giff.) G46	64	BM41
Thornley Av, G13	20	BD23
Thornliebank Ind Est,	63	BG42
(Thornlie.) G46		
Thornliebank Rd, G43	64	BJ40
Thornliebank Rd, (Thornlie.)	64	BJ41
G46		
Thornly Pk Av, Pais. PA2	48	AV37
Thornly Pk Dr, Pais. PA2	48	AV37
Thornly Pk Gdns, Pais. PA2	48	AU36
Thornly Pk Rd, Pais. PA2	48	AU36
Thorn Rd, (Bears.) G61	9	BE16
Thornside Rd, John. PA5	46	AJ34
Thornton La, G20	23	BN22
Thornton St, G20	23	BN22
Thorntree Way, (Both.) G71	71	CR42
Thornwood Av, G11	36	BJ27
Thornwood Av, (Kirk.) G66	14	CC16
Thornwood Cres, G11	21	BH26
Thornwood Dr, G11	35	BH27
Thornwood Dr, Pais. PA2	47	AR35
Thornwood Gdns, G11	36	BJ27
Thornwood Pl, G11	22	BJ26
Thornwood Quad, G11	21	BH26
off Thornwood Dr		
Thornwood Rd, G11	35	BH27
Thornwood Ter, G11	35	BH27
Thornyburn Dr, (Baill.) G69	58	CM33
Thornyburn Pl, (Baill.) G69	58	CL33
Threestonehill Av, G32	40	CD31
Thrums Av, (Bishop.) G64	13	BY20
Thrums Gdns, (Bishop.) G64	13	BY20
Thrushcraig Cres, Pais. PA2	48	AV35
Thrush Pl, John. PA5	45	AF38
Thurso St, G11	36	BL28
off Dunaskin St		
Thurston Rd, G52	34	BC32
Tianavaig, Ersk. PA8	18	AS22
Tibbermore Rd, G11	22	BJ26
Tillet Oval, Pais. PA3	32	AT30
Tillie St, G20	23	BP26
Tillycairn Av, G33	41	CF27
Tillycairn Dr, G33	41	CF27
Tillycairn Pl, G33	41	CG27
Tillycairn Rd, G33	41	CG27
Tillycairn St, G33	41	CG27
Tilt St, G33	40	CA27
Tintagel Gdns, (Chry.) G69	17	CP18
Tinto Dr, (Barr.) G78	61	AX44
Tinto Gro, (Baill.) G69	43	CR31
Tinto Rd, G43	64	BL40
Tinto Rd, (Bears.) G61	8	BD15
Tinto Rd, (Bishop.) G64	13	BY20
Tinto Sq, Renf. PA4	33	AX28
off Ochil Rd		
Tinwald Path, G52	34	BC32
Tiree Av, Pais. PA2	48	AT38
Tiree Av, Renf. PA4	33	AY29
Tiree Ct, (Cumb.) G67	72	CZ13
Tiree Dr, (Cumb.) G67	72	CZ13
Tiree Gdns, (Old Kil.) G60	6	AS15
Tiree Gdns, (Bears.) G61	8	BD15
Tiree Pl, (Old Kil.) G60	6	AS15
Tiree Rd, (Cumb.) G67	72	CZ13
Tiree St, G21	39	BY27
Tirry Av, Renf. PA4	34	BB27
Tirry Way, Renf. PA4	34	BB27
off Morriston Cres		
Titwood Rd, G41	53	BN36
Tiverton Av, G32	57	CF34
Tobago Pl, G40	38	BV32
Tobago St, G40	38	BU32
Tobermory Rd, (Ruther.) G73	67	BZ43
Todburn Dr, Pais. PA2	48	AV37
Todd St, G31	39	BY30
Todholm Cres, Pais. PA2	49	AX35
Todholm Rd, Pais. PA2	49	AX35
Todholm Ter, Pais. PA2	49	AW35
Tofthill Av, (Bishop.) G64	12	BV19

Name	Page	Grid
Tofthill Gdns, (Bishop.) G64	12	BU19
Tollcross Pk Gdns, G32	56	CA34
off Tollcross Park Vw		
Tollcross Pk Gro, G32	56	CB34
off Tollcross Park Vw		
Tollcross Rd, G32	56	CA34
Tollcross Rd, G31	39	BZ32
Tollcross Rd, G32	56	CA33
Tolsta St, G23	11	BN20
Tontine La, G1	5	BT31
Tontine Pl, (Ruther.) G73	68	CA41
Toppersfield, (Millik.) John. PA10	45	AE35
Torbreck St, G52	35	BH32
Torbrex Rd, (Cumb.) G67	73	DC12
Torburn Av, (Giff.) G46	64	BK41
Tordene Path, (Cumb.) G68	72	CZ10
Torgyle St, G23	10	BM20
Tormore St, G51	35	BF31
Tormusk Dr, G45	67	BW41
Tormusk Gdns, G45	67	BW41
Tormusk Gro, G45	67	BW41
Tormusk Rd, G45	67	BW41
Torness St, G11	36	BL27
Torogay Pl, G22	24	BU21
Torogay St, G22	24	BS22
Torogay Ter, G22	24	BS21
Toronto Wk, G32	57	CE37
Torphin Cres, G32	40	CC30
Torphin Wk, G32	40	CD31
Torrance St, G21	24	BV25
Torran Dr, Ersk. PA8	18	AU22
Torran Rd, G33	41	CH30
Torridon Av, G41	52	BK34
Torridon Path, G41	52	BJ34
off Dumbreck Av		
Torrington Cres, G32	57	CF34
Torrin Rd, G23	10	BM20
Torrisdale St, G42	53	BP35
Torr Rd, (Bishop.) G64	13	BZ20
Torr St, G22	24	BT25
Torryburn Rd, G21	25	BY25
Torwood La, (Mood.) G69	17	CQ19
off Burnbrae Av		
Toryglen Rd, (Ruther.) G73	54	BU37
Toryglen St, G5	54	BT35
Toward Ct, (Blan.) G72	71	CN44
Toward Rd, G33	41	CE30
Tower Av, (Barr.) G78	61	AZ41
Tower Cres, Renf. PA4	33	AX27
Tower Dr, Renf. PA4	33	AX27
Towerhill Rd, G13	9	BE20
Tower Pl, John. PA5	45	AH36
Tower Rd, John. PA5	45	AH36
Towerside Cres, G53	50	BC35
Towerside Rd, G53	50	BC35
Tower St, G41	37	BN32
Tower Ter, Pais. PA1	48	AT33
Towie Pl, G20	22	BM23
off Glenfinnan Dr		
Towie Pl, (Udd.) G71	71	CP39
Town Cen, (Cumb.) G67	73	DC12
off Cumbernauld Shop Cen		
Townhead Pl, (Udd.) G71	59	CQ37
Townhead Rd, Coat. ML5	43	CQ28
Townhead Ter, Pais. PA1	48	AT33
Townmill Rd, G31	38	BV29
Townsend St, G4	5	BS28
Tradeston St, G5	37	BQ32
Trafalgar St, G40	54	BV34
Trafalgar St, Clyde. G81	6	AV18
Trainard Av, G32	56	CB33
Tranent Pl, G33	40	CA29
Traquair Av, Pais. PA2	47	AN37
Traquair Dr, G52	50	BD33
Treeburn Av, (Giff.) G46	64	BK42
Trees Pk Av, (Barr.) G78	61	AX41
Trefoil Av, G41	52	BM37
Tresta Rd, G23	23	BP21
Trident Way, Renf. PA4	33	AY28
off Newmains Rd		
Trinity Av, G52	51	BE33
Trinity Dr, (Camb.) G72	69	CE42
Trinley Brae, G13	9	BE20
Trinley Rd, G13	9	BF20
Trondra Path, G34	41	CH29
Trondra Pl, G34	41	CH30
Trondra Rd, G34	41	CH29
Trongate, G1	5	BS31
Troon St, G40	55	BX34
Trossachs Ct, G20	23	BQ26
off Trossachs St		
Trossachs Rd, (Ruther.) G73	67	BZ43
Trossachs St, G20	23	BQ26
Troubridge Av, (Millik.) John. PA10	44	AD36
Troubridge Cres, (Millik.) John. PA10	44	AD35
Truce Rd, G13	20	BD21
Truro Av, (Chry.) G69	17	CP18
Tryst Rd, (Cumb.) G67	72	DB12
Tudor Rd, G14	21	BG26
Tudor St, (Baill.) G69	57	CH34
Tullis Ct, G40	54	BU33
Tullis St, G40	54	BU33
Tulloch-Ard Pl, (Ruther.) G73	67	BZ41
off Lochbrae Dr		
Tulloch St, G44	65	BQ39
Tummel Way, Pais. PA2	47	AP36
Tummel St, G33	40	CA27
Tummel Wk, (Cumb.) G67	72	DB11
off Cumbernauld Shop Cen		
Tunnel St, G3	37	BN30
Tureen St, G40	5	BU31
Turnberry Av, G11	22	BK26
off Turnberry Rd		
Turnberry Dr, (Ruther.) G73	66	BV41
Turnberry Gdns, (Cumb.) G68	72	DB8
Turnberry Pl, (Ruther.) G73	66	BV41
off Turnberry Dr		
Turnberry Rd, G11	22	BJ26
Turnberry Wynd, (Both.) G71	71	CN42
Turnbull St, G1	5	BT31
Turner Rd, G21	38	BV27
Turner Rd, Pais. PA3	32	AV29
Turners Av, Pais. PA1	47	AR34
Turnlaw Rd, (Camb.) G72	68	CC43
Turnlaw St, G5	54	BT33
Turret Cres, G13	21	BE21
Turret Rd, G13	21	BE21
Turriff St, G5	53	BR33
Tweed Av, Pais. PA2	47	AP35
Tweed Cres, G33	39	BZ28
Tweed Cres, Renf. PA4	20	BA26
Tweed Dr, (Bears.) G61	9	BF18
Tweed Pl, John. PA5	45	AE37
Tweedsmuir, (Bishop.) G64	13	BY19
Tweedsmuir Rd, G52	50	BD33
Tweedvale Av, G14	20	BA23
Tweedvale Pl, G14	20	BA23
off Tweedvale Av		
Tweed Wk, (Cumb.) G67	72	DB12
off Cumbernauld Shop Cen		
Twinlaw St, G34	42	CM28
Tylney Rd, Pais. PA1	33	AZ32
Tyndrum Rd, (Bears.) G61	10	BK16
off Rannoch Dr		
Tyndrum St, G4	5	BS28
Tynecastle Cres, G32	40	CD30
Tynecastle Path, G32	40	CD30
off Lightburn Pl		
Tynecastle Pl, G32	40	CD30
Tynecastle St, G32	40	CD30
Tyne St, G14	35	BF27
Tynwald Av, (Ruther.) G73	67	BZ41
U		
Uddingston Rd, (Both.) G71	71	CP42
Uig Pl, G33	41	CG32
Uist Cres, (Stepps) G33	27	CG25
Uist St, G51	35	BH30
Ulundi Rd, John. PA5	45	AF35
Ulva St, G52	35	BH32
Umachan, Ersk. PA8	18	AS22
Underwood La, Pais. PA1	32	AT32
Underwood Rd, (Ruther.) G73	67	BY39
Underwood Rd, Pais. PA3	32	AS32
Underwood St, G41	53	BN37
Union Ct, Pais. PA2	48	AU35
Union Pl, G1	4	BR30
off Gordon St		
Union St, G1	4	BR30
Union St, Clyde. G81	19	AY21
Union St, Pais. PA2	48	AU35
Unity Pl, G4	37	BQ27
University Av, G12	36	BM27
University Gdns, G12	36	BM27
University of Glasgow, G12	36	BM27
University Pl, G12	36	BM27
Unsted Pl, Pais. PA1	49	AW33
Uphall Pl, G33	40	CA29
Upland Rd, G14	21	BE25
Upper Bourtree Ct, (Ruther.) G73	67	BY41
Upper Bourtree Dr, (Ruther.) G73	67	BX41
Upper Glenburn Rd, (Bears.) G61	9	BE16
Urquhart Cres, Renf. PA4	33	AY27
Urrdale Rd, G41	36	BK32
Usmore Pl, G33	41	CG32
off Pendeen Cres		
V		
Vaila Pl, G23	23	BQ22
Vaila St, G23	23	BP22
Valetta Pl, Clyde. G81	6	AT17
Valeview Ter, G42	53	BQ37
Vale Wk, (Bishop.) G64	25	BY21
Vallantine Cres, (Udd.) G71	59	CQ37
Vallay St, G22	24	BT21
Valleyfield St, G21	24	BU26
off Ayr St		
Valley Vw, (Camb.) G72	69	CE39
Vancouver La, G14	21	BF25
off Vancouver Rd		
Vancouver Pl, Clyde. G81	6	AT17
Vancouver Rd, G14	21	BE25
Vanguard St, Clyde. G81	7	AY19
Vanguard Way, Renf. PA4	33	AY28
Varna La, G14	21	BG26
Varna Rd, G14	21	BG25
Vasart Pl, G20	23	BP24
Veitches Ct, Clyde. G81	7	AW15
Vennacher Rd, Renf. PA4	19	AW25
Vennard Gdns, G41	53	BN35
Vermont Av, (Ruther.) G73	55	BW38
Vermont St, G41	37	BN32
Vernon Dr, (Linw.) Pais. PA3	30	AJ31
Verona Av, G14	21	BE25
Verona Gdns, G14	21	BE25
Verona La, G14	21	BE25
Vesalius St, G32	40	CC32
Vicarfield Pl, G51	36	BK30
off Vicarfield St		
Vicarfield St, G51	36	BK30
Vicarland Pl, (Camb.) G72	68	CC41
Vicarland Rd, (Camb.) G72	68	CC40
Vicars Wk, (Camb.) G72	68	CQ40
Victoria Av, (Barr.) G78	61	AX41
Victoria Br, G1	5	BS31
Victoria Br, G5	5	BS31
Victoria Circ, G12	22	BL26
Victoria Cres, G12	22	BL26
off Dowanside Rd		
Victoria Cres, (Barr.) G78	61	AX41
Victoria Cres La, G12	22	BL26
Victoria Cres Pl, G12	22	BL26
off Bowmont Ter		
Victoria Cres Rd, G12	22	BL26
Victoria Cross, G42	53	BQ35
Victoria Dr, (Barr.) G78	61	AX41
Victoria Dr E, Renf. PA4	33	AY27
Victoria Dr W, Renf. PA4	19	AX26
Victoria Gdns, (Barr.) G78	61	AX41
off Victoria Rd		
Victoria Gdns, Pais. PA2	48	AS35
Victoria Gro, (Barr.) G78	61	AX41
Victoria Pk Cor, G14	21	BF25
Victoria Pk Dr N, G14	21	BF25
Victoria Pk Dr S, G14	21	BE26
Victoria Pk Gdns N, G11	21	BH26
Victoria Pk Gdns S, G11	21	BH26
Victoria Pk La N, G14	21	BF26
Victoria Pk La S, G14	21	BF26
off Westland Dr		
Victoria Pk St, G14	21	BF26
Victoria Pl, (Ruther.) G73	55	BW37
off Greenbank St		
Victoria Pl, (Barr.) G78	61	AY41
Victoria Rd, (Stepps) G33	27	CF24
Victoria Rd, G42	53	BQ36
Victoria Rd, (Lenz.) G66	15	CE17
Victoria Rd, (Ruther.) G73	67	BX39
Victoria Rd, (Barr.) G78	61	AX41
Victoria Rd, Pais. PA2	48	AS35
Victoria St, (Ruther.) G73	55	BW37
Victory Dr, (Kilb.) John. PA10	44	AC33
Victory Way, (Baill.) G69	58	CK33
Viewbank, (Thornlie.) G46	64	BJ42

Street		
Viewfield Av, (Bishop.) G64	24	BU21
Viewfield Av, (Lenz.) G66	15	CE16
Viewfield Av, (Baill.) G69	41	CH32
Viewfield Av, (Blan.) G72	71	CN44
Viewfield Dr, (Bishop.) G64	24	BU21
Viewfield Dr, (Baill.) G69	41	CH32
Viewfield La, G12	37	BN27
Viewfield Rd, (Bishop.) G64	24	BU21
Viewfield Rd, Coat. ML5	59	CR33
Viewglen Ct, G45	66	BT44
Viewmount Dr, G20	22	BM22
Viewpark Av, G31	39	BX29
Viewpark Dr, (Ruther.) G73	67	BX39
Viewpark Gdns, Renf. PA4	33	AX27
Viewpoint Pl, G21	24	BV23
Viewpoint Rd, G21	24	BV23
Viking Rd, (Thornlie.) G46	63	BH41
Viking Way, Renf. PA4	33	AY28
off Vanguard Way		
Villafield Av, (Bishop.) G64	13	BW18
Villafield Dr, (Bishop.) G64	13	BW18
Villafield Ln, (Bishop.) G64	13	BW18
off Villafield Av		
Village Gdns, (Blan.) G72	71	CN44
Village Rd, (Camb.) G72	69	CG40
Vine St, G11	36	BK27
Vinicombe La, G12	22	BM26
Vinicombe St, G12	22	BM26
Vintner St, G4	38	BS27
Violet St, Pais. PA1	49	AW33
Virginia Bldgs, G1	5	BS30
off Virginia St		
Virginia Ct, G1	5	BS30
off Virginia St		
Virginia Pl, G1	5	BS30
Virginia St, G1	5	BS30
Viscount Av, Renf. PA4	33	AY28
Viscount Gate, (Both.) G71	71	CN40
Voil Dr, G44	65	BQ41
Vorlich Ct, (Barr.) G78	61	AY44
off Eildon Dr		
Vulcan St, G21	24	BU25
off Springburn Way		
W		
Waddell Ct, G5	38	BT32
Waddell St, G5	54	BT33
Waldemar Rd, G13	21	BE22
Waldo St, G13	21	BH22
Walkerburn Rd, G52	50	BD33
Walker Ct, G11	36	BK28
Walker Dr, (Elder.) John. PA5	46	AK35
Walker Path, (Udd.) G71	59	CQ37
Walker St, G11	36	BK28
Walker St, Pais. PA1	48	AT33
Walkinshaw Cres, Pais. PA2	31	AR31
Walkinshaw Rd, Renf. PA4	18	AS26
Walkinshaw St, G40	55	BW33
Walkinshaw St, John. PA5	45	AH34
Wallace Av, (Elder.) John. PA5	46	AL34
Wallace Pl, (Blan.) G72	71	CN44
Wallace Rd, Renf. PA4	33	AW28
Wallace St, G5	4	BQ31
Wallace St, (Ruther.) G73	55	BW38
Wallace St, Clyde. G81	19	AX21
Wallace St, Pais. PA3	32	AU31
Wallacewell Cres, G21	25	BX24
Wallacewell Pl, G21	25	BX24
Wallacewell Quad, G21	25	BY23
Wallacewell Rd, G21	25	BX24
Wallbrae Rd, (Cumb.) G67	72	DB13
Wallneuk, Pais. PA1	32	AV32
off Incle St		
Wallneuk Rd, Pais. PA3	32	AV32
Walls St, G1	5	BT30
Walmer Cres, G51	36	BL31
Walnut Cres, G22	24	BT24
Walnut Cres, John. PA5	46	AJ36
Walnut Dr, (Kirk.) G66	14	CD15
Walnut Gate, (Camb.) G72	69	CH41
Walnut Pl, G22	24	BT24
Walnut Rd, G22	24	BT24
Walpole Pl, John. PA5	45	AF38
off Hallhill Rd		
Walter St, G31	39	BX30
Walton Ct, (Giff.) G46	64	BL43
Walton St, G41	53	BN37
Walton St, (Barr.) G78	61	AY42
Wamba Av, G13	21	BG21
Wamba Pl, G13	21	BG21
Wandilla Av, Clyde. G81	7	AZ19
Wanlock St, G51	36	BJ29
Warden Rd, G13	21	BF22
Wardhill Rd, G21	25	BX24
Wardhouse Rd, Pais. PA2	48	AS38
Wardie Path, G33	41	CH30
Wardie Pl, G33	41	CH30
Wardie Rd, G33	41	CH30
Wardie Rd, G34	42	CJ29
Wardlaw Av, (Ruther.) G73	55	BX38
Wardlaw Dr, (Ruther.) G73	55	BX37
Wardlaw Rd, (Bears.) G61	9	BH20
Wardrop St, G51	36	BJ29
Wardrop St, Pais. PA1	48	AU33
Ware Path, G34	42	CJ30
Ware Rd, G34	41	CH30
Warilda Av, Clyde. G81	7	AY19
Warnock St, G31	5	BU29
off Church St		
Warren St, G42	53	BR36
Warriston Cres, G33	39	BZ29
Warriston Pl, G32	40	CD30
Warriston St, G33	39	BZ29
Warriston Way, (Ruther.) G73	67	BZ41
off Lochaber Dr		
Warroch St, G3	4	BP30
Washington Rd, Pais. PA3	32	AV29
Washington St, G3	4	BQ30
Water Brae, Pais. PA1	48	AU33
off Forbes Pl		
Waterfoot Av, G53	51	BE37
Waterfoot Ter, G53	51	BE37
off Waterfoot Av		
Waterford Rd, (Giff.) G46	64	BK42
Waterhaughs Gdns, G33	25	BZ22
Waterhaughs Gro, G33	25	BZ22
Waterhaughs Pl, G33	25	BZ22
Waterloo La, G2	4	BR30
Waterloo St, G2	4	BQ30
Watermill Av, (Lenz.) G66	15	CF17
Water Rd, (Barr.) G78	61	AY42
Water Row, G51	36	BJ29
Waterside Gdns, (Camb.) G72	69	CG42
Waterside La, (Millik.) John. PA10	45	AE36
Waterside Pl, G5	54	BT33
Waterside St, G5	54	BT33
Waterside Ter, (Millik.) John. PA10	45	AE35
off Kilbarchan Rd		
Watling St, (Udd.) G71	59	CN37
Watson Av, (Ruther.) G73	54	BV38
Watson Av, (Linw.) Pais. PA3	30	AK31
Watson St, G1	5	BT31
Watson St, (Udd.) G71	71	CP40
Watt Av, G33	27	CH24
Watt Low Av, (Ruther.) G73	66	BV39
Watt Rd, G52	34	BB30
Watt St, G5	4	BP31
Waukglen Av, G53	62	BD43
Waukglen Cres, G53	63	BE42
Waukglen Dr, G53	62	BD42
Waukglen Gdns, G53	62	BD42
Waukglen Path, G53	62	BD42
off Waukglen Dr		
Waukglen Pl, G53	62	BD42
Waukglen Rd, G53	62	BD42
Waulkmill Av, (Barr.) G78	61	AZ41
Waulkmill St, (Thornlie.) G46	63	BG41
Waulkmill Way, (Barr.) G78	61	AZ41
off Waulkmill Av		
Waverley, Clyde. G81	7	AY19
off Onslow Rd		
Waverley Ct, (Both.) G71	71	CQ43
Waverley Dr, (Ruther.) G73	55	BY38
Waverley Gdns, G41	53	BN36
Waverley Gdns, (Elder.) John. PA5	46	AM35
Waverley Rd, Pais. PA2	47	AP37
Waverley St, G41	53	BN36
Waverley Ter, G31	39	BW31
off Whitevale St		
Waverley Way, Pais. PA2	47	AP38
off Waverley Rd		
Weardale La, G33	41	CE29
Weardale St, G33	41	CE29
Weaver La, (Kilb.) John. PA10	44	AC33
off Glentyan Av		
Weavers Av, Pais. PA2	47	AR34
Weavers Gate, Pais. PA1	47	AQ34
Weavers Rd, Pais. PA2	47	AR34
Weaver St, G4	5	BT30
Weaver Ter, Pais. PA2	49	AW34
Webster St, G40	55	BW34
Webster St, Clyde. G81	20	BA21
Wedderlea Dr, G52	34	BC32
Weensmoor Pl, G53	62	BC41
Weensmoor Rd, G53	62	BC40
off Willowford Rd		
Weeple Dr, (Linw.) Pais. PA3	30	AJ31
Weighhouse Cl, Pais. PA1	48	AU33
Weir Av, (Barr.) G78	61	AY43
Weir St, Pais. PA3	32	AU32
Weirwood Av, (Baill.) G69	57	CH33
Weirwood Gdns, (Baill.) G69	57	CH33
Welbeck Rd, G53	62	BD40
Welfare Av, (Camb.) G72	69	CF41
Wellbank Pl, (Udd.) G71	71	CP39
off Church St		
Wellbrae Ter, (Mood.) G69	17	CP19
Wellcroft Pl, G5	53	BR33
Wellfield Av, (Giff.) G46	64	BK42
Wellfield Ct, (Giff.) G46	64	BK42
off Wellfield Av		
Wellfield St, G21	24	BV25
Well Grn, G43	52	BL37
Wellgreen Ct, G43	52	BL37
off Well Grn		
Wellhouse Cres, G33	41	CG30
Wellhouse Gdns, G33	41	CH30
Wellhouse Path, G34	41	CH30
Wellhouse Rd, G33	41	CH29
Wellington La, G2	4	BQ30
Wellington Path, (Baill.) G69	58	CK33
off Nelson Pl		
Wellington Pl, Clyde. G81	6	AT17
Wellington Rd, (Bishop.) G64	13	BX17
Wellington St, G2	4	BR30
Wellington St, Pais. PA3	32	AT32
Wellington Way, Renf. PA4	33	AY28
off Tiree Av		
Wellmeadow Rd, G43	64	BJ39
Wellmeadow St, Pais. PA1	48	AT33
Wellpark St, G31	5	BU30
Well Rd, (Kilb.) John. PA10	44	AC34
Wellshot Dr, (Camb.) G72	68	CB40
Wellshot Rd, G32	56	CB34
Wellside Dr, (Camb.) G72	69	CE41
Wells St, Clyde. G81	6	AV18
Well St, Pais. PA1	32	AS32
Wemyss Gdns, (Baill.) G69	58	CJ34
Wendur Way, Pais. PA3	32	AU29
off Abbotsburn Way		
Wenlock Rd, Pais. PA2	48	AV35
Wentworth Dr, G23	11	BN20
off Dougalston Rd		
West Av, (Stepps) G33	27	CF24
West Av, (Udd.) G71	71	CR39
West Av, Renf. PA4	19	AZ26
Westbank Ct, G12	37	BN27
Westbank La, G12	37	BN27
Westbank Quad, G12	37	BN27
Westbourne Cres, (Bears.) G61	9	BE16
Westbourne Dr, (Bears.) G61	9	BE16
Westbourne Gdns La, G12	22	BL25
Westbourne Gdns N, G12	22	BL25
Westbourne Gdns S, G12	22	BL25
Westbourne Gdns W, G12	22	BL25
Westbourne Rd, G12	22	BK25
Westbourne Shop Cen, (Barr.) G78	61	AX43
Westbourne Ter La, G12	22	BK25
off Westbourne Rd		
West Brae, Pais. PA1	48	AT33
Westbrae Dr, G14	21	BG25
West Buchanan Pl, Pais. PA1	48	AT33
off Sir Michael Pl		
Westburn Av, (Camb.) G72	69	CF39
Westburn Av, Pais. PA3	31	AQ32
Westburn Cres, (Ruther.) G73	54	BV38
Westburn Dr, (Camb.) G72	56	CD38
Westburn Fm Rd, (Camb.) G72	68	CD39
Westburn Rd, (Camb.) G72	69	CE39
Westburn Way, Pais. PA3	31	AR32
off Westburn Av		
West Campbell St, G2	4	BQ30
West Campbell St, Pais. PA1	47	AR33
Westcastle Ct, G45	66	BS42
off Westcastle Cres		
Westcastle Cres, G45	66	BT42
Westcastle Gdns, G45	66	BT42

Street			Street			Street		
Westcastle Gro, G45	66	BS42	Westwood Av, (Giff.) G46	64	BK42	Whittingehame Dr, G12	21	BH24
off Westcastle Cres			Westwood Gdns, Pais. PA3	31	AR32	Whittingehame Dr, G13	21	BH24
West Chapelton Av, (Bears.) G61	9	BH17	Westwood Quad, Clyde. G81	7	AZ20	Whittingehame Gdns, G12	22	BJ24
West Chapelton Cres, (Bears.) G61	9	BH17	Westwood Rd, G43	64	BK39	Whittingehame La, G13	21	BH24
West Chapelton Dr, (Bears.) G61	9	BH17	Weymouth Dr, G12	22	BJ23	Whittingehame Pk, G12	21	BH24
West Chapelton La, (Bears.) G61	9	BH17	Whamflet Av, (Baill.) G69	42	CL30	Whitlemuir Av, G44	65	BP41
off West Chapelton Av			Wheatfield Rd, (Bears.) G61	9	BF18	Whitton Dr, (Giff.) G46	64	BM41
Westclyffe St, G41	53	BN36	Wheatlands Dr, (Kilb.) John. PA10	44	AC33	Whitton St, G20	22	BL21
West Coats Rd, (Camb.) G72	68	CB40	Wheatlands Fm Rd, (Kilb.) John. PA10	44	AC33	Whitworth Dr, G20	23	BQ23
West Cotts, (Gart.) G69	28	CK26	Wheatley Ct, G32	40	CC32	Whitworth Dr, Clyde. G81	7	AW19
West Ct, Clyde. G81	6	AU17	Wheatley Dr, G32	40	CC32	Whitworth Gdns, G20	23	BP23
West Ct, Pais. PA1	47	AQ33	Wheatley Ln, (Bishop.) G64	25	BY21	Whitworth Gate, G20	23	BQ24
Westend, (Bears.) G61	10	BJ19	Wheatley Pl, G32	40	CC32	Whyte Av, (Camb.) G72	68	CA39
West End Pk St, G3	4	BP28	Wheatley Rd, G32	40	CC32	Wickets, The, Pais. PA1	49	AW34
Westerburn St, G32	40	CB31	Whin Av, (Barr.) G78	61	AW41	Wigtoun Pl, (Cumb.) G67	73	DD9
Wester Carriagehill, Pais. PA2	48	AU35	Whinfield Av, (Camb.) G72	55	BZ38	Wilderness Brae, (Cumb.) G67	73	DD9
Wester Cleddens Rd, (Bishop.) G64	13	BW19	*off Cambuslang Rd*			Wilfred Av, G13	21	BF22
Wester Common Dr, G22	23	BQ24	Whinfield Path, G53	62	BC41	Wilkie Rd, (Udd.) G71	71	CQ40
Wester Common Rd, G22	23	BQ25	*off Parkhouse Rd*			Williamsburgh Ct, Pais. PA1	49	AW33
Wester Common Ter, G22	23	BR25	Whinfield Rd, G53	62	BC41	*off Lacy St*		
Westercraigs, G31	38	BV30	*off Parkhouse Rd*			Williamsburgh Ter, Pais. PA1	33	AW32
Westercraigs Ct, G31	38	BV30	Whinhill Gdns, G53	50	BC34	*off Lacy St*		
off Westercraigs			Whinhill Pl, G53	50	BC34	Williamson Pl, John. PA5	46	AK35
Westergreens Av, (Kirk.) G66	15	CE15	Whinhill Rd, G53	50	BC34	Williamson St, G31	55	BY33
Westerhill Rd, (Bishop.) G64	13	BY17	Whinhill Rd, Pais. PA2	49	AX35	Williamson St, Clyde. G81	7	AX17
Westerhouse Path, G34	41	CH29	Whins Rd, G41	52	BL36	William St, G3	4	BP29
off Kildermorie Rd			Whin St, Clyde. G81	7	AW17	William St, Clyde. G81	7	AW15
Westerhouse Rd, G34	42	CJ28	Whirlow Gdns, (Baill.) G69	42	CJ32	William St, John. PA5	45	AH34
Westerkirk Dr, G23	11	BN20	Whirlow Rd, (Baill.) G69	42	CJ32	William St, Pais. PA1	48	AS33
Westerlands, G12	21	BH23	Whistlefield Ct, (Bears.) G61	9	BH18	William Ure Pl, (Bishop.) G64	13	BX16
off Ascot Av			Whitacres Path, G53	62	BC41	Williamwood Dr, G44	65	BP43
Western Av, (Ruther.) G73	54	BV37	*off Wiltonburn Rd*			Williamwood Pk, G44	65	BP43
Western Isles Rd, (Old Kil.) G60	6	AS16	Whitacres Pl, G53	62	BC41	Williamwood Pk W, G44	65	BP43
Western Rd, (Camb.) G72	68	CA41	*off Whitacres Rd*			Willock Pl, G20	23	BN22
Wester Rd, G32	57	CF33	Whitacres Rd, G53	62	BB41	Willoughby Dr, G13	21	BH23
Westerton Av, (Bears.) G61	21	BH21	Whitburn St, G32	40	CB30	Willoughby La, G13	21	BH23
Westfield Av, (Ruther.) G73	54	BV38	Whitecart Rd, (Abbots.) Pais. PA3	32	AU29	*off Willoughby Dr*		
Westfield Cres, (Bears.) G61	9	BG19	*off Sanderling Rd*			Willow Av, (Bishop.) G64	25	BW21
Westfield Dr, G52	34	BC32	Whitecraigs Pl, G23	23	BN21	Willow Av, (Lenz.) G66	15	CE15
Westfield Dr, (Bears.) G61	9	BG19	*off Fairhaven Rd*			Willow Av, (Elder.) John. PA5	46	AL35
Westfield Rd, (Thornlie.) G46	64	BJ43	Whitecrook St, Clyde. G81	19	AX21	Willowbank Cres, G3	37	BP27
Westfields, (Bishop.) G64	12	BU18	Whitefield Av, (Camb.) G72	68	CC41	*off Woodlands Rd*		
Westfield Vil, (Ruther.) G73	54	BU38	Whitefield Rd, G51	36	BL32	Willowbank St, G3	37	BP27
West George La, G2	4	BQ29	Whitefield Ter, (Camb.) G72	68	CD40	Willowdale Cres, (Baill.) G69	58	CJ33
West George St, G2	4	BQ29	*off Croft Rd*			Willowdale Gdns, (Baill.) G69	58	CJ33
West Graham St, G4	4	BQ28	Whiteford Rd, G33	27	CH24	Willow Dr, John. PA5	45	AH36
West Greenhill Pl, G3	37	BN29	Whiteford Rd, Pais. PA2	49	AW35	Willowford Rd, G53	62	BB41
Westhorn Dr, G32	56	CC36	Whitehall St, G3	4	BP30	Willow La, G32	56	CD35
Westhouse Av, (Ruther.) G73	54	BU38	Whitehaugh Av, Pais. PA1	33	AX32	Willow Pl, John. PA5	46	AJ35
Westhouse Gdns, (Ruther.) G73	54	BU38	Whitehaugh Cres, G53	62	BC41	Willow St, G13	21	BH22
Westknowe Gdns, (Ruther.) G73	67	BX40	Whitehaugh Dr, Pais. PA1	33	AX32	Wilmot Rd, G13	21	BF23
Westland Dr, G14	21	BF26	Whitehaugh Path, G53	62	BC40	Wilson Av, (Linw.) Pais. PA3	30	AJ31
Westland Dr La, G14	21	BF26	*off Wiltonburn Rd*			Wilsons Pl, Pais. PA1	48	AV33
off Westland Dr			Whitehaugh Rd, G53	62	BC41	*off Seedhill*		
Westlands Gdns, Pais. PA2	48	AT33	Whitehill Av, (Stepps) G33	27	CF23	Wilson St, G1	5	BS30
West La, Pais. PA1	47	AR33	Whitehill Av, (Cumb.) G68	72	CZ11	Wilson St, Pais. PA1	48	AS33
West Lo Rd, Renf. PA4	19	AX25	Whitehill Fm Rd, (Stepps) G33	27	CF24	Wilson St, Renf. PA4	19	AZ25
Westminster Gdns, G12	22	BM26	Whitehill Gdns, G31	39	BW30	Wiltonburn Path, G53	62	BC41
off Kersland St			Whitehill La, (Bears.) G61	9	BF16	*off Wiltonburn Rd*		
Westminster Ter, G3	37	BN29	Whitehill Rd, (Stepps) G33	27	CF21	Wiltonburn Rd, G53	62	BC41
off Royal Ter			Whitehill Rd, (Bears.) G61	9	BF16	Wilton Cres, G20	23	BP26
Westmoreland St, G42	53	BQ35	Whitehill Rd, (Kirk.) G66	27	CF22	Wilton Cres La, G20	23	BP26
Westmuir Pl, (Ruther.) G73	54	BU37	Whitehill St, G31	39	BW30	Wilton Dr, G20	23	BP26
Westmuir St, G31	39	BZ32	Whitehill St La, G31	39	BW30	Wilton Gdns, G20	23	BP26
West Nile St, G1	4	BR30	Whitehill Ter, (Gart.) G69	29	CP25	Wilton St, G20	23	BN26
Westpark Dr, Pais. PA3	31	AQ32	Whitehurst, (Bears.) G61	9	BE15	Wilverton Rd, G13	21	BG21
West Princes St, G4	37	BP27	Whitehurst Pk, (Bears.) G61	9	BE15	Winchester Dr, G12	22	BK23
Westray Circ, G22	24	BT23	Whitekirk Pl, G15	8	BC19	Windhill Cres, G43	64	BK40
Westray Ct, (Cumb.) G67	72	DA13	Whitelaw St, G20	22	BL22	Windhill Pl, G43	64	BK40
Westray Pl, G22	24	BT23	Whiteloans, (Both.) G71	71	CR42	*off Windhill Rd*		
Westray Pl, (Bishop.) G64	13	BZ16	Whitemoss Av, G44	65	BP41	Windhill Rd, G43	64	BK40
Westray Rd, (Cumb.) G67	72	DA13	Whitesbridge Av, Pais. PA3	47	AP33	Windlaw Ct, G45	66	BT43
Westray Sq, G22	24	BS22	Whitesbridge Cl, Pais. PA3	31	AQ32	Windlaw Gdns, G44	65	BP42
Westray St, G22	24	BS22	*off Whitesbridge Av*			Windlaw Pk Gdns, G44	65	BP41
West Regent La, G2	4	BR29	White St, G11	36	BK27	Windlaw Rd, G45	66	BT44
West Regent St, G2	4	BQ29	White St, Clyde. G81	19	AZ22	Windmillcroft Quay, G5	4	BQ31
West Rd, (Kilb.) John. PA10	44	AC33	Whitevale St, G31	39	BW31	Windsor Cres, Clyde. G81	7	AW18
Westside Gdns, G11	36	BK27	Whithope Rd, G53	62	BB40	Windsor Cres, (Elder.) John. PA5	46	AK36
West St, G5	37	BQ32	Whithope Ter, G53	62	BB41	Windsor Cres, Pais. PA1	33	AW31
West St, Clyde. G81	20	BA21	*off Whithope Rd*			Windsor Path, (Baill.) G69	43	CP31
West St, Pais. PA1	48	AS33	Whithorn Cres, (Mood.) G69	17	CP18	*off Park Rd*		
West Thomson St, Clyde. G81	7	AW17	Whitlawburn Av, (Camb.) G72	68	CA41	Windsor Rd, Renf. PA4	33	AY27
West Whitby St, G31	55	BY33	Whitlawburn Rd, (Camb.) G72	68	CA41	Windsor St, G20	37	BQ27
			Whitlawburn Ter, (Camb.) G72	68	CA41	Windsor St, G32	41	CE31
			Whitriggs Rd, G53	62	BB40	Windsor Ter, G20	37	BQ27
			Whitslade Pl, G34	41	CH28	Windsor Wk, (Udd.) G71	59	CR38
			Whitslade St, G34	42	CJ28	Windyedge Cres, G13	21	BE24
						Windyedge Pl, G13	21	BE24

Wingfield Gdns, (Both.) G71	71	CR44	Woodland Cres, (Camb.) G72	68	CD41	Wright Av, (Barr.) G78	61	AW43
off Blairston Av			Woodlands Av, (Gart.) G69	29	CN23	Wrightlands Cres, Ersk. PA8	18	AU21
Winifred St, G33	25	BZ25	Woodlands Av, (Both.) G71	71	CQ42	Wright St, Renf. PA4	33	AW28
Winning Ct, (Blan.) G72	71	CN44	Woodlands Ct, (Thornlie.) G46	63	BH43	Wykeham Pl, G13	21	BE23
Winning Row, G31	39	BZ32	Woodlands Cres, (Thornlie.)	63	BH42	Wykeham Rd, G13	21	BE23
Winton Av, (Giff.) G46	64	BL43	G46			Wynd, The, (Cumb.) G67	73	DD8
Winton Dr, G12	22	BL24	Woodlands Cres, (Both.) G71	71	CP42	Wyndford Dr, G20	22	BM24
Winton Gdns, (Udd.) G71	59	CP38	Woodlands Cres, John. PA5	45	AF36	Wyndford Pl, G20	22	BM24
Winton La, G12	22	BL24	Woodlands Dr, G4	37	BP27	*off Wyndford Rd*		
Wirran Pl, G13	20	BA21	Woodlands Gdns, (Both.) G71	71	CP41	Wyndford Rd, G20	22	BL24
Wishart St, G31	5	BU30	Woodlands Gate, G3	4	BP28	Wyndham Ct, G12	22	BM25
Wisner Ct, (Thornlie.) G46	63	BH42	Woodlands Gate, (Thornlie.)	63	BH42	*off Wyndham St*		
Wiston St, (Camb.) G72	69	CF40	G46			Wyndham St, G12	22	BM25
Woddrop St, G40	55	BX35	Woodlands Pk, (Thornlie.) G46	63	BH43	Wynford Ter, (Udd.) G71	59	CR38
Wolseley St, G5	54	BT34	Woodlands Rd, G3	37	BP27	Wyper Pl, G40	38	BV31
Woodbank Cres, John. PA5	45	AH35	Woodlands Rd, (Thornlie.) G46	63	BH43	Wyvil Av, G13	9	BG20
Woodburn Ct, (Ruther.) G73	67	BX39	Woodlands Ter, G3	37	BN28	Wyvis Av, G13	20	BA21
Woodburn Rd, G43	64	BM40	Woodlands Ter, (Both.) G71	71	CP42	Wyvis Pl, G13	20	BB21
Woodburn Way, (Cumb.) G68	72	CY11	Woodland Way, (Cumb.) G67	73	DD10	Wyvis Quad, G13	20	BB21
Woodcroft Av, G11	21	BH26	Wood La, (Bishop.) G64	25	BY21			
Woodend Ct, G32	57	CG35	Woodlea Dr, (Giff.) G46	64	BM41	**Y**		
Woodend Dr, G13	21	BG24	Woodlinn Av, G44	65	BR40	Yair Dr, G52	34	BC31
Woodend Dr, Pais. PA1	49	AZ33	Woodneuk Ct, Pais. PA1	47	AR33	Yarrow Ct, (Camb.) G72	69	CG41
Woodend Gdns, G32	57	CG35	Woodneuk La, (Gart.) G69	29	CQ24	Yarrow Gdns, G20	23	BP26
Woodend La, G13	21	BG24	Woodneuk Rd, G53	62	BD41	Yarrow Gdns La, G20	23	BP26
Woodend Pl, (Elder.) John.	46	AK35	Woodneuk Rd, (Gart.) G69	29	CQ24	Yarrow Rd, (Bishop.) G64	13	BW17
PA5			Woodneuk Ter, (Gart.) G69	29	CQ24	Yate St, G31	39	BX32
Woodend Rd, G32	57	CF35	Wood Quad, Clyde. G81	20	BA21	Yetholm St, G14	20	BA23
Woodend Rd, (Ruther.) G73	67	BX41	Woodrow Circ, G41	52	BM33	*off Speirshall Ter*		
Wood Fm Rd, (Thornlie.) G46	64	BJ43	Woodrow Pl, G41	52	BL33	Yew Dr, G21	25	BW26
Woodfield Av, (Bishop.) G64	13	BX20	Woodrow Rd, G41	52	BM33	Yew Pl, John. PA5	45	AH36
Woodfoot Path, G53	62	BC41	Woodside Av, (Thornlie.) G46	64	BJ42	Yoker Burn Pl, G13	20	BA22
off Woodfoot Quad			Woodside Av, (Lenz.) G66	15	CF15	*off Yoker Mill Gdns*		
Woodfoot Pl, G53	62	BB41	Woodside Av, (Ruther.) G73	55	BY38	Yoker Ferry Rd, G14	20	BA23
off Woodfoot Rd			Woodside Cres, G3	4	BP28	Yoker Mill Gdns, G13	20	BA22
Woodfoot Quad, G53	62	BD41	Woodside Cres, (Barr.) G78	61	AZ43	Yoker Mill Rd, G13	20	BA22
Woodfoot Rd, G53	62	BC41	Woodside Cres, Pais. PA1	48	AS33	York Dr, (Ruther.) G73	67	BZ40
Woodford Pl, (Linw.) Pais. PA3	30	AJ31	Woodside Gro, (Ruther.) G73	55	BY38	Yorkhill Par, G3	36	BL28
Woodford St, G41	53	BN38	Woodside Pl, G3	4	BP28	Yorkhill Quay, G3	36	BL29
Woodgreen Av, G44	65	BR39	Woodside Pl La, G3	4	BP28	Yorkhill St, G3	36	BM29
Woodhall St, G40	55	BX35	Woodside Ter, G3	4	BP28	York St, G2	4	BQ31
Woodhead Cres, (Udd.) G71	59	CP38	Woodside Ter La, G3	4	BP28	York St, Clyde. G81	7	AZ19
Woodhead Ind Est, (Chry.) G69	28	CK23	Woodstock Av, G41	52	BM37	York Way, Renf. PA4	33	AZ28
Woodhead Path, G53	62	BC40	Woodstock Av, Pais. PA2	47	AN37	Younger Quad, (Bishop.) G64	13	BW20
off Woodhead Rd			Woodstock Way, Pais. PA2	47	AN37	*off Springfield Rd*		
Woodhead Rd, G53	62	BB40	*off Woodstock Av*			Young Pl, (Udd.) G71	59	CQ37
Woodhead Rd, (Chry.) G69	28	CK23	Wood St, G31	39	BX29	Young St, Clyde. G81	7	AX17
Woodhead Ter, (Chry.) G69	28	CK22	Wood St, Pais. PA2	49	AX34	Young Ter, G21	25	BW25
Woodhill Gro, (Bishop.) G64	25	BY21	Woodvale Av, (Bears.) G61	10	BK19			
Woodhill Rd, G21	25	BX23	Woodvale Dr, Pais. PA3	31	AQ32	**Z**		
Woodhill Rd, (Bishop.) G64	13	BY20	Woodville Pk, G51	36	BK31	Zambesi Dr, (Blan.) G72	70	CL44
Woodholm Av, G44	66	BS39	Woodville St, G51	36	BK31	Zena Cres, G33	25	BY25
Woodhouse St, G13	21	BG22	Wordsworth Way, (Both.) G71	71	CR42	Zena Pl, G33	25	BZ25
Woodilee Cotts, (Kirk.) G66	15	CH15	Works Av, (Camb.) G72	69	CG40	Zena St, G33	25	BZ25
Woodilee Ind Est, (Kirk.) G66	15	CG15	Wraes Av, (Barr.) G78	61	AZ41	Zetland Rd, G52	34	BB29
Woodilee Rd, (Kirk.) G66	15	CG16	Wraes Vw, (Barr.) G78	60	AV44			
Woodland Av, Pais. PA2	48	AU37	Wren Pl, John. PA5	45	AF38			

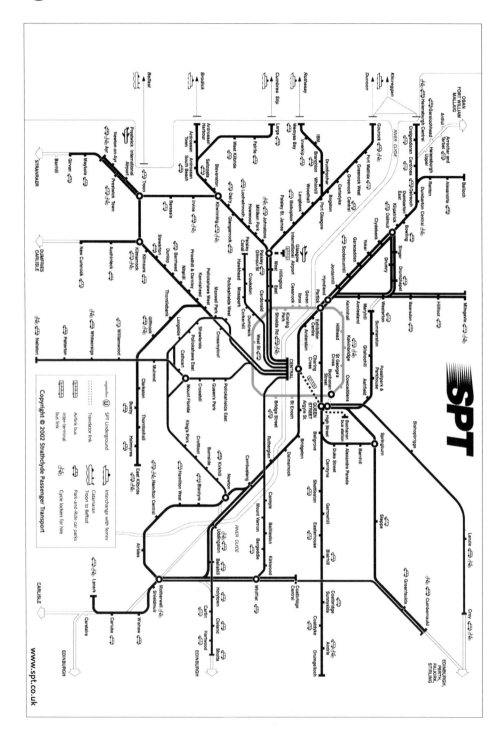